The New Regulation and Governance of Food

Routledge Studies in Human Geography

1. A Geography of Islands
Small Island Insularity
Stephen A. Royle

2. Citizenships, Contingency and the Countryside
Rights, Culture, Land and the Environment
Gavin Parker

3. The Differentiated Countryside
Jonathan Murdoch, Philip Lowe, Neil Ward and Terry Marsden

4. The Human Geography of East Central Europe
David Turnock

5. Imagined Regional Communities
Integration and Sovereignty in the Global South
James D Sidaway

6. Mapping Modernities
Geographies of Central and Eastern Europe 1920–2000
Alan Dingsdale

7. Rural Poverty
Marginalisation and Exclusion in Britain and the United States
Paul Milbourne

8. Poverty and the Third Way
Colin C. Williams and Jan Windebank

9. Ageing and Place
Edited by Gavin J. Andrews and David R. Phillips

10. Geographies of Commodity Chains
Edited by Alex Hughes and Suzanne Reimer

11. Queering Tourism
Paradoxical Performances at Gay Pride Parades
Lynda T. Johnston

12. Cross-Continental Food Chains
Edited by Niels Fold and Bill Pritchard

13. Private Cities
Edited by Georg Glasze, Chris Webster and Klaus Frantz

14. Global Geographies of Post Socialist Transition
Tassilo Herrschel

15. Urban Development in Post-Reform China
Fulong Wu, Jiang Xu and Anthony Gar-On Yeh

16. Rural Governance
International Perspectives
Edited by Lynda Cheshire, Vaughan Higgins and Geoffrey Lawrence

17. Global Perspectives on Rural Childhood and Youth
Young Rural Lives
Edited by Ruth Panelli, Samantha Punch, and Elsbeth Robson

18. World City Syndrome
Neoliberalism and Inequality in Cape Town
David A. McDonald

19. Exploring Post Development
Aram Ziai

20. Family Farms
Harold Brookfield and Helen Parsons

21. China on the Move
Migration, the State, and the Household
C. Cindy Fan

22. Participatory Action Research Approaches and Methods
Connecting People, Participation and Place
Sara Kindon, Rachel Pain and Mike Kesby

23. Time-Space Compression
Historical Geographies
Barney Warf

24. Sensing Cities
Monica Degen

25. International Migration and Knowledge
Allan Williams and Vladimir Balaz

26. Design Economies and the Changing World Economy
Innovation, Production and Competitiveness
John Bryson and Grete Rustin

27. Whose Urban Renaissance?
An International Comparison of Urban Regeneration Policies
Libby Porter and Katie Shaw

28. Tourism Geography
A New Synthesis, Second Edition
Stephen Williams

29. The New Regulation and Governance of Food
Beyond the Food Crisis?
Terry Marsden, Robert Lee, Andrew Flynn and Samarthia Thankappan

The New Regulation and Governance of Food

Beyond the Food Crisis?

Terry Marsden, Robert Lee, Andrew Flynn and Samarthia Thankappan

Routledge
Taylor & Francis Group
New York London

First published 2010
by Routledge
270 Madison Ave, New York, NY 10016

Simultaneously published in the UK
by Routledge
2 Park Square, Milton Park, Abingdon, Oxon OX14 4RN

Routledge is an imprint of the Taylor & Francis Group, an informa business

Typeset in Sabon by IBT Global.
Printed and bound in the United States of America on acid-free paper by IBT Global.

Library of Congress Cataloging-in-Publication Data

The new regulation and governance of food : beyond the food crisis? / by Terry Marsden . . . [et al.].
p. cm. — (Routledge studies in human geography ; 29)
Includes bibliographical references and index.
1. Food industry and trade—Government policy. 2. Food industry and trade—Safety measures. 3. Food—Europe—Safety measures. I. Marsden, Terry.
HD9000.6N435 2009
363.8—dc22
2008050788

ISBN10: 0-415-95674-9 (hbk)
ISBN10: 0-203-87772-1 (ebk)

ISBN13: 978-0-415-95674-1 (hbk)
ISBN13: 978-0-203-87772-2 (ebk)

Contents

PART III
Operating the Hybrid Model: Case Studies of Regulatory Supply Chains

PART IV
Key Contemporary Dynamics of Regulation

Figures

Tables

Abbreviations

AFSSA	Agence Francaise de Securite Sanitaire des Aliments
BRASS	Business Relationships Accountability Sustainability and Society
BRC	British Retail Consortium
BSE	Bovine Spongiform Encephalopathy
CIES	Food Business Forum
CPM	Commission on Phytosanitary Measures
DEFRA	Department of Environment, Food and Rural Affairs
EEC	European Economic Council
EHO	Environmental Health Officer
ESRC	Economic and Social Research Council
EU	European Union
EUREP	Euro-Retailer Produce Working Group
DG SANCO	Health and Consumer Protection Directorate General. Also known as Consumer Protection DG XXIV
FAO	Food and Agriculture Organisation
FMD	Foot and Mouth Disease
FSA	Food Standards Agency
GAP	Good Agricultural Practice

GFSI	Global Food Safety Initiative
GMO	Genetically Modified Organisms
HACCP	Hazard Analysis and Critical Control Point
IAEA	International Atomic Energy Agency
IFS	International Food Standards
IPPC	International Plant Protection Convention
ISO	International Standards Organisation
ISPM	International Standards for Phytosanitary Measures
MAFF	Ministry of Agriculture, Fisheries and Food
OIE	Organisation Mondiale de la Santé Animale/ World Organisation for Animal Health
QA	Quality Assessment
r-BST	recombinant Bovine Somatotropin
RPPO	Regional Plant Protection Organisation
SGQ	Norme du Système de Gestion de la Qualité/ Quality Management Systems
SPS	Sanitary and Phytosanitary Measures
SQF	Safe Quality Food
TBT	Technical Barriers to Trade
TSO	Trading Standards Officer
vCJD	variant Creutzfeldt-Jakob Disease
WHO	World Health Organisation
WTO	World Trade Organisation

Preface

This book is the result of several years of research (from 2002–2008) which was conducted under the auspices of the Economic and Social Research Council supported research centre on Business Relationships, Accountability, Sustainability and Society (BRASS), based at Cardiff University. It is an interdisciplinary research centre involving three Schools-Law, City and Regional Planning and Business Studies and Management. The research was led by Terry Marsden, Bob Lee and Andrew Flynn in collaboration with colleagues in BRASS. The authors would especially like to acknowledge the ESRC, BRASS and their host Schools for their support for the research, not least Ken Peattie, the Director of BRASS. Several researchers were also involved in conducting with the authors various parts of the research including: Dave Campbell, Elen Stokes, Taiwo Oriola, Lisa Carson, Everard Smith, Alice Percival and Natalia Yakalova. International research collaborators also played an important role, and we would wish to acknowledge Salete Barbosa Cavalcante, Maria Grazia Quieti, Larry Busch and Nicolien De Grijp. We would also wish to thank Denise Phillips and Emma Dean for assisting us in the production of the manuscript.

Most of all we are indebted to our wide range of interview respondents in this highly competitive, increasingly challenging and overwhelmingly fascinating field. Numerous informants from the private, public and NGO sectors gave evidence in our researches, both from the UK, the EU and wider afield, and their positive and generous responses and dialogues made this research possible. On a more personal level we would like to acknowledge the support of Mary Anne, Joseph and Hannah Marsden and Suki, Jake, Laura and Holly Flynn.

Methodological Note

Most of the chapters in this volume make reference directly or indirectly to primary interview data collected by the research team between the years 2002–2008. The primary research method was face-to-face interviews with key stakeholders and players in various sectors of the food industry—including the private sector, the public sector and the NGO and consumer sector. The majority of interviews were tape-recorded and then transcribed. When respondents declined the use of the tape recorder, detailed notes were recorded and transcribed afterwards. The interviews took place over three research phases and followed three key research objectives:

1. To identify the ways in which the state, corporate and non-corporate private interests, consumers and social interests build relationships in response to the need for accountability within the agri-food supply chain;
2. To identify how the establishment of the Food Standards Agency has impacted on the context and implementation of food regulation in the UK; and
3. To explore the potential impacts of European policy making (such as the setting up of the European Food Safety Agency) on the agri-food system in the UK.

The three phases of interviewing occurred at the EU, UK and then Global levels. At each level the researchers attempted to identify the key private, public and consumer organisations involved in the regulation and operation of the main food supply chains. At the EU level, for example, this involved over twenty-five interviews with senior representatives in the EU Commission, the main trade associations, and the key producer and consumer organisations operating at the EU level. At the UK level, senior members of corporate retailing and food processing firms were interviewed, key officials at DEFRA and the FSA, as well as those in the main consumer organisations. In addition, detailed, primary evidence was gained by informants engaged in the Red Meat and Fresh Fruit and Vegetable sectors in the UK and EU. These formed the basis for the analysis in Part III, Chapters 7 and 8. In the final phase of the research we undertook a series of interviews in the main global institutions which held some responsibility for food and agriculture. A series of interviews were thus conducted with officials in the World Trade Organisation (WTO), the UN Food and Agriculture Organisation (FAO) and their various subsidiary bodies.

The data emanating from these three phases of primary research, and related secondary analysis of reports and policy documents, form the empirical basis for most of the chapters in the book; and with the exception of the introductory and concluding chapters (Chapters 1 and 12), the analytical text is supported by the selection of anonymised quotations from the transcripts. These are, however, only illustrative of the more comprehensive analysis, argumentation and narrative which forms the basis of each of the chapters.

Part I

Exploring the Anatomy of the Food Crisis

1 The Anatomy of the Food Crisis
Regulating the Risk Geographies of Agri-Food in the 21st Century

INTRODUCTION

Agri-food studies are studies of the changing and ever more complex relationships between three spheres: economy, policy and space. At root, unlike other forms of commodity production or economic activity, however much the dominant systems of economic and political change may attempt to detach themselves from space, in their operation and regulation of the production and consumption of foods; space, through its embedded nature, geography, ecology, can never be entirely avoided or completely appropriated.

As we shall see in this book, particularly in the first years of 21st century, the relationships between these often contested spheres take on new and more complex dimensions. This is a period in which, however much the more liberalised food system celebrates its technological sophistication and increasing ability to service us all with an expanding array of novel food goods, this is tempered by the realisation that 'nature hits back'; often by creating what seem to be a continuing catalogue of new food 'crises', risks, concerns and scares. Indeed, as one result of this, contemporary 'food journalism' has now become a central feature of our mass media, focussing either on the 'scares' themselves or on how to create individual or more collective moralities which attempt to avoid them. It is truism to say that food has become a contested arena (Ansell and Vogel, 2006). It is a more academic question to ask who, how and by what means should key interests—government, private interests, consumers—hold the authority to decide on how these production and consumption arena should be organised and regulated. This is a central question of this book.

What seems to be clear is that however more sophisticated and globalised the food system becomes, the more it seems to be liable to increased contestations, periodic risk and crisis. This is indeed a major paradox of contemporary food system modernisation. This book is about conceptually and empirically understanding these tensions, and especially how current governments and regulatory bodies attempt to balance and deal with these economic, political and spatial demands that the conventional and increasingly globalised food system creates.

More specifically, it asks how the vast array of regulatory bodies balance and deal with the innate conundrum of continuing to stimulate an advanced capitalist and corporately -organised food production and consumption system at the same time as maintaining and reproducing a public and consumer-based legitimating framework for it. This is, of course, a dynamic, and as we shall see, a highly contingent process. It is also one which through its study demands conceptual as well as empirical development from an interdisciplinary social science perspective. More than ever, we can suggest, a focus on the question of food governance—that is the combinations of economic, political and spatial spheres which shape both how food is produced, processed, sold and eaten—is a key window on the public questioning and sustainability of the 20th and 21st century modernisation project itself.

THE ANATOMY OF AGRI-FOOD AS A LONG-RUN SUSTAINABLE ACTIVITY

In the second part of the 20th century the concept of sustainable agriculture and food became increasingly used to denote a variable but significant rupture with what has been termed the more dominant agri-industrial model of agriculture and rural development. The past twenty years, since the late 1980s, has been characterised by a growing crisis tendency in this latter dominant model, as well as an increasing call and search for alternative systems. In general terms these alternatives can be defined as referring to the environmental or ecological soundness of the agricultural production processes or the wider agri-food commodity chain. This implies that with respect to renewable nutrient cycles, such sustainable systems are those that are capable of being continued indefinitely, or at least continuous over considerable generational time. In many zones we might argue that agricultural systems have long been sustainable (since Neo-lithic times) in that whilst they have been subject to considerable adaptation and technical change, they have sustained in reasonable shape the main factors of production needed for the continuance of food production both *in* and *of* place. And they have managed to do this without significantly destroying the local and production-based ecologies on which they are based.

It has also long been established that agriculture, as a production process, is quite distinctive in that it both produces and transforms nature, through the (re-) production of livestock and plants, at the same time as being physically and geographically reliant upon nature as a *means* and *condition* of production (most notably soils, micro-climate, topography and vegetation complexes). Agriculture, and especially a sustainable agriculture, thus efficiently transforms as well as re-creates its space or *terriour* as part and parcel of the production process. Usually the indefiniteness of sustainable agriculture makes primary reference to a set of ecological principles, and it is also linked to not so much an end-point *sui generis*, but rather as a continual and increasing contested process. In this sense it needs to be recognised that there will always be ways in which agro-food systems can be adapted in ways which makes them more (or less) ecologically, economically and socially reproducible.

In general and abstract terms then we might argue that the process of sustainable agriculture and agri-food must infer a coordinated relationship between organisms and environment, which is adaptive to location, season, creating bio-physiologically or ecologically mutual benefits which give complementary status to the different components of the production system. Such explicit complementarities were a central part, for instance of ancient Chinese classical works written about 3000 years ago. Here agriculture needed to be practised as part of the harmony between heaven, earth and humans; and between the careful utilisation of the five key elements of the universe: metal, wood, water, fire and earth. These principles and adaptive techniques were passed down under systems of 'inherited experience'. For instance in the Tai Lake basin area of South-east China, the grain-livestock-mulberry-fish integrated production system has existed for more than a thousand years, by means of a cycling based on ecological food chains and synergies between the different but complimentary production systems.

In most advanced countries, and indeed progressively at a global scale, in the past twenty years there has developed a realisation that the dominant agri-industrial system has departed significantly from these long-running sustainable principles. There has developed what some authors have called a significant 'metabolic rift' (Foster, 1999) as the systems of ever more intensive production, processing and consuming foods have departed and detached themselves from the natural rhythms; and technologies have been progressively employed in ways to uphold the 'unsustainability' of this 'metabolic rift'.

The most notable but not exclusive crisis erupted in the UK in the late 1980s and throughout the 1990s with the arrival of BSE in British cattle and its reluctantly accepted transfer into vCJD in the human population. This was notable in that it created not only a long-running food safety crisis but also a political and economic challenge both inside central government and in the farming and agri-food sectors (see Zwanenburg and Millstone, 2003; Marsden et al., 2000). This chapter does not intend to re-analyse the causes and consequences of the BSE crisis (but see Chapter 4). Rather, it takes these as a point of departure to assess, in many ways what has been a period since the late 1990s, of crisis management in the agri-food sector, both in the UK and more widely in the EU. We see this process, in general terms, as the development of what we can term the development of a hygienic-bureaucratic State—that is, a model of a more complex set of state intervention and corporate responsibilities which attempted to ameliorate, as opposed to radically reform, the social and political architecture of agri-food governance, in ways which fend off and legitimate the risks of the intensive agri-industrial model.

In this introductory chapter to the book we will first trace some of the key developments in the private and public regulation of foods since the late 1990s—essentially what we might call the 'post-BSE period' of food regulation both in the UK and in Europe more generally. Second, we will explore how a combination of public risk factors surrounding foods have begun to shape this more complex and contingent regulatory terrain. In conclusion we will outline some key conceptual themes that this raises, and which will be subject to more detailed treatment in the rest of the volume. This chapter will then be followed by more detailed treatments of the specific regulatory handling of a series of new risks (Foot and Mouth and GM, Chapters 2 and 3), and the evolutionary development of the role of the State in agri-food in Chapter 4.

In our earlier studies of agri-food governance in the 1990s—a period in the midst of the BSE crisis—we concluded that in the UK at least, what we were witnessing was the emergence of a 'company state'. Quoting, Wyn Grant (1993), we argued that:

> Britain displays many characteristics of a company state. In a company state the most important form of business-state contract is the direct one between company and government. Government prioritises such forms of contract over associative intermediation. (1993:14)

We argued that it was not only at the level of policy formation that such relationships were found, but also at the level of policy implementation. Our extensive and multi-level evidence, gathered throughout the early 1990s, supported the view that combinations of public and private (particularly corporate retail) interests were now working together in sophisticated networks to secure the implementation of policy goals. This also created a marginalisation process with, for instance, consumer groups being largely outside both the central policy formation and implementation process. A primary goal of the new combinations of public and private interests was to both create and sustain vibrant, relatively low-cost and inflation-proof consumer markets in food. The rest of this chapter introduces how these food crisis tendencies have continued to be 'managed'; indeed, how they continue to 'maintain the unsustainable'. It also highlights some of the continuities and changes apparent in the continuing 'management of crisis' of the agri-industrial system.

THE ANATOMY OF THE (RISKY) CONTEMPORARY AGRI-INDUSTRIAL COMPLEX

The BSE crisis is now, of course, over twenty years old; and, over the past decade both governments and private sector interests have significantly adjusted to it. Nevertheless, as is witnessed with the proliferation of more recent risks, for instance, those associated with Foot and Mouth Disease, GM, Avian flu, or 'Blue-tongue', the agri-industrial model of agri-food has, quite strikingly and resiliently tightened its grip upon not only on UK and European, but also global food systems and spaces. Perhaps paradoxically, what is so striking about the contemporary governance of agri-food are the ways in which it has built up resilience in dealing with it's own unsustainable and metabolic vulnerabilities at the same time as protecting it abilities to create surplus values and profits. This book attempts to understand this conundrum.

We therefore need to recognise that the inherent 'crises' associated with the human and ecological health risks of the intensive agri-food system, which have, of course, been continually articulated over the past two decades, have (perhaps surprisingly) *avoided* a profound restructuring of the agri-food system itself, in ways which might have ushered in a more sustainable system of food provision and consumption. Indeed, the story is one which represents quite the opposite. As will be outlined below what we have witnessed has been an intensification and further embeddedness of the agri-industrial model. An initial and somewhat perplexing question has thus become: how, given the series of public and regulatory problems besetting contemporary food systems have they managed to 'sustain the unsustainable'?

This book will detail the complex processes of adjustment and regulation that has been made since the late 1990s with regard to the UK and Europe. However, underlying these, it needs to be recognised at the outset that it is an agri-industrial regulatory system, or anatomy, which is still crisis ridden, highly risky, and profoundly unsustainable with regard to the long-run historical principles of agri-food sustainability introduced previously. In the rest of this chapter we will first document some of the key developments in the agri-industrial model over the past decade. Second, this will be followed by an outline of how this has become part of wider social and regulatory concerns with contemporary food risks.

Key Developments in the Agri-Food System in the 2000s: Continuing to Sustain and Contain the Unsustainable?

Increasing Vulnerability

Twenty years after the onset of the BSE crises, why have food scares and risks seemingly become so endemic? It had become increasingly clear that increasing specialisation, monoculture and the spatial and physical intensity of production systems especially in countries like the UK, the US and the Netherlands have continued to heighten the vulnerability of animals, plants and humans to pest and disease risks. Whilst the onset of GM and other seed and plant technologies have been applied to reduce or avoid these vulnerabilities, and with the vast bulk of private and public research in the applied animal sciences, for instance, devoted to 'solving' the technical problems of intensively housed animal feeding operations (see Buttel, 2006; Marsden, 2008), it is now clear that these have only remained palliatives.

Reductions in ecological and plant and animal diversity, increasingly intensive production systems and the greater speed and 'time compression' associated with both production and logistics has made the food system more rather than less vulnerable to the development and mutation of diseases and their transfer across spaces and species.

The Careful Consumption of Risk

At the same time we have witnessed the twin processes of the *socialisation of food* on the one hand (within civil society) and the particular *scientification of food* on the part of the State. By socialisation here we mean that food itself, not least because of the heightened awareness of consumers, has become more of a socially and ethically constructed part of contemporary society. It has become, at least for some parts of the consuming population, a major factor in lifestyle, health and identity. Moreover, governments and the private sector have realised the increasing politicisation of consumption as markets have become more liberalised and the emphasis in macro-political terms has been to service the traditional role of citizenship through the allocation and attribution of more varied consumer rights. At the same time this has been linked to the imperative for the further global (as well as European) *liberalisation* and integration of markets and commodity flows through the continuing application of a supply chain logistics paradigm (see Busch, 2007).

Market Concentration

These trends have been re-enforced by the competitive advantages in the EU of a decade or more of the European Internal Market (EIM). The food and drink industry has become the largest manufacturing sector in the EU with growing amounts of added value, integration across national boundaries and food transportation. The trend has involved, both in food manufacturing and retail, a shift from a traditionally dispersed, fragmented industry subject to nationally-constructed regulations, to one where corporate power is placed in fewer hands and is increasingly pan-European. Vertical integration and higher levels of firm concentration have been based upon more sophisticated supply chain management logistics which have become more trans-national. This again, however, tends not to reduce the vulnerability of food risks. Quite the reverse in fact; with food ingredients and substances travelling across further geographical spaces at increasing speeds through privately managed supply chain control systems.

Rise and Rise of the Retailers

Since the 1990s the overall shape of this agri-industrial system has become even more corporate retailer-led. Socialisation, scientification and liberalisation have all assisted the corporate retailers over the more fragmented manufacturing sectors. Both in terms of concentration in the sector, levels of internationalisation of supply, and in the share of the overall food consumer market, the overall power of the retailers in supply chains has increased both economically and politically. Consumers today spend more of their household income in a small number of large supermarkets, and they visit these stores for an increasing array of goods and (more recently) services. Retailer loyalty cards enrol as well as track consumer trends and habits, building new social relationships with consumers (Guy, 2007).

As we shall see in the succeeding chapters, this process has occurred despite the multifarious food scares and crises that have affected the food sector more generally. Whether it has concerned BSE, Foot and Mouth, or the debates about GM, corporate retailers have continued on an entrenched, innovative and concentrated track; and despite growing calls for more regulatory control of their buying and selling power (see debates surrounding the setting up of the Competition Commission enquiries, both in 2000 and 2006; Marsden, 2004; Guy, 2007), they have been able to economically and politically distance themselves from the safety and quality problems inherent in other parts of the food chain.

This is, in many ways a remarkable achievement, and one which is documented in more detail in subsequent chapters. It is important to see this as both a *performative and contingent process*, rather than one which we might regard, more simplistically, as an inevitable or reductionist account of transitions and evolutions between industrial and merchant capitalism. It has, as we envisaged in the late 1990s, had to be *constantly achieved* through the production and reproduction of production, consumption and regulatory relationships. In short it has been achieved through the innovation in competitive practices, first, between retailers and their upstream suppliers; second, between themselves, as they have continually 'jockeyed' for competitive positioning in providing 'quality', mass and standardised products; and third, between themselves in terms of their sets of relationships between shareholders, on the one hand and segments of consumers on the other. As we shall also see, relationships with the state, whether national, EU or global have also been crucial.

In the early 1990s serious threats to established players in British retailing, for instance, came from the European food discounters (e.g. Aldi, Lidl and Netto). In the 2000s the greater threat comes from what is commonly known in the trade as 'Walmarterisation'; the arrival of the US-based international discount retailer in Britain, which ignited a new round of both retailer and supply chain competition across the entire sector.

An example of this continued dominance is the dynamic and highly competitive (and geographically expansive) positioning of the corporate retailer sector in the UK. Since 2000 the number of stores operated by the four largest grocery retailers (Tesco, Asda/Walmart, Sainsbury's and Morrisons) has more than doubled. Consumers have been prepared to spend more of their food expenditure in these stores. Retail sales of groceries in these stores in the UK amounted to 16% of total consumer expenditure in 2006, an increase of 17% since 2000. The number of product lines supplied by the 'big four' increased by 40%, whilst real prices of food declined by 7.3%. By 2006 in the UK, 72% of all grocery sales took place in supermarkets, an increase from 67% in 2000, with sales increasing by 26% over the same period.

By 2005 there was a corresponding decline in small independent specialist grocery stores by 7% (from 40,351 to 37,521). The largest increase over this period is represented by Tesco, which added 1200 more stores, nearly trebling its store count over the period. The 'big four' accounted for nearly three-quarters of all grocery sales by 2006. Another trend has been for the two leading players (Tesco's and Sainsbury's) to acquire significant local and regional convenience store chains; further embedding themselves in inner urban shopping districts as well as continuing the 'edge of town' developments. Indeed the number of convenience stores owned by the 'big four' increased from 54 to 1306. During this period, however (2000–2006), the competition between the group of key players has become more fierce, with operating margins slightly declining from 4.5% to 4.0%. The big four have also been responsible for increasing imports of foods into the UK, with imports of food and drink increasing by 24%, in real terms, from 17.7 billion in 2000 to 21.9 billion in 2004. As a result UK self-sufficiency in food has continued to decline dramatically.

A major instrument used by the corporate retailers in dealing with these different axes of intense competition, has been to both extend and to deepen their complex supply chain relationships over both time and space. In short they have strengthened their global as well as domestic grip on food supply through complex chain and logistics management. This has, for the time being at least, allowed them to succeed over the real geographies of natural production, through the continued and managed compression of space-time.

The Internationalisation of Retail Capital

This 'global grip' is now being seen as a new 'super-market revolution' by leading retailer analysts (see Reardon et al., 2007). And it is marked by both a growing internationalisation of corporate retailing, on the one hand, but also a deepening and more 'endogenous' and embedding process in different national states on the other. From their European and North American bases, there was first a sudden burst, and then an exponential diffusion of supermarkets in developing countries in the early 2000s. These were proactive strategies adopted by the retailers and encouraged by the global process of liberalisation of markets. For instance: an 'avalanche of retail foreign direct investment (FDI) into developing countries' was facilitated by the major policy change towards investment liberalisation. Moreover, this was given extra impetus by institutional and regulatory reforms in many developing countries. This has led to significant restructuring of national and regional procurement systems which are now retailer-led in developing countries; and, second, new local and regional supply chains developments. This is creating a new endogenous treadmill of competition and cost reduction for local producers and suppliers, as the new distribution and wholesale centres undercut the costs of pre-existing food supply chains.

This is thus a process not only of 'placing the firm' but also now 'firming the place' (Wrigley et al., 2005) with regard to embedding corporate retailer-led cost reduction into the fabric of developing as well as developed countries; both in the location of stores and in sourcing strategies of the retailers. It is now estimated that foreign direct investment (FDI) retail, in terms of total retail sales in developing countries represents 50%. This is remarkable growth given the first wave of FDI did not occur until the mid 1990s; and it has also sparked off considerable domestic retail corporate development which is largely organised along the same lines.

A further trend has been in vastly investing in 'quality management'. Whilst in the 1990s quality constructions were largely rudimentary and standardised, with an emphasis on individual competitive retailer definitions of quality food, by the 2000s both the quality thresholds had increased and the standards become far more diversified along not only retailer but supply chain lines. We are now in the decade of complex, quality 'category management'.

Squeezing the Suppliers

It is important to recognise the significant effects of retail power on the rest of the food supply sector both in developed and developing countries. Not only has the upstream sector been regarded as the source and the new alchemists of a succession of food crises, but because the concentrated retailer sector now so dominates the sale of food goods, both producers and manufacturers have been forced to react to their supply chain demands. This has unleashed more supply chain 'brand warfare' between the own brand products of the retailers and the more traditional branded goods of the major food manufacturers. It has reduced the margins in food manufacturing in ways which have made increasing levels of firm concentration in the manufacturing sector inevitable. As a result we now have within Europe a highly integrated and concentrated food manufacturing sector to match the competitive retailing sectors.

For example, currently in the UK there are some 400 major wholesalers (with sixteen accounting for 80% of wholesaling revenues) and 6000 main food manufacturers. There has been a net exit from this sector in the past decade such that in more than half of the food manufacturing categories, the sales of the largest three companies exceeds 50% of the total. For instance, Palmer & Harvey McLane as well as Booker Ltd account for more than 40% of the total wholesale market.

Ecological and Health Risks

Producers have also had to concentrate, develop economies of scale or face closure. Buttel (2006) has shown here that this has led to (i) the continuing spatial separation of livestock and arable production; (ii) the spatial concentration of production at a regional level, with the subsequent decline in mixed farming systems; and (iii) the continued intensification of production and the reliance upon external inputs (such as fertilisers, pesticides, and now genetically modified seeds). All this leads to far more transportation in the movement of animals and crops. This mobility becomes a major risk factor in the carrying and diffusion of disease (see Chapter 2).

These retailer-led trends at the production end of the chain have four other profound effects which increase ecological and health risks:

- (i) New technological developments in processing, transportation and distribution (but also in the ability to transform whole ecosystems) allow for an ever-widening *disconnection* between 'raw material' or locally processed foods and agricultural products, and final consumer products. These create new spatial and temporal arrangements;
- (ii) The global development of mega-farms, or the new latifundia, whereby concentration into one enterprise (melons, for example) creates a competitive advantage over several tens or hundreds of smaller family farms. These new latifundia enter into direct competition with surrounding family farms by 'appropriating, concentrating and recombining the available (and limited) resources, such as, land, water, quota, 'environmental space' and marketing possibilities' (van der Ploeg, 2006).
- (iii) Paradoxically the security of food supply may become more threatened under these circumstances, with the outsourcing of inputs into mega farms increasing the long-term fragility in food production, increasing environmental risks and giving opportunity for wholesale

'industry like' locational disinvestment from a region by mega farming interests.

(iv) Population movements in and then out of urban areas as a result of a reaction to the investment and disinvestment processes operating in agri-food systems—at the very least leading to more volatility and migration (e.g. Polish workers and cockle-pickers in the UK; new latifundia intensive poultry farms in Hungary).

Consumers Are Faced with a Vast Array of Food Goods

This is matched with an increasing array of quality labels and conventions in supply chains. Consumption patterns match more clearly onto socio-economic status and geographical location (both areas of plenty and 'food deserts'). The supply chain revolution that has developed has significantly restrained inflationary trends in food from getting out of hand with increasingly intensive 'price wars' between the major retailers.

Constructing Quality

A whole literature has developed around the sociology of food choice and quality (see Warde et al., 2004; Miele, 2006), which emphasises the social distinctions of food consumption. This production and proliferation of social distinctions is directly related to and built upon the emergence of the retail and catering supply chain revolution.

The Agri-Food System Increasingly Demands More of the Ecological System

The trends are underlain by 'metabolic rifts' between plants, animals and people. It creates all the more tensions. It continually attempts to detach itself from nature at the same time as transforming it. The retailer-led conventional system continues to revel in the opportunities of matching multifarious supply with growing consumer choices. At the very same time this continually denies natural and local geographies at the expense of providing wider consumer choices at increasing ecological costs. The analysis in the subsequent chapters will begin to show what a real conundrum this set of relationships really is. In one sense, nothing has changed. In another everything is changing.

State Management

These trends have also provided a paradoxical/contradictory problematic for the State in a context of growing concerns about food and ecological risks. The State has, in the first instance, been left standing within the socially hierarchical competitive environment which now constitutes food. It has had to follow innovation rather than lead or shape it. But at the same time the State cannot afford to relinquish its fundamental public responsibilities with regard to the safe and social provision of foods. The public will not stand for this, however addicted to the conventional system they may be. This fissure, left unresolved, lets in a whole range of hungry media interests with regard to the problems of food supply and provision, creating multiple moral panics with regard to the specificity and risks of food and eating. Again, at the same time the State, burdened, as it now is with continuing to promote a neo-liberal agenda, not least in stimulating a 'competitive' food sector, needs to be seen to be supportive to corporate agri-business capital. In short, jobs are on the line and mouths need to be fed. These contradictory problematics become the stage for the unfolding story of the 'new regulation of food'.

As a result of these trends in the 2000s we witness a transformation of the traditional agri-industrial model, as portrayed in much of the literature. This paradigm now has to accommodate and innovate significant supply chain management and cost-reduction strategies, which are, at the very least portrayed as 'consumer- led'. In fact they are retailer-led strategies which express their power in the supply chains. The 'consumer interest' is therefore being constantly 'reconstructed' by corporate firms in their performative and competitive strategies.

As we shall see in the rest of this book, however, retailers have not just achieved this central positioning in their own right, or in a sui generis fashion. As in the 1990s, the unfolding story of retailer-led expansionism has to be situated in its changing and contingent governance and regulatory context. For it is this interplay which begins to explain the circumstance.

To begin to understand these processes it is necessary to first consider some of the contemporary aspects of what we might call the contemporary 'anatomy' of food risk.

THE ANATOMY OF CONTEMPORARY FOOD RISK

The trends outlined above are leading to what we might call the increasing production/ manufacture of risks, at the same time as severely reducing the possibilities for sustainability of the agri-food system. However, we have to recognise that there have always been risks associated with food supply, however sustainable or otherwise they were. We need to, as well as critically situating current developments in the agri-industrial system, also critically situate our contemporary concepts of food risks. These are, as we shall see, now increasingly bound up with the three macro–societal trends identified at the start of this chapter: the socialisation of food, the increasing scientification of food (partly brought about by this socialisation process); and the further, but particular deepening of the (particular retail-led model of) liberalisation of markets.

Societies have had to continually devise innovative strategies to deal with the innumerable risks to health and well-being. Traditionally, these risks, such as famine, flooding, and predation, tended to be readily detectable and geographically circumscribed in their impacts. And, as understanding of the natural environment has improved, science and technologies have been applied to mitigate the potential human impacts of many of these natural hazards. Nevertheless, the successes that modernisation (especially over the last fifty years) has delivered have been marked by new social and environmental risks that are capable of manifesting deleterious impacts at indeterminate points in the future and over indefinite spatial realms. The significant differences, in characteristics and impacts, between contemporary risk and 'age-old' risk (i.e. the ability transcend ordinary sensory perception and to materialise without warning or geographical boundaries in the future) has been a feature recent sociological writing, for example *Risk Society* (Beck, 1992: see also Giddens, 1994 and Cohen, 1997).

According to Beck (1992), society is facing a new state of human insecurity, characterised not by the desire to satisfy basic and material needs, but by fear of the 'dark side of progress', i.e. the tangible and intangible by-products of (agri)industrial development. Confidence, therefore, that progress in human development has been synonymous with greater security is challenged by the recognition that modern day 'manufactured dragons', such as bovine spongiform encephalopathy (BSE) in cattle, may actually be a product of science and technology, and cannot easily be mitigated by it (Smith, 2002).

The crisis surrounding BSE (discovered first in British cattle during the mid-1980s) and its links with new variants of the Creutzfeldt-Jakob disease (vCJD) in humans, has been cited in the food risk literature as a classic illustration of what Beck (1992) means by 'manufactured risks'. This image of modernisation undermining feelings of confidence and security represents a formidable challenge to politicians, policy-makers, scientists, producers and others to find new ways of not only minimising these new threats to society, but to do so without creating hindrances to the modernisation process that is seen to have fulfilled many human needs. In other words, this post-modernisation era requires that economic and social development continues; but does so without minimising prudence or increasing public feelings of insecurity (Smith, 2002). In the context of the society being exposed to new types of food risks, public concern has extended beyond the mere occurrences of food borne diseases due to periodic microbial contamination. Instead, what has become significantly more important has been the increasing incidence of these microbial episodes, the emergence of new food pathogens, as well as infectious strains of familiar pathogens that bring resistance to customary anti-microbial treatments. *E. coli 0157* is a notable example. In the UK it is estimated that between 10–40% of cattle herds are infected with *E. coli 0157* and that infection has also diffused to a range of wildlife and domesticated animals that may be in contact with cattle. Overall infectious intestinal disease causes 300 deaths and 35,000 hospital admissions annually, and the UK Food Standards agency (FSA) estimate that 4.5 million people in the UK suffer annually from food poisoning. Food borne pathogens (such as E. coli and Campylobacter) primarily enter the food chain from contaminated meat products, but there are also outbreaks associated with contaminated water, soil and livestock. It can be introduced into the environment by cattle through faeces, but also in agricultural wastes spread on land. This can then pollute water supplies and the pathogens can survive in the soils for years.

In the case of non-infectious, food borne diseases, public concern surrounds the uncertain effects of a range of synthetic food additives, pesticide residues, nitrate residues, dioxins, heavy metals, hormones in beef, genetically modified organisms and so on (see Lang et al., 2001 and WHO, 1999). Public confidence in food is consequently undermined by the belief that chemical residues and genetic modification may harbour deleterious consequences for human health, such as mutagenic, carcinogenic and teratogenic effects (WHO, 1999).

In short, the mere complexity and diversity of food risks have become far more recognised. And this risk is seen to be bound up in a complex set of ways in which both supply chains and rural environments are managed and regulated both over space and time.

However, to attribute the erosion of public confidence in food (especially in the UK) during the 1980s and 1990s merely to a steady catalogue of food scares would be to ignore broader societal developments. These gave greater importance to broader expressions of public disaffection with how public responsibilities were being discharged. Notably, during the 1980s and into 1990s (and especially since 1997) the UK experienced its own period of social *glasnost*. This 'wind of social change'—towards greater openness and forthrightness in dealings between the public and public institutions—began to challenge the pre-existing ethos of authority and submission in transactions between the executive state and the client public. The ensuing transition from public administration through virtually closed policy avenues of *government* to the more socially inclusive notion of *governance*, gradually provided useful political space for new participants, such as environmental and social non-governmental organisations (NGOs) to contribute to the definition of problems of public significance as well as in devising likely solution options. Consequently, where previously, paternalistic statements of the diligence of regulators to reduce the range and number of breaches in food safety, for instance, may have ameliorated public concern, increasingly, this became inadequate in the late 1990s. Hence, issues of accountability within the food chain and effectiveness of mechanisms of food safety regulation, begun to take on greater national importance.

This wider process of governance in the UK, particularly in relation to its contribution to the construction of a new regulatory context for food, has been positively influenced by the parallel rise in participative democracy across Western Europe; as part—and—parcel of the wider 'European project'. Of particular importance has been the institutionalisation of greater openness in matters of public affairs that has been facilitated by the passage of key pieces of EU legislation such as 90/313/EC[1], 93/730/EC[2] and 95/46/EC[3], as well as the 'Treaty of the European Union' itself. These, together with legislation requiring the release of archived information, have opened the way for ordinary citizens, in the different Member States, to gain knowledge of the workings of the state; knowledge that previously would have been known only to governments, their advisors and to privileged insider individuals and groups. This process change in how, when and what types of information becomes public knowledge, meant that issues of public interest, such as food safety, began to be reported in the electronic and print media much earlier, and in much greater detail, than in the past. This easier access to information of public interest also facilitated NGO campaigning activities in areas such as animal welfare, application of the 'precautionary principle' to matters of food safety, as well as to environmental concerns generally.

Consequently, it is not sufficient to relate attempts at devising new strategies for assuring food safety in the UK and across the EU, simply to a raft of recent food scares. Important though this has been, the process has nevertheless been significantly influenced by the wider social, political and economic considerations shown in Figure 1.1 below.

There is now wider recognition that the above factors have been guiding how the public perceive food risks. This has challenged conventional food regulatory practices with their reliance on a combination of science, technology and expert advice to allay public fears. Governments across the EU began to acknowledge that the conventional approach dealt poorly with the crucial issue of scientific uncertainty. And, whilst absolute guarantees about the safety of foods cannot be given, or indeed, are not expected by the public, the fear that lives and wellbeing are being exposed to 'manufactured risks' raised public expectations for improvements in food regulation. The question for governments become: how can new food safety and quality assurances be established given these new food/governance pressures?

Beck's (1992) *Risk Society* thesis elucidates this contemporary risk/governance concern. Scientific research is not always able to provide a full and clear picture of what effects, for instance, widespread consumption of foods containing GMOs will have on human health (see Chapter 3 and Chapter 10). In view of this deficiency in 'science-based' decision-making, states, such as the UK, have become less resistant to value and culture-based advice infusing the conventional process of food safety regulation.

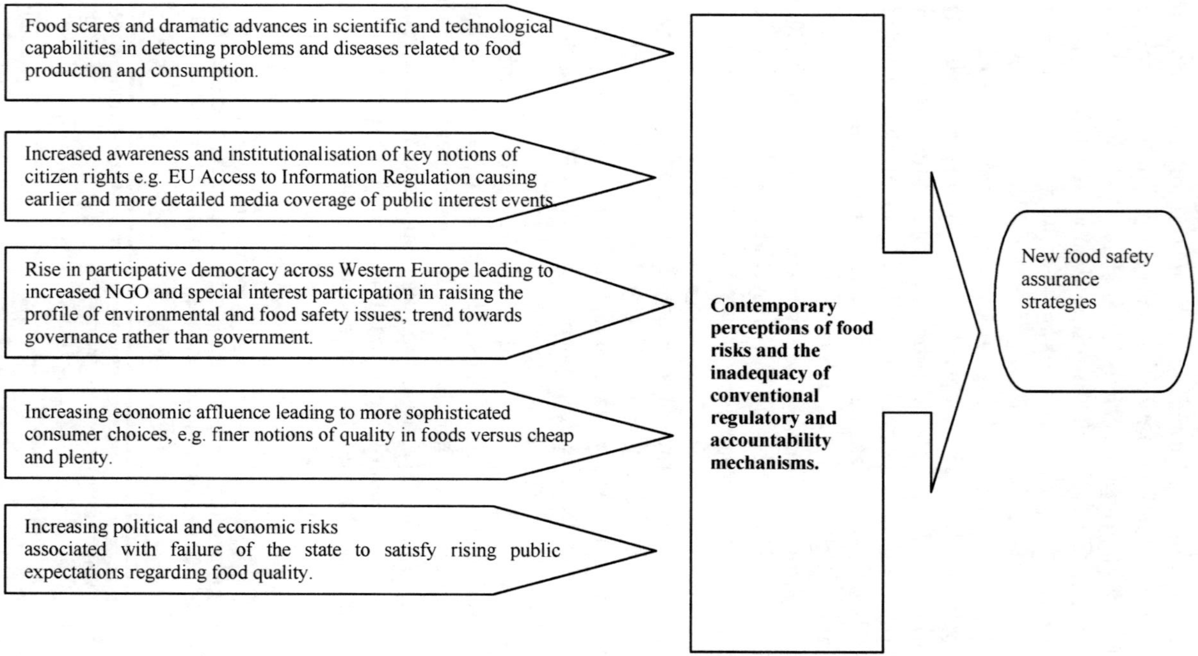

Figure 1.1 Factors contributing to contemporary perceptions of food risk and new regulatory approaches.

THE EMERGENCE OF A REVISED MODEL OF CONTESTED REGULATION AND ACCOUNTABILITY ACROSS EU FOOD MARKETS

From Enforcement of Minimum Standards to Managing Risk in Food

In the same way that public perception of food risks has been changing, so too have the regulatory and accountability approaches of governments and food processors/retailers. The latter consider their businesses to be at significant risk due to potential loss of market share as well as from civil liability claims. In the period up to the early 1980s, regulatory and accountability approaches focused primarily on managing age-old food risks, such as illnesses that were caused by direct microbial contamination of foods, elevated microbacterial counts, unhygienic food handling, poor transportation and storage of foods, and improper food preparation. Since the mid-1980s a discernible change in the perception, nature and extent of food risk began to emerge. In the case of the UK, public rejection of British beef following the outbreak of BSE, and the subsequent EU export ban on British beef, had adverse economic as well as social impacts on local farmers. And, the ensuing regulatory response to this threat (as well as to others such as pesticide, GMO and junk food) to human health, as well as to the rural and national economies, resulted in a fundamental shift in the way safety within the food supply chain would be assured in the future.

Looking back at the period before the mid-1980s, when food hygiene and public health were the highest concerns on the food safety regulatory agenda, strategies to manage food risk depended heavily upon science-based, technological approaches. Under the regulatory regimes that were in place then, food and agricultural production systems were regarded as being safe unless proven otherwise by technical and quantitative analyses. In this way, the state had a rational and scientific basis on which to rest relevant public health and food quality assurance policies. This time-honoured food regulatory approach, along with periodic on-site monitoring reinforced by a graduated scheme of penalties for breaches, allowed the state to play a key role in the food supply sector (Marsden et al., 2000). This conventional or *first phase* food regulatory regime, that is depicted in Figure 1.2, was, for an extended period, successful in addressing food safety and related public health concerns.

The transformation, since the mid-1980s, in how food risk is perceived and the new regulatory framework that has emerged to mediate the new concerns, have been traced by Marsden et al. (2000) in *Consuming Interests*. In depicting the evolution that was taking place in food safety assurance strategies in the UK from the 1980s into 1990s, they pointed to a transition from a traditional government-led corporatist regulatory and monitoring model (conservative, proof-based approach enforced at the

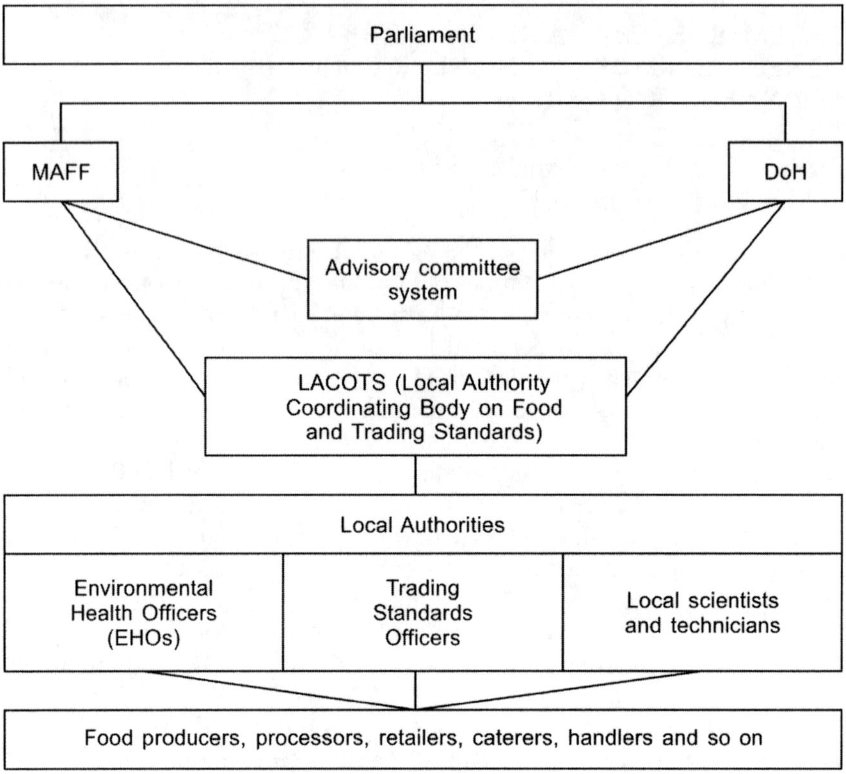

Figure 1.2 The conventional (or *first phase)* food regulatory regime in the UK. Source: Based on Marsden et al. (2000), p. 89.

local level by EHOs and TSOs) to a new phase dominated by supply chain management, and food standards strategies, designed and applied by the large multiple food retailers.

As Zwanenberg and Millstone (2003: 34) point out, this first phase of food regulation was incapable of dealing effectively with the expanding and long-running food risk crisis in the 1980s and early 1990s: they argue:

> A fundamental characteristic of the British approach to policy-making on BSE therefore, was that while policy was represented to the general public as if it were based upon, and only on, scientific evidence and the advice of the outstanding experts, in practice many of the important policy decisions were made before the scientists were recruited or consulted, and attempts were routinely made to obtain their endorsement of those prior decisions. The objectives of policy were concealed and/or misrepresented, risks were seriously and consistently

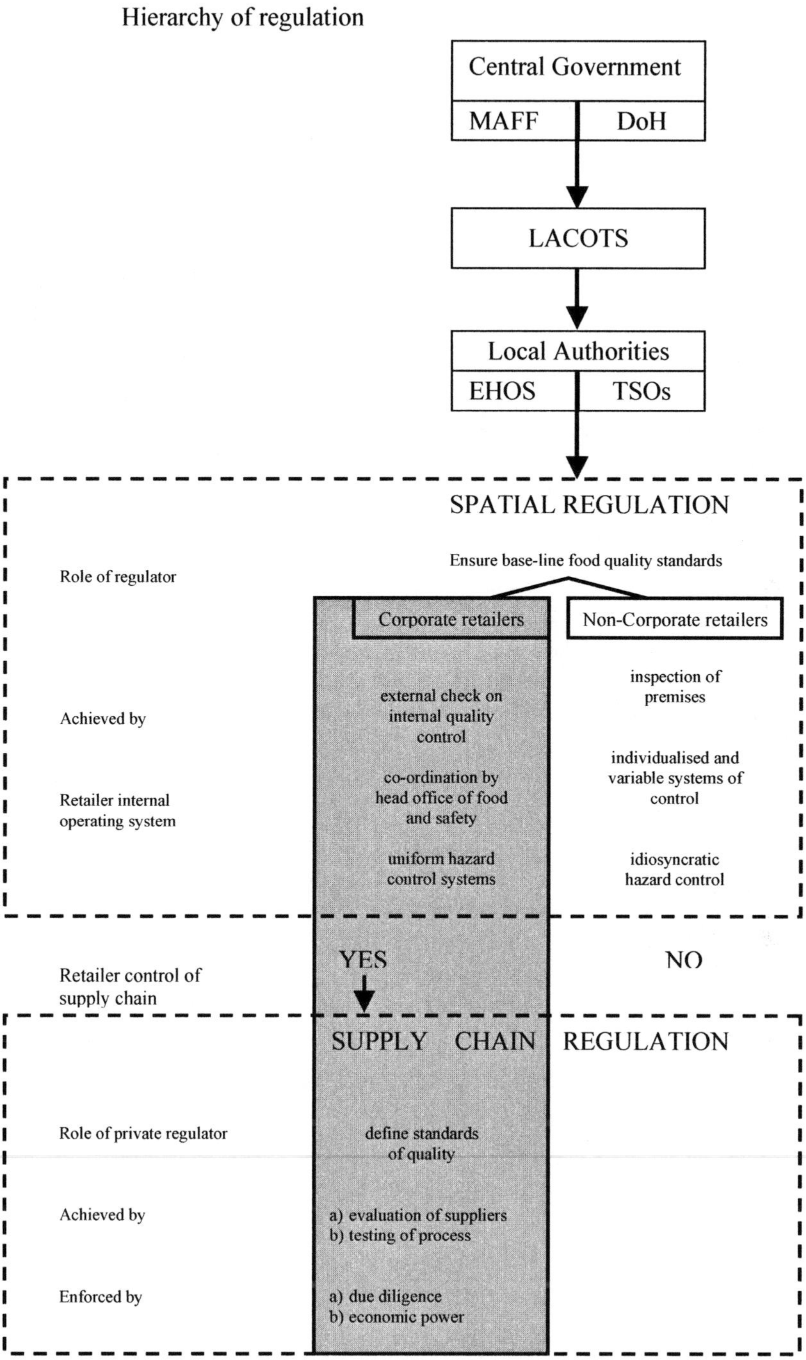

Figure 1.3 The private-public (or *second phase*) food regulatory regime in the UK (predating the Food Standards Agency of April 2000).

understated, and the degree to which the available evidence and expert advisors supported those policies was misrepresented.

The *second phase* in the evolution of food regulation in the UK is also corporatist in nature, but is, in this case, driven primarily by the way food safety issues are perceived by large food retailers; leaving the state to act mainly as auditors rather than standard-setters and enforcers of the mainstream process. A hierarchical, spatial and supply chain depiction of this evolved dual private-public interest food regulatory scheme is illustrated in Figure 1.3.

This two-tiered approach, whereby the state-centred system of spatial regulation continues for non-corporate producers and retailers on the one hand, but a new private-sector regulated supply chain approach operates for corporate retailers on the other, became an embedded feature of food regulation in the UK by the mid 1990s. But, despite offering certain clear improvements in food quality assurance, this two-tiered approach allowed corporate retailers to distinguish themselves from their non-corporate competitors, as well as from each other, on the basis of the assurance of quality that they are able to deliver through stringent supply chain management. However, because the greater assurance of food quality that the *second phase* (private-public) food regulation regime engenders does not encompass the entire food supply chain, and given the continuing diversity and intensity of food risk beyond the late 1990s, the pressure for further changes became apparent. It is to these new sets of relationships—a *third phase* in the evolution of food safety regulation—which this book will attempt to explore and assess.

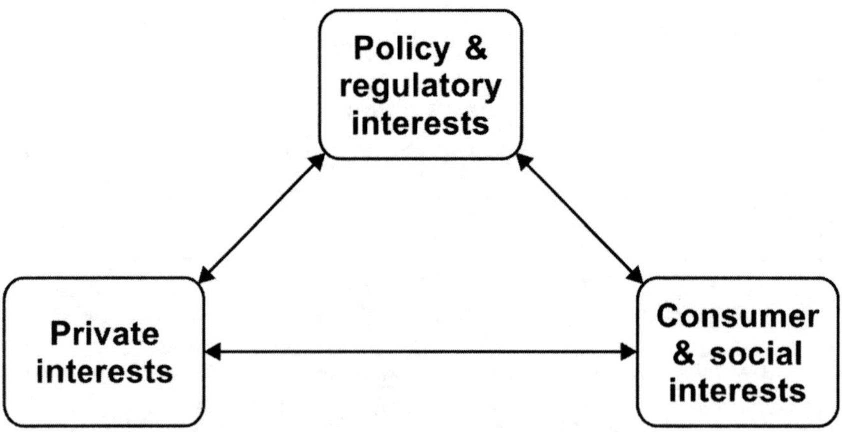

Figure 1.4 The formal food policy-formation network.

STRUCTURE OF THE BOOK

The following analysis will begin to assess some of the conceptual parameters and dynamics of this latest phase in the evolution of food safety regulation in the EU, and assess the influences shaping this contemporary regulatory and (wider governance) complex.

We can now conceptualise this focus as a set of interactions between the three sets of interests outlined in Figure 1.4. The succeeding analysis is divided into four subparts. Part I, together with this introductory chapter outline key aspects of the 'anatomy of the crisis'. We focus specifically on cases which post-date the BSE crisis of the 1980s and 1990s, by focussing on the Foot and Mouth outbreak in the early 2000s, and the unfolding regulatory and public controversies associated with the EU and UK management of the GM challenge. (See Chapters 2 and 3).

The second part of the book contains three chapters which detail our empirical and conceptual analysis of the new 'model' of food regulation which develops in the 2000s both at the EU and UK levels. Both interrelated levels are explored. This is followed, in Part III, by analysis of the operation of these regulatory systems as they apply to, first the fresh fruit and vegetable sector—a sector seen as a highly competitive market leader by retailers and governments in the unfolding health agenda—and then the red meat sector—a sector which has struggled to rid itself of the stigma associated with the BSE and FMD crises. Part IV of the book takes a more conceptual frame looking at aspects of: the management of risk (Chapter 9); the role of the precautionary principle (Chapter 10); and the positioning of global regulatory mechanisms (Chapter 11). In the concluding chapter (Chapter 12) we assess whether this model of regulation in the EU and the UK is sustainable, and whether it represents a palliative or a long-term solution to the continued governance of food in the 21st century. New challenges face the model of food governance analysed in this volume; and these provide a rich empirical and theoretical terrain to study the agri-food sector as a key arena for the broader understanding of economy, polity and spatial relationships.

2 Handling Biosecurity Risk
The Foot and Mouth Outbreak 2001

INTRODUCTION

This chapter offers an account of the foot and mouth disease outbreak of 2001. In many ways it is a story with such astonishing features that it almost requires little additional critique. However, we wish to pick up on some of the themes in the opening chapter. One of these, the globalisation and re-structuring of the food sector may seem surprising, since, although the disease did spread from Britain to Ireland, France and the Netherlands it was contained relatively quickly. The outbreak seemed largely a domestic character. In fact we will show that political handling of the crisis was dictated from the outset by the perceived need to protect global markets. Indeed the very seat of the infection almost certainly lay in imported meat.

A second theme is the intensification of agriculture and its generation of animal movement and the very risk of transmission of the disease. There are many features of this part of the story that shape the conditions that not only made the outbreak possible but which meant that by the time the disease was discovered it had spread nationwide. These include the loss of local abattoirs, the consumer sourcing of meat largely through the major retail chains, the vast distances covered by animals in the food chain and the perverse incentives against bio-security created by the presence of subsidy.

A third theme is devoted to the role of the State at the time of the outbreak. Here we can pick up on the multi-faceted nature of the State and the complex patterns of governance in which it is engaged. Historic systems of State engagement with a productivist agriculture do not rapidly disappear in a post-productivist era, but leave a legacy. So, whilst largely detached from the private ordering of the food chain, which, in the manner explained, shaped all elements of the risk of disease, the State was expected to step back in at the first moments of discovery of the disease and not only attempt to quell an already rampant virus, but also to pick up the entire bill for the costs of so doing. It provides, perhaps, the best possible example of the dichotomy that the State is increasingly detached from and even disinterested in food production, but unable to relinquish its role as the guardian of food safety and salubrity.

In particular we suggest that there are structural confusions inherent in the framework of disease control and response, whereby policies adopted to serve one outcome have precisely the opposite consequence. The primary example of this is that, in order to pursue a policy of stamping out the disease, the system provided for such levels of compensation that all risks of disease are externalised leaving little incentive for ongoing precaution. Similarly, payments set at generous levels to encourage the declaration of the disease to allow its stamping out reached such a level that it may have positively encouraged infection. The contrasts with newer models of food hygiene regulation could not be more marked. The private sector has increasingly assumed responsibility for the regulation of its supply chains and, with the support of national and EU policy, internalised risks (e.g. through Hazard and Critical Control Point [HACCP]).

Finally, the key decision making on how to control the spread of the disease once it is present brings together, in a single instance, arguments of the scientification and socialisation of food. Although as will be explained, meat from foot and mouth infected stock, or from animals vaccinated against the disease, has no human health impact whatsoever, and while such meat has for years been in the food chain, a central element of the decision making rested upon assumptions of what consumers would or would not accept. These were assumptions simply because there was little actual place for the consumer voice, and so, in this case, the consumer was represented by farmers and food manufacturers. At the same time, as is shown in following text, questions of what was scientifically possible in relation to vaccination were reconstructed under the influence of the economic consequences driven by concerns to access liberalised markets.

The foot and mouth outbreak of 2001 generated costs totalling no less than £9 billion, and with at least £3 billion in direct cost to the public sector (DEFRA and DCMS, 2002). Amongst these direct costs were significant sums of compensation. The largest single payment was some £4.2 million, but there were fifty-nine payments of more than £1 million and 323 of more than £500,000 (HM Comptroller and Auditor General, 2002). These figures represent compensation paid for losses incurred, but the private sector, particularly in tourism and supporting industries, but also in the food chain, suffered revenue losses of about £5 billion, much of which went uncompensated. Hundreds of businesses failed, and alongside this misery the outbreak produced unspeakable cruelty to animals.

THE NATURE OF FOOT AND MOUTH DISEASE

Foot and Mouth Disease (FMD) is an epidemic, viral infection to which all cloven-footed animals, including those commonly domesticated for agriculture, are susceptible (OIE, 2000: Ch. 2.1.1). It has been notorious everywhere in the world where livestock are reared as an extremely contagious disease but also one which is very rarely fatal. It can be transmitted by direct contact with infected, carrier animals, by contact with their discharges (FMD virus can survive for weeks or months in animal wastes), by being physically carried on other creatures which cannot actually contract the disease and on inanimate objects such as farm vehicles, and through the air over short and long distances as infected animals, especially pigs, exhale the virus. The incidence of long distance transmission by air is highly dependent on environmental factors and on the nature of the specific strain of FMD virus involved. Typically short-range transmission between animals brought into proximity or contact is the major source of infection.

FMD takes its name from a very unpleasant symptom infected animals may display, of the growth of vesicles or blisters chiefly in and around the mouth and feet which are painful and which can make chewing and walking difficult, sometimes to such an extent that the animal becomes lame. However, the principal symptom of FMD is fever. The severity of the symptoms infected animals display can differ widely. Infection may easily pass entirely unnoticed especially in herds of sheep, being very hard to detect in the context of normal husbandry practices. It is also a low mortality disease, for almost all adult cattle and sheep and over 90% of adult pigs will recover within two weeks. On the other hand, weak or young animals may die, and in particular mortality among newly born animals may be high as it induces myocarditis (heart disease). Adult cattle who recover may display 'reduced performance' in that their ability to gain weight and produce milk may be impaired. However, the point which must be stressed here is that FMD is far from an apocalyptic disease: adult animals very rarely die of it but rather recover from what in the literature is often compared to a bout of the flu (Houghton Brown, 2001). Significantly, there are only a tiny number of (disputed) cases of human beings ever contracting the disease, those cases being produced by extremely close contact with infected animals. Human beings cannot contract the disease by eating food products obtained from infected or vaccinated livestock (Prempeh et al., 2001). The Food Standards Agency (FSA) has said that FMD has 'no implications for the human food chain' (FSA 2001). Since the animal and human health aspects of FMD are limited, the wide ranging ramifications of the UK FMD outbreak of 2001 need to be explored in terms of the dynamics of the regulatory and supply chain context.

THE UK OUTBREAK OF 2001

First suspicions of the disease arose following a veterinary inspection on pigs at the Cheale Meats Abattoir at Brentwood, Essex on 19 February 2001. Although the disease was confirmed the following day, the five-mile exclusion zone at the Essex abattoir was not put into place until 21 February 2001. The tracing of the animals passing through the abattoir suggested a possible source of infection at a farm run by Bobby Waugh in Heddon-on-the-Wall, Northumbria. A five- mile exclusion zone was established around this farm on 23 February 2001. However, it is also known that sheep sent to Hexham Market on 13 February were infected. There were 3,800 sheep passing through Hexham Market on that day and 120 dealers attending the market (HM Comptroller and Auditor General, 2002). While the response of MAFF was to declare an exclusion zone in Essex, at that stage hundreds of potentially infected animals were dispersed widely across the country.

Supply Chain Restructuring

There are two aspects of the changing management of the red meat supply chain that impacted upon the spread of FMD: reduction in abattoirs and retailer own label dominance.

a) Decline of the Abattoir

Since the 1980s there has been a continual decline in the number of abattoirs (see Table 2.1).

In recent years in the UK there has been a significant number of abattoir closures (Shaoul, 1997; Kennard and Young 1999). Some closures resulted from the imposition of new EU standards that required an upgrading of facilities. In other cases, low margins arising from over-capacity have driven out the more inefficient operators. In both instances, though, the result has

Table 2.1 Decline in Abattoirs for Selected Years

Year	*Number of Abattoirs*
1984	817
1988	540
1992	491
2003–2004	311
2004–2005	297

Source: Schofield and Shaoul, 2000: 538; MLC, 2006: 13

been that smaller and medium sized operators have closed (MLC, 2006: 13). Inevitably, larger and more concentrated abattoir ownership means that animals have to travel further to slaughter.

b) Own Label Dominance

By 2002, 75% of the meat consumed was sold through major supermarket chains (VAO, 2005). At least as significant for the red meat industry as the supremacy of the supermarkets in sales, which is replicated for other foods, is their use of own labels to market meat. As the MLC (2006: 5) has noted, 'retailers' own label shares in meat are considerably higher than for total food'. In early 2006, for instance, 69% of red meat was sold by supermarkets under their own label, with the next highest category being dairy products at 46%. The desire of many such retailers to produce meat which is presented to the consumer, uniformly dressed and packaged, means the concentration of meat production in certain chosen abattoirs. This is turn demands considerable movement of live animals. At the outbreak of the disease, one transportation company based in Somerset disclosed that it moved over one million head of cattle per annum (O'Donnell, 2001). It feared that foot and mouth would kill its business. At the same time, many companies connected with agriculture found that they were not ruined by the outbreak of the disease, but actually made significant windfall profits helping with the slaughter and disposal of cattle. One Scottish waste contractor is reported to have billed £38.4 million for work undertaken at the time of the outbreak in facilitating the disposal of slaughtered stock (HM Comptroller and Auditor General, 2002).

However, one must question the utility of many such cattle movements. For example at the time of the outbreak Britain imported 125,000 tonnes of lamb, but exported 102,000 tonnes (Lucas, 2001). The Common Agricultural Policy in promoting intensive farming, and requiring ever- larger markets, rather than locally based patterns of rearing, supply and consumption actually increased the risk of epidemic disease. This can be explained by a simple example of a dealer from Ireland who purchased 271 hoggets, for between about £35–42 each, at Carlisle Market on 19 February 2001, illegally transhipping them through Scotland and Northern Ireland to the Republic of Ireland. The purpose of this exercise seems to have been to both attract a 4% rebate on VAT available in the Republic and to gain a £10 per head premium available to 'Irish' lamb (Sheenan and Kearney, 2001). The cost of this subterfuge was the spread of FMD to three jurisdictions. In introducing a twenty-one-day restriction on stock movements after initial shipment, a 'Cabinet Minister' is quoted as saying:

> 'Nobody took account of the extent to which dodgy farmers moved sheep around to claim quota payments. That is the true story'.(Prescott and Leake, 2001)

This is in the main a reference to the practice of 'bed and breakfasting' farm animals so that the numbers of animals forecast for the farm, early in the season, are actually available to the farmer at the time of inspection, thereby avoiding any shortfall in quota payments (Church of Scotland, 2001). If the farmer has a shortfall in forecasted numbers, the 'Cabinet Minister' is alleging that farmers merely borrow animals in order to ensure a higher quota payment.

The first of the Inquiry reports following foot and mouth, *The Future of Farming and Food* (Curry, 2002), points to many other unwelcome outcomes of the Common Agricultural Policy (CAP) system. These include: the separation of producers from their market; the distortion of price signals; and the masking of inefficiencies in production. As far as direct payments for livestock are concerned, the report calls for a decoupling of subsidies from levels of production as an interim measure:

> Farmers do need assistance in adjusting to reduced support and some compensation is justified for falling asset prices. However, anything other than short term assistance frustrates the objectives of reform, keeps farmers from the market and continues to encourage practices which may harm the environment. (21)

With the onset of the foot and mouth disease, cattle and sheep movements were tightly controlled. According to the 'Lessons to be Learned' Report, even in the aftermath of these controls there were over 700 investigations into illegal movements (Anderson, 2002).

HANDLING THE OUTBREAK

One of the many extraordinary aspects of the FMD outbreak was the initial confidence of MAFF that they could control the spread of disease, notwithstanding the widespread nature of the cattle and sheep movements. By the end of the first week in March the Chief Veterinary Officer issued the following statement:

> Most of the animals if they are going to develop the disease . . . should be showing signs last week and this week and possibly some overflow into next week. So the first evidence is that because we stopped all movements, we stop the spread of disease. (Henderson, 2001)

This can be placed alongside the similarly optimistic view expressed, on the same day by the Director of the Institute of Animal Health, whose laboratory was central to the control of the outbreak:

> My understanding is that the vast majority, if not all the current cases, are on farms with a link to the original outbreak and that is good news . . . everything that has happened so far might have been predicted. Had the disease taken off and moved out of control we would have expected to see cases with no connection to the original source by now. (Henderson, 2001)

With hindsight because these statements were issued before the cull of millions of animals it is easy to deride them as deluded. However we now also know that very high percentages of the cattle culled were not infected. In the Forest of Dean, a seat of opposition to the cull, thirty-four farms served with notices of slaughter resisted the cull. Not one animal on any of these farms was found to be infected (National Foot and Mouth Group, 2001).

Nonetheless statements such as those previously made produced the impression that MAFF was in control of the outbreak of FMD and in the process of eliminating it. The Anderson Inquiry states that 'the government departments were not greatly involved at this stage, largely because MAFF was not asking for help' (Anderson 2001, at para. 9.1). Moreover, the Anderson Inquiry suggests that the complacency within MAFF about disease control affected the entire Ministry:

> Individual groups and managers not directly involved with the outbreak remained focused on their own targets. There was no incentive to release staff to help in the fight against FMD'. (Anderson 2001, para. 9.2)

MAFF's faith in its capacity to survey farming and manage the FMD outbreak is revealing of the different regulatory practices that prevail in the food system. For FMD regulatory action was focussed on the producer—the traditional object of MAFF activities—and where well established patterns of behaviour could assert themselves. MAFF staff felt themselves to be confident in understanding farming practices, for example, sheep movements, and thus being able to introduce adequate control measures and to have them policed through the State Veterinary Service (SVS). To ensure that farmers complied with FMD controls generous financial compensation was provided. The contrast with the regulation of food hygiene is marked: MAFF traditionally had much weaker contacts with the consumer end of the food chain and responsibility for food safety is internalised by private actors (see Chapter 4) rather than, as in the case of FMD, externalised and responsibility taken by the State.

On 11 March, Nick Brown, Minister for Agriculture, appeared on 'Breakfast with Frost' and stated that the disease was under control; when pressed he repeated that he was 'absolutely certain' in this view (Anderson 2001, Annex E). As the Anderson Inquiry points out, there was no evidential basis for this view. Thirty-four cases of foot and mouth had been notified in the two days prior to that Sunday; 164 cases had been confirmed in total, and in Cumbria alone there were over 40,000 carcasses awaiting disposal. In the words of one farmer giving evidence to Anderson:

> We felt absolutely insulted and patronised by these lies that we were told. (Anderson, 2001: 81)

It was almost a further two weeks before the Cabinet Office Briefing Room (COBR) was open to co-ordinate work across all departments in handling the disaster. Coinciding with the introduction of COBR was the Contiguous Cull Policy. This was a policy to destroy on a precautionary basis 'animals within the 3 kilometre zones'.[1] The very announcement of this statement caused consternation, since, in effect, the policy only applied to sheep and pigs, but this was not immediately made clear. Alongside the Contiguous Cull Policy was a target to slaughter infected stock within twenty-four hours and dispose of the carcass within forty-eight hours. Overseeing the operation of this policy was the FMD Science Group.

What in effect the FMD Science Group did was to model the likely spread of infection from farm to farm in order to bring the disease on to a downward trajectory such that the rate of spread would always become smaller. Beyond doubt, this was achieved, but the approach was later admitted by the Chief Scientist's Advisory Group to have been 'over draconian' (Highfield, 2001). The approach took no account whatsoever of the possible variable conditions of spread according to factors such as geography. It made no allowance for natural barriers which might restrict spread. It made no distinction between inspected species, though it is clear that pigs present by far the greatest risk through exhalation. The model may well have overestimated wind spread. This is a common source of transmission of this highly infectious disease, but there is some evidence to suggest that in relation to this particular strain of virus, direct contact was a much more important mode of transmission. Finally, no distinction was made between different farming practices in different regions, and the Contiguous Cull Policy allowed for no assertion that a farmer had exercised rigorous bio-security measures. Any farm within a three-kilometre radius had its animals culled.

The Anderson Inquiry went on to show that the geographical information system deployed was generally used for the purpose of calculating CAP subsidies. In the words of the Inquiry:

> Information is frequently out of date, on occasion by several years. It was sometimes difficult to pinpoint the location of livestock accommodation within an individual holding, or identify the operator of that land. (Anderson, 2001: 72)

There are many stories of slaughter men arriving at the wrong location, but of course farmers could not know, however careful their own bio-security, that they were not within a contiguous cull area.

According to the FAO, 6.24 million animals were killed.[2] At least one-in-three diagnoses appears to have been incorrect. This is not surprising, given the generation of veterinary scientists with no effective experience of FMD. However, this figure relates to *confirmed* diagnoses (which were nonetheless wrong) but where there was thought to be no time for confirmation a policy of 'suspected slaughters' was pursued. Four in every five of these suspected slaughters did not involve an actual outbreak of foot and mouth. It is worth recalling when reading these figures, that each of these suspected slaughters then involved contiguous farming units often within the three-kilometre radius. On average, there would be four such units. This produced a ripple effect, and it meant that, long after the actual onset of disease had peaked, the numbers of animals killed continued to grow. In total, 2,026 farming premises said to be infected produced pre-emptive culling on a further 8,131 premises. In the first week of the Contiguous Cull Policy there were 48,000 animals slaughtered each day. In two days alone in Devon 32,000 animals were slaughtered (Mercer). In the week beginning 25 March, there were 293 infected premises 'confirmed' as suffering from FMD. By the week beginning 6 May 2001 there were forty-nine such premises, but by mid-May, the daily slaughter had risen to 80,000 animals (HM Comptroller and Auditor General, 2002).

Such levels of slaughter could only be achieved with the acquiescence of the farming community. In order to ensure that farmers did not resist the slaughter of animals, valuers were given an incentive to value generously by linking their payment to the value of the cattle destroyed. It became necessary to put a ceiling on the operation of this formula, and this was set at £1,500 per day (HM Comptroller and Auditor General, 2002).

Unsurprisingly in such circumstances, compensation payments rocketed. From the outset, MAFF were keen that there would be little argument in relation to the slaughter of infected stock. Payments were intended to be generous. However, as has been describedthat the top price for two-year-old sheep at the Carlisle Market at the outset of the outbreak was £42 per head. In contrast, the average value across the first four weeks of the outbreak was £100 per head in compensation. This figure eventually peaks at £300 in July 2001. Similarly, the average compensation payment for cattle tripled during the course of the outbreak (HM Comptroller and Auditor General, 2002). The Animal Health Act 1981 based compensation on the value of the animal immediately prior to infection. However there was no functioning market during the outbreak. Moreover, as millions of animals were destroyed, one might expect the valuation of stock to rise in order to reflect the subsequent shortage of stock. Also, although MAFF appointed valuers, under the legislation, it was open to the farmer to appoint a valuer also. It became clear from very early in the outbreak that over 90% of farmers were likely to do so, and the urgency of the cull made it easier to allow the farmer to choose the valuer, who in any case was paid on a sliding scale linked to value. In the end the Government paid £10 million in valuation fees, and in almost one in five valuation days the £1,500 cap was reached (HM Comptroller and Auditor General, 2002).

It must be stressed, however, that many farmers affected by the outbreak went uncompensated. Diseased cattle and those taken out in the contiguous cull (see next section) received compensation. There was also compensation assistance for 'welfare killings' of (e.g.) lambs born in the field that could not be moved, but which were literally drowning in the fields in an unusually wet spring. Many farmers could not get their animals to market and were not allowed to move them during the outbreak. These animals had to be fed and watered at significant cost with no outlet for sale, and long after their market value had peaked. These farmers joined many other people in the rural business community in suffering losses which effectively went uncompensated. Elsewhere we have argued (Campbell and Lee, 2003a) that to guarantee compensation for infection removes all incentives to precaution in a system that promotes the conditions whereby the outbreak and spread of the disease are promoted precisely because of this failure to internalise the risk. Here we have a curious regulatory system that rewards failure—and vividly illustrates the historically close links between MAFF and farmers (see Chapter 4) and suggests that farmers had managed to at least 'capture' part of the Ministry since the interests seemed to be so closely intertwined. Given the compensation guarantee, less than one in ten farmers carried insurance, but where this was so both the insurer and the Government paid out (Minoli, 2003). It is perhaps not surprising in view of the previous text that DEFRA—the successor to MAFF—felt the need to warn about the criminality of deliberate infection (DEFRA, 2001).

THE CULL

To slaughter so many animals within such short time frames proved not to be possible within the scope of the legal powers available. The initial policy for dealing with the foot and mouth outbreak was the 'stamping out' of the disease. This implies that swift localised action can isolate the disease before it is allowed to spread. It rests upon the slaughter of infected stock together with all other animals suspected of being at serious risk of contagion. However, this policy gave way to the contiguous cull. Such policy is different in nature. It was based upon the rapid slaughter (within twenty-four hours of suspected FMD) and disposal (within forty-eight hours of suspected FMD) of not merely cattle supposedly at risk through contact or otherwise, *but because they happen to be within a certain proximity of a suspected case.* As we have seen the radius of three kilometres of a suspected source of FMD was commonly employed, although not vital to the mathematical model. There are many questions about the legality of government action attached to the FMD outbreak. These include many civil liberties issues, many animal welfare issues, breaches of environmental laws and bio-security measures, and considerable examples of action that outstripped the formal legal powers available to the authorities (Campbell and Lee, 2003b; Chief Veterinary Officer, 2001;Tromans, 2002).

Essentially the problem facing the Government in relation to the contiguous cull was the Animal Health Act 1981 in giving powers to 'cause to be slaughtered' various categories of animal. These were restricted to: animals affected or suspected of being infected with FMD; animals in the same field, shed, or other place, or in the same herd or flock as FMD animals; animals in contact with FMD affected animals; or animals which appear to have been in any way exposed to FMD. One power that is not there is that of slaughtering apparently healthy animals merely on the basis that they are located on a site within a certain proximity to an outbreak of FMD.

In essence, this was admitted on a number of occasions. For example, the Animal Health Bill (which became the Animal Health Act 2002) was said to have introduced 'new disease control powers' for England and Wales by amending the Animal Health Act 1981. In the Consultation Paper (DEFRA, 2002) it was said that:

> The new powers to slaughter animals in order to prevent disease spread will ensure we have the means to control and eradicate an outbreak in a more effective and efficient manner than has been possible in the past.

In describing why the powers would be introduced, the new powers were described as 'precautionary'. However, on 26 March 2002, the Government was defeated in the Lords on the Animal Health Bill by 130 votes to 124. The motion to strike down the Bill was proposed by Lord Moran notwithstanding a three-line whip by the government. In the words of Lord Moran: 'The present Bill is based entirely on legalising and extending the mass slaughter of animals' (House of Lords Debates, 2001). Elsewhere, Lord Moran has described this Bill as 'of a positively Stalinist nature' which was an attempt to legalise the culling of 'many thousands of healthy animals. . .killed last year' (Moran, 2002).

The Government spokesman in the Lords at the time of the Animal Health Bill, Lord Whitty, told the Anderson Inquiry himself that the legality of the contiguous cull had been 'an issue' (Anderson, 2002: Annex B). The Anderson Report (2002: 163) concludes that:

> We consider the powers to be insufficiently clear. This lack of clarity contributed to a sense of mistrust of the Government, which was made worse by poor communication of the rationale of the cull.

It is interesting to note that in those areas of the country such as parts of Devon and the Forest of Dean where protestors against the contiguous cull were well organised, there were a number of appeals faxed immediately to MAFF upon the service of a notice seeking to slaughter animals. Notwithstanding continuing pressure by MAFF, in the overwhelming majority of cases, the resistance seems to have worked, and MAFF neither killed the animals nor litigated in the face of such resistance. One trainee solicitor is recorded as having saved 106 herds by this method. As explained previously none of the Forest of Dean animals proved to be infected. In total MAFF brought only fourteen further cases to legally overcome occasions of resistance to the cull in England and Wales, withdrawing from eleven and losing two of the three it took into court. At the same time it withdrew from at least 200 other proceedings which it had started. So low was its confidence in its position under the Animal Health Act 1981 that it was not prepared to test that position in the courts (Campbell and Lee, 2003b).

Where animals were slaughtered, there are accounts of significant cruelty including accounts of slaughter men shooting at herds of animals, with the ensuing panic making it necessary to take several shots to bring an animal down (Midgley, 2001). The RSPCA was given reports of animals alive twenty minutes after being shot, to then be finished off with a knife (Morrison, 2001). The regulations governing animal slaughter were clear. The Welfare of Animals (Slaughter or Killing) Regulations 1995 governed to the 'restraint, stunning, slaughter and killing' of animals and by virtue of Regulation 70 this included the killing of any animal for the purpose of disease control. This prohibits any 'avoidable excitement, pain or suffering to any animals'. Schedule 9 dictates the methods for slaughter or killing for the purpose of disease control. A captive bolt should be used to stun an animal, which then must be pithed or blood vessels in its neck severed without delay. Nothing more must be done to the animal until it is ascertained that it is dead. It follows that the activities described before in terms of random pot-shots at animals or in terms of lambs stunned but not promptly killed were yet another example of the illegality of the cull.

VACCINATION

In the light of this, one recurrent controversy is why the government did not resort to vaccination as a more efficient way of controlling the disease. This is a particularly significant debate because it begins to disclose levels of governance in relation to food and bio-security that were not apparent at the time in dealing with what seemed, on the face of it, an incident emanating in and largely confined to the UK. It is important to understand from the outset that prophylactic use of vaccines prior to any outbreak was not an option.[3] This is because of EU policy, as laid down in Directive

85/511/EEC as amended, had abandoned routine vaccination throughout Europe in favour of a policy of stamping out FMD outbreaks when they occur in Member States. Phasing out of routine vaccination was adopted as a policy in 1990 on the basis that stamping out would prove cost beneficial. In the event of an outbreak of FMD, vaccination could be used as an emergency measure once an outbreak had occurred but only if all vaccinated animals were then slaughtered.

EU policy cannot be divorced from wider international trade policy in this area. This, in particular, is influenced by the OIE (Office International des Epizooties, now generally referred to as the World Organisation for Animal Health) whose International Animal Health Code has been adopted by the WTO as the basis on which international trade might be restricted in the interests of disease control (see Chapter 11). The OIE is responsible for laying down international standards on animal health and international trade in animals and products of animal origin and for adopting resolutions on the control of animal diseases. Such standards are recognised by the World Trade Organisation (WTO) as appropriate international health regulations in accordance with which WTO member states can legitimately operate when applying bio-security measures that might otherwise restrict trade. In particular the code operates within the framework of the Agreement on the application of Sanitary and Phytosanitary Measures—the SPS Agreement (European Parliament, 2002) Directorate General for *Research Position of International Organisations on Vaccination against Foot and Mouth Disease* (EU Parliament, 22 May 2002). Under the Code, countries without FMD, which do not resort to vaccination to remain so, will achieve disease free status where there has been no outbreak within a twelve-month period. Where foot and mouth disease then occurs if the outbreak can be restricted by stamping out, then disease free status will be regained within a 3-month period of the last slaughter of diseased stock where this is followed by serological surveillance.

However, because FMD free status for Member States in Europe who do not use vaccination depends on there having been no vaccination within the last twelve months, it was clear that the UK was worried about the time that it might take to regain status as an FMD country not using vaccination. It is important to understand that FMD poses no questions of food safety. Historically British people ate FMD infected meat as is the case in many parts of the world still. Many countries of the world, outside Europe, pursue a policy of routine vaccination, in the manner of many other European states, including France and Germany, prior to the adoption of modern EU policy. There is no doubt, however, that the code offers more favourable treatment to the one-third of countries without FMD and choosing not to vaccinate, thereby giving market advantage to European and North American farmers. In part, therefore, insofar as FMD could have been prevented by vaccination or its outbreak curtailed by its usage, the immense costs of culling were incurred in order to comply with an entirely artificial rule of international trade less connected with food safety than with policies of competitive advantage. That this was a concern at EU level is clear from a press release which stated:

> Should the further development of the situation make it necessary for the EU to decide to introduce large-scale vaccination, the immediate consequence would be that third countries would prohibit the import of all live animals and non-treated products from the EU. This would lead to very severe losses in terms of trade and employment. (DG Health and Consumer Protection, 2001)

Given the legal restriction on preventative vaccination, the issue also arises as to whether or not the use of vaccination could have curbed the outbreak more effectively. Obviously, if this was to happen, it would have been necessary to act swiftly, using vaccination to limit the disease. This was the policy pursued by the Netherlands, which suffered an outbreak coinciding with that in the UK originating in calves imported from Ireland. The Netherlands adopted a policy of ring vaccination; vaccinating all animals in the radius of an outbreak. It nonetheless slaughtered the animals that were vaccinated, in order to restore its status as an FMD country without vaccination. The number of animals slaughtered was therefore significant (over one-quarter million) but in the event, this seems to compare well with the UK. It certainly allowed the more humane slaughter and orderly disposal of the animals.

There is an irony in comparing the trade implications of the Dutch action when compared to the UK. The Netherlands was disease free by 25 June 2001, and in the event only a three-month, rather than a one-year restriction, was applied by the OIE. This meant that the Netherlands was in a position to recommence animal export prior to the last case of foot and mouth in the UK on 30 September 2001. In contrast, as a result of the decision not to vaccinate, the UK was free to resume beef exports in February 2002. In fact, however, no exports took place until September 2002 because as part of the serological surveillance requirements, and perhaps in mind of the earlier history of BSE, the EU insisted on abattoirs handling only beef for export. In most situations this did not generate the throughput to allow the abattoir to operate economically, so it was not until permission was given to slaughter domestic and exported meat together that beef exports became a realistic proposition (Meat and Livestock Commission, 2002).

It seems that early vaccination in the face of the FMD outbreak was never considered as an option. The Chief Veterinary Officer has admitted that:

> No estimate (had) been made of the human resource requirements for a vaccination programme. . .The assumption (was) made that a stamping out policy would be operated first and that, if sufficient trade resources

> were immediately available as outlined, vaccination could be avoided. (Anderson, 2001: 124)

In fact, as part of its contingency planning requirement under EU law, issues such as the emergency use of vaccination should have been considered, and plans should have been in place to access emergency vaccine. Interestingly, the United States Department of Agriculture Policy for the Control of Foot and Mouth Disease contains the following statement:

> Emergency vaccination can play an important supporting role in the control of FMD outbreaks in FMD-free countries such as the United States. Vaccination can help contain the disease quickly if it is used strategically to create barriers between infected zones and disease free zones. (US Department of Agriculture, 2002)

However, even if MAFF was in no position to take the sort of action described previously, as an early means of suppressing the outbreak, as the Anderson Report shows it became necessary to consider vaccination on a number of occasions during the outbreak. This failure of advance planning meant that considerable time and effort was devoted to consideration of vaccination on many occasions during the course of the outbreak. On each occasion, it was ruled out. This was in the face of an almost doctrinaire approach adopted by the NFU (National Farmers' Union, 2001). Ben Gill stated that this position was adopted largely to protect international trade status:

> Vaccination would directly affect the marketing and trading of animals, meat, meat products and milk both within the UK and the EU and internationally. Yet it remains quite unclear as to how or why such restrictions would be and how long they would be in place. (Gill 2002)

Complicit also in this approach were the major food manufacturers though, not apparently, the retailers. This was on the basis of supposed consumer opposition to the sale of products from vaccinated stock. This is notwithstanding the fact that they were widely consumed over many years in Europe prior to 1989; that cattle are regularly exposed to vast numbers of injections for other purposes; and that, the consumer voice seems to have been represented only through the farming union and the food manufacturers.

In truth, once the early opportunity of control was missed, the options became stark. Either one could have vaccinated the farm animal population on a long-term basis (an option not available under EU law), or, vaccination could have been used in order to promote the more humane and orderly killing and disposal of stock. One might have expected the NFU to have supported this, but it did not. Arguably, consumer attitudes to meat consumption may have been more adversely affected by the cruel killing and pyre burning of animals than by any policy of vaccination. Eventually the

NFU was to recognise that its position is unsustainable as indicated by the following statement upon the publication of the Anderson Inquiry Report:

> The NFU recognises the recent developments in vaccination research. All reports have recommended that emergency vaccination should be considered as an addition to the slaughter of infected animals and dangerous contacts. The NFU welcomes the call from the Royal Society for swift action to put the final scientific and practical steps in place to allow emergency vaccination to become a real option. (Gill 2002)

The vaccination debate is bedevilled by confusion and misunderstanding. For example, in terms of consumer resistance, the UK imports an estimated 70,000 tonnes of beef each year from countries that vaccinate against foot and mouth though the exact figure is not known (National Foot and Mouth Group, 2003). This meat is not marked in any separate way or subject to any special treatment. Yet apparently the NFU position was that domestic meat from vaccinated animals would have to be labelled, which as the National Foot and Mouth Group (NFMG, 2003: Appendix 2) point out produced the position that the NFU sought to have 'more onerous restrictions placed on the domestic market' than on the import market. During the Dutch outbreak, once cows were vaccinated but prior to their slaughter, their milk nonetheless went into the food chain. The same would have happened in the UK had cattle in Carlisle been vaccinated (as was the decision at one point in time).

To take another example, Professor David King, Chief Scientific Adviser, in speaking out against vaccination, issued the following statement:

> Nation-wide mass vaccination would make it impossible to tell the extent to which the virus is present in the country's livestock. There are currently no internationally recognised tests that are able to distinguish between vaccinated and infected animals. (King 2001)

The first part of this statement seems hard to reconcile with the Anderson Report which offers the following analysis:

> All viruses, including the FMD virus are made up of protein stock. These proteins can be structural or non-structural. Infected animals produce antibodies against both. However, vaccinated animals produce antibodies against structural proteins only. A positive NSP test detects antibodies against non-structural proteins and therefore identifies an infected animal. (Anderson, 2002: 123)

This is endorsed by the European Parliament's view that it was possible—at least on a herd by herd basis—to distinguish between infected and vaccinated animals (European Parliament 2002).

The second part of David King's statement provides the real insight, however, into why vaccination was rejected. The NSP tests were not internationally recognised at the time of the 2001 outbreak by the OIE. Therefore, although the test might help to distinguish between vaccinated and infected animals, this would have done little to assist in the restoration of FMD disease free status. This was said to have been 'a vital element in decision-making on vaccination in the event of an outbreak of FMD' (European Parliament, 2002b). In short, while to all concerned the absolute reluctance to vaccinate animals seemed perplexing, it was driven by a system of international governance that remained hidden to most observers. Rules emanating from the WTO and the OIE and endorsed in policy terms by the EU meant that the UK did not consider the use of vaccine on a contingency basis to attempt to suppress any early outbreak of FMD. It was continually rejected thereafter during the outbreak, notwithstanding the widespread cruelty and chaos brought about by policies of mass destruction of animals. In order to preserve meat exports worth a gross figure of £5m per annum (and as Lucas [2001] points out we are net importers of meat) the government was ready to kill millions of animals a cost of billions of pounds.

LESSONS TO BE LEARNED?

At the time of the 1967 epidemic, there were 2,200 abattoirs in the UK, but this had shrunk to 360 by the time of the 2001 epidemic (Anderson, 2001: 26). During the 1990s, notwithstanding the risks attaching to movements of the livestock population, more than two thirds of existing abattoirs were closed (Kennard and Young, 1999). The increase in the volume of animal movements within the UK as a result is hard to estimate but the BSE inquiry found that, in 1994, as a result of abattoir closures, 20% of cattle travelled very long distances to slaughter, literally including movement from northern Scotland to the south east of England (Phillips, 2000: vol. 12, para. 4.14). Although as we have stated abattoir closures were not unconnected with the imposition of EU hygiene standards (Shaoul, 1997), alongside this were significant changes in food production and consumption, notably the domination of red meat sales by retailers' own labels.

Although it seems apparent that the greater the animal movement the higher the degree of risk, this may be offset by the reduced number of destinations to which animals may travel. But the real difficulty about the distances which livestock travel is best seen in relation to problems of tracing the disease, so that in 2001, by the time infection is spotted it is seated in over 120 locations. The necessary but draconian controls of animal movements once the epidemic was recognised is a very strong indication that there is no longer localized supply in which controlling movements from local farms to the nearby abattoir is a sufficient response. Moreover, once the disease breaks out, conditions of modern livestock production implies the inevitable slaughter of many more animals than would have been the case at a time when units of production were so much smaller.

In this complex pattern of private production and public regulation, the profits of intensification accrue to the private actors, but the risk is borne by the public purse. Of course not all in the private production chain profit equally and ironically this inequity became apparent in the FMD outbreak. Those with the cheques for hundreds of thousands of pounds were not hill sheep farmers or those with local dairy herds, but were largely the dealers whose animal transhipments had created the risk in the first place. Those with most to lose were those whose stock had been carefully bred over generations, and such farmers most commonly resisted the cull rather than accept the compensation cheque. Those who lost most of all financially, as explained earlier, were those whose stock remained without disease but also without a ready market.

In 1967 at the time of the previous outbreak, the State could have been exemplified as an interventionist, Fordist, welfare State. Given the close relationship between the National Farmers' Union and MAFF through to the late 1970s at least it was not so surprising that the tentacles of the State extended even to acting as guarantor or insurer of those in the food supply line. What is remarkable is how in the early 2000s, and in spite of the heavy programmes of privatisation and liberalisation in this intervening period, *the State still subsumed the risk of animal disease*. This reveals not only how 'fixed' patterns of governance can be over time but also how within one broadly conceived policy area, that of food, we can find highly divergent relationships between State and private interests. Of course, whether we analyse FMD or food hygiene the configuration of State and private interests is there ostensibly to deliver wider public policy goals. In reality, though, as we have shown in relation to FMD, those whose activity heightened the risk by devising intensified systems of production of specialised dimensions bore no risk of loss; this is true not only of their own loss in losing stock through disease, but they bore no liability loss for the spread of disease to others, however derelict their behaviour. In spite of the general political distancing of the State from questions of sufficiency of food supply, the loss of stock through disease remained a public good.

Indeed there is a curious attachment to models pursued in previous outbreaks (Woods, 2004). It seems that much of DEFRA's contingency planning prior to 2001 was based on an influential 1973 cost-benefit analysis using data from the 1967 FMD outbreak. This argued for stamping out FMD without vaccination (Power and Harris, 1973). However, the intervening quarter of a century, during which the geography of the rural economy and therefore the economics of vaccination had, of course, changed dramatically, rendered this study obsolete in many respects (Roberts, 2001). There was no recalculation of the equation and mass slaughter continued to be portrayed as maximising welfare. It committed enormous public expenditure to the defence of livestock exports at the cost of inflicting huge damage on the rural tourist industry, and, whilst the precise figures are open to dispute, it is beyond doubt that the former is of much smaller economic significance than the latter (DEFRA/

DCMS, 2002). Indeed it is said that 'the losses to the livestock sector . . . were dwarfed by the . . . losses to the tourist sector' (Rushton et al., 2002). In a masterpiece of understatement, Anderson (2001: para. 14.4) called for a revision of the costs and benefits used by MAFF as this was 'overdue' because a 'number of factors is likely to have changed since the 1960s'.

There is an enormous contrast and disjuncture here between the dynamism of the private interest re-ordering of the sector in this timeframe and the static and inert nature of the public regulatory framework. With the former, change is continual and is effected potentially by each and every contract in the food chain, whereas with the latter, the structures of regulation demand formal legal change, which might be prompted only by crisis and which is slow to effect. Arguably understanding the disjuncture between the two is crucial to a full appreciation of the problems thrown up by FMD in 2001. The disease spread in a manner beyond all expectations because those expectations showed little awareness of the scale of animal shipments. Similarly, when dealing with the outbreak, there were significant shortfalls in the regulatory response to risk essentially because the modelling of the contiguous cull was geographically and intellectually remote from the infected areas, and made assumptions not borne out in the conditions of modern agriculture. Measures taken as a result led to a loss of trust not least through the exercise of highly questionable powers and fed an existing disenchantment with government on the part of the farming community already convinced that government had neither enthusiasm nor empathy for the pressure brought to bear upon it in this changed time.

In a sense the FMD outbreak was one of those crisis events that provoked change, and one of the main ones was to dispense with a separate Ministry for Agriculture Fisheries and Food and create a Department for Environment, Food and Rural Affairs. Apart from the public relations value of dispensing with the much criticised MAFF, this was at least an acknowledgement of wider rural interests than merely agriculture and the linkages, pointed to in the Curry Report between food production and environment (Curry, 2002). It had useful synergies with the creation of the Food Standards Agency, which is considered in Chapter 9. In many other respects, however, little has changed. The compensation structures remain in place providing little incentive to change production methods in favour of greater bio-security. A Royal Society Report almost four years after the start of the epidemic stated that the government was in no position to effectively tackle foot and mouth disease using emergency vaccination if there was another outbreak. Rather than resolving to handle matters differently in the future, significant effort was invested in ensuring and more extensive, sweeping powers to slaughter yet more animals in a mass cull. In a de facto admission of earlier illegality the government reserved to itself all the powers it would need to repeat the mistakes of 2001.

3 Genetic Disorders

Resistance, Regulation and GM Food and Feed

INTRODUCTION

The previous chapter examined an episode which, though largely affecting the UK, had undertones of the global governance of food production not immediately apparent on first hearing. Changing geographical scales, we now turn to a case study of genetically modified (GM) food[1] and feed. This concerns consumption as much as it concerns production and it also offers further insights into the multi-level governance of food that may be more obvious as conflicts between national sovereignty in matters of food regulation are pitched against powerful institutional forces of trade liberalisation. The matter is one of high politics as nation states battle to hold back forces of globalization in this case by resisting technological advance. Although the crisis that this engenders ends in a formal dispute between the USA and the EU regarding the blocking of that technology, it is an important part of our thesis that these actors were more akin to allies than enemies and that the real dispute was more on of neo-functional dynamics of regional integration in Europe set against neo-realist capacities of member States in Europe.

These tensions are not only apparent in the history offered subsequently, but as an integral part of the background to the establishment of the European Food Safety Agency, which we consider later, the in-fighting over GM approvals in Europe allows insights into the centralisation of food regulation in Europe. Moreover, while the previous chapter demonstrated that the risk of animal disease was treated as a public good and a central responsibility of the State, here we see that while there are systems of approval for GM in Europe, potential problems thrown up by the technology are treated as the subject of private ordering and the risks and responsibilities allocated accordingly. Whereas in the case of animal biosecurity the UK appears locked into command and control structures based on inspection, notices, and governmental action in culling out the disease, the development of a new technology offers new regulatory opportunities and ultimately builds upon tracing and labeling through the supply chain and the internalisation of risk and costs into private contracting and away from the public purse.

The resistance in the UK and Europe would seem to be deeply rooted in the public perception of risk and public scepticism of science (Wynne et al., 2001). Quite apart from arguments that plant modification by genetic modification is no different than that practised throughout the history of agriculture by plant breeding, there is now quite longstanding experience in more countries of GM crop production and consumption without the reporting of widespread health disorders. Yet even now in many European countries opposition to GM food has not abated. This may indicate that the scepticism is not or is not solely based on health concerns. Of course, as we outlined in Chapter 1, the late 20th century saw a series of food 'crises' in the UK arising out of human health concerns. Some such as salmonella and E-coli were grounded in identifiable and well-established risk, though poor risk communication may have produced a scare that outweighed the ongoing risk posed (Miller and Reilly, 1995). Other concerns, such as that posed by BSE, related to risks that were much more contingent and more controversial as a matter of science. It was a key finding of the BSE Inquiry that the rigour with which policy measures were implemented for the protection of human health was affected by the belief of many prior to early 1996 that BSE was not a potential threat to human life (Phillips, 2000). When in March 1996 it was admitted that previous assurances were incorrect and that BSE had in all likelihood already been transmitted to humans, this was seen as a betrayal. This feeling of mistrust was compounded as cases of new variant CJD emerged at a point at which it was impossible to predict how widespread the problem might be.

Suggesting that concerns about GM are not primarily health driven is not to say that these earlier food scares were irrelevant, for when the European Community comes to regulate GM crops it finds it must do so in the face of wider scientific mistrust and better mobilised consumer pressures. We argue that this gave rise to pragmatic and piecemeal measures which at times smacked of political compromise rather than planned policy and which resulted in an uncoordinated network of regulation notwithstanding an industry view that these would prove impractical, unworkable and unnecessary (Select Committee of the EU, 2002). On the whole, while highly contested, the regulatory system should be depicted as a widely supportive largely neo-liberal regime. As we will illustrate it is highly dependent on private-interest governance principles, and while at some points there is dispute as to the cost and complexity of such governance, ultimately such a system is possible because biotechnology provides the basis for capital accumulation, appropriation of farming practice, and the integration and internationalization of the corporate agri-food sector (Marsden, 2008; Lappe and Bailey, 1999). Much of what happens in relation to GM provides an historic explanation of the changing regulation of food within the EU; but there is much besides that provides a platform from which to observe wider developments in food governance.

We argue that GM technologies in food and feed production generate both integrative and contested effects (Marsden, 2008) and that these are reflected in the regulatory frameworks. A telling part of the legal argument in WTO circles is that there is no substantial or significant difference between plant modification through conventional and biotechnical means. Be this as it may, this notion of a move away from the conventional towards a technological fix has become one of huge import because it is seen as a signifier of resistance to or support for agri- industrial models. Although not always clearly articulated, the technology is seen as a prop to shore up homogenised, intensive, concentrated models of agricultural production; to sustain the unsustainable agri-industrial model (Buttel, 2006). This conventional/technological division is keenly felt particularly by those advocating an alternative model based upon re-localisation of food around technically simpler, more diverse and less intensive patterns of production. This is because of the fear of the irreversible impact of GM crops; that once the genie is out of the bottle, all is lost. With so much at stake pressures mounted on most member states to reach decisions concerning GM within a European Union system that devolved regulatory supervision to competent authorities. At the beginning of our story, responsibility for approvals lay with the member states but the failure of these states to process applications for GM approvals necessitates the intervention of the European Commission and the construction of a new and more centralised regulatory structure.

The chapter argues that the Commission placed itself in an impossible position as a result of its instinctive support of biotechnology innovation and enterprise while dealing with a significant number of Member States departing from this agenda under considerable pressure from their own citizens. This represents a very good example of the wider conundra of the EU project—deregulating a fast moving food system but having to 'protect' consumer risks (see Chapter 5). Ironically at the same time the EU is required by forces of market liberalisation to rationalise and explain to other members of the WTO the continuing barriers to GM products. Eventually these pressures found articulation in a WTO formal dispute, and, in response, the European Union produced defences to this challenge based upon health risk and precaution, but the truth is that the concerns of citizens throughout Europe could not be so described or so easily confined (Gaskell et al., 2004). For many European citizens the issue was about the very nature of how and where they lived and sustained themselves. These may seem vital issues but ironically the forces of global trade could not allow, could not even contemplate such arguments since local and historic preferences smacked so obviously of inherent trade protectionism. Interestingly, however, within all of these arenas the debate on GM is conducted in the language of risk. Under WTO structures health concerns provided one of the few compelling legal responses to explain the reluctance in the EU to accept GM such that health risk generated far greater attention than concerns of rural sustainability or bio-diversity loss (Wales and Mythen, 2002).

THE TROUBLED HISTORY OF GM REGULATION

GM regulation has a short history, with the first laws coming into force only within the last decade of the 20th century, but it is a crowded history typified by rapid and intensive regulation. The law has been driven throughout by the European Community and through a series of regulations and directives. Wider European domestic regulation has been forced to follow, albeit often reluctantly, the European lead. In an earlier paper (Carson and Lee, 2005) we produced tables to assist with the complexity of charting the relevant EU legislation and to provide an ease of reference. A summary table is included here. Table 3.1 represents a timeline of European GM regulation from 1990 onwards, with the main pieces of legislation highlighted illustrating the changing nature of the regulation in response to perceived shortfalls. As this may suggest the story is in part one in which law trails in the shadow of scientific advance (Gent, 1999) but this is not the full story because there is little doubt that at a political level the strength and nature of opposition to the technology was misunderstood (Toke, 2004a). As the tables illustrate, the early legislation concerns the regulation of activity—such as research and development or release to the environment—and it is only at a much later stage is any thought given to informational rights to the consumer or measures that might allow the exercise of choice over consumption.

In 1990 Directive 90/220 defined GMO as 'an organism in which genetic material has been altered in a way that does not occur naturally by mating and/or natural recombination'. For such activity, the Directive introduced a GMO application procedure. Before a GMO could be released into the environment for any reason (including for research development) the competent authority in the Member State had to be notified in the form of a technical dossier containing detailed information. The Member State examined the dossier and evaluated the risk and sent a summary to the Commission. The Commission would then send a summary to the other Member States, which had thirty days to ask for more information if they so wished. In theory the applicant should have received, thereafter, a response within ninety days of submission of the dossier but, in practice, this proved to be much longer. If the application was successful there were terms and conditions attached e.g. the use of pollen barriers. Alongside this, Directive 90/219 required Member States to regulate the contained use of GM micro-organisms in

Table 3.1 History of EU Legislation on GMOs

Year	*Title*	*Contents*
1990	Directive 90/219	The contained use of GM micro-organisms
1990	Directive 90/220	The deliberate release into the environment of GMOs
1994	Directive 94/51	Adapting to technical progress for the first time 90/220 on the deliberate release into the environment of GMOs
1997	Regulation 258/97	Novel Foods and Novel Foods Ingredients
1997	Regulation 1813/97	The compulsory indication on the labelling of certain foodstuffs produced from GMOs in addition to the particulars required in food labelling laws
1997	Directive 97/35	Labelling of new agriculture producing or containing GMOs notified under Directive 90/220
1998	Directive 98/81	Amending Directive 90/219/EEC on the contained use of genetically modified micro-organisms
1998	Regulation 1139/98	The compulsory indication of the labelling of GM Soya/Maize foodstuffs, repealing Regulation 1813/97
2000	Regulation 49/2000	Adventitious presence of GMOs in soya or maize: labelling requirements under Regulation 1139/89 not applying if the proportion is no higher than 1% of the food ingredient
2000	Regulation 50/2000	The labelling of foodstuffs and food ingredients containing additives and flavourings genetically modified or produced from GMOs
2001	Directive 2001/18	The deliberate release into the environment of GMOs and repealing Directive 90/220
2003	Regulation 1829/2003	Genetically modified food and feed
2003	Regulation 1830/2003	Traceability and labelling of GMOs
2003	Regulation1946/2003	Trans-boundary movement of GMOs
2004	Regulation 65/2004	Establishing a system for the development and assignment of unique identifiers for GMOs
2004	Regulation 641/2004	Detailed rules for the implementation of Regulation (EC) 1829/2003 (above)

order to minimise their potential negative effects on human health and the environment. The Directive classified GM micro-organisms into two groups according to their level of hazard. In order to minimise the risk to human health and the environment, the user was required to adhere to health and safety principles including notification before first use.

There are two comments that can be made rather simply with the benefit of hindsight. The first relates to the diffuse nature of the controls. Essentially the primary obligation for approvals is placed upon Member States, putting other Member States in a position where they are forced to respond to an approval elsewhere in Europe in line with the principle of mutual recognition. Clearly this allows a degree of forum shopping on the part of biotech multinationals, which may have real choices in respect of the location of the regulation of their activity. While these arrangements support notions of subsidiarity and national sovereignty, since any approval would eventually lead to market approval within the EU as a whole, there was obviously a place for central co-ordination which the structure ignored. This structure made it very difficult to defend challenges by GM producing countries that the EU itself had persistently failed to progress GM approvals. In fact of course the dragging of heels was on the part of Member States whose stance was very much in opposition to the biotech enterprise and, as we will show, eventually this structure had to be replaced by a centralised European system of approvals.

Secondly, the Directives had many gaps and weaknesses in terms of the conditions under which and the transparency with which GM produce would be placed upon the market. Being nationally determined, these might not be inclusive, certainly not inclusive of all European consumers, and might vary greatly in the strictness of conditions under which GM crops might be grown. It was not until a later phase of GM legislation more than a decade later that these problems would be addressed. In terms of transparency the very titles of the Directives which speak of 'deliberate release' and 'contained use' is worthy of note; there is little indication that crops might be grown. The language speaks more of the control of some curious but remote scientific process that might pose some unspecified risk of the 'release of GMOs' into the environment. The obscurity accords with arguments that scientists in biotechnology may engage with the public at times only from their own linguistic and social domain (Cook et al., 2004). It begins a track of dependence on science, within the Commission's approach to food regulation in particular to legitimate activity, which continues as regulation is reformed. As such it begins a path which concludes at the door, years later, of the European Food Safety Agency. It may go some way to explaining also why the GM issue came as a surprise to and created such opposition within the European rural domain (Marsden et al., 2003).

By the mid 1990s, thanks in no small part to the work of various European NGOs (Levidow and Murphy, 2003) there was a forced response to growing consumer anxiety. Unlike their counterparts in the USA, European

NGOs were better placed to resist GM crop production as it had no effective market penetration in Europe. The focus of those NGOs was wide-ranging but was environmentally driven to a large degree being concerned both at biodiversity protection and the promotion of sustainable agriculture. GM production was strongly linked to intensification of agriculture representing opportunity for agri-industrial players and as such could be juxtaposed against an increasingly successful agenda of multi-functional, agro-environmental food production (Levidow and Murphy, 2003). Significantly for what was to follow, the response at a European level was not to revisit arrangements for crop approvals but instead to choose to modify Directive 90/220 by introducing a new annex to that legislation requiring 'compulsory labelling of all new agriculture producing or containing GMOs notified under Directive 90/220' (see Directive 97/35). As we shall see this labelling response is a favoured mechanism to quell unease about biotechnology by asserting choice, although the extent to which labelling allows the consumer (as opposed to the retailer) to actually exercise choice is doubtful and at best it provides a very limited and indirect response to the wider sustainability doubts voiced by the NGO community.

In an attempt to quell doubts about the technical composition of food, by the mid-1990s the Commission moved to impose tighter controls on foodstuffs through a Regulation (258/97) which sought to control novel ingredients in food. The notion of an ingredient was fairly narrowly drawn so that the Regulation failed to cover food additives, flavourings or extraction solvents. The Regulation had a wider coverage than GM food but it did include categories of novel food where foods/food ingredients contained or consisted of GMOs or where foods/food ingredients were produced from, though did not contain GMOs. As a Regulation this measure was immediately applicable in all Member States and it demanded official review and approval of all novel ingredients. Again, however, this produced a highly decentralised and therefore variable model of Member State approval. A product coming on to the market in one Member State could gain approval there, and could then circulate freely in the single market. Moreover the Regulation applied only to novel foods introduced into the EU after the date of the Regulation (15 May 1997) meaning that GM products already in use for human consumption were subject to no further scrutiny. The main products on the market at this time were Monsanto's Ready Round-Up Soya and Novartis BT maize. Under pressure, and in a stop gap measure pending more careful consideration, the Commission introduced a further Regulation in 1997 (Regulation 1813/97) demanding that labelling requirements for novel foods be extended to foods containing GM Soya/Maize.

Approvals under the Novel Foods Regulation depended on the foodstuff being shown through safety assessment to be as safe as an equivalent conventional food. This is a curious notion given that food inevitably poses risk to health in a wide variety of circumstances. It did little to speed approvals. Syngenta's Bt11 sweet corn was submitted for approval in the

Netherlands in February 1999 but not authorised until May 2004. The then Health and Consumer Protection Commissioner, Byrne, described the corn as having been subject to 'the most rigorous pre-marketing assessment in the world' (EU Commission, 2004). Under the Novel Foods Regulation an applicant ingredient was required to undergo an official safety review and approval before being sold to the public. Applications were submitted to the competent authority in the Member State in which the applicant wished to first market the product although such approval would then open up the entire European Market. In the UK the assessment was carried out by the Advisory Committee on Novel Foods and Processes (ACNFP) which after April 2000 advised the Food Standards Agency (FSA) which determined approvals.

Employing such procedures by October 1998, the EU had approved nine agricultural biotech products for planting or import, but it was facing a *de facto* revolt as it became apparent that Member States including France, Germany, Italy, Greece and Luxembourg banned GM crops, notwithstanding their approval elsewhere in the market. Mutual recognition broke down and a regulatory structure designed to ensure market access was employed to erect market barriers. The EU singly failed to take action to challenge these bans notwithstanding their apparent illegality giving rise to what became known as the moratorium on GM, which was to last almost six years and provoke litigation before a Dispute Panel of the WTO.

The GM moratorium, which lasted from 1998 to 2004, was hardly a planned move on the part of the EU. In October 1998 the EU authorised two biotech carnation varieties (to improve vase life and modify flower colour), and these became the last live GMO plants to gain approval—making 18 GMOs in total authorised for commercial release prior to the moratorium. In June 1999, France and Greece called for the moratorium on new GMO approvals at a meeting of EU environment ministers and won backing from Italy, Denmark and Luxembourg. Later agreement to the moratorium by Belgium and Austria helped form a powerful bloc that could effectively vote down approvals in any case.

That the moratorium was proposed by the environment ministers is noteworthy in the face of a growing bifurcation between the agenda of the EU to chase the economic opportunity to exploit biotechnology and remedy the now significant lag in Europe in GM products when compared with the USA, and the agenda of Member States. The latter agenda varied from State to State, but it includes some attempt to: protect local agriculture as an integral part of a rural development agenda; preserve local foods cultures; and maintain rural landscapes and preserve biodiversity. The response to this by the Commission was that the easiest point of contest was the point of purchase so that consumers should be offered the choice of GM. The Commission continued along a path which placed unerring belief in the power of market choice for goods which they perceived would change once this value of GM was realised—indeed comments by the Environment

Commission Wallstrom that 'the value of biotechnology is poorly appreciated in Europe' found their way into the US submission to the WTO Disputes Panel (United States-European Communities, 2004). In September 1998 the EU re-introduced on a more permanent footing compulsory labelling of food products containing soya/maize (in which GMOs were most likely to be found) unless no DNA/protein was present. In an indication that the task was seen as one of appeasing the European consumer in the supermarket, bizarrely this Regulation (1139/98) failed to impose any requirement upon suppliers to catering establishments to inform the supply chain of the GM status of foods/ingredients—an omission that was not remedied until 2000 (Regulation 49/2000).

Also missing from the original labelling measure in 1998 and again remedied by the 2000 Regulation was any consideration of when genetically modified material might be said to be present; this effectively created a zero tolerance. The solution was the introduction of a de minimis threshold of 1% for the accidental or adventitious content of DNA or proteins resulting from genetic modification of food, below which the products need not be labelled. Given that the organic sector worked to a zero tolerance standard the very idea of non-GM products actually and legally containing GM also became and remained a point of opposition for organic growers. In an accompanying Regulation (50/2000) all foods, not just soya/maize containing or produced from GM additives and flavourings had to be labelled. In practice, however, because of the two- year gap between the 1998 and 2000 Regulations, and to be sure of avoiding criminal liabilities for breach of labelling, the European supply chain had begun by this time to self-audit. This realisation that effective information was dependent on tracing through the supply chain marks an important stage in the development of regulation with a simple public face—a label—disguising a complex process of private governance—tracing within the supply chain. Ultimately, tracing and labelling became the main policy instruments used by the EU Commission to cajole recalcitrant Member States to accept the presence of GM foods on the European market.

Commission attempts to modify and in particular to simplify administration of crop approvals met with much less success because, of course, these would lead, as intended, to the agri-industrial plantation of GM crops within Member States. Directive 98/81 amongst other provisions included a list of GM micro-organisms thought to pose no risk to human health or the environment in the hope of creating the basis of fast track procedures. But by the time of the Commission Report on Member State's approval processes (EU Commission, 2001), only Sweden, Finland and Denmark had transposed the 1998 Directive fully and accurately. In 2001 the Commission moved to a more centralised model in the face of Member State intransigence.

Directive 2001/18 introduced a common procedure and common principles for granting consent to the deliberate release and placing on the market of GMOs in Europe. It sought a more efficient, transparent and participative approach, replacing and strengthening the provisions of Directive 90/220. Expert and public consultations prior to consents GMO labelling were made compulsory. The Directive also limited consents to a period of ten years, which could be subject to renewal, and consents incorporated compulsory monitoring once GMOs were placed on the market. The Directive introduced an obligation to implement monitoring plans in order to trace and identify any direct or indirect, immediate, delayed or unforeseen effects on human health or the environment of GMOs as (or in) products after they have been placed on the market. In particular the monitoring plans sought to make provision for potential long-term effects such as new allergies. Finally the Directive also provided for a common methodology to assess the risks associated with the release of GMOs and a mechanism allowing the release of GMOs to be modified, suspended or terminated where new information became available on risks.

Before moving to an explanation of the present regime for regulation of GM crops/food in Europe, it is useful to reflect upon the impact of this fluid and uneven pattern of regulation up until the reforms from 2003 onwards and to reflect how this affected the attitudes of those in the food supply chain. Left with few other options, the industry went to great lengths to look to source foods and ingredients from non-GM suppliers as the means of compliance with labelling rules. With no initial tolerance for adventitious contamination, and given a strong anti-GM stance of many governments within Europe, the regulatory compliance and the avoidance of administrative penalties required considerable investment in in-house systems of monitoring of the supply chain. Food companies, wishing to rebuild trust and confidence in the aftermath of episodes such as BSE were prepared to make this investment. In a paradigm example of private interest regulation (Marsden et al., 2000) this policing of the supply chain was well in advance of anything formally demanded under legislation. In some cases also, food manufacturers re-engineered their product rather than source from GM supplies, though the slow rate of approvals of GM crops together with the GM moratorium made this a far easier option in the European market. Consequently, even before regulation formally moved in this direction, public assurance had become based on private policing of the supply chain.

It is significant also that those crops in which genetic modification was most common were feed crops such as soybeans, in which by 2002 the majority of product was represented by GM varieties (LMC International). Alternative sourcing was more difficult therefore because of the growing dominance of GM, but as it happened the regulatory rules did not require the labelling of GM feed allowing a route to compliance. In short, although not a cost free exercise, the industry found it relatively easy to avoid GM lines in the face of consumer resistance and chose for the most part to avoid GM ingredients through a process of self-policing.

In relation to consumers, after a rather slow start, regulation shifts to focus on the labelling of pre-packaged foods containing GM where there was an actual presence of novel DNA or protein. This was indicative of a wish to meet the consumers' right to know rather than of any attendant concerns with the safety as such of these products. Moreover, it is not difficult to isolate gaps in the information offered to consumers, suggesting, possibly, that the task was one of employing regulation to build confidence rather than offering complete transparency. Controversy over testing methods and the reliability of results created much uncertainty notwithstanding the apparently simple labelling requirement. The requirements were not exhaustive and in the case of highly processed ingredients such as refined vegetable oils produced from a GM source but no longer containing GM DNA/protein, there was no requirement for labelling. Other gaps in the 'right to know' involved feed and also products produced by animals fed GM feed, and the retail chain was subject to earlier more stringent regulation than were catering outlets. Finally, as previously shown, absolute standards are altered to allow for adventitious (accidental) contamination. Importantly for companies, however, there was a requirement to prove that any such presence was accidental demanding due diligence especially in the face of NGO pressures not to allow even the adventitious presence of GMOs which extended throughout the supply chain.

Consumer choice, exercised on the back of labelling and underpinned by tracing of GMOs in the supply of food, increasingly became the way forward for the European institutions in the face of Member State antipathy. There was no doubt that trust in food had become a major political issue across a sizeable part of the Community. Even in States such as the UK where government seemed implicitly sympathetic to biotechnology, these attitudes were not reflected in the citizenry at large (GM Nation Public Debate Steering Board, 2003). From a quiet beginning in which a permitting regime for GM passes into EU law almost unnoticed in 1990, by the middle of that decade genetically modified foods had become a point of resistance among European consumers and for a significant majority of these consumers, price made no difference (Noussair and Ruffieux , 2004) as did claims that the technology was beneficial (Pidgeon et al., 2005). The food industry in the USA argued that, since most foods are genetically modified, albeit using traditional techniques of plant modification, it is puzzling to differentiate on the basis of the safety of the process rather than the product (see Chapter 11). There was scientific sympathy with this view. Amidst the final arguments about the moratorium on GM approvals the International Council for Science stated that:

> Currently available genetically modified foods are safe to eat. Food safety assessments by national regulatory agencies in several countries have deemed currently available GM foods to be as safe to eat as their conventional counterparts and suitable for human consumption. (International Council for Science, 2003: 8)

Either such arguments were met with deep distrust by European consumers, or, as we shall argue, , they failed to address the real concerns of those opposing GM food, which were never purely, or even mainly, safety related. Nonetheless, it was convenient for the EU Commission to be able to assert that on the back of clear marking the consumer could exercise choice in relation to GM produce including a continuing boycott if desired. It may be that the adoption of a regulatory solution based on market choice had an appeal to eurocrats besieged by biotechnology companies wishing to access the European market in the name of trade liberalisation. Although we examine the elements of tracing and labelling in the following section, it remains to be seen how complete a solution it actually is. From the perspective of the biotechnology companies, the wish is not only to export GM food into Europe but also to grow GM crops in Europe; tracing and labelling regulation do little to address the wider problem of crop approvals. Moreover, the demand that a GM food be labelled means that it is not treated as a like food when compared with a crop subject to more traditional forms of plant modification. Biotechnology companies would reject this thinking and may choose to do so formally in the future under the auspices of the World Trade Organisation.

THE MORATORIUM AND ITS CONSEQUENCES

In view of the de facto moratorium on processing applications for GM crop approvals in Europe, in May 2003, Argentina, Canada and the USA. requested the WTO to constitute a Disputes Settlement Panel (O'Rourke, 2004). The EU, through its Trade Commissioner, was to express regret at this 'unnecessary litigation' arguing that the legal action would confuse already sceptical European consumers (European Commission, 2003a). The Environment Commissioner stated that:

> There should be no doubt that it is not our intention to create trade barriers. But my concern is that this request will muddy the waters of the debate in Europe. We have to create confidence among citizens for GMOs and then allow them to choose.

The US authorities did not agree and went on to argue in the opening of the submission to the Dispute Panel that:

> The United States is confident that once the European Commission allows its scientific and regulatory procedures to reach their conclusion, it will once again approve new biotech products, benefiting EC consumers and biotech producers around the world. (United States, 2004 at para. 6)

Allowing for the fact that these remarks are made in the context of a WTO dispute, it appears, nonetheless, from these statements that the shared philosophy of trade liberalisation and globalisation serves more to unite than divide the parties notwithstanding the litigation between them. Equally, both parties, including, as suggested earlier, the EU Commission, look to the benefit of GM for consumers to be made clear through scientific processes which will eliminate the doubts of a sceptical public.

From the Environmental Council in July 2000 the environment ministers of EU Member States had expressed support for a moratorium pending the development of proposals on the labelling and tracing of GMOs, reflecting the political pressure felt by the national politicians in the face of considerable popular resistance. Under Article 16 of Directive 90/220/EEC the so-called safeguard clause provided that where a Member State has justifiable reasons to consider that a GMO, which has received written consent for placing on the market, nonetheless constitutes a risk to human health or the environment, it may provisionally restrict or prohibit the use and/or sale of that product on its territory. By the time of the moratorium, Austria (three times) France (twice) and Germany, Luxembourg, Greece and the United Kingdom (once each) had all invoked the safeguard clause. In all cases, the relevant Scientific Committee at EU level could find no case to support safeguard action denying authorisation. In addition, Italy invoked the safeguard clause in the Novel Food Regulation (Regulation 1813/97 on Review and Approval of Novel Foods, reg. 12) in August 2000 suspending trade in and use of products derived from four GM maize varieties, notwithstanding their approval as products 'substantially equivalent' to those already on the market. Within a month the Scientific Committee for Food concluded that the information provided by the Italian Authorities did not provide detailed scientific grounds for any restriction (Dabrowska, 2004).

Such decisive rejections by the Scientific Committee for Food suggests that Member States were invoking the safeguard clauses on rather wider terms that those adopted by the expert committee indicating a more diverse and deeper seated unease about the genetic modification of crops at a national level. The Scientific Committee became the institutional mechanism by which the EU sought to override national objections as unscientific and ungrounded. Yet even after the WTO action began, Austria sought to introduce national measures banning GMOs in the region of Upper Austria for a three-year period. The Upper Austrian Regional Government promoted this measure in an attempt to protect organic and traditional methods of agricultural production in its area. The European Food Safety

Authority, which was by this time in place (created by Regulation (EC) No 178/2002 discussed further in Chapters 5 and 6) again concluded that there was no new data upon which a ban might be justified. The Environment Commissioner expressed 'full respect for the concerns of the Austrian authorities' but, in striking down the measure, said 'legally speaking, this seems a clear-cut case'. (European Commission, 2003)

It took until April 2004 for the European Commission to end the moratorium with the approval of a modified sweetcorn developed by Syngenta. Yet even agriculture ministers from the Member States had refused to approve the sweetcorn prompting unilateral action by the Commission. In response to criticism that such a move overrode national sovereignty, the then Consumer and Health Commissioner, Byrne, responded that:

> The fact that ministers were unable to make a logical response is a matter for them . . . (the decision was) fully in conformity with democratic systems we've put in place in the EU . . . the more the public realise they're protected and informed, this will filter through to elected representatives and it'll perhaps be easier in the Council. (European Commission, 2004)

In Britain, GM Nation, an unprecedented canvassing of public opinion, involving 675 public meetings and more than 36,000 written responses, demonstrated how far away this task of public realisation might be. The report (PDSB, 2003) found (at para. 6) that: 'the more people engage in GM issues, the harder their attitudes and more intense their concerns'" The Financial Times concluded that:

> Most people turn out to have an intelligent understanding of the issues, a rational scepticism about the benefits and a healthy mistrust of GM advocates. (Financial Times, 2003)

Broadly the report configured the public as doubtful that they rather than the biotechnology companies would benefit from GM. In the face of the findings, the UK Environment Secretary promised: 'We said we would listen and we will' (Vidal and Sample, 2003). Yet as is shown next, plans for the co-existence of GM crops to be grown alongside conventional and organic crops continued. Minutes of a cabinet sub-committee in early 2004 (Guardian, 2004) record the UK Government questioning the GM nation findings because 'it was unclear whether participants in this part of the debate had received balanced information'. It would seem to be true that public opinion was not as united as GM Nation had portrayed but instead was fragmented and ambivalent (Pidgeon et al., 2005) but to state (as did Ministers—Guardian, 2004) that calls for a ban were an 'irrational way for the government to proceed, particularly given the symbolic importance of the decision for the government's science policy and the UK science base' denies the lack of enthusiasm for the technology and promotes a merit good framework in which Government knows best. In so doing the government missed a major message of the GM Nation Report, namely that their handling of the ongoing debate was not fostering trust but building scepticism. It equally neglects the opportunity to begin to build a context for risk assessment that might properly allow a wider debate on technologies in order to bring much needed consensus and resolution. Ultimately, the government's prior commitment to what it sees as 'the UK science base' is quite as lacking in balance as the participation exercise it decries.

Although there may have been other lines of argument to pursue (Zedalis, 2002) the complainants in the WTO Dispute Panel, rightly as it turned out, centred their arguments on breaches of the WTO's Sanitary and Phytosanitary Agreement (SPS). The essential argument, in relation to the general moratorium, put by the USA (United States-European Communities, 2004) was that the moratorium constituted a measure under the SPS agreement likely to affect international trade. At the very least this amounted to undue delay under Article 8 of the agreement and procedurally this was flawed under Article 8 and Article 7 (in the latter case because of a failure to publish promptly details of the moratorium). The submission pointed also to the need for any moratorium to be based upon risk assessment in line with the requirements of Article 5.1. Alongside this the USA argued that the moratorium was not based on scientific principles and maintained without sufficient scientific evidence contrary to Article 2.2. Finally these measures were said to be discriminatory in their effect (infringing Article 5.50 and amounting to disguised restrictions on imports contrary to Article 2.3 of the agreement).

Reviewing the requirements for risk assessment in this formulation, Article 5.1 of the SPS Agreement demands:

> an assessment, as appropriate to the circumstances, of the risks to human, animal or plant life or health, taking into account risk assessment techniques developed by the relevant international organizations.

Moreover any response (such as a moratorium) must be based on such an assessment. Risk assessments under this framework must address either threats of pests or disease or the effects of food or feed on human or animal health. This is narrowly drawn and does not encompass wider social and environmental fears that might have engaged the European public. Moreover, in the aftermath of a series of food risks, a great deal of effort may be needed to restore trust and confidence in the regulation of food risks in European consumers. This is unlikely to be achieved simply by experts unveiling the results of risk assessment, but may require the active support and participation of a dubious citizenry (Toke, 2004b).

The factors of genetic modification that trouble Europeans extend far beyond human health concerns to include a diverse collection of concerns relating to the environment not narrowly drawn around questions of plant health. There are uncertainties too about technology and change in a culture that is more hesitant to see technological innovation as obviously beneficial. Irrespective of the potential benefits of technology there may be doubts as to how and if these may be realised in practice. Famously, according to George Bush:

> we can greatly reduce the long-term problem of hunger in Africa by applying the latest developments of science . . . Our partners in Europe are impeding this effort. They have blocked all new bio-crops because of unfounded, unscientific fears . . . (Newsmax, 2003)

Unsurprisingly in doubting the benefits of GM technology (Pidgeon et al., 2005) Europeans may be sceptical that problems of world hunger are so simple that the production of yet more food presents an immediate solution. It is ironic that in castigating fears as unscientific Bush places the debate firmly in the socio-political context by resorting to appeals based on human starvation. Although not so lofty, the socio-political aspirations of the European population for sustainable systems of agriculture based on non-intensive and locally sourced food which match wider aspirations for the preservation of cultures, lifestyles and national difference are not allowed to count.

It is important to realise that as a body committed to trade liberalisation and the opening up of markets, the aspirations previously expressed are values that the WTO cannot accommodate as they must be perceived as explicitly protectionist (Perdikis et al., 2001); more importantly, neither can the EU in its neoliberalist pursuit of a single and integrated market in goods and services. The EU must be characterised as the reluctant litigant in the WTO Dispute Panel case on biotech products. Notwithstanding the ability of the American countries to point to their lead in agricultural biotechnology (United States-European Communities, 2004), there was little to indicate in the run up to the Panel hearing that the European Commission was resistant to the opening up of markets in these products. For example, the then Health and Consumer Affairs Commissioner, Byrne, is on record (Die Ziet, 2001) as conceding in advance of the hearing that:

> There is no scientific proof that GM-Food is more dangerous per se than any other form of food.

At about this time, Frits Bolkestein as Commissioner for the Internal Market reflected that:

> It's rather a saddening spectacle to see that 0.03% of worldwide acreage producing GMs is within the confines of the EU compared to about 60 to 70% in the US . . . We want to hold our own and we want to lead in

> new technologies and this is a new technology of prime importance. . . (Plant Biotech Co-operative Centre, 2001)

Rather than promoting EU regulation as inhibiting the development and marketing of GM crops, the Commission strove hard to permit these things to happen in the face of resistance from a highly sceptical European public. Regulation was the intended mechanism to facilitate the growth and sale of GM crops. Within this regulatory structure the European Food Safety Authority (EFSA) now provides a more centralised approach to approvals that will prove much less problematic than Member State approvals. Member State scientists will retain a role in the process but it is one which will assert scientific certainty as a first stage in an approval system. In describing this development one Commission Official claimed that the creation of the EFSA took matters away from the Commission itself in a manner that:

> would hopefully lead to policy being made with other objectives in view than the economic interest of the sector including for example a very big emphasis on making policy which is science based, in a quite structured way. (Interview)

The aspirations for this approach are well summed up in the following statement:

> The science, basically the Food Safety Authority is going to be the key player for science I would say, so they are going to assess the risk; there is a piece of meat/wheat and we don't know if its harmful or dangerous, so the scientists are going to analyse and then they are going to send their scientific decision to the Commission. (Interview)

We see here a willingness to invest in what is seen as a neutral and untainted assessment of questions of harm in the hope of diffusing dispute and resistance. Interestingly, however, at a political level, the ultimate risk management decisions reside with the Commission. We explore these structures in Chapter 5 but it would seem that the European Commission feels itself well placed to gauge the public temperature and proceed at an achievable pace, albeit one that is rather more brisk on the back of scientific approval. It appears then that the Commission seek the best of both worlds: the accreditation of science based decision making where validity rests on its lack of outside influence, alongside the right to reject scientific findings in the face of political difficulty.

The EU moratorium on approvals was no simple matter. It was borne out of the capacity of GM products to create deep rifts between Member States and the EU institutions, as the manner of the ending of the moratorium and as the stand off between the Commission and the Council indicates. Nonetheless with the moratorium gone there is no reason to doubt that the EU will pursue its agenda of trade liberalisation in this area as for all other goods. The question is how, not whether, it will proceed in this direction. The EU view the mechanisms that have brought about the ending of the moratorium, tracing of GMOs and labelling of GM products, as the minimum assurances need to gain public acceptance of GM products. The American litigants may well yet take the view that these are further barriers to trade (Sheldon, 2002) as they are said to:

> extend far beyond health protections for consumers and in fact create onerous and impractical regulatory barriers. (Lee, 2005)

The invocation of a WTO dispute Panel demonstrated the lack of any appreciation of the tight spot in which the EU finds itself in coaxing reluctant Member States faced with widespread domestic opposition. The adverse finding by a WTO dispute Panel, which the EU did not appeal, meant little to and received little attention from the general public. Indeed although Europe has now introduced mechanisms through EFSA that address questions of risk assessment in the manner promoted by the WTO with expert determination at the primary and leading phase in risk governance, these structures are more not less remote from European citizens. They are torn from a national context that may have been vital in shaping views of GM products. They are less likely to incorporate the range of concerns that will inevitably shape the development of the technology in Europe and which a holistic system of risk assessment ought really to embrace.

All of the evidence shows that social, cultural and ethical attitudes to the technology have driven the dispute from the outset. Any process that seeks to marginalize such concerns, re-educate towards a 'correct view' of the value of innovation, or, for that matter, rule in favour of one side over the other runs the risk of deepening distrust in a way that, as the EU institutions have already witnessed, threatens the very goal of advancing world trade, as the WTO itself becomes the point of resistance.

THE PRESENT REGIME—TRACING AND LABELLING

The UK among other Member States welcomed the suggestion of labelling and traceability provisions but argued that the approach to tracing could be harmonised and made more specific, and that there were gaps in the labelling provisions. Because those Member States that had led the opposition in the Council of Ministers were in a position to impede the working of Directive 2001/18, pending its reform (Hervey, 2001) by the autumn of 2002 Regulations were proposed on: GM food and feed, Traceability and Labelling and Trans-boundary Movement. These proposals produced three regulations in 2003, which took effect in 2004, and which now represent the current law on assessment, authorisation, labelling, tracing and moving genetically modified food and feed. A survey commissioned by the FSA on the total financial compliance cost to businesses of the proposed Regulation estimated the then net cost of £93 million would increase to £720 million on the back of new regulation. (NERA 2001, see also Cabinet Office 2003). Nonetheless, this suite of regulations has allowed the Commission to effectively override all continuing objections from Member States and put an end to the moratorium on the basis that effective regulation is in place.

Labelling and Adventitious Contamination

The tone for this new balance between an effectively operating market for biotechnology products and transparent dealing with the consumer is apparent from the Food and Feed Regulation (1829/2003). This states an objective to provide a high level of protection for human life and health, the environment and the interest of the consumer in relation to GM food and feed, whilst ensuring an effective working of the internal market. It expands the labelling regime to include GM food or feed regardless of whether the GM DNA/protein is detectable or not. A product (including flavours and additives) which is analytically indistinguishable from a conventionally produced equivalent would have to be labelled as containing GM. For example, products containing highly refined oils, previously outside the labelling law, must now be declared as of GM origin. Indeed common and highly processed foodstuffs such as maize oils or starches, soy and vegetable oils lecithin and hydrolysed vegetable protein may well be caught. It would seem that independently from tracing requirements in the partner Regulation, the supply chain must bear the responsibility for a full traceability system to verify any labelling.

Yet the Food and Feed Regulation is limited to food/feed containing or derived 'from' a GMO. It does not cover food/feed made 'with' a GMO (such as a processing aid or foods made with the help of a GMO such as genetically modified enzyme). The enzyme, chymosin, which is used to make cheese from milk, rather than being produced by scraping calves stomachs, can be obtained from bacteria that have been altered to produce large amounts of chymosin. The bacteria used to produce the chymosin have been genetically modified but the chymosin itself has not, meaning that such products would still not need to be labelled under the new reforms. It seems a little odd that this distinction between made 'from' and made 'with' is not made apparent to the consumer if the regime is based on consumer choice. Similarly, there is no obligation placed on the farmer to tell the consumer whether an animal has been reared on GM or non-GM feed. If the farmer is to have this right to information and if GM legislation is indeed based upon consumer information and sovereignty then it might be thought that the consumer would be given information on animal feed and also possibly on whether the animal has been treated with genetically engineered medicinal products? It is hard to escape the sense that these are pragmatic judgments and political compromises at the heart of the regulatory system. GM products are so pervasive in the feed market that the labelling of animal products as bred on GM products could cause major disruption to the food chain if consumer sovereignty was to go so far better not to tell.

Significant debate has surrounded permissible levels of adventitious contamination. Indeed such debate was even more significant than one might have imagined at the time, because as is explained latterly, although introduced as a limit to trigger requirements for labelling, it was later suggested in the UK as the threshold for liability for cross pollination. There had been an earlier threshold of 1% adventitious contamination, but in the Second Reading in the European Parliament in July 2003 a compromise reset the limit at 0.9% on EU approved GMs, in spite of a recommendation of a 0.5% limit proposed by the Environment Committee of the European Parliament (Levidow and Boschert, 2008). A temporary limit of 0.5% was agreed, however, for GMOs with a positive safety assessment even though not yet formally approved. This compromise was endorsed by the European Commission, so that in July 2003 the Regulation was adopted by the Parliament and the Council (Regulation (EC) No 1829/2003 of the European Parliament and of the Council on Genetically Modified Food and Feed, OJ L268) and it took effect on 18 April 2004. This effective reduction in the threshold by 0.1% was roundly criticised as hardly worthwhile by campaigning NGOs, who were particularly critical also of the 0.5% allowance of adventitious contamination by GM products that have been subject to a favourable risk assessment but not yet approved. Indeed, the allowance of adventitious contamination as such allowed Friends of the Earth (FoE, 2004) to make the following claim concerning the Regulation:

> the contamination thresholds will allow unauthorised GMOs to enter the food chain; furthermore these GMOs will not have to be labelled.

In response to the EU Regulation, the Genetically Modified Food (England) Regulations 2004 (S.I. 2004/2334) create (mis)labelling offences by tying in the main obligations of Regulation 1829/2003 to offences already available under English law. Where marketing claims of "GM feed free" are adopted, as producers respond to consumer pressure for greater transparency, in the UK these may need to be regulated under existing controls in the Food Safety Act 1990 and/or the Trade Descriptions Act 1968. There are difficulties for trading standards officers checking food claims, however, because the presence of GM residues in a product may not always be discernible on testing. It may well be then that the most effective policing takes place not under formal public regulation but through supply chain policing to serve the private interest of the major food retailers.

One major issue regarding the labelling of foodstuff concerns animal food and feed. Under the Regulation animal feed if derived from GMOs has to be labelled as such. Approximately 2,000,000 tonnes of soyabean meal and 1,000,000 tonnes of maize gluten feed, much of which comes from GM crops, are imported into the UK for use in animal feed. The FSA stance is that there is no evidence that DNA survives processing and passage through an animal's digestive tract such that it is present in milk, eggs or meat. The FSA has completed studies on whether GM material can survive the passage through the entire human digestive tract (FSA, 2002). Some DNA survived the laboratory created environments but none survived human tests. Nonetheless these studies and the risk communication employed by the FSA became a point of media attention shortly after the introduction of the Regulation when the former Environment Minister questioned whether the FSA stance was sufficiently precautionary (Meacher, 2003). In the event there is no obligation anywhere to inform the consumer whether the animal has been reared on GM or non-GM feed.

The impact of labelling laws is not yet fully apparent given the lack of market penetration in Europe of GM products. GM ingredients have to be labelled regardless of detectability, which may mean that very many foodstuffs will carry the GM warning. This includes GM additives and flavourings. Highly refined soya and maize oil and lecithin will have to be labelled regardless of detectability. However given the instances in which consumers will lack full information it is hard to escape the conclusion that certain lines have been drawn pragmatically, so that, for example, GM feed is so prevalent that informing the consumer that meat is from animals reared on GM feed might provoke massive dislocation in the European market for meat if consumer resistance was not overcome.

Traceability and Labelling

The 2003 reforms produced a harmonised Community framework for tracing and identifying food products and feed derived from GMOs at all stages of their life on the market (Regulation 1830/2003, OJ L 268). Clearly this shifts the burden to the private production and distribution chains which are charged with responsibility for constructing a coherent and consistent approach such that it might appease European consumers. In the face of opposition from countries with significant biotechnology production such as the USA and Canada, the OECD introduced a system of unique identifier codes to be applied to each authorised GMO in order to allow access to specific registered information on GMOs in the supply chain (OECD, 2002). These identifiers form part of the fabric of the Cartagena Protocol on Biosafety and information on GMOs which can be accessed through the Biosafety Clearing House. The onus will be on the importer to obtain necessary documentation and/or testing, though in practical terms the responsibility is apportioned by means of contracting within the supply chain to allocate risk of regulatory failure.

This Regulation and the one on Food and Feed are inter-linked because any effective labelling system depends on the traceability of food ingredients. Traceability also facilitates product recall when necessary either because of the identification of human health effects or because of regulatory breach. In order to trace live GMOs and products derived from them operators are required to transmit information to the effect that a product contains, consists of, or is derived from GMOs. The unique identifiers will form the basis for conveying information on GMOs throughout the supply chain. For importers appropriate documentation will be required from their suppliers or every batch imported will need to be tested. For many products, particularly derived products, testing will not be possible due to the product being indistinguishable from its unmodified counterpart.

The effect of this is that food businesses will have to track down the movement of GM products through the production and distribution chain whilst transmitting and keeping information at each stage of placing a product on the market. These documents will need to be kept for at least five years. The consumer will see little of the tracing system, short, at least, of some major event of recall. Nonetheless the tracing system is vital to the consumer in underpinning the integrity of GM labelling. Labelling is only as good as the validation processes that underpin it. Yet on one hand, levels of adventitious GM content are permitted, even from products yet to be fully approved. On the other, industry harbours serious doubts as to whether testing methods and protocols can be developed to ensure accurate verified labelling. In heavily processed foods modified DNA or protein can be difficult to detect. As we have seen, to date industry has tended to steer completely clear of GM supply chains in the absence of recognised tests for determining biotech methods in food production.

It is difficult to escape the conclusion that traceability will work in an uneven manner. Large-scale entities, corporate retailers and major manufacturers may be able to rely upon their supply chain knowledge, robust contracting and testing procedures. This may be less true for smaller companies which will be in a position to provide less assurance to their consumers. Similarly in comparison with the private sector operations, trading standards or environmental health officers or other competent authorities may be less well placed to test and monitor supply leaving public regulation highly reliant on the private policing of supply chains.

Trans-boundary Spread of GM

In order to meet the EU obligations under the 2000 Cartagena Protocol on Bio-safety (Falkner 2000; Street, 2001) which the European Union ratified in August 2002, a Regulation on Trans-boundary Movements of GMOs (17/2003) completed the suite of GM regulations in 2003. In the UK, responsibility for this issue falls to DEFRA rather than the FSA since it deals with environmental protection rather than food labelling. In implementing the provisions of the Cartagena Protocol (Hilson and French, 2003), the Regulation attempts to ensure an adequate level of protection for the transfer, handling and use of GMOs that may have an adverse effect on the environment and human health and specifically focuses on trans-boundary movements outside the EU. The Regulation sets up a system for notifying and exchanging information on GMO exports to third countries, and specifies procedures for exporters, importers, Member States and the Commission itself, in the case of notifications to the Biosafety Clearing House set up by the Cartagena Protocol.

Although trans-boundary issues were regulated in this way, other problems of coping with co-existence of GM and conventional crops were left entirely to Member States. On 20 July 2006 DEFRA issued a consultation paper on proposals for managing the coexistence of GM, conventional and organic crops in England (DEFRA, 2006). In introducing the consultation paper, Ian Pearson, the then Environment Minister, is reported (Miekle, 2006) as saying: 'in the real world, you can't have zero cross-pollination' calling instead for a 'precautionary, science-based and pragmatic co-existence'. Rather oddly, since it was never intended for this purpose, the 0.9% threshold for adventitious contamination was adopted as the threshold now proposed for co-existence. This involves the rejection, even at the consultation stage of a suggested 0.1% threshold by the Soil Association, on behalf of organic farmers on the basis (in the words of the Minister) that 'we should not kid ourselves that levels of nought or 0.1% are either practical or realistic.' This view largely reflects that of the European Commission's own research (Bock et al., 2002) and adopts the assumption made in countries such as New Zealand that 'the organics industry is likely to have to adopt acceptable limits for accidental GM contamination' (Christey and Woodfield, 2001). Regulation is no easy matter because it is not yet known whether GM and non GM crops will be mixed in an undifferentiated production chain or whether distinct chains will emerge, though, given opposition to date to GM production, the immediate emergence of a single supply chain seems somewhat unlikely. Nonetheless, the depiction of the regulation of co-existence to inform consumer choice helps to justify the 0.9% threshold. It is important in this context to realise that the 0.9% threshold is itself 'adventitious' in the sense that it has little to do with any scientific assessment of levels of points at which cross pollination or the adventitious presence of GMOs is likely to occur; rather than this, it reflected a political compromise that could be achieved in the Parliament (Levidow and Boschert, 2008).

The DEFRA Consultation Paper rejected the concept of 'GM free' in that 'there is no practical distance that will guarantee that cross-pollination can never occur'. The view of the paper is that 'a perfect system of control is unlikely to be achievable in a real world situation' such that the suggested 0.1% threshold (set at the limit of detection) would present serious difficulties and 'ultimately (would) not be in the best interests of the organic sector' (because it could not be maintained) (DEFRA, 2006). This then raises the question of whether the threshold for organic crops should be set at some point below the 0.9% threshold and the paper consults on this. It points out, however, that amendments to the EU Regulation on organic production (EU Regulation 2092/91) might in any case be amended to make certain that products labelled organic could not contain GMOs beyond an adventitious threshold. The situation in organic farming is that the use of GM varieties is not permitted (EC Regulation 1804/1999), but the threshold for adventitious GM presence for labelling purposes might be set at 0.9% in any case. Interestingly, throughout its analysis, the paper treats the problem of co-existence of GM and organic crops as a reciprocal problem, asking, for example, 'how would organic growers cope with a threshold lower than 0.9% if the onus for meeting it was placed upon them'. Equally in discussing the very great distances that might need to be imposed to work a very low threshold the paper suggests that 'expecting organic growers to apply such distances would effectively preclude them from growing the crop in question'. The paper makes the point that the likely types of crops to be grown under GM are in very small quantities of production within the organic sector. There is no production of organic beet hardly any sweetcorn and very little maize or oilseed rape. The largest likely GM crop in organic production is potatoes, which are not so likely to be affected by GM materials.

Under the consultation proposals GM farmers in England would have to inform neighbouring farmers of the presence of GM crops, but proposals for a public register of farms growing GM crops are not supported in the paper on the grounds that this would be too bureaucratic and offer information to protesters. The consultation paper suggests strict separation barrier distances between fields growing GM and conventional crops, of the same species, suggested as 35 metres for oilseed rape, and 80 and 110 metres for forage maize and grain maize respectively. Such barriers would be subject to inspection with fines for failure to meet requirements. The paper accepts that barriers might be possible in the form of strips of non-GM crops grown alongside the GM crops to act as a barrier between non-GM crops in a neighbouring field. The idea is that the barrier crop would absorb pollen from the GM crop. This raises questions as to whether the barrier strip would count towards the separation distance, but DEFRA clearly envisage this or even that it might help reduce that distance since the paper states that barriers may be 'an attractive option if it is difficult to observe a separation distance.'

The paper considers not only *ex ante* regulation but *ex post* liability rules, the combination of which is said to increase the value of waiting, and so as to result in the less immediate adoption of the GM technology (Beckmann et al., 2006). In an interesting section of the Consultation

Paper, it considers the possible remedies for losses for non-GM farmers whose crops develop an adventitious presence above the 0.9% threshold without fault on the part of the farmer in question. Interestingly the paper describes such losses as 'financial' which begs the question of whether this form of cross contamination constitutes physical damage. The paper expresses the view that claims based on GM cross pollination are 'untested and uncertain' as a matter of common law. One might add that cross pollination itself is largely of this nature being based on limited farm scale trials (Jamieson, 2004). The Consultation Paper suggests that it might be difficult to establish 'the proper defendant'. Given that the claim may be in nuisance (and therefore against a neighbour with an interest in land) this presumably posits a difficulty of causation in showing which particular source of GM material has caused the problem. The paper is in favour of redress mechanisms and considers the possibility of leaving claims for redress simply to be resolved under existing law, or an industry-led (voluntary) redress mechanism, or a statutory redress scheme. It assumes that GM affected crops above the threshold level will still have a market, but that the value will be less than that for non-GM crops. It also assumes that cases will be infrequent (since separation measures will work) and that only direct financial losses will be covered. The non-GM farmer would have to meet strict conditions in order to establish liability including compliance with any guidance or legislation relating to co-existence; once again emphasising the reciprocal nature of liabilities.

Experience of North American farmers has shown that contamination of non-GM crops by GM crops is inevitable, due to forces of nature, and the high propensity for crops contamination during post-harvest sorting or handling of crops. Consequently, achieving the EU minimum 0.9% threshold of adventitious GM presence in non-GM crops would be a daunting challenge, once GM crops become widespread in the United Kingdom. For this reason, and in the absence of insurance cover for crops contamination risk, any co-existence policy regime faces the challenge of evolving a comprehensive measure that would insulate non-GM farmers from all forms of financial injuries arising from contamination of non-GM by GM crops. While DEFRA's consultation paper rightly aims to achieve this objective, it surprisingly glossed over intellectual property infringement risk posed by contamination of non-GM crops by proprietary GM crops. As evidenced by the experience of the North American non-GM commercial farmers who were bankrupted by patent infringement lawsuits, liability for intellectual property rights infringement arising from cross-pollination of GM and non-GM crops is a crucial co-existence problem and a significant legal externality that any viable co-existence policy must reckon with and address.

GM seeds and the ensuing crops are proprietary and are protected in the United Kingdom by either the Patent Act, 1977 or Plant Varieties Act, 1997. The application of these laws in the United Kingdom is held to the minimum standards of protection prescribed by the relevant provisions of the 1994 WTO Agreement on Trade-Related Aspects of Intellectual Property Rights (TRIPS); and the 1961 UPOV Convention for the Protection of New Varieties (as revised in 1991) to which the UK is a signatory. Seed companies are known to rigorously enforce their property rights in GM seeds via 'technology contract agreements', which inter alia, vest a restrictive non-exclusive licence in GM farmers. Monsanto successfully sued an American canola farmer for saving proprietary seed from previous harvest for replanting (*Monsanto v Homan McFarling* 302 F.3d 1291 (Fed. Cir. 2002) though on appeal the award of $780,000 was ordered to be reduced to reflect the actual benefit gained by saving and replanting of genetically altered seeds in violation of Monsanto's rights (*Monsanto v Homan McFarling* (No. 2) 363 F.3d 1336 (Fed. Cir. 2004). Under section 60(1) (a) of the UK Patent Act, a patented product such as genetically modified seed and the ensuing crop, is deemed to have been infringed where the alleged infringer 'makes, disposes of, offer to dispose of, uses, or imports the product or keeps it whether for disposal or otherwise.'

UK non-GM commercial farmers whose farms were contaminated would be vulnerable to the strict liability regime of the patent law, since they would naturally want to do all or any of those acts forbidden by section 60(1) (a). They would also not be able to claim the defence of the right to save, use, sell, or propagate proprietary seeds/crops, under section 60(5);(g) of the Patent Act, since they did not buy any proprietary seeds from seed companies. Additionally, non-GM farmers would not be assisted by the defence that their farms were contaminated or that the presence of GM crops on their farms was adventitious. In order to prevent in the United Kingdom, the scenarios in *Monsanto Canada Inc., v. Percy Schmeiser* (2004) SCC 34, (2004) 1 S.C.R. 902, where a farmer was sued in Canada for adventitious presence of GM crops on his canola farm, it is imperative that a statutory defence against intellectual property rights infringement be put in place for the protection of non-GM commercial farmers who had their farm contaminated by adventitious GM crops.

CONCLUSION

The handling of cross contamination issues demonstrates many of the points raised in this analysis. We see GM becoming an integral part of the changing agri-industrial landscape, such that there is no question of its right to grow alongside conventional crops not withstanding its potentially irreversible effects. At the same time there is the recognition, within the plans for a compensation structure that the impacts of GM will be heavily contested. In part this is because it forms a wider picture of the appropriation of agriculture by agri-business. The controversy around GM has caused some stock taking and some re-evaluation of the sustainability of modern agricultural practice. Proponents of GM might claim that the technology is a good example of eco-modernisation since the case made for it is in terms of win/win claims—less pesticide use, fewer nitrates/phosphates etc. However these claims only exhibit value or demonstrate the 'win/win' scenario if one accepts the dominant agri-industrial framework in which the claims have value. If one rejects that framework itself as unsustainable (Buttel, 2006) then the eco-modernisation case begins to fall away.

In order to accommodate biotechnology, at least when based on GM, in the face of significant opposition, the regulatory structures have been over almost twenty years in a continuing state of developmental flux. Slowly, however, we have seen the centralisation of governance structures and their relocation to a European level. The crisis that prompted a European moratorium of processing approvals for the release of GM crops has been answered at a European level by addressing an entirely different question, namely that of consumer rights to know about products that might contain GM. In this adaptation, the question of release is sidelined and implicitly accepted and arguments about biodiversity loss or the rural landscape are transmuted into questions only of the market acceptability of products and away from questions of their production.

In so doing science has played a considerable role, and the use of scientific expertise within the EFSA framework effectively operates as a legitimating mechanism—an issue explored in Part II. This process is aided by the WTO agreements which focus on narrow questions of product safety for human health rather than opening up wider questions that might form part of any assessment including those connected to environmental protection and sustainable agriculture. Another remarkable element of this transformation in regulation is the involvement of the private sector through supply chain tracing and product labelling. As the public agencies retire to the shadows on the basis that assurance can be offered by private interest regulation, the next stage of the contest will conveniently pitch civil society against private providers. This may leave a form of governance that re-enforces rather than challenges changes to the dominant power relationships within agri-industrial production.

Part II

The Evolving Hybrid Model

4 State Failures and Failures of the State

INTRODUCTION

In this chapter, we analyse the manner in which the food crisis discussed in Chapter 1 makes itself manifest in patterns of governance. More specifically, we examine the nature of state failures in the management of food safety, and how, as a result, the state at both a national and European level has been searching for credibility to reassert its authority and legitimacy. At the European level, the networks that operate in the area of food safety and that bring together scientific communities, policy actors, economic interests, NGOs and policy makers raise an important question about the extent to which these networks complement or compete with traditional forms of state authority.

The chapter analyses the development of food policy in the UK and the EU in the post-war years and concentrates particularly on the period from the late 1980s to the early 2000s when food crises flared into public and political prominence and then waned as food safety appeared to be better managed. Amongst the common trends at both the European and national level there were at least three that are worth commenting on further. First, the moves from partial, agriculture dominated perceptions of food policy to ones which are more comprehensive and consumer oriented. Second, political crises in ensuring safe foods are critical in both policy development and institutional innovations (the demise of the Ministry of Agriculture, Fisheries and Food (MAFF) and the creation of the Department of Food and Rural Affairs (DEFRA) and of the Food Standards Agency (FSA) in Britain, and the creation of DG SANCO and the European Food Safety Authority at the European level. Third, there have been increasing links between national and European food policy development and the spill over of political crises between the two levels of government. Over time, the EU dimension to food policy has become ever more important and so we pay particular attention to it.

The chapter begins by discussing food policy in Britain, where we have witnessed a relative decline in the significance of food debates linked to production and the rise of rather different debates linked to consumption.

Next the chapter analyses the policy and institutional development of food policy in Europe. Finally, the chapter discusses the changing nature of food governance in Europe in relation to policy and institutional innovation.

PRODUCER-LED CHOICE: FOOD POLICY IN BRITAIN

The early post-war years in the UK were characterised by a producer-led domination of food choices. Its essential features were pervasive and have only relatively recently been usurped as the major food retailers began to imprint their own characteristics on the regulatory process (see Chapter 1). Perhaps two factors more than any other were responsible for the initial producer domination of post-war food choice. One was the political strategy of the National Farmers' Union (NFU) and the other the Government's response to food shortages (see Self and Storing, 1962; Wilson, 1977; Grant, 1983; Cox et al., 1986; and Foreman, 1989).

Compared to other elements within the food system, farmers are distinguished by their sheer number—though that has fallen markedly—and thus the minute market influence of any individual farmer. Faced with ever more concentrated operations upstream and downstream (that is those who provide them with inputs such as fertilisers and purchase their products like food manufacturers), who could use their market position to squeeze the profit margins of farmers, the latter have been successful at organising themselves to protect and promote their interests through political means. The NFU had an enviable reputation for its expertise and skilful lobbying and long enjoyed close contacts with the then Ministry of Agriculture, Fisheries and Food (MAFF). Indeed, the closeness of the links with MAFF provided a source of comment and, perhaps, these contacts did go much deeper than those of any other interest group and government department. The NFU had supported successive post-war government's policy of making farming more productive through increasing intensification as, it was believed, this would ensure the long-term prosperity of farming.

The political strategy of the NFU dovetailed neatly with the concern of the post-war Labour Government (Williams, 1965) and its Conservative successors to increase food supplies. The war years and early years of peace were marked by considerable government intervention in the management of food. At a time of genuine food scarcity, which worsened with the ending of hostilities, government had to play a role in ensuring food reached a largely urban population. Obviously a key means was through the stimulation and control of domestic agriculture. Farmers received guaranteed prices for the major agricultural products and sold to an assured market. In short, farmers were directed as to what to grow and the government engaged in bulk purchase.

The close links between farmers and government were crystallised in the 1947 Agriculture Act. This provided for a privileged position for the

National Farmers' Union, as the representative of farmers to engage in annual negotiations with government through an annual review of the general economic conditions facing agriculture in the year ahead and to set prices for products accordingly. Other interests, such as consumers, were marginalised. With the easing of food scarcity concerns in the 1950s and the election in 1951 of a Conservative Government that was committed to relaxing controls on food a more liberal pricing and distribution system emerged, although rationing on such staples as butter, margarine and meat lasted until 1954 (Foreman, 1989:56). Nevertheless, the NFU retained its pre-eminent position and, along with the then Ministry of Agriculture, set the tone for much of the post-war agricultural and, by default, food policy. In terms of choice, the over-riding emphasis was ensuring adequate supplies of affordable, safe food for a largely urban population. In terms of food rights, it can be expressed as government action to provide collective food security, that is, *freedom from want*. The role of regulation here may be characterised as *public-interest regulation* in which government takes a leading, strategic and directive role. It is to be contrasted with that of private interest regulation which characterises corporate food regulation in the late 1990s (see Harrison et al., 1997). In short, choice was in large part determined by the state-induced construction of supply: the interactions between what farmers produced and what government wanted them to produce. Indeed, the rights emerged from the common interest (i.e. expectation) at the time in the need to safeguard food supplies, requiring positive state action (i.e. duties upon the government) in the agricultural policy sphere.

Economic Interests and MAFF

Through a combination of factors farmers, since the 1970s, generally found themselves in a difficult position. They were squeezed between their suppliers and food manufacturers and retailers who increasingly dictated how products must be farmed by setting stringent quality standards. Also, the favourable political framework within which farmers had been accustomed to operate came under closer scrutiny. At the time farming practices were increasingly questioned for their effects on animal welfare and the environment and the costs of supporting farming were no longer unquestioned (see, for example, National Consumer Council, 1988; Cottrell, 1987; Clunies-Ross and Hildyard, 1992; Body, 1991; Clark and Lowe, 1992). Almost inevitably the close links between the NFU and MAFF came under critical scrutiny, not least from some Conservative MPs who had traditionally been regarded as natural allies (see, for example, Body, 1982; 1984; 1987). Thus, economically and politically farmers increasingly found themselves in a defensive position.

The protracted relative economic and political decline of farming has been accentuated by the dramatic rise to prominence of first food manufacturers

(Flynn, Marsden and Ward, 1991) and more recently retailers (Wrigley, 1991; 1992; 1994). These have proved to be the two most buoyant sectors within the food system, and are dominated by a small number of large firms. Key food manufacturers include AB Foods, Booker, Allied Lyons, Grand Metropolitan and Unigate, whilst the most important food retailers are Tesco, Walmart-Asda, Sainsbury and Morrisons. Throughout the 1980s and into the 1990s the major retailers underwent considerable expansion such that today they have captured about two thirds of food retail sales. In contrast the smaller independent retailers account for an ever-declining proportion of sales. It is the major multiples which increasingly determine the shape of the British food sector and are able to influence the food choices on offer. Together retailers and manufacturers have been sources of considerable innovation across a range of areas from new products, to the distribution and storage of those products.

Within the food system it is the manufacturers and increasingly the major retailers who will be exercising influence (Flynn and Marsden, 1992; Marsden and Wrigley, 1995). Such influence carries with it a regulatory dimension. Retailers, in particular, have found themselves both drawn into and actively seeking a regulatory role. For example, during the late 1980s–1990s it was by no means apparent that key retailers would move into the dominant position within the food system they enjoy today. Retailers faced intense internal competition and growing criticisms of their sourcing strategies and as a result had to grapple with the challenge of market maintenance (Marsden, Harrison and Flynn, 1997). This involved them in a more diversified set of relationships with the state at both the national and European level. Perhaps fortuitously, at the same time, MAFF, which had considerable regulatory responsibility throughout the food chain, had been seeking to share some of its regulatory burden, often under the mantle of deregulation (see also the next section). That such a coincidence of regulatory interests could be realised owed much to MAFF's knowledge of, and involvement with, the industry built up over long years of its support. As one industry interviewee reflected on the situation at the time: 'the food industry has always had a good working relationship with MAFF because MAFF needs such a relationship. You see MAFF is sponsoring the food industry'. Up until its demise in the 1990s MAFF retained close contacts with the food sector which it was keen to foster (interview with MAFF official). Contacts between retailers and government occurred on a regular basis and at a variety of levels from the highest circles of policy making to local level policy implementation.

Consumer Groups and MAFF

The position of the supermarkets in relation to government is in marked contrast to that of consumer groups and consumers. It is worthwhile briefly contrasting their experiences with those of key producer interests in the aftermath of the Second World War. Whilst the NFU was embraced by government and its privileged position with the then Ministry of Agriculture protected, consumers had their interests looked after by the Ministry of Food. As long as food shortages and rationing remained, so there was a role for the Ministry of Food, which had been formed in 1939 (it had previously been disbanded in 1921 following the easing of food supplies after WWI). Once those conditions changed then the rationale for a separate Ministry was lost.

In October 1954 it was announced that the Ministry of Food would merge, but very much as junior partner, with the Ministry of Agriculture. The proposed reform provoked considerable controversy, with significant implications for the subsequent construction of food choice. One junior Minister of Food, Dr Charles Hill, was moved to argue that 'in essence it (the Ministry of Food) had been a consumer's organisation and I doubted whether the consumer's interests could be fully protected if what remained of the Ministry of Food passed to the Ministry of Agriculture' (quoted in Foreman, 1989: 57). Similarly critical comments were made in *The Times*: 'The worst of the possible alternatives has been chosen. If there could not be a separate Minister of Food, his remaining responsibilities should have gone anywhere rather than the Minister of Agriculture. It is asking too much of any Minister to be able to hold the balance fairly between the interests of the consumer and the powerful agricultural interest' (quoted in Foreman, 1989: 57).

Concerns about consumer representation within MAFF never entirely disappeared (Smith, 1990) but were muted whilst food itself remained a politically quiescent issue. Once that changed in the 1980s and 1990s MAFF found itself encountering real difficulties fending off charges that it put producers before consumers. In the early 1990s, in response to criticism of its aloofness from consumers, MAFF formed a consumer panel. Various consumer groups have members on this committee and they have welcomed the opportunity this has opened up for them to represent consumer views to government. As one interviewee put it: 'I think . . . our influence has grown . . . [This is] [p]artly through the setting up of the consumer panel, partly because we have quite a lot of people now on MAFF committees'. A more sober assessment of the Panel is provided by Millstone and van Zwanenberg (2001: 601) who claim that 'Ministers and officials saw it as forum through which MAFF's messages could be disseminated, rather than as an occasion for listening or engaging substantively with consumer concerns'.

Cultivating links with MAFF depends upon groups observing codes of behaviour and practice. Consumer groups must show to government that they are responsible, credible and sources of useful information. Indeed, as one consumer group interviewee argued 'we have built up the relationship with government departments, . . . built up the trust of government in that all our work is usually based on sound research'. Another interviewee, however, hinted that at the time links between MAFF and consumer groups were not that strong: 'in common with the other consumer organisations we were extremely sceptical when (the consumer panel) . . . was set up. But I think they've (MAFF) largely won us over, in that it isn't a hollow PR exercise, and they have moved quite considerably on a lot of things that the consumer panel has been pressing for'. Whilst the influence of consumer groups within MAFF may have grown it is from a low base. Moreover, it is largely confined by MAFF, to the less central (i.e. non-economic) areas of its work. There is, for example, little evidence to show that consumer groups have anything limited or sporadic influence on agricultural policy. In any case, consumer groups find their ability to make inputs into the policy process constrained by limited resources. For example, in the summer of 1996 it was announced that the National Consumer Council faced swingeing cuts in funding from government and was to make one third of its staff redundant.

CENTRAL GOVERNMENT AND THE REGULATION OF FOOD

By changing the regulatory and policy styles of government, merging the Ministries of Food and Agriculture, changed the way food choices were structured. As the Ministry of Agriculture, the department's preferred administrative style was to incorporate favoured (i.e. economic) interests into the decision making structure in an attempt to ensure that the two move together. When the need to ensure food supplies was a national priority the incorporation of farmers, presumably, made much sense. The merger with the Ministry of Food did not change the department's operating style. Thus, as part of the merger the Ministry of Agriculture took over the Ministry of Food's responsibility for food standards. For example, the latter had set up a Food Standards Committee in 1947, to be followed in 1964 by a Food Additives and Contaminants Committee (Foreman, 1989: 56). These Committees, exist to help protect the consumer, they also assist in the co-ordination of government and industry activities (National Consumer Council, 1988). They were replaced in 1983 by the Food Advisory Committee but like its predecessors it has been increasingly criticised for its lack of independence, unrepresentative membership and secrecy of proceedings. (For a critique of the voluntarisitc and secretive style of food committees, see Millstone and van Zwanenberg, 2001) When, for the first time in 1993 the financial links between members of the Food Advisory Committee and food companies were published, 'Twelve out of 17 members . . .declared some cash reward' and that may have been an underreporting (The Guardian 12 May 1993).

The deliberations of food related committees and their recommendations are significant for food choice because they are able to propose modifications to the boundaries of existing regulations. As the food companies and retailers search for new products and processes there is frequently a need for new regulations or the amendment of existing regulations. A good example of the types of changes that may be made were reflected in MAFF's attitude to food regulations which have 'tended to move away from imposing compositional standards on food . . . to provide more effective ingredient and nutritional labelling' (Foreman, 1989: 118). The extra flexibility this modified stance has given food manufacturers is reflected, for example, in low-fat products which were previously outlawed by specifications on minimum fat content.

The case of food composition provides a good example of how rights related to food choice have been reformulated. The move towards more 'effective labelling' is one based upon the assumption that the informed individual is best placed to make decisions on consumption. In other words, the consumer is being given the right, the freedom to, consume. Such a notion of rights is quite different from that which prevailed at the end of WWII. Then there was a sense of a collective consumer interest whose choice was largely determined by government. The role of governments was to ensure freedom from want through the provision of affordable and safe food. Now it is the corporate retailers who play a central role in promoting to individualised consumers their vision of quality and diversity of consumption. This is one of variety and a hierarchy of standards. Different retailers seek to imbue their products with notions of quality and to do this they must be able to exercise considerable influence over the supply of products. This may be termed private interest regulation (Harrison, Flynn and Marsden, 1997), because retailers are creating their own standards and operating food safety systems which go beyond that required by more traditional forms of public regulation.

FROM MAFF TO DEFRA: RECOGNISING THE CONSUMER INTEREST

The Conservative Governments of the 1980s and 1990s had been plagued by a series of food crises, such as salmonella in eggs and BSE. Throughout these crises, the Conservative Government resisted calls for the reorganisation of central government, particularly to reform or, indeed disband, MAFF. When the Labour Government was elected in 1997 it was already committed to structural reform with a promise to create a new Food Standards Agency (for a discussion of the Agency see Chapter 9). At the time, and to some surprise, Labour's reformist and modernising agenda did not appear to have much further impact on MAFF other than the removal of its food safety functions to the FSA. Nevertheless, disquiet at the Ministry's performance persisted, its production outlook and perceived defence of established interests meant that it appeared ever more anachronistic. So, too no great surprise MAFFs demise followed Labour's 2001 election victory.

Rather less expected was the organisation that emerged to take on MAFFs former functions. Rather than, say a Ministry of Rural Affairs that had been championed by bodies such as the Country Landowners Association (now known as the Country Land & Business Association), a new Department for the Environment, Food and Rural Affairs (DEFRA) emerged. The naming of the new department had some symbolic significance: farming had disappeared from the title to be replaced by food. Alongside the functions of MAFF, DEFRA also inherited responsibilities for sustainable development, environmental protection and water, rural development, countryside and energy efficiency. DEFRA may be well placed to help in the 'greening' of agricultural policies but of, perhaps, even greater import is the shift in focus to thinking of food beyond the farm gate rather than simply behind it. The result has been much greater emphasis on food supply chains and understanding the links between production and consumption (for example, DEFRA's Sustainable Food programme). Perhaps the most high profile recognition of the need for a rethinking of public policy to reconnect farmers with their markets and the rest of the food chain came from the Report of the Policy Commission on the Future of Farming and Food (popularly known as the Curry Report after its chair Sir Donald Curry[Curry, 2002]).

Crises in UK food production and consumption policy had spill over effects at the European level as we shall see subsequently. The globalisation of food supply chains means that food crises can quickly move beyond national boundaries and also draw in different national governments and levels of government. The severity of food crises in Europe, notably that of BSE, showed that they can take place over wide spatial scales, involve many different economic and consumer interests as well multiple levels of government. As a result, Europe found that food crises can be very difficult to manage and the credibility of existing systems of governance are severely tested. Political crises, though, often result in institutional innovations, and that of food was no exception (Hellebo, 2004: 9).

EUROPEANISING FOOD POLICY: AGRICULTURE AND FOOD PRODUCTION

Historically DG Agriculture has been one of the most influential directorate generals. Agriculture was at the heart of the founding of the European Community, and the Common Agricultural Policy (CAP) has long been its most well known policy. Whilst agriculture was to the fore, however, food policy as a distinctive area of activity remained underdeveloped and viewed through a productivist lens. Millstone and van Zwanenberg (2001: 595), remark that 'consumer and health interests have routinely been subordinated to the objectives of furthering the commercial interests of farming and the food industry.' For instance, support for European farmers and growth in farm output was partly justified on grounds of food security.

Even the slow, incremental growth in consumer policy up to the 1980s did not initially lead to the development of a food policy. Instead, food issues forced their way higher up the policy agenda as the Commission and Member States grappled with the mechanics of developing the Single European Act (1986). Engagement with food issues at a European level emerged mainly as the result of efforts to eliminate trade barriers to the operation of the internal market (Alemanno, 2006; Voss 2000: 228). The Commission sought to remove potential trade barriers by specifying the composition of individual products. Not surprisingly, in attempting to specify in detail the ingredients in a product, the Commission found itself embroiled in debates over national and regional culinary traditions and tastes. Food law at the national and regional level is well established and across Europe and there are numerous and long-standing regulations to combat adulteration, fraud and unsafe foods.

As a result, progress in the agreement of so-called recipe laws (vertical directives for individual foods) was slow and controversial. By the mid 1980s only about fifty directives had been adopted and the Commission abandoned the approach and replaced it with the mutual recognition principle based upon a judgement of the European Court of Justice on the 1979 *Cassis de Dijon* case (Alemanno, 2006: 241). With this approach to regulation, goods produced or marketed in one country could be circulated elsewhere as long they met rules, standards or tests to be found in another Member State.

EUROPEAN FOOD CONSUMER POLICY AND ITS ORGANISATION

The Organisation of Food Policy Before BSE

It is important to recognise that early European actions in relation to food safety were justified on market rather than consumer protection grounds. The consumer as an object of policy was not mentioned in the Treaty of Rome and, as we shall see in the following text, was largely marginalised at an institutional and political level. Alemanno (2006: 243) has noted that up until the emergence of food crises in the late 1990s,

> European food law continued to develop in a fragmented fashion. . . . EC food law was still mainly focused on issues of trade and the free movement of goods rather than on safety issues. Although a significant number of EC legislative texts were adopted, one could not properly speak of a pan-European common food policy.

The development of consumer policy has not come about through recourse to a strong legal base but rather the gradual accretion of efforts from consumer organisations, the European Parliament and Commission staff. The extension of Community activities in the 1970s and 1980s in the area of consumer policy was mirrored in other areas of social policy, such as education, environment and R&D.

At a formal, though largely symbolic level, it was at the EC Summit meeting in Paris in 1972 when Heads of Government formally recognised that economic development must be accompanied by improvements in the quality of life of Europe's citizens. This gave licence for both institutional and policy developments. With regard to the former, this initially consisted of the creation of a service for consumer affairs; which, in effect meant, recognition of the issue within the Commission but it was not regarded as sufficiently worthy to require DG status. Alongside the service for consumer affairs, and serviced by it, was the creation of a Consumers Consultative Committee (renamed the Consumers Consultative Council in 1989), and subsequently restructured as the Consumer Commission in 1995. Membership of the body was drawn from a diverse range of organisations, including the major representative bodies: BEUC, Euroco-op, COFACE and ETUC (European Confederation of Trade Unions). The principal role of the organisation was to act as a sounding board, a consultative forum, for Commission work that had implications for consumers.

The low political profile assigned to food policy and the weak institutional arrangements attached to food and consumer issues, meant that it was very difficult to develop a distinctive, consumer oriented food policy. This is not to suggest that food issues were a marginal issue. Clearly, food is important to consumers and to the operation of the European market. Much discussion of food, therefore, related to regulatory issues that largely took place outside of the gaze of the public and of politicians in a small number of scientific committees: the Scientific Committee on Foodstuffs (SCF) composed of independent scientific experts, the Standing Committee on Foodstuffs (StCF) consisting of national representatives, and the Advisory Committee on Foodstuffs (ACF), whose membership is drawn from interest groups. The latter committee was the more marginal, while the other two played a much more important role in decision making. The SCF was consulted on scientific advice by the Commission and so provided the risk assessment, whilst the StCF—as the body that represented the interests of the Member States—provided the forum that undertook risk management (Voss, 2000: 229–230). The committees allowed a scientific rationale to play alongside the food sensitivities of national governments and generally worked well and provided a means for mediating forms of interest formation and . . . and [could] thus contribute to the legitimacy of Community decision making" (Voss, 2000: 231).

A similar committee structure existed for animal health where there was a Scientific Veterinary Committee composed of scientists with a high standing, and a Standing Veterinary Committee drawn from national representatives (Voss, 2000: 232). In short, up until the time of BSE the food and animal committees operated with a relatively low profile, some in a secretive way, but with considerable credibility.

The BSE crisis, however, exposed the weaknesses of the committee-based approach since national interests were able to prevail over collective consumer interests and thus delay Community level decision-making on tackling BSE. The workings and reportings of Committee deliberations also did not assist in developing a co-ordinated approach to BSE from the relevant DGs (Voss, 2000: 232). The failings of food safety management at the European level were brutally exposed by the Report of the European Parliament (1997: 14) (the so-called Medina report) into the Commission's handling of the BSE crisis which found that

> Public health protection competencies are compartmentalized between a number of different Commission departments (as regards possible food risks). The BSE affair has been handled variously by: DG VI (Agriculture), DG III (ex-Internal Market, now Industry), the Consumer Protection Service (currently DG XXIV), and the Directorate for Health and Safety (DG V). This compartmentalization has hampered the coordination and efficiency of the services concerned, has facilitated the shifting of responsibility for maladministration between the various services of the Commission and points up the lack of an integrated approach. (Buonanno: 14)

BSE and the Reorganisation of Food Safety: Institutions and Policy—1986–1996

The BSE saga had wide-ranging ramifications for the management and organisation of food safety in both Britain and Europe. The way in which BSE was tackled illustrates the increasing interconnectedness of food systems and of levels of governance. It is not only that food crises can 'spill over' from one political arena to another but that there is then established a dynamic, in which governments seek to establish their legitimacy and credibility in relation to their own constituencies (UK and EU consumers) and to one another (UK government to Commission and Commission to other Member States and the European Parliament). BSE was first identified in the laboratory in 1986. It was not until two years later, however, in August 1988 that the decision was made to slaughter all BSE-affected cattle in the UK. In the following July (1989), the Commission banned the export of British cattle that were more than one year old and then later in the year banned the use of cows brain and spinal cord for human consumption. Over the following years there followed further tightening of the use of materials in human and animal foods.

Any sense that the BSE crisis was being 'successfully' managed was undermined by the announcement by the UK government on 21 March 1996, based on a report of the Bovine Spongiform Encephalopathy Committee that a link may exist between BSE and human equivalent Creutzfeldt-Jakob disease. The announcement caused alarm amongst consumers in the UK (and the rest of

Europe) and concern amongst European beef producers. For governments across Europe, there was a desire to take action to protect consumers and reassure meat markets. Faced with the threat of unilateral action by Member State governments against British beef and pressure from the British government to question the legality of such moves, the Commission was compelled to act.

Commission decisions on animal health are based upon the work of the Scientific Veterinary Committee (SVC), whose members are appointed by the Commission on the basis of nominations by Member State governments (Westlake, 1997: 12). At its meeting on 25 March 1996, the Committee proposed by fourteen votes to one an immediate ban on British beef and by-products, a decision that it reaffirmed at a subsequent meeting the following day. On the next day (27 March 1996), the Commission met and unanimously agreed to follow the advice of the SVC. During meetings in April and May of the SVC and the Commission there were suggestions that the SVC may recommend a relaxation of the ban on a very small number of bovine products (e.g. gelatine) however, there was never the necessary qualified majority vote on the SVC (Westlake, 1997: 14–15). The British Conservative government, already in a difficult position in Parliament and under regular attack from Euro sceptic MPs, responded by refusing to co-operate with EU decision-making. It was not until the meeting of a European Heads of Government meeting in Florence on 20–21 June 1996 that a gradual lifting of the export ban was agreed, but there was no timetable, and was conditional upon an even wider cull of cattle than had been expected (Westlake, 1997: 22).

Whilst at the level of high politics, the British government, other Member State governments and senior Commission officials had been able to formulate a compromise on the export of British beef that would allow all to claim a measure of victory and enable European government to once again resume normal working, at another European institution, the Parliament, there were serious concerns about the way in which BSE had been managed. As Roederer-Rynning (2003: 123) has noted 'the E[uropean] P[arliament] played a key role in turning . . . [the BSE] epidemic into an EU-wide political crisis'. On 18 July 1996 the Parliament set up a temporary committee of inquiry to review the Commission's handling of BSE. The committee made a number of detailed recommendations, and one of the outcomes was the adoption by the Parliament on 18 February 1997 of a 'conditional censure', by which the Parliament could monitor through a further temporary committee whether the Commission adopted its recommendations.

Food Policy and Institutional Development: Post-BSE Developments—1996–1967

Under considerable pressure, Commission President Santer in a major statement of 18 February 1997 met many of the Parliament's concerns. He announced a number of measures (Westlake, 1997: 23–24), amongst the most significant of which were:

- Creation of a group of Commissioners, to be chaired by Santer, that would have overall responsibility for food matters;
- The relocation of all the Commission's food health advisory and consultative committees to DGXXIV in an attempt to strengthen the science that underlay decisions and assure internal and external audiences of its independence from producer interests;
- DGXXIV was to be reformed and given overall responsibility for consumer health (from DGVI).

There were also two other noteworthy and related developments in the early part of 1997. The first was the formulation of a revised approach to food law and policy in the Green Paper on the General Principles of Food Law in the EU and the Commission Communication on Consumer Health and Food Safety. Second, were the Commission proposals for a new food agency. Initially both Santer and his successor as Commission President, Prodi, favoured an organisation similar to the US Food and Drug Administration but the latter soon moved towards a more modest science driven, risk assessment focussed agency. (An outline of the Agency is discussed subsequently and also in Chapter 9).

In a speech to the European Parliament on 18 February 1997 Santer proposed the 'gradual establishment of a proper food policy, which gives pride of place to consumer protection and consumer health'. On 30 April 1997 in a Communication from the Commission*:* Consumer Health and Food Safety the new approach to food policy was outlined. Three principles would now underlay policy:

1. Separation of legislative responsibilities (for risk management) from scientific advice (for risk assessment).
2. Separation of legislative responsibilities from controls and inspections.
3. Transparency in decision-making.

Food safety was to be achieved by three complementary instruments:

1. Risk analysis—covering the scientific evaluation of risks, risk management (i.e. an assessment of the measures required to reduce risk to an acceptable level), and communication of risks to decision-makers, consumers and producers;
2. Reform of the scientific committees; and
3. Controls and inspections involving the introduction of risk assessment procedures, monitoring of the entire food chain, and auditing of national monitoring systems.

It is also important to recognise that during the reformist phase in food management of the late 1980s and 1990s food was amongst the most important issues on the European public policy agenda. Food moved to prominence because of a series of crises, most notably, BSE, in food safety. These crises exposed the limitations of EU institutions to manage food safety and consumption and in turn induced a wider political crisis in Europe. As a result Commission Presidents Santer and Prodi were to claim that consumer interests were at the heart of their administrations. In reality they could probably do little else. Member State governments, key producer interests and consumer organisations demanded reassurance that the Commission could competently tackle food safety issues. Equally pertinently, the European Parliament with its threat of 'conditional censure' hanging over the Commission ensured that policy and institutional change had to be implemented. Indeed, consumer issues became a means by which the Parliament could bolster its own significance and helped further nurture relations between itself and DG SANCO (Roederer-Rynining, 2003: 123). Roederer-Rynining (2003: 124) argues that following the BSE crisis at a European level there was a shift of 'political resources away from producers towards consumers. This situation provided consumer and environmental groups in the E[uropean] P[arliament] with unprecedented opportunities to expand their influence'.

It is worthwhile briefly speculating on why the food crises led to a deepening of European integration rather than its rolling back and the re-nationalisation of food safety responsibilities. Perhaps rather remarkably there were no overt efforts to relocate or reassert the primacy of the nation state as the key site for food safety responsibilities but instead an unquestioning assumption of the need for further European integration, most notably with the creation of the European Food Safety Authority (EFSA). Efforts to promote Europe-wide regulation might have been justified on the basis of the internationalisation of food sourcing and manufacture. However, the key policy documents on EU food law and the Commission Communication of 1997 have a curiously Eurocentric model of food production and consumption systems rather than operating with a more globalised model. Thus, farm to fork food safety regulation are largely confined to what happens within the EU. So, whilst consumers can be reassured that there can be some standardisation of public food safety regulation across Europe and thus, perhaps, a break with previously dominant national systems of food regulation that such a transition can take place implies that there are important elements of symbolism rather than changes in substance involved. The operating model and constraints within which EFSA operates are discussed further in this chapter and in Chapter 9.

A Proposed Food Agency

Criticism of the Commission's management of food safety, particularly in relation to BSE, by the European Parliament culminated in a threatened vote of no confidence. Santer made the media and consumer friendly Emma

Bonino Director General for Consumer Protection. Bonino continually promised that the consumer was now at the centre of the Commission's agenda. However, the Santer Commission could not overcome questions over its competence or honesty and resigned in March 1999.

Prior to the resignation of his Commission Santer had promoted the idea of a US-style Food and Drug Administration for the EU. The successor Prodi Commission appointed David Byrne as Director General (DG) of DGXXIV. Restoring public confidence in food safety was made a priority issue. Food and consumer issues were ratcheted still further up the public policy agenda. For Prodi food safety was a priority from the outset and he too expressed initial sympathy for an agency modelled on the US FDA.

Through the summer of 1999 there had been much debate within the Commission, the food industry and consumer bodies over the remit and functions of the proposed food authority. Initially, drawing upon his predecessor's idea Prodi had advocated a body similar to that of the US FDA. Such an organisation would have far-reaching executive powers. However, Prodi and a number of others in the Commission were subsequently persuaded that the food authority should have more limited powers, similar to those of the European Medicines Evaluation Agency (EMEA) (European Voice, 1999). The reasons for the shift in thinking appear to have been twofold: first, a more modest agency was much easier to implement in legislative terms, and second, there was a feeling that it was technical and scientific expertise that the Commission needed to bolster. As Prodi informed MEPs although EMEA only made technical decisions, it did so "with notable swiftness and authority" (European Voice, 1999). Such thinking was sympathetic to that of the food industry, where there had been little desire to see an EU version of the FDA. Rather as a spokesperson for the CIAA noted 'The agency should take the good bits from the FDA and the good bits from the EMEA.' The spokesperson continued, 'There are many issues related to risk assessment where there is need for scientific advice at European level. The agency should maximise scientific advice and bring coherence to food legislation' (European Voice, 1999).

Similar issues were raised by the Commission and in its justification for the Food Authority argued:

> The Commission believes that major structural changes are necessary in the way food safety issues are handled, having regard to the experience over the last few years and the generally accepted need functionally to separate risk assessment and risk management. The establishment of a new Authority will provide the most effective instrument in achieving the changes required to protect public health and to restore consumer confidence. It is clear therefore that the primary focus of such an Authority will be the public interest. (CEC, 2000: 14)

The Commission rejected the idea of including risk management within the scope of EFSA on the grounds that risk management was properly the preserve of political decision makers and bestowing such responsibilities on an independent body would require changes to the EC Treaty (CEC, 2000: 15). Similarly, responsibility for new food legislation and ensuring rules are properly enforced was to remain with the Commission and national authorities rather than be devolved to the new Agency (European Voice, 2000).

Following the White Paper on Food Safety the Commission still had to formulate the detailed proposals on the Agency. Here, the Commission found itself having to deal with divisions amongst the Member States. On the one side, Spain demanded that the Agency should issue opinions only at the Commission's request, and on the other side, Sweden demanded that it be free to launch its own initiatives (European Voice, 2000). At the core of the debate was whether or not the proposed Agency should be able to override the views of national food agencies. Giving the Agency pre-eminence in scientific matters would make it harder for countries to justify national consumer protection measures if the agency disagreed with a national government's claims about food safety.

The Commission's proposals for a food agency were examined in detail by the European Parliament, since this was an area subject to co-decision. In a report drafted by the British MEP Philip Whitehead, it was argued that the grandiose vision of the Commission should be curbed and that 'the remit of the authority should be sharply focused on issues related to food safety only' (European Voice, 2001). For Whitehead, like the Commission in its original proposal, risk management was the concern of Member States and the Commission, whilst risk assessment was an appropriate function. Where Whitehead and the Commission differed was over the agency's role in the approval of new varieties of GMOs: the former maintained it was too large a task for a body working on a small budget, whilst the latter successfully argued that the agency could take on board this task (European Voice, 2002).

The first head of the EFSA, Geoffrey Podger was formerly Chief Executive of the FSA. The FSA is responsible for risk management, risk assessment and risk communication, whilst in Europe risk management is undertaken by the Commission. In seeking to justify the separation of risk assessment and management, Podger claimed it depended on 'objective scientific analysis' and an 'independent risk assessment body like . . . [EFSA] . . . [who can] give our view without fear or favour'. He continued: 'it is then up to the risk managers to decide what they want to do'. And added 'It's a very deliberate attempt to separate the process out [risk assessment and management] and to *force* the risk managers to *actually take decisions* in the light of already published objective advice' (quoted in European Voice, 2003, emphasis added).

Strengthening DGXXIV

At the organisational level the Commission undertook a major shake up of its responsibilities for consumer protection. In 1989 the Commission had created the Consumer Policy Service (CPS). Historically a marginal body with a tiny budget in April 1997 it underwent a massive change and became the Directorate General for Consumer Policy and Health Protection. It was later renamed Consumer Protection (DG XXIV) and is now more commonly known as DG SANCO. Its staff was boosted from 96 to 322 with a further increase to about 350 planned for 1999.

The reorganisation was the first of the measures that were outlined by Santer in response to the European Parliament's committee of inquiry on BSE. The aim was to make activities on food safety and health more efficient, transparent and balanced, and the approach of the reforms was to be based on three principles: separation of the functions of drawing up legislation and providing scientific advice; separation of the drawing-up and monitoring of legislation; and strengthening transparency and the dissemination of information throughout decision-making and monitoring operations (CEC, 1997).

DGXXIVs remit for consumer health also meant that it had responsibility for control and inspection services. Here the language of the Commission was highly revealing of the tensions that it had to manage, principally in extending its activities whilst working within budget constraints and Member State sensitivities about the competence of their own national inspection regimes. In a Communication, the Commission announced that:

> The new approach for control and inspection will be based on the following three main orientations. Firstly, in view of the wide range of areas covered by legislation, and the limited resources available, risk assessment procedures will be introduced to allow control priorities to be established. Secondly, control activities will be reorganised to ensure that the whole of the food production chain is properly covered ("plough to plate" approach). Thirdly, the approach will be further developed through the general introduction of formal audit procedures [i.e. HACCP], to allow an assessment of the control systems operated by the competent national authorities. (CEC, 1997: 12)

The principal scientific advisory committees that had been based in industrial and agricultural DGs were transferred to DGXXIV in what 'was seen to reflect a fundamental change in thinking for the Commission' (James et al., 1999: 11). These committees were responsible for analysing the latest developments in a whole range of food issues and would now report to a DG with the interests of the consumer to the fore (Alamanno, 2006: 245). DG SANCO was also given responsibility for the food and veterinary office based in Ireland.

'Science' and Food Safety

As already noted, the scientific committees were reorganised and placed under the responsibility of DGXXIV. Alamanno (2006: 245) reports that placing the scientific committees under the remit of DGXXIV removes them from 'direct industrial pressures'. However such an assumption may be rather naïve on two grounds. First, producer and manufacturing interests will undoubtedly change the focus of their lobbying activities towards DGXXIV. Second, some industrial interests, such as food retailers, already enjoyed good relations with DGXXIV and were likely to see those deepened as they shared its consumer oriented focus.

The functioning of the scientific committees was based upon the promotion of a traditional model of science that privileged scientific knowledge above other forms of knowledge and expertise. The primacy of science was to be based upon three factors: (i) the excellence of science as evaluatory work was only to be undertaken by eminent scientists; (ii) the independence of scientific work was to be assured as scientists were to be free from interests that might subvert their ability to provide independent advice; and (iii) there was to be transparency in decision making (Alemanno, 2006: 245). However, the approach simply reinforced the use of a narrow scientific base for risk assessment, since it continued to marginalise broader social concerns about food production and safety; these were the very factors that had done so much to undermine the credibility of the scientific model of risk assessment and communication (Millstone and van Zwanenberg, 2001). Chapter 3 analyses the treatment of risk in relation to GM food where the perceptions of civil society differed markedly from those of natural scientists. Moreover, as Millstone and van Zwanenberg (2001: 599) point out, decisions that are represented as based on 'sound science' are 'in practice . . . based on implicit and covert economic and political considerations and judgements'.

The Commission Communication on Consumer Health and Safety distinguished between risk assessment and risk management. The idea was that independent scientific experts (later largely to be found in EFSA) would be able to produce the risk assessment, it would then be left to risk managers (those working in the Commission and Member States) to decide whether to take action or approve a substance on (or for) the market (Alemanno, 2006: 246). The relationship between risk assessment, risk management and risk communication was further elucidated in the White Paper on Food Safety (EC 2000) that heralded the EFSA. EFSA was given responsibility for risk assessment and communication but not risk management (unlike the UK where the roles are integrated within the Food Standards Agency).

The EFSA role in scientific analysis and risk assessment provides a key pointer into the likely effectiveness of the organisation. As Alemanno (2006: 249) has pointed out EFSA 'lacks the formal authority to reach binding resolutions on potentially contentious scientific issues'. In other words, where other Community or Member State scientific bodies reach different conclusions to those of EFSA, the latter must seek to reach an accommodation with them or if that is not possible to identify where areas of disagreement lie. Despite the scientific credibility and authority that EFSA seeks to promote, it cannot simply impose its own views on those of others. In an area such as food, where different notions of risk and food culture come into play, EFSA can find itself as one competing scientific voice clamouring to be heard.

In the following section of the chapter, we analyse the relationships between different organisations, how authority to speak on matters of food safety is shared, and how groups coalesce around key institutions.

THE CHANGING NATURE OF MULTI-LEVEL FOOD GOVERNANCE

Prior to the recent organisational changes in Britain and Europe relations between the two levels of government were reasonably straightforward. In Britain MAFF had the main responsibility for food and agricultural policy. The Department of Health had lead responsibility for general food hygiene. At a European level DG 3 had responsibility for industry directives and DG 6 was involved with meat hygiene rules. One former MAFF official has claimed that 'The relationships between DG 3 and ourselves were close, there were people, Commission officials, we knew them personally. . . We had a good liaison' (Interview).

The creation of the British FSA and the demise of MAFF changed the relationships with Brussels. 'Negotiating responsibility [for food safety] went across from MAFF to the FSA. Ultimately whatever decisions are taken have to be endorsed by the responsible minister, who is now the Secretary of State of Health. It is unlikely that the Secretary of State will disagree with what the FSA Board decide, unless there's a political reason (Interview).

The changing organisational responsibilities in Europe have also impacted on relations with London. Commission food responsibilities that were in DG 3 and DG 6 have been consolidated in DG SANCO. As one interviewee commented 'Although ostensibly their responsibility is still the same, the discussions and mechanics are the same, however, the emphasis is probably different, because like the FSA DG SANCO has a different mission from what DG 3 and DG 6 had'. So whilst some staff contacts between London and Brussels may be the same, the more important development is that the focus of key organisations and the nature of their relationships with external groups has been altered. Economic interests may no longer enjoy such close relationships with government as they once did and consumer groups find that their ideas are more attuned to the rhetoric of government.

The organisational changes relating to the management of food that have taken place in Britain and Europe provide the backdrop against which networks and coalition building are played out. Within these networks food interests and governments seek to promote their agendas and marginalise that of others, sometimes seek alliances to better promote their case and share knowledge, and collectively continually engage in the construction of the food policy agenda and pattern of governance. Next we outline how this pattern of food governance operates at the European level. The key themes that illustrate the pattern of governance are: the organisation of food groups, the links between groups and the Commission and Parliament, the representation of interests, the priorities and resources of key groups, their approach to coalition building, and agenda setting.

ORGANISATION OF FOOD GROUPS

There are a number of key characteristics of the representation of food interests in Brussels. Each element of the food supply chain is well represented in Brussels. Indeed, for many of the parts of the food chain there will be multiple forms of representation, with primary and secondary representative organisations (e.g. the CIAA is a key food manufacturing organisation but there are also bodies such as the Fresh Fruit and Vegetable Association which is a much more minor player and caters for much more specific interests). Some groups concentrate their activities solely on food and agriculture, such as COPA-COGECA and the CIAA whereas for others, such as Eurocommerce or BEUC, food is an important issue for them but not their only concern. Finally, there are other groups, particularly environmental groups, such as Greenpeace or Friends of the Earth, for who food is but a minor interest but one that they link to their broader agenda.

Four important outcomes result from these features of food governance. The first is that there is a dense network of groups with differing interests in the development of food policy and its management. Some groups will be consistent players whilst others will be involved on a temporary basis. There is, therefore, no settled pattern of groups contributing to food policy but rather groups seek to involve themselves on any particular issue as they see fit for their purposes. Second, but again depending on the food issue involved, there can be considerable competition between groups to assert their expertise and authority. Sometimes the competition will be between groups representing different parts of the food chain (e.g. between retailers and food manufactures) but it can also be between groups seeking to represent the same part of the food chain (e.g. between consumer groups like BEUC and Eurocoop) as they struggle to determine their primacy. Third, no group is able to impose its interests over all the others in the food chain. Fourth, that means that groups are generally keen to engage in tactical coalition building exercises to better promote their views to the Commission and parliament and to indicate to the rest of the food lobby that they are serious players. When coalitions are being put together groups that miss out on membership may feel themselves to be marginalised and that is also likely to be the perception of other groups. So groups need continually and actively to insinuate themselves with others. Nevertheless some groups are more likely to engage in coalition building than others are. If groups believe that they are politically strong and have good access to the Commission they are less likely to wish to work with others. Similarly if a group feels that its particular message will be unduly diluted in the compromises necessary to put together a coalition it too may wish to work more independently. Meanwhile groups that lack strong economic and political resources are much more likely to be coalition partners as they seek different avenues through which to promote their views.

Much of the efforts of food groups will be targeted at lobbying the Commission. The Commission, though, is not simply an empty vessel responding to the arguments of the strongest group or the best-organised coalition, as a pluralist perspective would suggest. The Commission also has its own agenda, for example on reform of the CAP. However, the Commission does not have the power to impose its strategy on those that it wishes to manage. It cannot govern because it must work through and with the Member States and representative organisations. What emerges therefore is a sophisticated pattern of multi-level governance in which the Commission and Brussels based representative organisations will work at and with different levels of government to steer policy development.

The key economic food interests are: COPA-COGECA (representing farmers), CIAA (representing food manufacturers) and Eurocommerce (representing retailers). Key groups representing consumer interests are BEUC and Eurocoop (both are mainstream consumer groups) and Eurogroup (whose interest is in farm animal welfare). A temporary member of the network on an issue like GM food is Greenpeace.

Groups recognise that they cannot always promote their views directly because of the resistance that they may provoke. So, for instance, fifteen major food companies, including Danone, Craft, Nestle and Unilever, have funded EUFIC which was founded in 1996. Its purpose is 'to provide science based information on food and food related topics to health nutrition professionals, educators, opinion leaders and the news media in a form understandable to the general public'. The reason behind the formation of EUFIC was that although the companies behind it had their own information dissemination strategies the information that they gave out was too linked to the brand or company name. It was therefore discredited. What was needed was an organisation that could communicate with the consumer the basics of food safety and nutrition (EUFIC interview). Moreover, activist groups will not talk to the major food manufacturers but EUFIC might be able to develop a dialogue with them and so build a bridge to the manufacturers.

LINKS TO THE DIRECTORATE GENERALS AND THE PARLIAMENT

Major pressure groups all find access to policy makers in Brussels relatively easy. The policy community, consisting of both Commission staff and pressure groups, is small and through the networks that exist people either know each other or will know of each other's reputation. Contacts are maintained through a regular round of formal and informal meetings, lunches and receptions. What distinguishes the groups, therefore, is the degree of access that they enjoy and the influence that they are perceived to wield. A typical interview comment is that from Eurocommerce who claim that they 'have very good links with the Commission'. The interviewee continued: 'I consider DG SANCO to be very open . . . and they consult us, they come to our meetings and they talk very openly with the [Eurocommerce] members, they discuss and they accept criticism and they listen to what we say'. Similarly from the consumer perspective a BEUC official claimed 'I have a lot of links in DG SANCO. Before legislation is published I am usually in contact with the technical person in legislation so we have the opportunity to bring some input beforehand' (BEUC interview).

The relationship between DG SANCO and consumer groups is a deep and subtle one. On the surface relations are straightforward. For its part key staff in DG SANCO also believe that they have good relations with consumer groups. Indeed, 'the consumer organisations have a privileged relationship with the old DG XXIV [now part of the revamped DG SANCO] . . . we have a rather privileged position with the consumer and it's not a bad relationship either. They [consumer groups] have a feeling that they are more involved than they used to be' (DG SANCO interview). The relationship with consumer groups can be contrasted with that of environmental NGOs.

> The environment organisations we don't see so much of, we see them occasionally. When we do see them our relations tend to be a bit more difficult because they are not permanent visitors with ourselves, so we don't know each other very well. Greenpeace is the one that we tend to deal with the most but they tend to take for us, rather extreme precautionary positions, they are non-science based as far as we are concerned and that makes the dialogue more difficult. (DG SANCO interview)

Beneath the formal mechanisms and networks a more subtle set of relationships can be observed. Here it is important to note that the Commission recognised that consumer groups compared to economic interests were late to organise at a Brussels level and were weakly represented. So the Commission made the decision to fund a small number of consumer organisations. As an official from DG SANCO commented:

> It's a curious relationship as they often criticise us. We have special institutions, we have a consumer committee where we meet the representatives of the consumer organisations regularly. . . . We act as a kind of sponsoring department in the consumer world.

DG SANCO is therefore in the peculiar position of both sponsoring consumer organisations and being responsible for consumer policy. Officials are however quick to point out that 'I don't think we can be criticised for being captured by these organisations as they are not really powerful enough' (DG SANCO interview). Indeed, rather than 'capturing' DG SANCO its officials find it useful to have a consumer constituency to hand who can provide them with information and expertise. Perhaps even more important DG SANCO, which like its predecessor DG XXIV is weak compared to the major economic DGs, can use consumer groups to bolster their own agenda. This is because these groups can lobby to influence the wider Commission policy-making machinery and engage with national governments, the Council and MEPs (DG SANCO interview).

What we are observing here is the way in which a DG, through a variety of means, nurtures networks and NGOs that in turn can be used to bolster its own position (Mazey and Richardson, 2001). By helping to raise the profile of consumer groups and a consumer agenda on food, DG SANCO and its predecessors has in turn been able to ratchet up the profile of a more consumer oriented food policy and so provide a credible alternative to the traditional market dominated perspective on food. Food policy becomes more mainstream as historically weak and marginal actors in the Commission and NGO movement engage in a symbiotic relationship to mutual benefit. As one interviewee in DG SANCO explained:

> We [DG SANCO] find it valuable because they [consumer groups] enable us to influence the policy-making machine. After we make proposals, we are able to use these [consumer] organisations as sources of information and expertise as well as a avenue of feedback to the national level, to national governments, to the Council, to MEP's and to Parliament. We're consciously engaged in this level of *orchestrating* certain dialogue and thinking. I wouldn't suggest that it's terribly neat or straightforward, but I think it's necessary (Emphasis added).

A similar process can be detected in the way in which the European Parliament has also been able to raise its own profile and legitimacy through championing the case of food safety (see the description of the work of the Parliament in relation to BSE previously discussed).

From the perspective of DG SANCO it appears that consumer groups are helpful to their strategy but not central. The contrast with retailers is stark. 'The big players are fully aware of what we're doing for them. We're also aware of how valuable our relations with them are. They know better than anybody what consumers are doing as opposed to what they are saying' (DG SANCO interview).

DG SANCO also organises their own consultation or stakeholder meetings and to which they invite representatives of all relevant organisations (Eurocommerce interview, BEUC interview). Although groups welcome the openness of the DG they also find that it raises challenges for them. One test for example, is that the Commission timetable may be very compressed so that groups have only a short time to digest proposals and little time to consult internally. Specialists within groups can therefore feel vulnerable in meetings: they are expected to speak for their group but are wary of advancing ideas in case they should later be challenged by their members. One interviewee described the meetings as 'very live and very organic. You have to be able to react to what has been said before . . . and also use the opportunity presented to you by what another organisation will say to in turn enhance your own position' (Eurocoop interview).

Despite the sophistication of the membership of groups, the prominence of Brussels in policy making and the fact that the Brussels food policy making machine is very well established groups can still encounter difficulties legitimising their actions. 'The problem is that the people in the member groups do not always realise the importance of Brussels and the fact that it is much more important that we lobby at a European level rather than waiting for national authorities [to act]' (Eurocommerce interview).

Lobbying the European Parliament is becoming increasingly important for food groups. Once again they will adopt common strategies to try and influence MEPs. Groups will provide briefings for MEPs and organise meetings with MEPs. The key person, though, who groups want to influence is the rapporteur as they draft the report. As one person explained

> Once you know the rapporteur you go there [to the Parliament] and you say okay these are our problems with the Commission proposal and you convince him to table the amendments you want. Now if this is done it is a very big success. If you have the rapporteur with you this is great because normally the committee follows, he has a lot of influence. Then you also have to go to meet the other . . . [MEPs] to say, yes these are the amendments we think are very good and you should support the rapporteur.

If groups cannot persuade the rapporteur to support their views then they have to embark on a more extensive lobbying process. To begin with groups would turn to the deputy rapporteur, a MEP from a different part to that of the rapporteur, but who still has considerable influence. Key MEPs would then be identified for intensive briefings in the hope that they would be able to introduce sympathetic amendments. National member organisations will also be contacted so that they can lobby to support an organisation's European position (Eurocommerce interview).

REPRESENTATION OF INTERESTS

Clearly as the case of membership of the Board of the EFSA shows, the retailers are regarded by senior policy makers in Brussels as able at least partly to represent consumer interests. However, Eurocommerce remain wary of associating themselves too closely with consumers. They recognise that they are more consumer oriented than the CIAA.

> It's true that we always put forward our role on . . . food consumers . . . and their requests and needs, but this is a particularity in the food chain and also one that distinguishes our sector . . . we have something which links us very strongly with consumers but we can't replace consumer [organisations]. Don't forget supermarkets remain economic operators and yes food safety and customer satisfaction remain the top priority as this is what makes the business work but they remain economic operators. I think our [retailers and consumers] positions are very specific and add value to the European institutions but they [retailers] cannot replace consumers.

BEUC have also recognised that retailers are sometimes recognised as consumers representatives. An official from DG SANCO commented that 'they [the retailers] know better than anybody what consumers are doing as opposed to saying'. Consumer groups are well aware of such sentiments and one BEUC official commented '"You have heard the Commission saying, "if you want to know the consumer opinion ask the retailers", which I believe is a wrong statement'. BEUC are therefore keen to 'make it very clear who is a recognised consumer organisation' and to challenge those who they believe falsely present themselves as consumer representatives. Such thoughts have implications for the willingness of BEUC to engage in coalition building exercises.

One group that recognises that it is vulnerable to challenges to its consumer credentials is Eurocoop. Although it was one of the founders of the Consumer Committee its membership base is drawn from the co-operative movement. Some of its members have become successful and now they face the challenge that

> really our members are businesses and not really consumer organisations. So there is a constant struggle here in Brussels between ourselves and other organisations. They say "we are the true consumers, you are not really consumers". Naturally there are some people in the Commission that take the same view (Eurocoop interview).

The Commission funds a small number of consumer groups to provide a counter balance to economic interests. So who is regarded as a legitimate consumer group can be very important in securing funding. In 2002 Eurocoop lost their Commission funding because they did not meet the new Commission criteria of a consumer body. Although this has not affected their good working relationships with Commission staff it does have a direct impact on their activities. One of the ironies of Commission funding is that it expects groups to be able to work across a wide range of consumer issues. The result is that their resources are spread thinly with duplication of effort.

PRIORITIES AND RESOURCING

None of the major pressure groups is devoted exclusively to food safety issues. Instead food safety and hygiene is but one part of a broader agenda that they seek to further. For example, from the producer side COPA–COGECA will have as a major concern the development of the Common Agricultural Policy, food manufacturers will also be interested in trade issues, retailers in labour relations and competition policy and consumer groups in the full range of consumer issues, such as labelling. So, for all of the groups in the food policy community, food must compete internally with other issues for resources and the setting of priorities. All of our interviewees have claimed that food is one of the most, or the most, important issue for their organisation. The Eurocommerce interviewee commented: 'Eurocommerce is a very big organisation and there are a lot of priorities, and food safety is one of the most important'. However, as food is becoming a more complex policy issue nearly all of the groups feel under resourced. As a BEUC interviewee commented 'We are getting additional work and staying longer hours in the office'. Eurocommerce is one of the most well resourced pressure groups operating in Brussels. Even though nearly all of its members have an interest in food the resourcing given to the issue remains modest with one full time appointment and another person shared with the consumer department.

In an effort to overcome the resource constraints that they face and to ensure that they devote their efforts as best they can to meeting their members interests groups seek to utilise and capture their members knowledge. For example, Eurocommerce has a food committee made up of about thirty-five experts who meet quarterly in Brussels and analyse individual Commission proposals and provide direction for the organisation's responses. Similarly BEUC rely heavily on their national members for professional expertise (BEUC interview). In Eurocoop the officer responsible for food will expect to meet with their national food experts about three or four times a year. At these meetings priorities will be set that will then go to the Eurocoop Board for approval. The priorities are largely set by the officer's knowledge of likely Commission initiatives 'because we are on the inside we know what is coming down the track' (Eurocoop interview).

In practice both much of the day-to-day agenda of pressure groups and their strategic thinking will be set by proposed Commission legislation. The groups, though, do not simply act in a responsive mode they also seek to shape Commission thinking and that of others in the food lobby.

When lobbying, groups know that their arguments are stronger when they speak with one voice. Failure to agree a common position is widely perceived to 'weaken our position' (BEUC interview). Groups like to work on a consensual basis and this also places great pressures on members to agree. Whilst there is a priority on members working together, groups can find it very time consuming to agree priorities and positions. All groups have to deal with the challenge of reconciling the interests of their national members. For some groups such as COPA-COGECA members will often start from different positions and have quite different objectives when, for example, discussing CAP reform. COPA-COGECA therefore can appear to be introspective but must have sophisticated mechanisms for promoting internal unity. Also national groups will bring quite different resources and organisational skills to their European bodies. For instance, the RSPCA are much better funded and professional than a number of their counterparts in other European countries. Eurogroup has to ensure that its agenda reflects its European membership and is not dominated by, say the RSPCA, and also that it does not place undue demands on the RSPCA, for instance in relation to funding research. If members cannot reach consensus then groups may submit two responses to a Commission proposal. For instance, Eurocommerce experienced difficulties in reconciling the interests of its retailer members and those who dealt in produce in relation to GMOs labelling. Eurocommerce did not wish to undermine the position it had developed on GMO labelling and which many of its members favoured and so attached an annex with a dissenting view to its position paper that it submitted to the Commission. Internal divisions on GMOs have been even more severe for the CIAA. It has found it very difficult to stop its members regarding GMOs as a competitive issue rather than an issue on which they need to adopt a common position. As it is no longer possible for CIAA members to unite around GMOs, temporarily the organisation does not contribute to Commission led debates or policy. On such a crucial European issue, that is very important to CIAA members, the organisation itself is silent and leaves it to individual members to develop their own approach.

COALITION BUILDING

Coalition building between many of the groups in the food lobby is an essential part of their activities. One interviewee described the situation as follows:

> Brussels is very small and it is very lobby friendly. People are always meeting. . . . It is very open and people are free to contact and there are informal get togethers. So it is very easy to lobby in Brussels terms of networking . . . and there is a lot of sharing of information to see

can we build a coalition here, or what information do you have we can trade (Eurocoop interview).

Eurocommerce are one of the key actors in the food network. They argue that it is good to create coalitions with organisations where there are common interests. Joint actions may only involve signing a letter together, for example, between Eurocommerce and the BEUC and the CIAA. Eurocommerce are much more reluctant to work with Greenpeace, though this has happened on GMOs.

Another outward looking organisation is Eurocoop. They claim to have good relations with other consumer bodies as well as economic interests. For them coalitions are 'a kind of love hate. We build alliances but also we are sort of competitors. It depends on the particular subject. I think we all recognise how difficult it is [to build coalitions]' (Eurocoop interview). Interestingly because of their co-operative roots Eurocoop have been able to work with COPA-COGECA which also has a strong co-operative base but they have never issued a press release together. This is because COPA-COGECA is much more insular than consumer or environmental groups.

BEUC jealously guard their privileged position as a Commission recognised voice of the consumer. They are unwilling to work in partnership with other groups that have a consumer remit, such as Eurocoop, and there is clearly a great deal of rivalry between the two organisations. For example, the consumer representative on the EFSA Board is Deirdre Hutton from the UK National Consumer Council and they are members of BEUC. As a Eurocoop official noted in a comment symptomatic of the distant relations between the two consumer groups 'we have no relationship with her' and they clearly did not expect one in the future. BEUC is also cautious about working with Eurocommerce, doing so only occasionally.

A good example of where a range of organisations in the food system can come together is GM. Here Eurocoop became involved in an alliance with environmental NGOs such as Friends of the Earth and Greenpeace as well as Eurocommerce and their British counterpart the BRC. The formation of such an unusual coalition seems to owe much to the issue, the personalities involved and the small world of European lobbying. The first steps in putting the coalition together involved a meeting between individuals from Eurocoop and Friends of the Earth. They had never previously met but knew of each other's interests. It was then agreed that Friends of the Earth would seek to draw in other environmental groups and Eurocoop would do the same for the consumer side. In the coalition 'we were mainly NGOs and we got along and complemented each other in terms of knowledge and personality' (Eurocoop interview). One of the largest members of Eurocommerce is a co-operative and that provided an important link between the retailers and the alliance that Eurocoop helped put together.

The involvement of the retailers was widely believed to have enhanced the credibility of the coalition position.

CONCLUSIONS

There are four issues to be borne in mind when considering the changing food policy agenda and its relationship to food governance: the first of these is the rise of consumerism within policy. This has had two impacts. On the one side it has enhanced the role of consumer and retailer organisations in the policy process. On the other hand it has led to the relative marginalisation of food producer and manufacturing interests. For example, at both the London and Brussels levels the food manufacturing industry has found itself increasingly challenged by other elements in the food chain. Whilst in London the Food and Drink Federation has to cope with a number of other voices clamouring to be heard by the FSA and the Department of Health, the industry may feel that its loss of influence is marginal. This is because the industry is organised on a transnational basis and as Brussels is increasingly the locus of decision making it can pay greater attention to working through the CIAA. However, 'one of the problems [faced by the food manufacturers] is that the same kind of sea change between the policy makers . . . and the food representatives' that has happened in Britain is also happening in Europe. The economic base of policy has moved to one in which policy makers 'are now putting the consumer first' (Interview). In a rapidly shifting policy climate food manufacturers are finding it difficult to reposition themselves and are being outmanoeuvred by retailers and consumer groups.

Second, the increasing policy focus on consumers places greater pressures on retailers and on state organisations to continually construct a positive consumer interest in food. Retailers are acutely aware of the vulnerability of their position: 'consumers have higher expectations regarding food safety and food quality and retailers because of their direct contact with consumers remain the first persons who are faced with a problem' (Eurocommerce interview).

Third, policy at the European and UK level has increasingly emphasised 'farm-to-fork' regulation. Eurocommerce (interview), for example, has been very supportive of the Commission's position on food safety. They are keen to establish clear responsibilities in the food chain. They believe that each part of the food chain should be responsible for their own activities.

Fourth, as we shall explore in more depth in the next chapter, the model of food governance that has emerged raises issues for the role of the state. Even if policy is in large part driven by a consumerist rhetoric that in itself raises new challenges. The Commission on its own does not have the power or authority to meet these policy challenges and neither will the EFSA given its power to govern. Rather, as we have seen the issues raised by the retailers over the communication of risk, the Commission must work with *other key actors* to deliver on food policy. Clearly economic interests are to the fore in policy delivery. The question is: has a policy framework been constructed with the necessary drivers that allow the Commission to steer policy in the direction that it would like it to go? A 'hollowed out' British state relies heavily on private interest regulation by the major supermarkets to deliver public policy goals, is the same to happen at a European level?

5 A New Regulatory Terrain

The Emerging Public/Private Model in Europe

INTRODUCTION

This chapter asks a key question emerging from the previous analysis. How can and should contemporary governments respond more effectively to the growth of food risks, while at the same time encouraging the further economic development and integration of the European internal market? Taking the case of European food regulation and accountability, the interplay of influences that are beginning to shape this new regulatory terrain are explored using primary empirical data and analysis. More specifically we examine the three critical dimensions of change in the 2000s. These are organised in terms of: (i) the maturing of Europeanisation and its impact and relationships with the UK; (ii) the consumerisation and new institutionalisation of food policy, and the wider participation of interest groups; and (iii) the development of a more complex private interest model of food regulation. This chapter thus outlines a revised conceptual model of contested regulation which incorporates the State, corporate and non-corporate interests, consumer organisations, and a variety of other social interests.

THE MATURING EUROPEANISATION OF UK FOOD

In our earlier work (see Marsden et al., 2000) we began to show, through, both the design and implementation of European food hygiene Directives, how corporate retailer-led supply regulation became empowered, and the use of quality control and risk management techniques, such as Hazard and Critical Control Point (HACCP), tended to empower the retailer-led forms of food regulation. The failure in reducing food risks and legitimacy concerns since the mid 1990s, and indeed, their diversification and differential spatial spread across member states (like Swine Fever in the Netherlands, Dioxins in Belgium) tended to further press the EU to develop wider powers and ambitions. This was represented in the Food Safety White Paper of 2000, as follows:

> Consumers should be offered a wide range of safe and high quality products coming from all Member States. This is the essential role of the Internal Market. . . . An effective food safety policy must recognise the inter-linked nature of food production. It requires assessment and monitoring of the risks to consumer health associated with raw materials, farming practices and food processing activities; it requires effective regulatory action to manage risk; and it requires the establishment and operation of control systems to monitor and enforce the operation of these regulations. . . .
>
> Historically, these measures have mainly been developed on a sectoral basis. However, the increasing integration of national economies within the Single Market, developments in farming and food processing, and new handling and distribution patterns require the new approach in this White Paper. (CEC, 2000: 6–7)

With the preceding concerns in mind, the crucial priority of the White Paper was the establishment of an independent European Food Safety Authority to provide:

> scientific advice on all aspects relating to food safety, operation of rapid alert systems, communication and dialogue with consumers on food safety and health issues, as well as networking with national agencies and scientific bodies. (CEC, 2000: 3)

And, while the White Paper prepared the underlying aims of this more comprehensive European approach to monitoring and enforcing food safety and assurance, a further challenge was the building of multi-interest support for the process of implementing and institutionalising this new EU-led food safety regime.

Despite the leadership position held by DG SANCO, the view from DG Agriculture is that 'good communication exists between Commissioners David Byrne (DG SANCO) and Franz Fischler (DG Agriculture) because their jobs overlap a lot and they have common views' (DG Agriculture, 2002). Similarly, DG Trade, which is primarily responsible for the EU's compliance with WTO rules, and in particular the Sanitary and Phytosanitary Agreement (SPS), is satisfied with the opportunities open to it to contribute to the development of the new food safety regime.

In reference to the establishment of the EFSA—the centrepiece of the new Commission's new food safety regime—DG Trade is satisfied that its somewhat long-distance relationship with DG SANCO does not prevent its key concerns from being taken into consideration. According to an interview in DG Trade, 'our interest in the EFSA is in ensuring that the right questions are asked, and that third countries have access to it' (DG Trade, 2002). This is very important as, despite advocating 'health before trade,' the key operating principle of the SPS Agreement is that measures designed to protect health (and the environment) 'have to be based in science' (WTO, 2003). This 'science-based approach' to food/trade policy is one of the key features of the new food safety regime emerging from Brussels.

Collaboration between DGS and Stakeholder Umbrella Groups in the Formation of Food Safety

In furtherance of the EU's objective of participative governance (see Article 1, Treaty on European Union), the Commission has been engaged in what Mazey and Richardson (2001) describe as the 'opportunistic creation of new institutions as a means of locking diverse interests into the ongoing process of Europeanisation' (p. 227). In particular, and as our own research has confirmed, the European Commission 'has been a strategic actor in constructing constellations of stakeholders concerned with each of the Commission's policy sectors' (Mazey and Richardson, 2001: 227). Consequently, a number of the more visible and influential consumer and farming lobby groups in Brussels, such as the European Consumers' Organisation (BEUC), Eurocoop, COPA-COGECA, Association des Consommateurs Europeens (AEC), and the European Association for the Coordination of Consumer Representation (ANEC), receive financial support from the Commission.

The following excerpts from our interviews illustrate some of the key trends in this process that seek to deepen the Europeanisation of food policy; and expose some of its implications for Member States, like the UK. According to COPA-COGECA, for instance, the organisation, which was founded more than forty years ago, is a kind of partner for the Commission. 'It was a farmers' body, working in their interests, and . . . everytime there are new members in the European Union, there are new members in COPA. To begin with, our strength was related to the fact that 30% of the European Community's population were farmers; now we are only 5%. Currently, the strength of our position comes from the fact that the Commission and especially the Council and Parliament have exactly the same problems as we have. So when we produce a policy document, the strength of it is that those who are dealing in Parliament encounter the same problem, and the positions we take often contribute to the establishment of compromise situations. So, for instance, when we don't have a position on matters of importance we get some angry comments from Parliament saying 'where is your paper' (COPA-COGECA, 2002)

At the same time, regulatory interests, such as DG Agriculture and DG SANCO, have not been satisfied simply to be the focus of lobbying activities by private and consumer interest organisations. 'In fact, from the viewpoint of DG SANCO, sponsorship of EU-level consumer groups became necessary because these organisations were late in starting to organise themselves at a community level, and the Commission, began to be aware of the consumer wanting to be more involved, and complaining that there was a mismatch in that they weren't getting the kind of input that would enable them to sustain the consumer points of view in the policy. So the Commission, decided that we would actually pay these organisations to exist, we actually fund several organisations at European level to carry out their activities. It's a curious relationship, as they (consumer organisations) often criticise us (DG SANCO, 2002)'.

Commission sponsorship of umbrella stakeholder groups, however, is not limited only to those resident in Brussels, but extends to organisations with the specific characteristics even in member states:

> We don't provide finance to organisations at the national level for overheads and general expenses. We finance what are called the Euro enquiry offices. It's a specific function which gives us a special relationship with even national organisations. It's a slightly curious business, because we are both the sponsoring department but we also make policy, but I don't think we can be criticised for being captured by these organisations, as they're not really powerful enough. But this is why we don't finance beyond a certain level. (DG SANCO, 2002)

This process of financing the establishment of stakeholder groups benefits the Commission. For instance, DG SANCO argues that:

> [o]ur sponsorship, for example, has led to the conceiving and development of a Trans-Atlantic consumer dialogue as a kind of parallel to the Trans-Atlantic business line. It's been rather successful, and we see it as quite a legitimate way of addressing the balance. (DG SANCO, 2002)

Like DG SANCO, DG Agriculture fails to see any conflicts of purpose or ethical problems associated with the funding that the Commission provides to specific stakeholder groups and the residual obligation that this might engender. The feeling is that both the Directorates and the stakeholder organisations that the co-sponsor are able to maintain their respective objectivity (DG Agriculture, 2002)

Yet, despite the preceding semblance of inclusiveness at the EU food policy level, and DG SANCO's annual sponsorship of a 'consumer assembly' which meets over two days to discuss relevant Community policies, for some groups, the process includes a considerable degree of symbolism. For instance, whilst endorsing the notion that the Commission uses it as 'a counter-force—to have some kind of balance in policies' COPA-COGECA is concerned that the process may be too tightly controlled by the Commission. Referring to its experience as participants in the Mid-term Review (MTR) of the Common Agriculture Policy (CAP), COPA-COGECA is critical:

> . . . the Commission fools us all the time. We are now very frustrated. They were misleading us for almost half a year. The Commission

> officially told us, at the end of April (2001) that it will request a review from us, but they had already made the decision on the contents of the report from December. So the Commission, for me and for many of us (NGOs), is such an undemocratic operator despite all these formal consultative committees and seemingly decent open communication.
>
> The Commission has been, for most of us, more populist than ever. They have, very rationally, been developing policies arising from their own perspective. About consumers and the environment, all things are beautiful whilst consistently pushing European agriculture to deliver more. (COPA-COGECA, 2002)

In addition to the formal consultative routes that insider groups tend to use to engage with the EU food policy-making process, some stakeholder groups have found that more fluid arrangements are also effective. Eurogroup for Animal Welfare, for instance, reports that, in addition to networking with other lobby groups

> we influenced a French Minister once because his daughter went to the same school as the Director of the Animal Welfare Organisation. So he met the minister and talked about cosmetics. To be a good lobbyist you've got to be recognised. You don't necessarily have to do anything except get to know people. So much of good lobbying are personal contacts. If they don't like you then they're probably not going to listen to you, so you must try to be all things to all people. (Eurogroup, 2002)

Compared with Eurogroup, which has a rather narrow focus—animal welfare—the European Food Information Council (EUFIC) concentrates on a broader public service role. EUFIC's mission is related directly to the increase in public demand for information, particularly the enhancement of the public's understanding of nutrition and food safety. This is accomplished, not by seeking to influence the nature and content of communiqués from the Commission itself, but through exerting indirect influence on the policy-making process by building up good relations with key journalists. By so doing, EUFIC becomes one of the first points of contact for comment, interpretation or elaboration on key pieces of EU food policies. The organisation's comments, be they of concern, reservation or endorsement, can easily become a part of the public debate, which in turn, influences the politico-policy-making process. This food policy engagement via journalists takes place both at the EU as well as at national levels, and in national languages.

From the preceding extracts we can identify some of the key facets, and more specifically dynamics, of the gradual Europeanisation of food policy (outlined in Chapter 4). First, the role and reform of the Common Agricultural Policy remains traditionally pan-European, but now espouses deeper notions of subsidiarity and consumerisation. More emphasis is being placed upon its complex policy packages and instruments delivering 'quality' products to the consumer through an increasing variety of European-wide supply chains—many of which are locally embedded but also available to the 'European consumer' through the European Single Market. Farmers, consumers and food processors are increasingly seen as providers of quality products for this European market, with some producers able to obtain protected area status for the local monopoly production of certain speciality products (e.g. Protected Description of Origin (PDO)s and Protected Geographical Indication (PGI)s).

This transition in the function and operation of the CAP produces new challenges for traditional producer interests, like COPA-COGECA, which are now faced with the lateral challenge of EU enlargement, the vertical challenge of more regional and local subsidiarity, as well as the more macro-European challenge of identifying with the consumer. Their long-established relationships and committee structures thus come under considerable stress, as do their traditionally bi-lateral and corporatist relationships with DG Agriculture. Thus producer interests, more than any, feel the full brunt of this new period of Europeanisation; and there are considerable expectations raised more broadly about how the producer sector can rise to these more European and cross sectoral challenges.

Second, whilst Europeanisation as we have seen brings new and quite profound challenges for existing interest group relationships, it is also based upon a new faith in new organisations and relationships—most notably the setting up of the EFSA. This new, and largely untested, structure also represents a wider and deeper European commitment to food safety and assurance, and a stronger belief in the need for European-based enforcement and monitoring of member state procedures. Carefully learning from the US and the UK, the developments in setting up an independent body based upon a 'scientific approach', the EFSA is seen as a central assurance system for meeting the economic aims of the European internal food market (see CEC, 2000).

Third, increasingly we see a wider diversity of organisations playing a European role and seeking to influence as well as to articulate different knowledges concerning foods, health and ethical issues. For example, animal welfare groups, European information agencies (like EUFIC and the European Food Law Association [EFLA]), and the consumer groups now have to grapple with the complexities of such issues as the precautionary principle, GM and traceability. Part of the greater Europeanisation Project now involves accommodating a wider and more diverse array of concerns and interests than those simply associated with the quality of foods. Increasingly then, the policy arena has been attracting a moral and ethical dimension associated not only with foods, but with wider risk relationships associated with the transparency of scientific applications and their role and consequence for European civil society.

THE GROWING CONSUMERISATION AND INSTITUTIONALISATION OF EUROPEAN FOOD POLICY AND THE EMPOWERMENT OF A WIDER RANGE OF INTEREST GROUPS

The growing power of the European Parliament (EP) and in particular European policies which have strengthened the role of the consumer in policy-making have, rather ironically, coincided with the significant decline in agricultural productionist interests and the power and responsibility of the Directorate for Agriculture in food safety and quality matters. The new and ensuing 'consumerist' approach emphasises the role of consumer concerns at each stage in the product chain. The following comment from DG Agriculture, regarding the Mid-Term Review of the CAP, underscores just how much the previously corporatist policy-making landscape has shifted: 'DG Agriculture is not here for the farmers, but is involved with rural development and agriculture' (DG Agriculture, 2002).

Despite being fully aware that farmers' groups like COPA-COGECA and their national counterpart-organisations like the UK's National Farmers' Union (NFU), are decidedly dissatisfied with the new direction that the review seems to be taking the CAP, DG Agriculture feels the need to highlight the growing number of other related concerns that it must balance for the good of the greater 'European Project'. Consequently, a diverse range of organisations (in addition to farmer' groups) representing competing and sometimes complementary interests, seek constantly to exert influence on the DG Agriculture, SANCO as well as on the European Parliament.

The imperative to show consistency with the new focus on consumer concerns in the Commission's new food regime, across the different Directorates, can be seen also in the philosophy that guides the proposals for EU-funded food research (under Framework 6). DG Research uses the classical 'farm-to-fork' philosophy to illustrate its commitment to consumers having the right to high quality and safe foods (see Figure 5.1). This 'farm to fork' approach—with the consumer at the centre- is

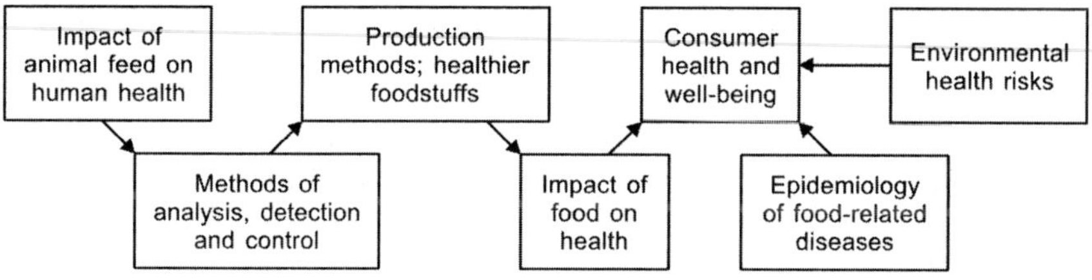

Figure 5.1 Food Quality and Safety, DG Research, 2002. Source: Breslin, (2002); TP5/II/DOC I/WP16 (Framework 6).

used as 'the primary driver for developing new and safer food production chains and foods, relying in particular on biotechnology tools and taking into account the latest results of genomics research' (Breslin, DG Research, 2002).

Despite clear evidence that consumer demands exert strong influence on food policy at the level of the European Commission as well within individual member states, it is important to recognise here that this process of growing *consumerisation* is underlain by a series of significant tensions and shifting positions associated with production versus consumption interests; public policy versus private sector interests; the differential authority of communication about risks, and, finally, competing conceptions about sustainable production methods. A more consumerist approach can conveniently ally and elide the questions of intensive and more extensive farming systems, genomic research and development and the protection of the consumer. Also, such a consumerist approach tends to place a thin veil over the intensely competing interests of the corporate retailers, food manufacturers versus the public legitimacy and communication role of public authorities like the DGs and the EFSA.

Our evidence identifies some of these tensions as they emerge out of the process of consumerisation and institutionalisation. While becoming increasingly involved in the shaping of new legislation and policy on food, retailers and manufacturers are also keen to demonstrate that the very purpose of such policy shifts *must be to ensure the effective workings of the internal market*; that is to provide a more cast-iron set of assurances for consumer protection such that their competitive spaces in the markets for food can be maintained and developed. *This private interest objective* of preserving the legitimacy and effective workings of the internal market coincides with one of the key objectives outlined in the White Paper (CEC, 2000). To corporate retailers and food processors, these geo-commercial issues are far more important than the rather more myopic concerns about the actual membership of the board of the EFSA; or indeed the actual micro-biological business of 'closed-door' scientific testing for new manufactured disease agents such as Acrylamide, for instance. What seems to unite all parties, however, is the need for more *effective and scientifically based communication.* Without this it is argued, food markets will continue to be de-stabilised and vulnerable to media speculation and NGO inspired moral panics.

The new institutionalisation process occurring in European food policy then, can be likened to an attempt at killing two birds with one stone, i.e. seeking a double-dividend effect. On the one hand, the response seeks to provide an improved basis for the vast array of competing interests to be consulted and to come together in ways which will make policy making more inclusive, effective and implementable. On the other hand, it provides a more sophisticated science and defence-based communication system of food and health risks aimed at stabilising and relegitimating European food markets. In fact, significant importance was being given by the Commission to lessons learned from the FMD crisis in the UK (see Chapter 2). One significant outcome of the UK FMD crisis is that it helps to provide an even firmer basis for the creation of the semi-autonomous EFSA. Another Commission-level reaction to FMD can be seen in its attempts to harness the competitive energies of all of the food interests under a banner of consumerism based upon a more widespread precautionary approach (see Chapter 10).

The importance of embedding a science-based approach to policy-making across the entire agro-food supply chain, and the pivotal role that the EFSA can play in this, have been expressed by a range of interests at the EU level. From the perspective of DG SANCO, for instance, science-based decision-making 'protects against political indiscretion especially regarding precautionary measures' (DG SANCO, 2002). DG Trade, with responsibility for external trade issues such as the SPS Agreement (cited earlier) believes that the establishment of the EFSA will go a long way in helping to 'separate out science from legislation' (DG Trade, 2002). Using the ban on hormones in beef as an example, DG Trade believes that the key motivation for the ban was 'political' rather than based on concerns for health:

> The hormones case is partly fact and partly folklore. Parliament had concerns about whether hormones were a risk to human health. In fact, there was a scientific committee which hadn't reported at that stage, but was more or less poised to say that the risk was not so great. Despite this, the ban was imposed anyway. Upon strong challenge from the US, and because our scientific risk assessment of the potential impacts was not adequate, the EU was found to have infringed international trading rules (DG Trade, 2002).

Clearly then, the institutionalization of the EFSA—which is free from concerns about risk management and impacts of decisions on the internal market, instead is dedicated strictly to risk assessment and risk communication—ought to improve the basis and quality of EU food safety legislation. Ostensibly, this is the governmental expectation.

Figure 5.2 attempts to illustrate the major elements and functions of the new food safety regime that has been forming in Europe. The centrepiece is clearly the EFSA, with responsibilities for risk management and communication, leaving DG SANCO in particular to pilot risk management and food safety enforcement strategies throughout the different Member States.

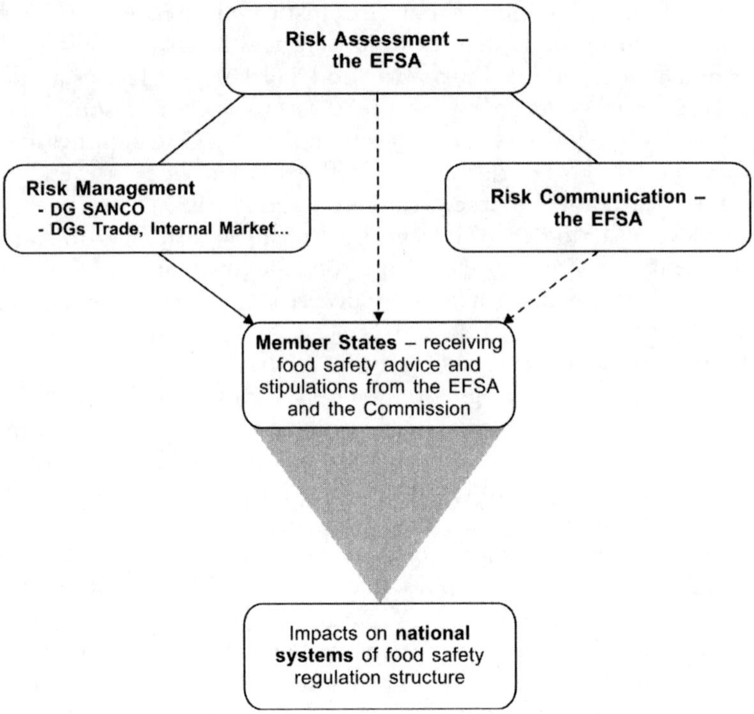

Figure 5.2 The major elements and functions of the EU's new food safety regime.

Consumerisation and Internal Food Markets

From the perspective of internal food markets consumer organizations, like DG SANCO, seem to welcome the creation of the EFSA and the standardisation of food policy across the EU that the new organisation aims to institutionalise. Consumer representative, BEUC, for instance, has long held the view that strategies for assuring food safety across the EU were being undermined by the differences in food safety policies that exist at the level of the European Commission, and between the different Member States. Eurocoop, another established consumer lobby group, perceives the creation of the EFSA as a response to the 'rapid increase in new European food standards and the erosion of borders within the EU internal market.' In their view, the 'EFSA provides a forum for discussing standards and setting parameters'. As a result, the EFSA is viewed as 'a good initiative, but one which may ultimately function to re-legitimate business-as-usual practices in the food industry' (BEUC, 2002). It is perceived to be imbued with 'both a scientific and political agenda' (Eurocoop, 2002).

Private interest groups, in particular, have responded positively to the process to formalise a science-based approach in European food policy-making. Looking back at the two-tiered, retailer-devised food quality and regulatory framework that developed in the UK during the 1990s, it can be argued that the emerging EU food regime has been significantly influenced by the process used by large UK food retailers to manage risk within their product supply chains. In fact, according to DG SANCO, industry has 'no real problem with the science-based approach. It, in fact, provides them with a basis for non-arbitrary decision-making' (DG SANCO, 2002). This kind of support for the new food regime appears to be implying that science-based decision-making is the same as politically neutral decision-making. And despite their support for the new, non-arbitrary science-based approach to food policy, DG SANCO noted that corporate retailers, like Tesco

> are here at least once a year. The big players are fully aware of what we are doing for them. We are also aware of how valuable our relations with them are. They know, better than anyone, what consumers are doing as opposed to saying. (DG SANCO, 2002)

We return to these particular relationships between retailers and EU regulators, and the influence they exert on the new food safety regime.

The EFSA So Far

Whilst recognising that it may be too early in the process to form an opinion on the EFSA, Eurocommerce, a major private interest umbrella organisation, believes that the EFSA has a very important role to play but since it does not have any legislative powers, its impact will be somewhat similar to that of a scientific lobby body. 'Food safety policy itself will continue to be made by the European commission with DG SANCO (at the heart of the process) whilst the EFSA will be responsible for communicating food risks to member states and the public' (Eurocommerce, 2002).

Whilst recognising the importance of a science-based approach to the EFSA's two main tasks: risk assessment and risk communication, Eurocommerce is nevertheless concerned that often 'scientific opinions are not very clear and not very understandable, and everybody can interpret them in different ways.' This concern engages with the issue of scientific autonomy, the destabilising impacts of which can be prevented if when facing scientific uncertainties, the risk assessment work of the EFSA is promptly complemented with clear decisions from risk managers before the EFSA is called upon to communicate with member states and the public.

The EFSA and Transparency in Food Safety Policies

The overwhelming consensus amongst our sample of regulatory, private interest and consumer/social interest representatives is that the air of independence and multi-sectoral representation which is meant to typify the board of the EFSA will enhance its operational transparency. According to BEUC (2000), for example, 'being able to attend open sessions of EFSA team management meetings and listen to the deliberations is one element of the transparency we wanted to achieve—the right of access'. But, despite recognising the importance of transparency, the following comment from Eurocommerce reveal a telling variation in objectives between private interest bodies and consumer/social interest groups:

> Yes. I fully agree that we must have transparency, but transparency must not be there for the sake of transparency. It must be there for the sake of communication. An example is the recent Acrylamide issue. Acrylamide is a chemical that is created in baked foods such as breads, chips, biscuits and crisps, and which is carcinogenic.
>
> There was information in the newspapers recently which caused some amount of panic. For its part, the scientific committee of the European Commission failed to ameliorate the significant degree of scientific uncertainty that surround issues such as the degree of risk, and what preventive actions might be taken. At the same time, public pressure was being placed on Eurocommerce and its members to communicate with consumers, giving them instructions how to cook and to avoid exposing themselves to this new cancer-causing agent. The real concern is that to communicate if there is scientific uncertainty often means that you can give out mistaken messages. This is not the way to inform the consumer. That's why it's not that we are against transparency, but you have to be very careful not to spread any information concerning scientific findings without appropriate verification and controls. (Eurocommerce, 2002)

Clearly, retailers are somewhat uncomfortable with being situated at the centre of the food risk communication process whilst being peripheral, at best, to the scientific process that assesses the risk. For retailers in particular, the risks extend beyond considerations of human health, and encompass risks to very competitive market shares as well as those surrounding civil liability issues.

Composition of the EFSA Management Board: Institutionalizing Multi-Sectoral Participation

Despite the preceding concern of corporate retailers in terms of risk communication, the food safety White Paper lays responsibility for 'communication and dialogue with consumers on food safety and health issues as well as networking with national agencies and scientific bodies' at the feet of the EFSA (CEC, 2000: 3). And, with official discourse placing consumer interests at the centre of food deliberations and policy-making at the EC level, dialogue with consumers has been taken to mean that consumer organisations should be allowed to participate in the formation and implementation of the new food safety regulatory regime. As a result, consumer groups were expecting to enjoy a stronger presence on the EFSA management board; a desire which, BEUC informed us, has failed to materialise:

> At the beginning we thought there would be a total of four representatives from consumer and industry representative bodies. The speculation was a fifty–fifty split. Then Parliament amended this to four representatives of consumers and other interested parties. This has potentially diluted the voice of consumers on the EFSA management board, especially considering that two of the four places have since been taken by farmers' groups. It certainly is something that we are disappointed with. This is a bad starting point (BEUC, 2002).

Nevertheless, and despite the appointment of only *one* consumer representative to the 14-member EFSA board (without an alternate to cover periods when the appointed representative is unable to attend board meetings), consumer groups like BEUC have chosen to remain optimistic that the new EU food safety regime will deliver on its promise to keep consumer interests at the heart of food safety policies. At the same time, farmers' umbrella groups, like COPA-COGECA, believe that through continued network-building with other NGOs, a good working balance between producer, retailer and consumer interests will develop.

FROM PRODUCTIVISM TO CONSUMERISM: THE EMERGING MODEL OF PUBLIC/PRIVATE REGULATION

We have seen, so far in this analysis, how the new, or at least revised processes of Europeanisation, consumerisation and institution building are developing in both a contingent and dynamic way. Our evidence has allowed us to explore, how these macro processes are engendering two more deeper and micro regulatory trends. The *first* involve the (differential) empowerment of a wider range of interest groups and consultation procedures in food policy-making. These become more fluid than before in that they are networks based around significant issues rather than simply group-led. For instance, we see new (but potentially ephemeral) alliances being formed around issues like GM by consumer, environmental, animal welfare and retailing groups. This acts as a significant counterweight to the 'industry-led' manufacturers and producer interests and alliances.

Also, we see the boundaries between the traditional 'insider-groups' and outside groups becoming much more blurred, with the DG SANCO and the EFSA now establishing new clientelistic relationships with some consumer organisations, but not with others. Indeed, we have discovered significant fluidity both in the means of networking and the content of inter-mediation on the one hand, and in terms of variable 'state-capture' and influence on the other.

The second micro-regulatory trend which is exposed, concerns the contemporaneous and co-evolving model of private-interest food regulation. At the same time as we see a more complex, fluid and networked policy process operating at the EU level (as discussed in Chapter 4); interestingly, we also see a re-affirmation of a more complex, yet authoritative private interest model of food regulation embedding itself in the conventional food supply chains in Europe. In other words, the regulatory stronghold that, for instance, major food retailers in the UK have over their supply chains is being reproduced throughout the Union and beyond. Evidence of this hegemonic process already underway in regions beyond the borders of the EU can also be found in the principles and operation of the Euro-Retailer Produce Working Group (EUREPGAP, and see Chapters 7 and 11). Based on the UK's experience of corporate retailers virtually capturing the food quality assurance process, and a strong private-interest endorsed, science-based food risk assessment process at the EU level, plus corporate retailers defining and enforcing the standards that overseas farmers must meet in order to gain/retain access to European markets, corporate retailer-led regulation becomes a central pillar of the new European food regulatory regime.

The more hybrid private interest model has had to both adjust and Europeanise to rapidly changing circumstances. This has not reduced its relevance, but its character has been modified in the sense that it now also has to sit alongside stronger public sector agencies and actions and a stronger reliance upon independent 'scientific' mitigation and assessment of food risks. Hence, having originally developed out of the limitations of the state, the private-interest food regulatory model is now more contextualised again by state intervention. In addition, it now has to project itself as an effective, market-based and efficient system for policing the food chain in a more complex, and as we have seen, more networked, participatory and fluid policy-making community; one in which some private sector interests—particularly farmers and food manufacturers—have been increasingly questioned as the rightful custodians of the European food system. In doing this it would seem that British retailer-practices and business models have been to the fore.

The British influence in shaping the European food safety agenda has thus not only been associated with it being the unique source of BSE or FMD. Rather, the now established practices of the concentrated British retail sector in policing their food chains through arms-length control mechanisms and developing innovative baskets of own-brand goods has led to this being seen as a preferred model at the European level. Issues of traceability, labelling, implementing a pre-cautionary approach, and the specific debates about the regulation of GM products (see Chapter 3), have all tended to reinforce the private-interest model of food regulation that has been projected and implemented by these retailers. The trick, therefore, becomes how to dovetail the existing private interest model within the newly enhanced public-interest regime that is being projected by the EU, and outlined previously.

Private-interest umbrella organisations, such as Eurocommerce and the Confederation of the Food and Drink Industries (CIAA) at the EU level, and the British Retail Consortium in the UK, see and project these public-interest developments as a positive European step as long as they remain focussed upon assuring the stability of European food markets and allowing the full operation of the European, and indeed the global food market to operate as freely as possible under these circumstances. According to CIAA,

> although retailers don't like each other, especially the large ones. . . , on food safety we manage to make it a non-competitive issue. Thanks to the input of large companies, we are now working in a much more proactive and efficient way. And, we have very good contacts with DG SANCO because we bring them something that helps them with their job. We also work with (EU) Parliament.
>
> We act by first building coalitions across different sectors and countries, then working through special committees we discuss technical issues ranging from food contaminants to the revision of the Common Agricultural Policy. We build coalitions at the international level also. For instance, we prepared a sustainable development report on the food industry for the United Nations. (CIAA, 2002)

It is clear from the evidence that private-interest representative groups at the European level have equipped themselves well to influence the new EU food policy regime. By demonstrating their technical competence in matters of food safety, the evolving policy for them becomes one of mutual co-evolution of both public and private systems with the belief that it is for the public sector to set in place minimum guarantees and risk assessment and assurance mechanisms, and for the private sector, given this more stable risk environment, to compete for the attentions of the more risk-averse and selective European food consumer. Moreover, the costs of compliance in this mutually reinforcing system will tend to always fall more heavily upon the upstream sectors; for it is they—for instance in the case of traceability of GM grains (Chapter 3)—who will have to find the necessary hardware and software to ensure compliance with the private and public systems of regulation.

However, whilst the EU's emerging food safety regime is clearly increasing the grip of retailer-led regulation, these mutually reinforcing private and public interest mechanisms must also ensure that globalised and liberalised trade in foods continues to flow as freely as possible. This could create increasingly difficult headaches for the retailers with regard to traceability and quality regulation. However, according to CIAA, this might not be the case:

> We have done traceability for a long time. Lots of people seem to re-invent things. Traceability in the food industry is something that you do, otherwise you cannot operate. But, as always, regulators want to regulate. (CIAA, 2002)

In fact, the new EU food supply chain stipulations seem only now to be catching-up with quality assurance initiatives that were imposed upon foreign supplies by EU corporate food retailers in the 1990s. These pre-emptive quality assurance mechanisms not only make it relatively easy for retailers to become compliant with emerging food safety legislations, but they enhance their ability to source foods more cheaply and to continue to increase the variety available on their shelves (e.g. organics and fruits and vegetables from South America and elsewhere, see Chapter 7).

Whilst private-interest organisations are largely supportive of the new food safety model that is being advocated by the Commission, despite having a voice in the policy-making process, many social and consumer groups are concerned that food standards that serve the purposes of harmonisation and protect the smooth functioning of the Single Internal Market may not go beyond very minimum standards. This is particularly evident in matters such as animal welfare.

The main aim of this chapter has been to begin to re-conceptualise European food regulation during a continuing period of food risk and insecurity. We have begun to identify some of the key parameters of change at the European level, including: (i) the gradual but significant *Europeanisation of policy*, through not least, the implementation of the recommendations of the European Food Safety White Paper, and the overall commitment to a stronger 'top-down' and standard European approach to both the assessment and the management of risks; (ii) the growing *consumerisation and institutionalisation* of these policies and the empowerment of a wider set of interest groups; and (iii) the increasing use and legitimacy of a *more complex private-interest model of food regulation*. This latter tendency is acting to further entrench retailer and commercially-led regulation in and through supply chains at the same time as the public authorities are attempting to further guarantee minimum standards of food safety and quality, and take the bulk of the responsibility if and when major food scares occur.

Hence, we can begin to see, perhaps with hindsight, how the somewhat peculiarly British dual model of food regulation depicted in *Consuming Interests* in the late 1990s (what we termed the *second phase* of food regulation), has now mutated at the European level (to the *third phase*), both as European food markets have become more integrated and developed, and as the diversity and intensity of food risks have tended to grow. We are now then more firmly in a 'post-BSE" phase of European food regulation; one which has established new 'independent' food institutions in which to assess and manage these risks; and one which divests considerable power to selected commercial and consumer organisations in delivering food through more accountable supply chains. This is very much then a *state-private sector hybrid model of food regulation*; one which is a particular type of public and private sector response to the five pressures on food regulation (as identified in Figure 1.1).

It is important to see this more complex, multi-level system as a response to these pressures in ways which preserve particular notions of the internal (and 'free') market and exchange in food goods within and beyond Europe, at the same time as expressing new controls in the name of the 'consumer' and 'public interest'. In this sense it is also consistent with other branches of the European project which stress supply chain double-dividends and consumerisation of public policy (see, for instance, Folkerts and Koehorst, 1998; and Skogerbo, 1997). Food safety regulation is now then far more embedded and integrated into the European political project. Indeed it carries a far bigger political punch than its actual economic weight in Europe, and perhaps as agriculture and the CAP were viewed over fifty years ago (Chapter 4), now food policy is again seen as a major plank for the further overall integration of the European project. It follows then that as agricultural producer corporatism has declined in its political and economic power in many of the member states, as well as in European policy-making (as discussed in Chapter 4), this has not weakened the political and economic significance of food in Europe as a major and dynamic regulatory activity. Rather, it has laid a foundation for a more comprehensive and commercially led regulatory system—a hybrid model—based upon appeasing consumer and private sector concerns. It is increasingly systemic, scientific and standardised; global as well as local

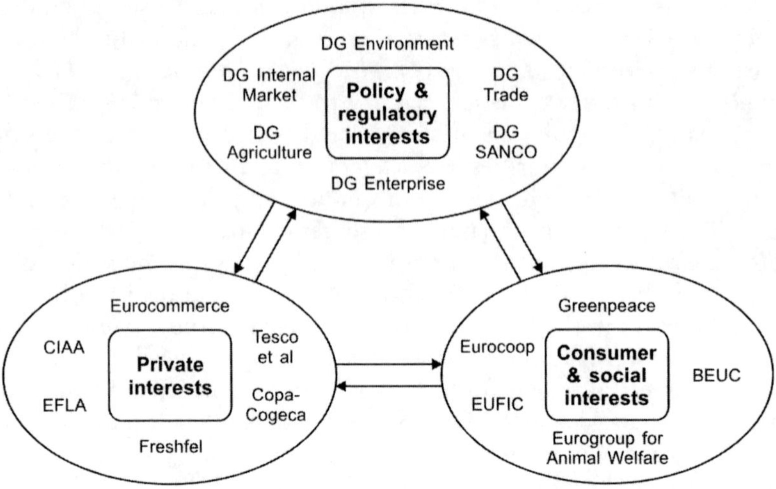

Figure 5.3 The emergent and more fluid food policy-formation network.

in reach as well as inter-sectoral. And, as we have seen in this analysis, it has emerged out of, and will be maintained by, the interaction of a larger number of actors and policy networks. This makes the evolution of public policy all the more complex and reliant upon different combinations of public-private interest.

More specifically, these influences and shifts reflect a reconstituted and multi-dimensional set of relationships between private interests, policy and regulatory interests and consumer and social interests. This is illustrated in Figure 5.3, moving from what might be called a formal or corporatist food policy network (Figure 1.4) to a more fluid and participatory model in which, for instance, key Directorates seek as much to influence what private and consumer groups think as being the focus of their lobbying activities.

This new policy-making landscape and its differentiated influences have arisen partly due to the more challenging and complex food risk environment outlined in Part I. In addition, they provide a central challenge or test for the wider European Project in attempting to incorporate consumer and public concerns (i.e. uncertainty and risk), at the same time as fostering an integrated and a globally competitive European food market. This, after over a decade of operating the European Single Market, make the requirements for effective transnational regulation and food assurance systems much more pressing than in earlier periods.

However, from the perspective of the wider European Project—as we shall see in succeeding chapters—major questions remain not only about what types of regulation are required but also how those types of regulation should be formed and then implemented. In this sense, a focus upon the *contemporary evolutionary governance and regulation of food* tends to expose some of the broader contradictory tendencies of EU policy-making, whereby more regulatory and policy-making fluidity becomes partly a response to regulating uncertainty in a more Europe-wide way.

The very fact that EU food in recent years has been policy-making as more of a collective exercise, involving large numbers of participants, often in intermittent and unpredictable 'relationships', is likely to reinforce the processes by which national autonomy is being eroded, as well as the capacity for consistent EU-level political leadership. The likelihood of any one government or any one national system of policy actors (e.g. governments and interest groups combined) imposing their will in the rest is now challenged. National governments know this. We can therefore expect to see the emergence of two apparently contradictory trends: First, the need to construct complex transnational coalitions of actors which will force all actors to become less focussed on the nations states as the 'venue' for policy-making. Just as many large firms have long since abandoned the notion of the nation-state, so will other policy-actors. They will seek to create and participate in a multi-layered system of transnational coalitions. Second, the continued 'politics of uncertainty' will lead national governments and national interest groups to try to coordinate *their* national Euro-strategies (e.g. DTI, 1993; 1994). In that sense, Euro-policy-making may bring them closer together (Richardson, 2001: 21).

Food regulation, in this more fluid context therefore, becomes a key 'battlefield of knowledge' and power in the fulcrum of Europe on the one hand, and in the re-orientation of Member States and pan-European policy-making and implementing relationships on the other. The overall tendency, it appears, is for uncertainty and risk to generate more regulatory complexity, as well as to re-arrange the power relations between different food supply chain actors. This, in a preliminary and more formal manner, is leading to a more complex institutional and policy-making *structure* which is now both multi-level and multi-interest. The drive to minimise food risks for European consumers without creating hindrances to the internal market is resulting in significant standardisation in practice and philosophy across the entire agro-food chain. And, although the new relationships between the state, corporate and non-corporate private and public interests promise a more viable and accountable food system, it is our view that food safety benefits will be accompanied by important spatial diversity costs, such as a loss of regional diversity in food production and preparation. These are food quality concerns which, also, will need to infuse the food policy-making domain. Indeed, the question of diversity, the sanctity of local and short production trends, and the growing political concerns over ethical and animal welfare issues (see Lucus et al., 2002) are likely to continue to pressure the newly established policy community which is outlined and conceptualised here.

6 Building Relationships in a New Phase of Contested Accountability in the UK

Incorporating the New Public-Private Model of Food Regulation

INTRODUCTION: RESEARCHING THE IMPLICATIONS OF THE FOOD SAFETY CRISIS IN THE UK

We have seen in Chapters 4 and 5 that food safety crises and problems have led to major institutional changes across the EU and attempts were made to introduce policy-making processes that are more open and consultative. The premise is that, consumer involvement in policy making provides an opportunity to restore consumer trust and confidence. The UK Government, for example, set up the Food Standards Agency (FSA) in 2000, and this was followed by the inception of Department of Environment, Fisheries and Rural Affairs (DEFRA) in 2001 (see Chapter 9). The Government believed that creation of the FSA would put an end to the climate of confusion and suspicion which resulted in the way food safety and standards issues have been handled in the past. This was thought to ensure that all future Government activity relating to food will be subject to public and scientific scrutiny, and that the public's voice will be fully heard in the decision-taking process.

The UK Government's decisions were drawn up in the light of Professor Philip James's report and the responses to the consultation exercise carried out in May and June 1997. They were designed to address the key factors which James identified as contributing to the erosion of public and producer confidence in the current system of food controls: the potential for conflicts of interest within the Ministry of Agriculture, Food and Fisheries (MAFF) arising from its dual responsibility for protecting public health and for sponsoring the agriculture and food industries; fragmentation and lack of co-ordination between the various government bodies involved in food safety; and the uneven enforcement of food law. The UK Government supposedly sought a clear separation between promoting safe food in the consumer interest on the one hand and promoting the interests of business on the other.

Responsibility has now been devolved to a single body, whose essential aim is the protection of public health and which has the right to make public its advice to Ministers. The UK Government hopes that the effectiveness of controls on food will not in future be undermined by overlaps, conflicting objectives or incoherence. Therefore, in creating the FSA, the UK government sought to remove the conflict of interest that lay at the heart of the MAFF, which was charged both with promoting the food industry and protecting the consumer interest.

The chapter explores the effects of the gradual *Europeanisation,* increasing consumerist approach and institutionalisation of food policy in the UK, the complexities of private interest model of food regulation and the role played by retailers in the food sector in trying to influence consumers.

The chapter analyses the key emergent themes evolving as a result of the private, institutional and consumer pressures on food regulation. There are clear evidences of the growing significance of incorporating consumer and public concerns and constructions in policy making, along with fostering a pivotal and globally competitive European food market. The riding of these two 'horses'—one associated with the deepening spatial mobility and manipulation of food; the other associated with continuously giving this mobility some degree of public legitimacy—defines the agenda for the new complex model of food regulation. A model, which has re-cast the private interest regulation, within a new publicly defined set of parameters supposedly in the (European) public interest.

THE CHANGING SCOPE OF GOVERNANCE: POST-BSE FOOD POLICY IN THE UK

As we have proposed in earlier chapters, the evolution of the UK food policy can be categorised into three phases: The *first phase* represented a period (before the mid 1980s) of a regulatory regime when food and agricultural production systems were regarded as being safe unless scientifically proven otherwise. The State had a rational and scientific basis on which to test relevant public health and food quality assurance policies. This food regulatory approach, allowed the State to play a key role in the food supply sector (Marsden et al., 2000), and was, for a considerable period, successful in addressing food safety and other public health concerns relating to food.

In *Consuming Interests,* Marsden et al. (2000) map out the changes and adaptations, that have taken place since the mid 1980s, and in how food risk is perceived and new regulatory frameworks emerged. They point to advancement from a government-led regulatory and monitoring model to a new phase (the *second phase*) dominated by supply chain management, and food standards strategies, designed and applied increasingly by the large multiple food retailers. This *second phase* of food regulation was driven primarily by the way food safety issues are perceived by large food retailers; leaving the State to act mainly as auditors rather than enforcers of the mainstream process.

Regardless of the fact that the *second phase* was offering clear improvements in food quality assurance, this approach allowed corporate retailers to distinguish themselves from their non-corporate competitors, and from each other, on the basis of the assurance of quality that they are able to deliver through rigorous supply chain management.

A *third phase* in the UK was marked by the establishment of the UK Food Standards Agency (FSA) in April 2000, with an aim to promote food safety and food standards as a non-ministerial department focussing on the protection of consumers and their interests. The James Report had revealed a public unease in relation to the corporatist style of decision-making in the British food and agriculture sector. There was a public perception that the process of decision making was steeped in an ethos of secrecy (involving Ministry of Agriculture Food and Fisheries (MAFF) and powerful farming, industrial and retailer groups). This *modus operandi* was seen as both benefiting those with vested interests and functioned to the detriment of the public. As a consequence, the government agreed to remove certain key functions and responsibilities from the MAFF and Department of Health (DoH), and vest them in the more independent FSA, with the powers to set stringent food safety standards, as well as to enforce them.

An assessment of the key conceptual parameters and dynamics of this *third phase* in the evolution of food safety regulation in the UK, and the powers responsible for shaping this current regulatory framework are presented in the following sections based upon interview evidence.

THE EVOLVING FOOD SAFETY MODEL I: EUROPEANISATION OF UK FOOD POLICY

In its most explicit form, *Europeanisation* is conceptualised as the process of downloading EU Directives, regulations and institutional structures to the domestic level (Howell, 2004). According to Bulmer and Radaelli (2004) *Europeanisation* consists of processes of (i) construction, (ii) diffusion and (iii) institutionalisation of formal and informal rules, procedures, policy paradigms, styles, 'ways of doing things' and shared beliefs and norms. These are first defined and consolidated in the EU policy process, and then incorporated in the logic of domestic discourse, political structures and public policies.

The nature of *Europeanisation* involves adjustment to the EU process of aligning two institutional logics: that of the EU *and* that of the UK governance. This adjustment process entails two separate steps. As a first and necessary stage, domestic institutions must find suitable ways of processing EU business. The lowest adjustment cost is incurred by incorporating EU business into the pre-existing domestic logic of governance through some switching mechanism. Bulmer and Burch (2001) refer to the two components of institutional response to *Europeanisation* as *reception* and *projection*. *Reception* is the first response to *Europeanisation*. It is a prior step to the *projection* response, where projection refers to the development of machinery for securing an effective voice in the formulation of policy in Brussels. This means, learning 'the rules of the game' in Brussels and how they may be different from those in the domestic political system.

The adaptation of UK governance to integration over the period up to 1997 was principally one of absorbing EU business into the practices established domestically over past decades. Post-1997, the UK government built on established trends in the UK/EU policy handling, but it has also set up new structures and processes (Bulmer and Burch, 2001), which potentially shift the field on which European policy is played out at the domestic level. While these changes have not yet led to significant alterations in outcomes, they have the potential to do so and they have particularly influenced UK food policy.

The effects of *Europeanisation* can be measured along three distinct interrelated variables namely: *policy content*, *policy structure* and *policy style*. According to Hall (1993), policy content can be divided into three different levels. The first relates to the precise setting of policy instruments. The second is the instruments or techniques by which policy goals are attained. The third level comprises the overall goals that guide policy. The concept of policy structure is potentially very broad, raising some problems in defining its boundaries. National institutional structures range from the basic building blocks of the State through to policy coordination networks, codes, guidelines and ways of working (Peters, 1999; Bulmer and Burch, 2000).

It is recognised that the EU is increasingly the main source of food law that needs to be formulated in the UK. Directives covering food composition, food labelling, food marketing standards, additives, contaminants, nutrition, adulteration and food fraud provide a constant stream of new legislation. A clear example is the sentiment, expressed by the Department for Environment, Food and Rural Affairs (DEFRA) and the FSA, that the UK government did all that was possible to consult with key UK stakeholders on the implementation of UK food law, but that the decisions on standards were often made at EU, rather than national level. This thinking was reflected in our interviews with retailers: 'the vast majority of legislation now is definitely European'. Similar views are held by consumer interest groups, who argue for example that legislation on all aspects of farm animal welfare has been European-based, and has come from a directive that's been agreed upon on a European level and has been taken by the UK and implemented directly into UK law with very few changes. It follows therefore that any directive will be almost verbatim translated into UK legislation and that nothing else will be brought in and changed.

In continuing to pursue the EU's objective of participative governance (Article 1, Treaty on European Union), the European Commission has been engaged in the creation of new institutions as a means of securing different interests into the ongoing process of *Europeanisation* (Richardson, 2000). In particular, and as we saw in Chapter 5, it 'has been a strategic actor in constructing assemblage of stakeholders concerned with each of the Commission's policy sectors' (Mazey and Richardson, 2001). As a result of which, various influential consumer and farming lobby groups in Brussels, for example, the European Consumers' Organisation (BEUC), Eurocoop, Committee of Agricultural Organisations in the European Union (COPA), General Confederation of Agricultural Co-operatives in the European Union (COGECA), Association des Consommateurs Europeens (AEC), and the European Association for the Coordination of Consumer Representation (ANEC), receive financial and policy support from the Commission.

The general pattern so far has been one of a gradually increasing set of rules on how to conduct European business. Thus there has been a proliferation of 'guidance,' whether through the use of precedents or of codified rules. It is now possible to identify some of the key facets, and more specifically dynamics, of this gradual *Europeanisation* of UK food policy. This new transition brings about challenges for the various interest groups and their inter-relationships.

First, as we analysed in Chapter 5, we now see an increasingly wider diversity of organisations playing a European role and seeking to influence as well as to articulate different knowledges concerning foods, health and ethical issues. For example, animal welfare groups and the consumer groups now have to tackle the intricacies of issues such as the precautionary principle (see Chapter 10), GM and traceability (Chapter 3). Part of *Europeanisation* now involves accommodating a wider and more disparate range of concerns and interests than those just associated with the quality of foods.

Second, there is a fundamental issue which *Europeanisation* and European policy raises in the context of devolution in the UK: European policy is reserved to the UK government, but much of its substance is devolved thereafter. Hence much European business needs agreement between the UK and the devolved authorities. Thus according to the UK government 'around 80% of the policy areas devolved to the Scottish Parliament has an EU dimension' (Bulmer and Burch, 2001). This situation heralds the arrival of a new multi-level governance of European policy within the UK. At the same time it means that the new devolved authorities (executive and parliamentary) must address the issues of *Europeanisation* as well as the UK national context.

THE EVOLVING FOOD MODEL II: RISING CONSUMERIST AND INSTITUTIONALISATION OF POLICIES AND RECONSTRUCTING THE CONSUMER INTEREST

The Role of the UK State in Building Consumer Trust

The most universal needs and expectations of all consumers about the food they consume are safety, price and availability. The most basic role of public policy is to ensure that these fundamental consumer needs are met. Once they are met, consumers often exercise personal preference in their purchasing decisions. At this point, the market, it is assumed, should be relied upon to provide consumers with such choices, and government's role thereafter becomes one of ensuring that claims made by industry are not false or misleading.

One suggested lesson from the UK government's response to the BSE crisis was that its preference for a 'comforting' approach to communicating with the public, rather than being more open about what was known and unknown, created 'greater damage to commercial interests and triggered virtually unmanageable levels of public distrust' (Randall, 2003). Under these conditions actors fail to recognise that 'rival rationalities' and loss of trust are fundamental to the success or failure of risk communication, and contribute to a more politically controversial risk situation (Gutteling and Kuttschreuter, 2002; Margolis, 1996). In the face of an untrusting audience, *using more science* (and risk assessment) is believed to feed public concerns, because evidence for a lack of risk often carries little weight with the public. Trying to address risk controversies primarily with *more science* is in fact likely to exacerbate conflict (Slovic, 1999).

In the face of these challenges, increasing attention is being paid to trust in public institutions *and* science and technology and how greater understanding of *trust issues* can improve risk management and communication. A number of studies cite declining levels of trust in public institutions and science and technology (Randall, 2003; Petts and Leach, 2000; Trettin and Musham, 2000; Slovic, 1999). Trust is thought to be one of the most important influences on how people perceive risk and respond to risk communication (Petts and Leach, 2000; Finucane, 2000; Siegrist & Cvetovich, 2000). 'Trust' in this context can be defined as a person's expectation that other individuals and institutions (in social relationships) can be relied on in ways that are competent, caring and predictable (Beckwith et al., 1999). Public trust may rest more on a faith in the capacity of the authorities to cope with the risk rather than remove it completely (Star, 1984).

Trust is also thought to be fragile, it is easily broken, but it is considerably harder to rebuild, and in some cases cannot be rebuilt (Slovic, 1999). The fragile nature of trust can create difficulties in risk management and communication. Langford (2002: 103) cites the British public's response to the BSE crisis as an example of a loss of trust accompanied by considerable outrage, changing 'not only attitudes and opinions, but something deeper to do with our accepted or taken-for-granted view of the world'.

Marsh (2001) cites a need for re-skilling in agencies, which would enable more complex analyses of communities; shrewder strategies for engaging diverse communities and mediating between competing interests; more advanced skills and techniques for incorporating diverse aspirations into policies and programs. In the UK, in the *third phase* of food regulation, many institutions are adopting more interactive and constructive dialogues with the public, and their degree of success is related to whether:

- Clear objectives for engaging in dialogue with the public have been set;
- It can be established that the exercise is fair, matches methods to particular purpose and situations, is well-timed, and uses principles of inclusivity to select participants with wide ranging interests;
- The quality of the processes can be assessed and outcomes can be examined; and
- Sufficient training and resources have been allocated bearing in mind the full economic and political costs of not doing so (Parliamentary Office of Science and Technology, 2001).

Kjaenes, Harvey and Warde (2007) from an extensive EU study argue that there are almost continuous demands from consumers and representative groups regarding new forms of governance which can institutionalise trust. *Representation in decision-making* of the public as consumers, *independence* from both business interest and political influence and *transparency* through more democratic monitoring become more important. They argue this does not imply a new form of trust but rather

> another episode in a long series of recurring phases of reconstruction of confidence in food through institutional realignment. This confidence is based on more complex motivational arrangements than before, and therefore also more complex conditions for the investiture of trustworthiness. (p. 201)

This has been a major objective of the Food Standards Agency in the UK. It emerged that they were striving to build consumer confidence, by *first* explaining in clear, unambiguous terms what the risks associated with food safety are.

> I think it (consumer understanding of food risk) is improving, yes it can be quite technical and it can be quite difficult but if you have people there together it forces the scientists and the technical people to explain things in a way that everybody else can understand . . . (FSA)

Second, clear and effective communication strategies could be achieved through increased transparency and stakeholder involvement (Podger, 2003)[1], as it is widely accepted that trust and confidence in risk management are key to risk acceptance. Through 'good' communication, trust is increased and therefore the acceptance of risk:

> Because we operate in this open way, we consult on a day to day basis, both with food industry contacts and with consumer organisations. We have consumer representatives on all our scientific advisory committees, we have a consumer committee, so we can quote real consumers as opposed to consumer lobbyists, actually advising us on the actual decisions we're taking. And one of the ways we've been working which we started right from the beginning, is using what we call Stakeholder Groups, in other words we have meetings, often in public, with a range of all our stakeholders all together so they're interacting with each other as well as with us. . . (FSA)

Third, by making people aware of the risk and supplying appropriate advice on action to be taken by them:

> We have to think about things like, when we're doing risk management, is it appropriate to ban something, or is it more important to focus on the risk communication and say 'this is the situation' and we're giving you the choice, we've given you the information and you decide whether to eat this or not. I think we're doing this more than we used to. . . . we put more emphasis on risk communication than we did before we were in business. We're saying we think there's a risk there but we can't quantify it, but we think you should be aware so that you can decide whether or not you want to be a bit choosier about what you eat. (FSA)

Other studies have shown that an increased public understanding of science alone is unlikely to influence acceptance of a particular technology that is perceived as potentially risky (Frewer, 1999). In the food sector especially traditional risk communication strategies, which focus solely on public education, are bound to fail. Experience has shown that presenting the public with educational material does not necessarily lead to better public acceptance. On the contrary, people tend to select information which is consistent with already held views and values. The Food Standards Agency (FSA) seems to adopt the latter strategy. However, much remains to be seen, about the effectiveness of the strategy (see Chapter 9). As Frewer (1999) states, the public is quite capable of understanding the concept of uncertainty and thus should be provided with clear information about the uncertainties around risk. This in turn will increase perceptions of trust in information sources and better acceptance of emerging technologies.

Further, consumer reactions to information are often difficult to predict. This is true even for shopping behaviour after food scares have been widely publicised. Some will translate anxiety into changed behaviour immediately, while others will not change either through habit or in consequence of their belief in producer, retailer and government reassurances.

It is increasingly recognised that mutual understanding and consensus-building are the best ways to address the elements of values and fairness in risk decision-making. This in turn forms the foundation for public trust and confidence in public institutions. Because objective facts are not always the basis for decisions, participation and citizen engagement in policy making is necessary in the formation of acceptable public policy. This has been attempted by the FSA in the form of citizen's juries, for example (see Chapter 9).

Such a theory dictates that a successful model for risk communication must reconcile the views of scientists, the public and politicians in order to achieve a common understanding of complex risks leading to credible management options and credible policy development around risk.

Role of Consumers and Other Interest Groups in Policy Making

The old debate about consumer concern as rarely leading to action no longer completely holds. Private and public bodies of the food sector now realise that increasing consumer advocacy is set to be a powerful force in the marketplace as a result of a combination of factors. Consumer power should not be under–estimated. Powerful lobbying groups can facilitate consumer action. For example, in the case of GM foods, the call for action has been seen in the increased sales of organic foods. Effective and appropriate consumer involvement are essential to ensure consumer interests are taken into account to improve the quality of decision making, and to help avoid a recurrence of problems that have led to a decline in consumer trust and confidence in food and food policy-making institutions.

It was clear from the UK interviews that most of the UK consumer interest groups now claimed to play a pivotal role in influencing policy making. They seemed to be more vociferous and responsive to consumer advocacy. For instance:

> . . . it's (food safety) an important issue because it's what consumers are really, are very much concerned about, and we are aware that consumers tend to see these issues as a bit of a package, there is safety, there's animal welfare, there is a natural form of production, there are these various values that consumers go for . . . (Consumer Group)

> . . . in some ways we know that consumers have more power than government these days. At least that is what is said, and in some ways

that's true. So, we go for trying to persuade consumers that they could buy animal-friendly products. And we do that either through the media or education . . . (Consumer Group)

Some consumer interest groups were of the opinion that they can exercise more power in influencing the government in policy making, only because they have the strong backing of the public. This is evident in the following excerpt of the interview with one of the consumer interest group:

> . . . we have the power in as much as we tend to have public support on our side generally, and so if we can make that more obvious then we can hope to influence policy and things like that. . . . the very large farmers have the time to be on National Farmers' Union (NFU) boards and to get represented at the higher levels of the NFU where again, they have a great deal of power and influence within government although they have made themselves unpopular with foot-and-mouth and so forth . . .

The views reflected by the private interest groups were similar in line to the consumer interest groups, in that the consumers play a vital role in the policy-making process, and the private interest groups in turn, value and communicate the consumers' perceptions into the decision- making process.

> I've got personal views on consumer groups. A lot of the consumer groups do an awful lot of good, they are almost a kind of conscience of society and I think have a very important role to play in terms of ensuring that consumers perceptions are fed into the decision making process, but at the end of the day there has to be a balance at the various levels. I think they are knowledgeable, they are articulate. (Retailer)

Considering the importance of consumers in the policy-making process, regulatory activity of food control should establish well-designed and well-publicized procedures for receiving and considering consumer and industry inputs at the policy-making level. A regulatory body interviewed stated:

> We have a division which is marketing and consumers and that provides us focus for consumer considerations. (DEFRA)

There is no doubt that the consumers in the UK are increasingly influencing food regulation by selection or rejection of food considered healthy or hazardous. Therefore large scale retailing organisations and various consumer interest groups acting as intermediaries between the spheres of production and consumption are very sensitive to consumers' preferences and practices.

THE IMPLOSION OF THE (NOW FAR MORE SENSITIVE) CONSUMER AND PRODUCER DIVIDE

Over the course of the late 20th century, market dominance by distributors and wholesalers gave way to dominance by manufacturers, followed by the current period of dominance by integrated distributor-retailers. One of the most controversial elements of supermarket's dominance of the food retail sector is their impact on farming. For many years in the UK there have been accusations that the big multiples are reaping excessive profits from the agri-food chain by 'turning the screw' on suppliers and primary producers. The squeeze on farming (and farm-gate prices, specifically) is by extension, said to be affecting the resilience of the rural economy and quality of the environment.

Although the retail industry has been found to be broadly competitive (Supermarkets, 2000; Competition Commission, 2006), the sheer scale and buying power of the global retailers makes them subject to increasing scrutiny, and a level of discontent in farming which has occasionally been expressed in militant action against stores and depots. Around 230,000 UK farmers trade with the majority of consumers via only a handful of supermarket companies, where UK consumers purchase 75–80% of their groceries (Euro Monitor, 2003). The profit of all those 230,000 farms has been roughly equivalent with the profit of just six major supermarket chains (Euro Monitor, 2003)

In comparison, to the producers' eroding power, retailers and traders have a powerful economic position, which enables them to wield a powerful position in the industry, to influence policy decisions. This was also highlighted in our interviews with the consumer interests groups.

> . . . If you're talking about small farmers, medium sized farmers, family farmers, I think that they probably don't have very much influence at all. (Consumer Group*)*

> . . . what we have to do is to make processors and farmers work with the retailer rules. The retailers are short hand for customers; they translate what the customer wants. Whatever people might think of retailers, they are very good at translating the customer needs. So, in that case we have no choice but to follow them, because they represent the customer. (Farmers Union)

From the preceding extracts it is evident that there is a widespread recognition among the various groups interviewed that effective and appropriate consumer involvement is essential; so as to ensure consumers interests are taken into account to improve the quality of decision-making, and to help avoid a recurrence of the problems that have led to a decline in consumer trust and confidence in food and food policy-making institutions. However, this consumer involvement is seen as increasingly (and effectively) mediated through the corporate retailers. In the *third phase* of food regulation it was also recognized that there has to be a shift in attitudes, policies and practices so that consumer involvement is more at the heart of decision-making. There has been increasing government emphasis in recent years on greater public involvement in decision-making and service provision both in the UK and the EU. However, it is unclear whether the so-called consumer involvement these organisations promote is carried out to fulfil a formal requirement to do so as a 'box-ticking' exercise or whether it is done to legitimise or avoid taking what might be an unpopular decision. It also emerges from the interviews that consumer voices from Non-Governmental Organisations (NGOs) and other consumer organisations are often regarded as 'self-appointed' and are not necessarily representative of the mass of consumers. Interviewees acknowledged that the setting up of the Food Standards Agency in the UK in 2000 represented a significant move towards greater consumer involvement in the food sector. The more recently created DEFRA has also committed itself to new ways of working but is seen as still at an early stage in developing more consumers -focussed strategies.

THE EVOLVING FOOD REGIME III: THE ENSUING COMPLEX PRIVATE INTERESTIN FOOD REGULATION

Role of Retailers

The distinctive feature of the recent restructuring of the UK food chain is that it is retailer-driven. Retailers have a powerful position in the food system (Dobson and Waterson, 1996; Fiddis, 1997), and through their traceability and quality assurance schemes (QAS) are able to influence the entire food production chain, and also importantly to define its margins. Due to retailer initiatives in new product development, and vertical and horizontal alliances, they play a particularly influential role in the market place, in terms of both food use and acceptability (Ellahi, 1996). Indeed, the quality/value system that each retailer applies, and the policies adopted, can have significant impacts on many of the other interested parties, such as producers and consumers.

The retailers' continued influential position is further heightened by the current retailer market and related management strategies. Innovations in own-brand products in the UK market further strengthen this position. These not only give retailers better margins, but also increase their negotiating position with manufacturer brands. Manufacturers find themselves in the position of both trading partner and competitor. The following excerpt from our interviews with a consumer interest group draws attention to the powerful position of retailers.

> . . . the retailers influence the policy making and the decision making quite significantly because they are extremely powerful and can influence the decision making in the products around the supermarket shelves. I think their role is may be one of too much strength. (Consumer group)

However, to remain profitable in a competitive environment, they must meet consumer needs. In order to facilitate competitiveness and ensure that share of the market is maintained, they endeavour to identify and anticipate consumer expectations in advance of sales (Hill and Merton, 1995). This is becoming more difficult. The behaviour of consumers is becoming increasingly volatile and concerned with the instant satisfaction of their wants (NRLO, 1998), and therefore, some retail policies can be of a speculative nature.

Customers are today perceived as no longer prepared to be dictated to by suppliers, and have become more assertive, more demanding, individualistic and generally more affluent in their tastes. The market power of consumers is seen as growing stronger as a result of fierce retailer competition; new technology and new business practices. The retailers are the self-selected barometers of this process.

Consumer market power is becoming ingrained through the increased use of retail scanning data to decide product assortment, prices and marketing strategies. Successful retailers have perfected the art of customising their service offering both hierarchically in socio-economic terms, and spatially in the judicious location of stores. This ensures they produce what customers want, when they want it, and at a price they are willing to pay; as one of the consumer interest group interviewed said:

> Sometimes there's been a tendency in the past to try and present themselves (retailers) as though they should really be the consumer organisations because they know their consumers; but they have the information for different reasons, for commercial reasons in order to take advantage of that. Sometimes we've found it very useful to work with the retailers, like on GM, they had a crucial role to play and completely were able to shift the supply chain and ensure non-GM supplies and at a time when the government wasn't accepting any responsibility at all for GM and lack of consumer choice. So it was down to them that consumers could have a choice. (Consumer group)

Another consumer interest group argues,

> The retailers have a huge amount of influence on certain issues, in the sense that they can determine what is sold in the shops and they're very receptive to consumer pressure. So for example on GM crops they have effectively stopped the market through, because consumer pressure asked them to practically. In terms of government policy, we have found that some of the big corporations input, or the bio-tech companies, pesticide companies, and their associations like the Crop Protection Association, seem to be able to wield an enormous amount of lobbying power, and in many cases they seem to have very good links into the particular branches of government that deal with these issues. (Consumer group)

An explanation to this movement of power substitution of the state regulation seems to come from the change in food habits. The increase in consumers' income and the transition to more 'sophisticated' consumption has reduced the demand for undifferentiated products. The labelling and defining characteristics of quality are therefore directly linked to the competitive food retail market.

Additional influences on retailers' roles and responsibilities are the potential failings in the market system. In the present 'free-market economy', although the government intervenes to protect consumers from health and safety market failures, consumer autonomy and choice is highly valued; so that non-interference is favoured above paternalistic intervention as a guiding principle of government policy (i.e. the 'nanny state' versus the freedom of choice). While consumers may ultimately influence or veto whether a new technology is successfully adopted through their purchasing power, consumer autonomy can be compromised by several factors. For example, if there are limitations on the availability and accuracy of information on a food product, market mechanisms may not always ensure that the desired controls are in place to maintain consumer confidence. In these situations, trust is transferred from legislators and the market to the retailer. These are increasingly perceived to act as a mediator of consumer interest. Hill and Merton (1995:9) note that 'probably most consumers consider ensuring the acceptability of practices (production methods) is the responsibility of the retailer'.

It is argued that retailers have been able to respond to consumer needs, thanks to the 'information age', which has created significant new forms of marketing, communication and business. Customer information at all points of communication (such as loyalty cards) means that production can be tailored to an increasingly accurate degree, thereby saving money and increasing profit margin.

> You keep an eye on what's going on generally in the market and look at other market research, you can really try and predict where things

> are going to go, going to develop. Other than that, try and predict what they think latest trends would be to probably give us some idea, of what we can or cannot do. (Retailer)

Moreover, in the light of the dynamics of the retailer-consumer relationship, retailers see their responsibilities as lying in several distinct areas of safe food and facilitating consumer choice. This is discernible from the excerpts of the interviews carried out with some private interest groups.

> . . . what we need to make sure is we've got all the right procedures in place to supply those products to our customers so that they're safe, good quality and legal. (Retailer)

> . . . yes we want to chuck in things for the customers benefit and we do need to understand our customers and what they need. (Retailer)

The consumer interest groups were of the opinion that, on one hand, there were some retailers who were very forthcoming and innovative in satisfying customer demands.

> Some of the big supermarkets have been far more reticent about making concrete moves in the right direction on animal feed, certainly people like TESCOs. Whereas, on the other hand, you have more progressive supermarkets like the Co-op and definitely M&S who are just far more helpful. So you often hear from someone like TESCO who will say well actually we can't source non-GM animal feed even though our customers might want it. It's impossible. And then you'll hear from M&S the next day who say well actually we've already done it so it's an interesting situation. (Consumer Group)

> There is a great deal of evidence to show that food manufacturers have improved the food supply in the UK over the last twenty years. In terms of food manufacturers they make some attempt, for example, to reduce sugar and salt in processed food but it is very marginal of what they have done, and it is also variable, so you have got some retailers who have been very good and very proactive in trying to provide some health initiative. (Consumer Group)

And, on the other hand, there were also some who for the fear of being "named and shamed" would adopt measures to satisfy and meet consumer needs.

> I think it's a similar sort of line to the supermarkets because a lot of them, especially the bigger ones, had this idea that they weren't going

> to be doing anything more on GM so they were quite happy to just give us the cold shoulder, and last week we re-launched our shoppers' guide on the website and people have been phoning in and saying oh please, take us off the orange or the red list. (NGO)

> Yes, [in] some things they are very influential but I think it has its limitations working with them as well because of the way that they operate. (Consumer Group)

Consumer demand and its dynamic construction by retailers drive the entire food network. This demand is shaped by many factors. The most influential is the impact of the large multiple retailers on consumer selection and choice; through their supplier relationships with primary producers and food manufacturers, and their extensive promotional activity. A large majority of choices and decisions regarding food consumption are made just prior to the act of consumer purchasing. The success of retailers in their own eyes has in the main been due to their ability to anticipate the needs and expectations of consumers, and to deliver to them a wide range of products of high quality and freshness at competitive prices.

> . . . The freedom of retailers to provide their customers with the choice on what they want to buy, not the freedom to rip off or the freedom to poison, or the freedom to pull the wool over peoples eyes, what it is about is the freedom to provide the customer with the choices of the products they want to buy. . . . (Retailer Trade Group)

The retailing industry maintains its central position in the food system due to its capability to create and respond to the customers' preferences. For example, when the distributors decide to label the products with GMO, or eliminate the ingredients of their own brands, this action has a cascading effect throughout the food industry, grain traders, and producers.

As competing interests from consumer lobbies and regulatory bodies have grown, retailers have been skilful in accommodating a wider range of the overall political shifts into their approach to promote their wellbeing. Corporate retailers at the EU level now operate both independently and jointly through organisations like Euro Commerce (Flynn et al., 2004). In the UK, retailers have to position themselves continuously and carefully as custodians of the consumer, distinguishing themselves from both the producer and food manufacturing interests. As the increasingly integrated European food market continues to show major food safety problems, the retailers have taken the opportunity to further embed retailer-led supply chain management.

THE EVOLVING FOOD MODEL IV: THE FOOD STANDARDS AGENCY IN THE CONTEXT OF PRIVATE INTEREST REGULATION

Despite the rising dominance and legitimacy of private interest groups the Food Standards Agency was established in the UK (in April 2000) to promote food safety and food standards as a non-ministerial department, focussing on the protection of consumers and their interests. Food quality and safety, it learned, were back in the public (non-competitive) domain. The main aim of the Food Standards Agency (FSA) as set out in the enabling legislation in 1999 was: 'to protect public health from risks which may arise in connection with the consumption of food (including risks caused by way in which it is produced or supplied) and otherwise protect the interests of consumers in relation to food' (FSA, 2001). Unlike its predecessor unit in MAFF, the FSA could claim to be free from direct sponsorship of any food industry sector and is answerable to the minister for public health.

The evolution of food regulation in the UK is driven primarily by the way food safety issues are perceived by large food retailers; leaving the state to act mainly as auditors rather than standard-setters and enforcers of the mainstream process.

It is important, therefore, to evaluate the formal role played by the FSA in creating a difference to food governance in the UK given the continued development of private interest regulation. The private interest, consumer and social interest, and regulatory interest groups were asked about their views on the FSA's move towards a more transparent and inclusive process of governance, that contrasts sharply with the seemingly closed style of governance by the Ministry of Agriculture Fisheries and Food (MAFF). The views expressed by the three major interest groups interviewed in the research are summarised here.

Private Interest Groups: 'Not enough to name and shame!'

The FSA's *modus operandi* in restoring consumer confidence by adopting the naming and shaming process was severely criticised by most of the private interest groups.

> Does name and shame really restore in the consumer confidence in food? What it has done (the FSA) is that it has established the Food Standards Agency as an independent organisation that is willing to "blow the whistle" on big commerce, big commercial companies in the way that MAFF was perceived by consumer groups as not doing. It would be good if it (FSA) actually really took on its mantel of restoring confidence, restoring consumer confidence, if it actually adopted a policy of name and praise. (Retailer)

One of the guiding principles of the FSA is to be open and accessible (to which it is being seen in Government circles as achieving). However, the private interest groups see it differently:

> Transparency does not necessarily equate with effectiveness. They've (FSA) not quite grasped that yet . . . (Retailer)

The FSA's definition of 'consumer interest' was questioned by one of the private interest group, who stated:

> we're not sure what they (FSA) mean by consumer interests. Do they mean the interests of consumer organisations? If they're talking about the interests of individual consumers, there are fifty-nine million individual consumers in this country—each with a different set of priorities. (Retailer)

They further branded the functioning of the FSA to be politically motivated, by stating:

> . . . the big problem is they (FSA) don't have the evidence to determine why they're seeking to change policy or to intervene in a particular area. And to that extent the FSA's political. Now who the political drivers are within the FSA, on country of origin labelling or on assurance schemes or whatever—is in some areas difficult to say. But that is political. There is no doubt about it. Because they don't have the evidence. (Retailer)

While there were criticisms on the way the Food Standards Agency functioned, some suppliers/manufacturers were of the view that the Agency has done a commendable job; and that it is now more willing to consult the industry. The transparent policy adopted by the Agency and the efforts made to dispel panic through its vast communication procedures among consumers were also appreciated.

> . . . things have changed now, for the better in the last few years, with the creation of the Food Standards Agency and DEFRA and they're much more willing to consult with the industry. (Food manufacturer)

Views expressed by one of the private interest organisation reflect the fact that they appreciate the different mechanism of functioning of the FSA, as compared to the MAFF.

> The Food Standards Agency definitely thinks differently to what MAFF used to be, they are far more willing to discuss complicated

> issues in public and through that come to sensible certain decisions, where MAFF would have been absolutely petrified of having the discretion in the first place. So the FSA is dealing with actually the most noticeable things, it's done easy, its just that everything is open. We don't have secrets and their view is very clear that their view is to protect the customer. (Retailer)

Regulatory Interest Groups

The regulatory interest groups exhibited a very cautious attitude regarding their views about the setting up and functioning of the FSA.

> If consumers are going to have confidence in food they need to have a champion out there who's guided by sound science, guided by and not dictated by the politicians and that was the suggested place for the FSA.

Two of the local authorities interviewed, felt that the FSA had been helpful in their overall (local authority's) functioning, as is evident from the following excerpts of the interviews with them.

> . . . FSA was quite helpful and checking now and then we were happy with the way we were going.

> . . . since they were established. We have, a good relationship with them, and there's a lot of mechanisms been put in place, and there is a good exchange of information between ourselves and the Agency.

Consumer & Social Interest Groups

The views gathered from the consumer and social interest group reflect criticisms on the lack of co-ordination between the FSA and the DEFRA; and unease in the way the FSA dealt with the GM issue:

> . . . in terms of the objectives, in principle, clearly it's positive we have an Agency now disconnected from other influences, supposedly and apparently. They're purely and simply looking at what's best from a food safety point of view, giving a view, whether that view is then accepted and put into implementation. So on the face of it that can be very positive. The negative side of that is from our experience, unless there's an improvement in the co-operation between the FSA and for example DEFRA, there can be times when they will give a view in isolation and not really appreciate the implications of what they're saying.

On the issue over the GM free labelling, one of the consumer interest group had the following view about the manner in which the FSA acted:

> . . . we couldn't really understand why the FSA . . . this independent food watchdog was acting so outrageously . . . the FSA was an independent food watchdog, but everything they've ever done on GM and organics proves that they're not . . . it just strikes me that they're not being balanced and they're not really being independent. . . .

However, some consumer organisations appreciated the role played by the FSA, and were impressed by the consumer focussed approach adopted by the FSA.

> Some things have changed since the formation of the FSA. There is a difference between transparency and openness which is difficult to measure and it is early days to know and there are also issues about whether always being transparent is beneficial. . . .
>
> We have been quite impressed with the consumer focussed approach that they've taken and that's been helped by the way that the board meets in public and when we talk to individual board members they do feel personally responsible for the FSA and it fulfilling its role.

What is evident from these analyses is that most consumer interest groups appreciate the new role played by the FSA, especially in putting consumers first and having consultations with many consumer groups. However, not many are in favour of the transparency approach adopted by the FSA, as they feel this approach may stifle new evidence.

The scope of the FSA's remit offers potential for joined-up policy thinking along the whole food chain, but it has been interpreted in fairly bounded terms. In practice, its rationale remains rooted in the dominant retailer-led paradigm. The Agency's responsibility extends beyond food safety to include matters concerned with food quality, consumer protection and choice; but, as demonstrated with it's posturing with regard to GM and organics it steers clear of engaging in systemic discussions about supply chains, and how they might be redeveloped. Its effectiveness however, depends in part on the extent to which it is trusted by the public to provide reliable and impartial advice. Securing this trust largely depends on how the Agency identifies and takes appropriate action in response to risks to food safety and the public's concerns; the extent to which the public recognise the Agency as the authoritative source of advice and information on food standards; and how transparent the Agency is in its decision making and engages those who have an interest in food standards.

THE NEW EMERGING HYBRID MODEL IN THE UK

The chapter has identified four significant recent developments in which the State, corporate and private interests, consumers and social interest groups build relationships in response to the need for accountability within the agri-food chain. This represents the development of a more complex public/private set of relationships—*a third phase* of regulation—which now embodies new public institutions (like the EFSA and the UK FSA) and a greater competitive 'battle' to win over the hearts and minds of consumers.

The results of the research show *first*, that there is indeed a significant trend towards a 'national' *Europeanisation* of food policy in the UK. *Second*, there is a growing institutionalisation of these policies, and the related empowerment of a different set of interest groups when specific issues, e.g. GM- food, BSE and a multitude of other food safety issues are concerned. *Third*, private interest groups (particularly retailers) are increasingly playing a major role in (re)shaping the UK food policy.

Nevertheless, there was consensus on issues of common interest, and there is a more flexible and participatory relationship between the private interest, policy and regulatory interest and consumer and social interest groups. The latter indicates that this *is an amalgamation of a state-private sector model of food regulation*; where there is a specific response from public and private sectors to the various pressures on food regulation (for example see Smith et al., 2004). It is worth noticing that this complex and hybrid model is emerging as a response to the (post BSE) food regulation pressures in ways which safeguard the broader macro-economic and political concepts of the European Internal Market (EIM) and increasingly integrated exchange of food goods within and beyond Europe, while also simultaneously enunciating new standardised and 'non-competitive' controls in the name of the European consumer and public interest (as discussed in Chapters 4 and 5).

This emerging model of food regulation may have begun to lay a foundation for a more, all-inclusive and business-led regulatory system based on appeasing consumer and private sector apprehensions. The new and distinctive stimuli for this have arisen partly due to the more exigent and intricate food risk environment. And it appears (in the context of the UK at least) as though this trend will be maintained by the interaction of a larger number of actors and policy networks (Figure 6.1), which, in turn, makes the evolution process more complex and potentially contingent.

This does not diminish the role of retailer-led private regulation as suggested in the earlier second phase of food regulation. It came out very strongly in the research that retailers, in the name of the consumer and public interest, are more influential in food policy making in the UK, partly as a result of their knowledge of and authority over the competitive constructions of the consumer interest. As one consumer interest organisation stated: 'both legislators and consumers, are pushing (policy making), certainly from the consumer point of view'. 'The consolidation and internationalisation of the food retail and manufacturing industry can be expected to continue', according to the conclusions of an influential report[2]. One question therefore is: what does this mean for consumers? Despite the increasing power of both manufacturers and retailers, it suggests that it will be these bodies most able to adequately represent and construct the consumers who will drive the food supply chain in future.

In this sense, the new consumer is increasingly influencing the food system by selection or rejection of food considered healthy or hazardous; and large scale retailer's organisations acting as intermediaries between the production and consumption are very sensitive to consumers' 'preferences'.

The importance of some key consumer trends (e.g. comfort, health, variety, individuality, enjoyment and security) can be evidenced in several important developments. *First*, the different links in the supply chain are increasingly attempting to communicate more directly with the end customer as they vie for that consumer's business. *Second*, all the players want to have a greater impact on the shopper's buying behaviour. Retailers are trying to influence the consumer mindset by presenting themselves as a brand. Indeed, brand competition is a key battleground between retailers themselves, and between them and the large food manufacturers.

Marsden et al. (2000) noticed a pendulum movement during the 1990s in which the deregulation in food markets and the disappearance of representative (production-based) corporate organisations were gradually occupied by large-scale retailer's organisations. According to the authors, 'retailers, given their pivotal position in supplying choices and enhanced degrees of freedom conferred on them by government, become acutely important for the legitimisation of the state and more specifically for the management of the food system on behalf of the state and the consumer interest' (p. 193). While this power has been maintained and developed as they have sustained their market and regulatory power, the governance of food has now also, again become a territory for new state and consumer bodies.

The overall tendency of food regulation, in this emerging and flexible framework, therefore, appears to generate more complexity due to uncertainty and risk related to food safety, as well as to constantly reshuffle the power relations between different food supply chain players. In an effort to minimise food risks for consumers without creating impediments to the internal markets, these new relationships between the State, corporate and non-corporate private and public interests has begun to offer a more practical and accountable food system. However, these new relationships could usher in other costs, such as a loss of local and regional diversity in food production and preparation (Smith et al., 2004).

Thus, the new emerging UK third phase model of food regulation outlined in this chapter; developing through the four dimensions analysed, suggests that retailers are now much more influential in controlling the quality and 'value pathways' of foods from 'farm to fork'. However, the emergence

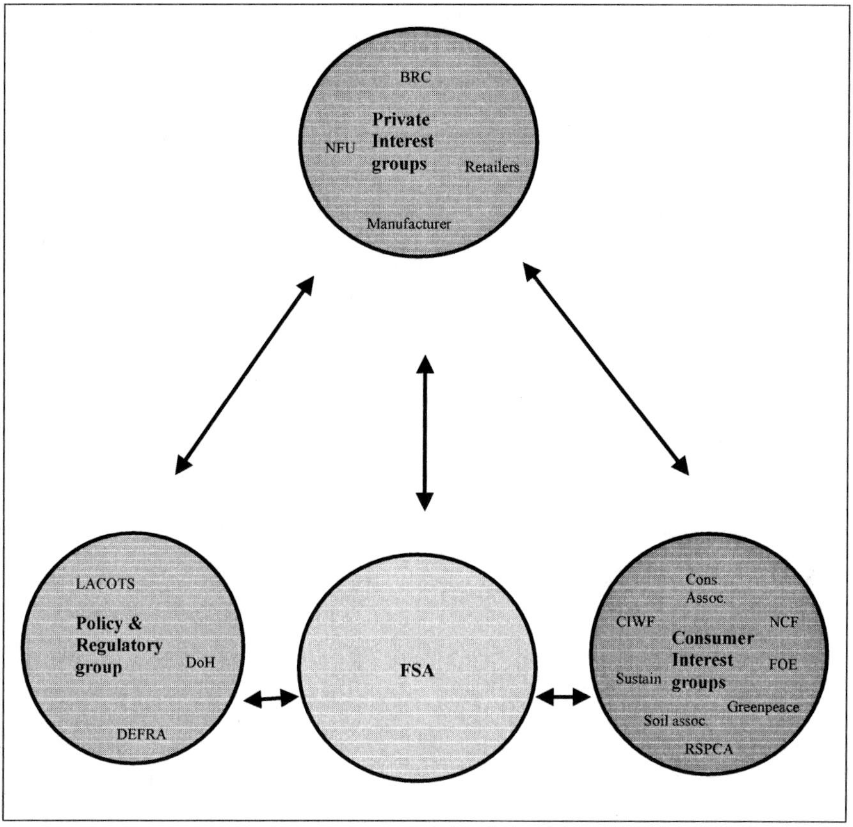

BRC	-	British Retail Consortium
NFU	-	National Farmers' Union
LACOTS	-	Local Authorities Coordinating Body on Food and Trading Standards
DoH	-	Department of Health
DEFRA	-	Department of Environment, Food and Rural Affairs
FSA	-	Food Standards Agency
CIWF	-	Compassion in World farming
NCF	-	National Consumers' Forum
FoE	-	Friends of Earth
RSPCA	-	Royal Society for the Prevention of Cruelty against Animals

Figure 6.1 The emerging food policy formation network in the UK.

of private-interest regulation does not steer clear of the need for the State to protect the consumer interest as it once might have done. Now, private interest regulation needs a consultative and 'stake-holder' State at both UK and EU levels such that it can appease growing consumer concerns about the conventional food supply system. However, it does shape the ability of the State to act in the interest of the consumer. The need therefore is to map out its effects and impacts, and to assess how this model continually metamorphoses to the constantly emerging pressures of 'risk society'. The re-organisation of public food regulation through the setting up of the Food Standards Agency (analysed in more detail in Chapter 9) has been a significant introductory step in this regard. In this research we also set out to seek the formal role played by the FSA in creating a difference to food governance in the UK. The views held by the regulatory, private and consumer interest groups on FSA's moves towards a more transparent and inclusive process of governance, positions the FSA as still in its infancy. And its effective functioning and acceptance as one of the UK's reliable source of advice and information on food needs to be seen in its broader complex, public/private regulatory context which has begun to be outlined here.

Part III

Operating the Hybrid Model

Case Studies of Regulatory Supply Chains

7 The Cutting Edge of Retail Grocery Competition

The Case of the Fresh Fruit and Vegetable Supply Chain

THE EMERGENCE OF A HYBRID MODEL

We have seen how private interests (particularly retailers) increasingly play a role in (re)shaping the UK food policy; and that this is done in a more flexible and participatory relationship between the private interest, policy and regulatory interest and consumer and social interest groups. This is an evolutionary state–private sector model of food regulation; where there is a specific response from public and private sectors to the various pressures of food concerns.

This complex model emerges as a response to the (post BSE) food regulation pressures in ways which safeguard the broader macro-economic and political concepts of the European Internal Market (EIM) and increasingly integrated exchange of food goods within and beyond Europe, while also simultaneously enunciating new standardised controls in the name of the European consumer and public interest. This emerging model of food regulation has begun to lay a foundation for a more business-led regulatory system based on appeasing consumer and private sector risks. And it appears (in the context of the UK at least) as though this trend will be maintained by the interaction of a larger number of actors and policy networks, which, in turn, makes the evolution process more complex and potentially contingent. In this chapter, the case of fresh fruit and vegetable sector is used to explore this hybrid model. This chapter examines the in-depth operation of this model with reference to fresh fruit and vegetables.

This has been a leading sector for food retail innovation and sales during the 2000s. After reviewing the market and regulatory frameworks involved in the sector this analysis, using interview data from retailers and regulatory bodies outlines the specific ways in which the public private systems interact. It has, as we shall see, been a sector which has experienced the proliferation of private standards and third-party certifiers. It is a sector which experiences the heightened pressures of private sector retail competition and public sector concerns over food safety.

The Global Fruit and Vegetable Sector

The world annual production of FFV totals approximately 1 billion tonnes, and global trade in fruits and vegetables is worth US $70 billion. However, Cook (1998) reports fruit and vegetables are by their nature local, with only 4.4% of global vegetable production and 8.9% of fruit production traded internationally. After bananas, the primary internationally traded commodities are citrus, apples, tomatoes and grapes. China, India and Brazil account for 30% of the world fruit production. The US and EU are the largest fruit and vegetable importers and exporters, with 40% and 11% global market share respectively.

The European Fresh Produce Sector

The EU is a major player in world horticulture, with 9% of world production. Around 15% of the value of EU agricultural production comes from the horticulture sector, and it is both a major importer and exporter. It accounts for around 11% of world exports and 25% of world imports. It is the second largest exporter and the biggest importer of fruit and vegetables in the world. Leading products traded are citrus fruit, apples, tomatoes and onions.

Figure 7.1 highlights the size of the EU fresh fruit and vegetable production. Total vegetable production in the EU was 51 million tonnes in 2004, while fresh fruit production stood at 62 million tonnes for the same year. Consumption of fresh fruit and vegetables has been generally stable at 44 million tonnes and 46 million tonnes respectively in 2002. The leading fruit and vegetable producing Member States are Italy, Spain and France.

The EU's main imports are bananas, citrus fruit, apples, grapes, and pineapples; fruit juices are also important imports. The EU's main exports are citrus fruit, apples, grapes, peaches and nectarines, onions and tomatoes.

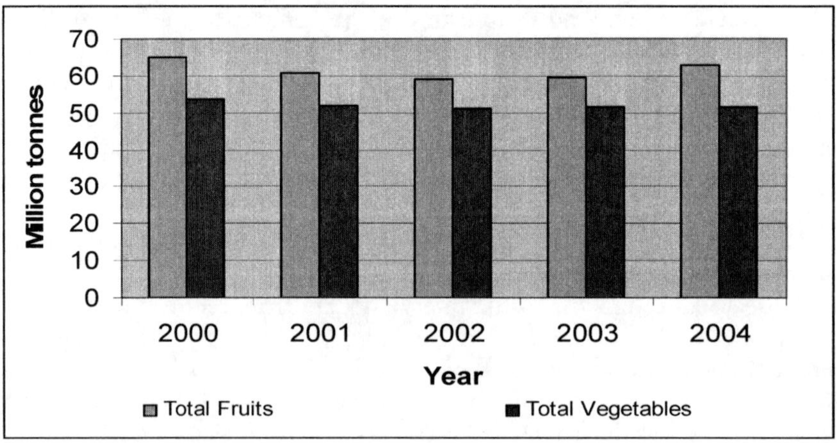

Figure 7.1 Production of fresh fruit and vegetables in the EU.
Source: FAO STAT online database

EU support programmes in the sector are largely implemented through producer organisations. Support programmes are financed by members of producer organisations and the EU on a 50/50 basis. EU aid however is limited to 4.1% of the value of the production handled by the producer organisations. Funds can be used to finance withdrawal of products from the market at times of surpluses or to top-up compensation payments. They can also be used to finance operational programmes of support. In the EU nearly 1,400 producer organisations are recognised, channelling 40% of all fruit and vegetables to the market.

The EU budget for the fruit-and-vegetable sector was €1,650 million in 2002 (3.7% of the agricultural budget). About 56% of this budget is for fresh fruit and vegetables. Specific aid schemes exist for processing of tomatoes, peaches, pears and citrus fruit; dried figs and dried prunes; cultivation of grapes for drying; the storage of sultanas, currents and dried figs and nuts.

The UK has been an increasingly major importer of fresh produce. Over the past decade, UK domestic growers of fresh produce have lost out substantially to imported products. By 2001, the UK producer value shares of domestic vegetables (including potatoes) and fruit markets were 71% and 10.4% respectively. When potatoes are excluded national self-sufficiency in vegetables is much lower. Despite successive health campaigns to increase consumption of fruits and vegetables there is a growing crisis in national primary production, partly driven by a mismatch between domestic varieties, changing consumer preferences and retailer strategies.

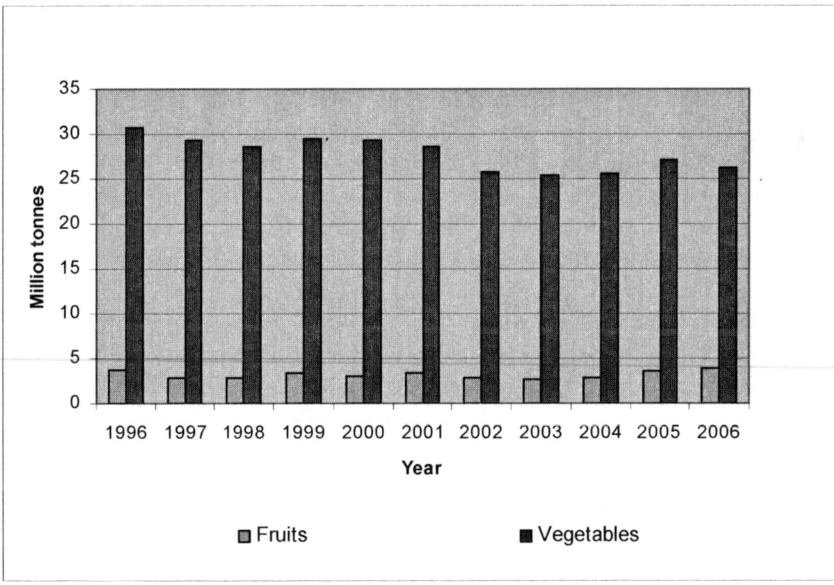

Figure 7.2 Production of fresh fruit and vegetables in the UK.
Source: DEFRA 2007, Chapter 5

The decline in domestic production is mirrored in data of planted area with the area under vegetables declining from 156,264 ha in 1993/94 to 119,351 ha in 2002/03 and under fruit from 37,339 ha in 1993/94 to 27,648 ha in 2002/03.

UK fruit and vegetable production (Figure 7.2) is nevertheless successful and competes well in some areas with the best in the world; for example, in protected tomatoes and root and green vegetables, soft fruit, quick frozen vegetables and added value prepared salads and other vegetables. The structure of the primary production sector is currently fragmented with some very large but also many small growers. In the past, the fragmentation and the segmentation of added value has meant that a consolidated sector view on priorities and policies has been difficult to obtain.

Globalisation of FFV Trade

Consumer spending in the convenience store sector is growing and fresh produce is set to play a key role in the battle for market share. IGD's 2005 report on convenience retailing states that 20p in every pound is spent on food and grocery in convenience stores in a market which is now worth £23.9 billion. According to a survey of 6,000 stores in the UK by the IGD, fruit and vegetable sales have almost doubled. Sales have grown from 2.3% in 2003 to 4.1% in 2005. FFV is growing significantly in terms of sales contribution. The forecourt area has also seen significant change. Many stores have seen strong growth, with 18.8% of forecourts now stocking fresh produce. Fresh fruit and vegetables accounts for 61.3% of all sales, and this sector has grown by 1.2% at current prices in 2000, primarily as a result of increased sales of fresh fruit and fresh green vegetables (UK Food Market Review, 2001). Trade liberalisation and advances in post harvest technology and long distance chains have driven rapid increases in trade in fresh produce. Over recent years, a process of fragmentation and segmentation is occurring amongst the UK consumers (Barrett et al., 1999), who tend to give more emphasis to aspects of quality and convenience than to price and quantity. Further there is an increasing demand for healthy foods and foods from market 'niches' often reflecting ethnic variety and traditions.

To meet the growing consumer demands for FFV in the western world; international trade of FFV is increasing in scale and variety. This is a trend that has been encouraged by a liberalising international and national regulatory framework associated with GATT/WTO, IMF and World Bank policies, and has been further facilitated by considerable improvements in communications and packaging technologies (Barrett et al., 1999). FFV exports from the developing world, has become a major growth sector in international trade (Friedland, 1994; Jaffe, 1995; Thrupp, 1995). At the same time agricultural networks have become increasingly global (Bonnano et al., 1994; Friedland, 1994).

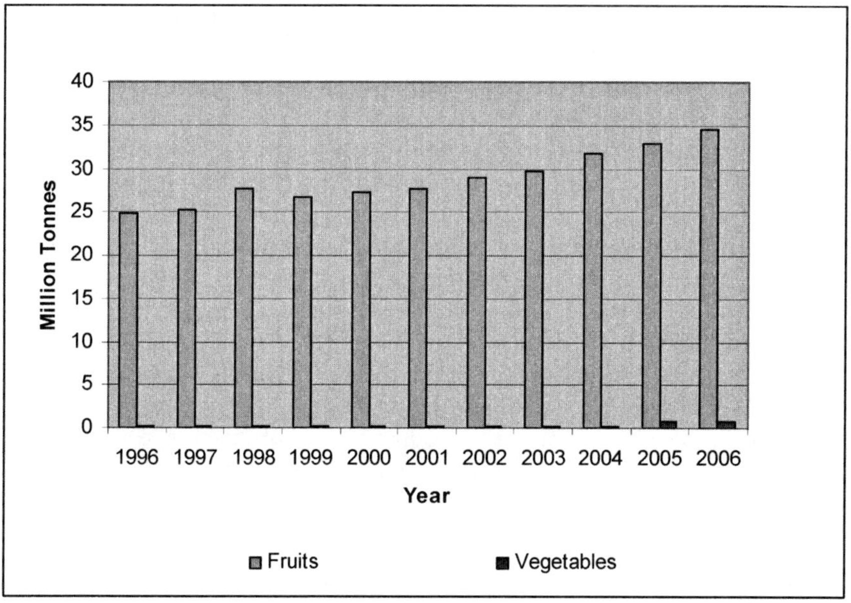

Figure 7.3 Fresh fruit and vegetables imports in the UK.
Source: DEFRA 2007, Chapter 5

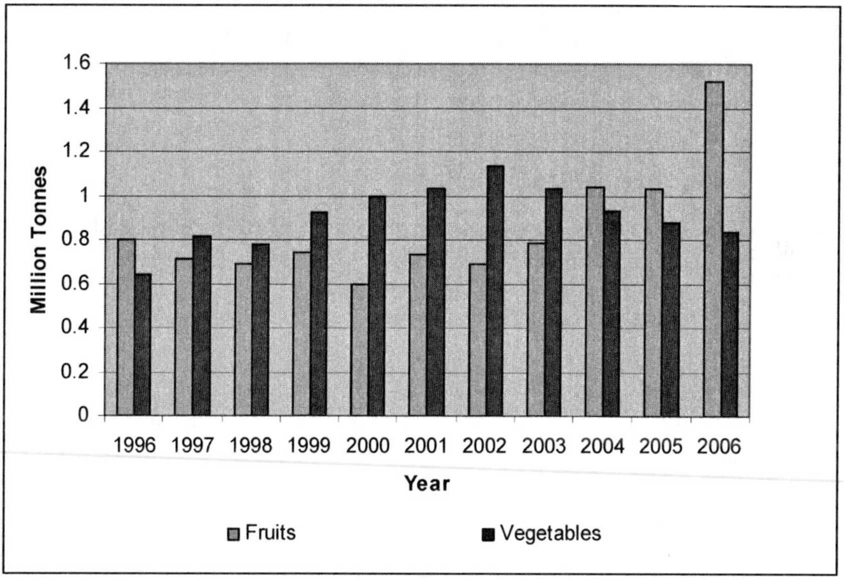

Figure 7.4 Fresh fruit and vegetables exports from the UK.
Source: DEFRA 2007, Chapter 5

This growth in demand is retailer-led, with retailers, increasingly adopting a global sourcing policy to satisfy these new demands (Barrett et al., 1999).

With more emphasis given to consumption of fruit and vegetables as part of a healthy diet, and the importance of a varied and year-round supply of high-quality fruit and vegetables for enhancing the image and competitiveness of supermarkets, demand for imported fruit and vegetables in Europe is substantial and likely to increase. Many non-EU exporting countries have responded to this demand due to the relatively high returns per volume for horticultural crops compared to other agricultural exports, seasonal and climatic advantages, lower labour costs, and promotion and support for export horticulture from international aid agencies. Labour intensity is high, and an estimated 45 million people depend on export horticulture for their livelihoods in African, Caribbean and Pacific (ACP) countries. The growing emphasis on quality standards and public concern about food safety in the developed world have led both governments and retailers to set increasingly high standards on production and processing methods, and these are putting increasing pressures on suppliers. The European Union (EU) pesticide legislation has contributed to this trend towards increasingly stringent standards, and has generated particular concerns amongst those involved in the fresh produce industry.

Implications of EU Legislation in the FFV Sector

There are two main and interlinked EU legislative processes associated with pesticide use which are affecting growers exporting fruits and vegetables to the EU: the Maximum Residue Level (MRL) Harmonisation Programme and the Pesticide Approvals Review Programme.

MRL Harmonisation Programme

Since 1993 the EU has been implementing a programme to establish harmonised maximum residue levels (MRLs) which restrict levels of pesticide residues in foodstuffs sold in Europe. MRLs for foodstuffs are established both nationally and internationally with the key objectives of:

(a) controlling the correct use of pesticides in terms of the registered use;
(b) permitting the free circulation of food commodities that have been treated with approved pesticides and comply with the established MRLs; and
(c) minimising the exposure of consumers to harmful or unnecessary intake of pesticide residues.

The stated aims of the EU harmonisation programme are to iron out current inconsistencies in national MRLs in the different member states, by establishing common and obligatory MRLs for all active ingredients approved for use within the EU, based on systematic and scientific procedures. The relevant EU Directives establish obligatory MRLs for specific crop/active ingredient combinations where sufficient data is available, and also specify what data is required to establish an MRL where data are not currently available. Where there is insufficient data, the EU has left the MRL position as an 'open position' for a limited period of time. During this period, data collected and analysed according to defined procedures can be submitted to the EU to defend the establishment of an MRL, which is usually done by agrochemical companies, but can also be done by other parties. If the period expires and no acceptable data has been received, then the MRL is set at the limit of determination (LOD), i.e. analytical zero.

Pesticide Approvals Review Programme

This programme aims to systematically review the registration of the 823 active ingredients approved for use within the EU prior to 25 July 1993. As with the MRL harmonisation programme, the continued registration of a pesticide depends on appropriate data being generated and submitted by interested parties, again usually agrochemical companies. This is indicative of the fact that, in practice, only those active ingredients which are commercially important are likely to remain registered for use.

Consequences of the Regulation

It is clear that the two programmes together have led to:

(i) withdrawal of approximately 350 of the 823 active ingredients from the approved list (although producers outside of the EU may be able to secure import tolerances for some of the 350);
(ii) a substantial increase in the number of crop/active ingredient combinations for which MRLs will be set at LOD.

These programmes continue to cause problems for EU growers and the impact on growers exporting from non-EU countries to the EU is often seen to be particularly harsh.

Growers of tropical, sub-tropical and out-of-season fruit and vegetables are being particularly hard hit by the legislation because a disproportionately high number of relevant MRLs are set at LOD, and many of the most widely used active ingredients are likely to be phased out through the approvals review programme. This situation has arisen because, first, agrochemical companies are not likely to want to invest in generating and collating datasets to defend registration of, or set MRLs for, older, out of- patent pesticides; yet these pesticides also tend to be cheaper and more widely available, and hence widely used, in developing countries. Second, agrochemical companies have in general only been interested in generating data for establishment of MRLs for crops they classify as 'major crops' i.e. crops of major economic significance, for example bananas and citrus fruits. In the UK, the fresh produce industry has worked with the government to generate data for establishment of MRLs for key crop/active ingredient combinations which were not being defended by agrochemical companies.

While the two programmes could potentially benefit exporting countries through encouraging more rational use of pesticides, which in turn could lead to health, environmental and sometimes economic benefits; the current process of implementation is such that these benefits are not easily realised. The communication of the legislation and its implications has been poor, as a result of which exporting countries have not had time to respond by defending essential MRLs or by making alternative pest control measures available to their growers.

European markets are currently not willing to lower cosmetic and other quality standards, so growers cannot risk anything but very low levels of pest and disease infestation. As a result, growers and exporters especially from the developing countries are likely to face increased costs of production at least in the short run, due to the reduced options for pest control, making export production even more risky. Further, the increasing demand from importers for traceability systems allow any irregularities to be traced to the 'offending' producer. These factors are likely to have a negative impact in the affected exporting countries, in particular. There is a risk that smaller and less well organised export industries may be abandoned by EU importers because they are not able to provide appropriate pest management/IPM training to growers, set up robust traceability systems, or to conduct their own trials on new pesticides to speed up the process of national registration of EU-approved pesticides. Small-scale growers, especially independent smallholders, may be abandoned by exporters, because exporters may consider the costs of training and running traceability systems for a large number of dispersed, small production units, outweigh the benefits of sourcing from smallholders. Even if smallholders still have the opportunity to supply exporters, they may find it difficult to continue exporting due to the higher cost of EU-approved pesticides, extra costs passed down by the exporter, and/or unacceptable increases in labour requirements for implementing non-chemical pest control methods.

ROLE OF RETAILERS IN FFV SUPPLY CHAIN

Retailer Driven Chains

For many FFV producers and farmers, retailers have become their only possible outlet. For fear of loosing their business, many farmers and producers accept some of the low prices offered by large retailers and sell with low or no profit margins. In contrast, retailers often take very high margins on the fresh fruit and vegetable products they sell (see Figure 7.8 and the section on 'Impact of Retail Governance on FFV Production in the Developing Countries' later in this chapter).

Figure 7.5 shows the retailers' role of 'gatekeeper' at the narrowest point of the 'hourglass' or 'bottleneck' between farmers and consumers. This has led to a wave of civil society and regulatory scrutiny of this sector in recent years. This is partly driven by contestations around the farm-retail price gap, and different levels of alleged profitability between the farming and retail industries.

In the UK, the total profit of all 230,000 farms has been roughly equivalent to the profit of just six supermarket chains in the recent years. The top five retailers have around 70% of the grocery market in the UK. The average return to capital in the UK is around 10–15% in the entire retailing sector compared to 0.5% in the UK agriculture (Qualmam, 2001).

The retail sector has concentrated rapidly, with the top 30 retailers accounting for 33% of global sales in 2003 compared to 29% in 1999. The buying power of the retailers in a number of countries is threatening high ranking national supermarket players. European retailers also pool their buying power together into large buyer alliances such as European Marketing Distribution (EMD) and Associated Marketing Services (AMS), which raises buyer concentration to a higher level (the narrowest part in Figure 7.5; Dobson Consulting, 1999; Dobson et al., 2003).

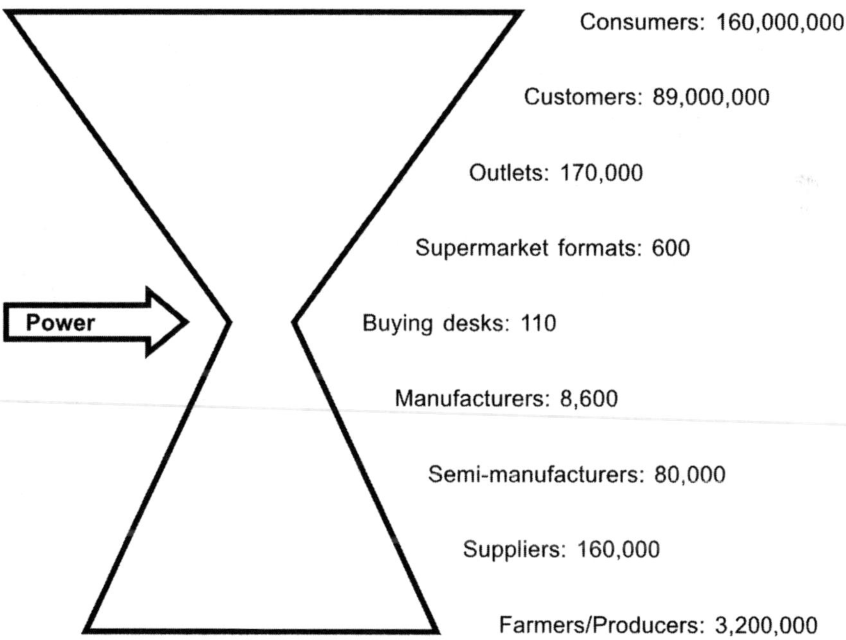

Figure 7.5 The food supply chain 'bottleneck' in Europe. Source: Adapted from Grievink (2003).

The FFV sector is at the sharp end of this competitive approach. Governance of the chain resides at the retail end. In the FFV sector, uniformity and high quality are necessary for further processing, branding and large-scale buying by food service and retailers. To ensure this, ways of preserving traceability and identity are needed, buyer-driven chains have therefore evolved in this sector (Gereffi, 1994). These are more regulated and characterised by high levels of governance and long-term vertical co-ordination between the producers, supplier-integrators, processors and retailers. The resulting chains have barriers to entry such as voluntary standards, codes and benchmarks.

The two main factors driving the restructuring of the FFV sector and the increasing role of supermarkets in explicit co-ordination of the chain can be attributed to both the competitive strategies of the supermarkets around product differentiation, and the need to control risk in the face of a more complex regulatory and consumer environment.

For the UK supermarkets, FFV is a key (entry) item in the competition for market share in food sales. It is not only profitable (as it has some of the highest profit margins per square metre of shelf space of any product category in the store rivalled only by wine and chilled food (see for example Garcia and Poole, 2002); but also one of the few categories of products that further influences consumer's choice of stores (Burch and Goss, 1999). Hence the FFV sector holds a disproportionate element in retailers' competitive strategies.

Retailers have tended to narrow their fresh produce supply base, which is driving consolidation at all levels of the chain. Preferred suppliers or 'category managers' are often integrated with grower-packers providing year round supply, through alliances with overseas suppliers. Mack Multiples, for example sells £270 million of fresh fruits and vegetables to UK retailers from over sixty countries.

> . . . the majority of whole fruits, specifically in the south, come through Mack Multiples. . . . They (retailers) will give us a spec. and they will say, you can use these three or four suppliers and that's the product, these are the brands . . . (MACK-UK FFV Supplier).

Fresh vegetable production and packing in the UK has a trend towards very narrow specialisation in response to supermarket, processor and caterer requirements for category management and traceability. An example of a specialist grower–packer, is Geest, with 2002 sales of £762 million. Geest is very active in the UK convenience/prepared salad market with a 40% share.

The level of private sector governance of the FFV sector is high especially by multiple retailers. As the fresh produce chain is relatively short, primary producers get involved in standards and due diligence issues at an early stage. Price pressure is very important, however, and the brunt is felt by labour. UK horticulture is sustained by a casual labour force of migrant and often undocumented workers. Half of the 72,000 people employed for planting, harvesting and packing in the UK food industry are supplied by 'gangmasters'. They provide the industry with a flexible workforce to meet the seasonal demands of planting, harvesting and packing crops and the market demands of fluctuating daily and seasonal retail requirements.

> . . . we employ a lot of East European labour and we also use labour providers. That's the polite word for 'gangmasters'. We are trying to be a little bit more sophisticated about it, seeing as it is so much in the public eye. . . . I have no problem getting East European labour, and it is all legal. As far as the labour providers, we've had problems there in trying to get them to be legal. And in actual fact, we are currently going through the process now. We've actually weeded quite a lot out over the last year or two, because they seem to be getting more and more of the illegal people, and we are sorting that out . . . (UK salad crop grower)

As competing interests from consumer lobbies and regulatory bodies have grown, retailers have been skilful in accommodating a wider range of the overall political shifts into their approach to promote their wellbeing. Corporate retailers at the EU level now operate both independently and jointly through organisations like Euro Commerce (Flynn, et al., 2004). In the UK, retailers have to position themselves continuously and carefully as custodians of the consumer, distinguishing themselves from both the producer and food manufacturing interests. As the increasingly integrated European food market continues to show major food safety problems, the retailers have taken the opportunity to further embed retailer-led FFV supply chain management.

> We have given them (retailers) the power'. (REO—Veiling-Belgian Vegetable Auction body)

> . . . what you have to do in retail is to be as close as you possibly can to what your customers actually want. At the end of the day we exist to meet the needs of our retail customers, . . . everything is largely governed by what the customer wants and what the sales of a particular line are . . . (Retailer)

As the direct interface between the consumers and the food industry, retailers are likely to remain the main force in setting the agenda for the FFV food supply chain. Retailers have the commercial power to force business process change further down the supply chain.

> . . . in terms of the products that we want and the standards that we want to meet, then obviously we have a fair degree of influence in what our supply base actually does, even for branded lines, . . . And for own label we can direct whatever standards we actually want. Down on the ethical trading front, which is more difficult, we can in theory . . . theoretically we can specify whatever we want wherever we want it . . . (Retailer)

One example of this in practice is the case of pesticides. Retailers are constantly seeking to reduce pesticide residues on the fruit and vegetable products sold in their stores and have required that the level of residues should be below what is required by the EU regulatory standards. Some retailers have a long-term objective of making all the produce they sell free from pesticide residues. It is not entirely clear how this will be reconciled with the demands for produce to be free of pest damage and to have a long shelf life.

Trends Affecting the Retailers

Among the many tools available to retailers, private FFV labels can be viewed as one of the most effective instruments for actively securing customer loyalty to a store, as labels help ensure the same product cannot be available in any other store in the local market. In implementing the private label strategy, retailers seek dual objectives: lowering retail price and enhancing product value. Retailer brands offer consumers products perceived to be of higher quality than the standard product at prices below recognised leading brand products of similar quality. Retailers across Europe have implemented private label strategies to cater to particular consumer demands, and there has been a trend to develop high-quality, differentiated private label products. The retail share of private labels among food products is high in many European countries, especially the UK where over 45% of volume and value share of retail food consumption is private label.

Demand influenced changes in retail strategy have implications for the way retailers choose suppliers. In deciding to implement a private label strategy, retailers consider a set of criteria when selecting suppliers and the type of product for branding. Research by Skytte & Blunch (2001) show, in addition to traditional factors like price, quality, and the ability to supply required volume, the ability to trace back products and the willingness of suppliers to engage in long-term relationships with retailers are important selection criteria. The prominence of private labels has affected this shift.

In response to increasing consumer demand for safety, quality, and convenience in food, retailers have adopted more proactive marketing strategies, where they try to achieve customer loyalty not only by improving service, location, and store layout but also by having more influence on the overall value creation process in the food chain.

In the FFV sector, retailer private label strategies are largely geared to provide assurances regarding sensory and aesthetic attributes and the levels of chemical residues in products. Retailer brands for produce are generally associated with 'integrated farming', which consumers have associated with a lower use of chemicals, and, to a lesser degree, better land stewardship. In addition, private labels are also required to meet the necessary grades specified by retailers with regard to sugar content, firmness, size, and other product characteristics. Sensory attributes, much valued by consumers, are difficult for retailers to guarantee and measure and the implementation of control and the monitoring of such characteristics can be costly. However, cooperation between suppliers and retailers can be mutually beneficial and tends to reduce the quality assurance costs for retailers (Brousseau and Codron, 1998). Given the risks and uncertainties associated with growing and marketing produce, suppliers on the other hand, appreciate the guarantee of an outlet provided under the cooperation with retailers.

The retail branding scheme practiced in the FFV sector is mainly of the substitution type, where the retailer draws up production standards for suppliers.

> They give specifications in terms of how they want the crop grown and then . . . well, our customer will give us the specification, which happens to be, as far as Marks & Spencer is concerned it's Geest and G's marketing. So they will receive whatever it is that they would receive in that area from Marks & Spencer's, they will then tell us. (UK salad crop grower)

The farming practices prescribed are not always precise, and sometimes it may be necessary to ascertain whether the suppliers meet the necessary standards. Production practices can be measured by maintaining a register of chemical treatments, planting dates and growth measurements, soil analysis results, and other practices. However, suppliers may be granted some leeway, for instance, if chemical treatments are employed when pest populations exceed a certain threshold. To avoid this contingency resulting in an erosion of consumer confidence, retailers may employ a set of clear standard operating rules and ensure that suppliers are knowledgeable about the procedures to be adopted. A good example of a similar case was highlighted by one of the UK growers interviewed.

> . . . as far as we are concerned, the people who are supplying us, the stuff during the winter, are supplying to the same level and standard that we are. We know what they are entitled to use, we know where we get into problems is they are allowed to use certain chemicals and we are not.

> And there is not a lot you can do about that. We accept that there is a difference. They are not breaking the law. (UK salad crop grower)

A third party may be employed to ensure that suppliers adhere to the standard. This produce scheme does not lead to the type of extensive cooperation that exists when a retail brand product is produced. However, retailers may also employ more complex schemes where producers and retailers mutually set standards with the view of adopting measures to enhance environmental quality as well as the safety and sensory attributes of products.

> . . . we are not (audited by each customer), because . . . and this is where the game starts to get a bit interesting in that if you are an M&S supplier and people know you are, then they haven't got to worry too much. (UK salad crop grower)

Such arrangements require confidence and long-term relationships between the parties involved and may result in a well-differentiated product on the retail shelf (Codron et al., 2002).

The major retailers continue to consolidate their share of the UK market through the opening of new store formats especially in the convenience sector. This will further increase the pressure retailers put on the suppliers to increase efficiency. Retailers also aim to consolidate the number of suppliers they use.

> I think inevitably you will see consolidation in the supply bases as people pursue efficiencies in terms of costs. (Retailer)

In the supply networks, globalisation continues in terms of international retail networks. These are now managed often on a collaborative basis across both countries and continents. In search of greater efficiency, retailers are looking for stable and predictable supply chains as it enables them to drive cost out of the system. Marketing initiatives such as consistent everyday low pricing are also driving the need to have stability in the cost of goods. This drives different kinds of commercial relationships with suppliers.

Despite the drive for consistency and standardisation this also has to cope with the need for more differentiation of product. The rate at which consumers' needs are changing is seen as accelerating and creating more flexibility and innovation in the supply chain. This means demand is becoming less homogenous and more segmented as a result of changing lifestyles, household structures and demographics. This in turn creates the need for a wider range of product quality, price and food solutions.

The supply chain literature suggests the existence of three models between the retailers and supplier relationship.

a) A partially vertically integrated supply chain, where there is a level of retailer ownership of processors but not farms—*Integration*
b) A close and long term commercial relationship with processor—*Partnership*
c) A short term arrangement, with the suppliers—*Trading*

There has been a growth in the partnership model. This includes true collaborative partnership arrangements but also encompasses pragmatic partnerships which are not necessarily long term, but are a simple way to achieve short term needs. Both, however, are driven by the need for consistency, predictability and lower prices all of which are easier to deliver within a partnership framework.

Each retailer uses a combination of these models to varying degrees. Even where there is integration, this does not represent the totality of trade in a particular sector, and partnerships are often loose groupings with relatively weak formal agreements. Growth in the partnership model is a key area of opportunity for those suppliers and producers capable of delivering the requisite goods. Most retailers see further growth in this area as a route to a more efficient supply chain.

Retailers' rationalisation of their supply base and more international competition has led to FFV food processors consolidating through merger or acquisition. Retailers are demanding higher technical standards from their processors and producers and traceability of supply is gaining importance. For example, Wal-Mart's North American Pallet, Carton, and Case Initiative (NAPCCI) and its Radio Frequency Identification (RFID) tracking initiative seeks to supplant generic barcodes with supply chain identifiers that will result in a unique number on each pallet, carton, and case. The initiative has put suppliers into a more dependent position, where they are attempting to understand technologies that are largely new to their supply chains in order to remain compliant.

There has been an associated proliferation of private standards often as part of retailer Corporate Social responsibility (CSR) or risk management initiatives. Voluntary standards and associated codes and certification schemes are emblematic of globalisation, linked as they are to the growth of international supply chains, a reduced role for state organisations and recasting of regulatory systems and voluntary self-regulation (Jenkins, 2001).

One sign of the importance attached to sourcing was the 1999 establishment of the Euro Retailer Produce Working Group (EUREP) guidelines for Good Agricultural Practice (GAP). The GAP protocol became the industry standard against which national assurance schemes are benchmarked. Where there is no equivalent national scheme, producers are inspected against GAP by a EUREP accredited verification body. Central to GAP is a commitment to adopt Integrated Crop Management (ICM) practices.

DEVELOPMENT OF EUREPGAP PROGRAMME FOR FRESH FRUIT AND VEGETABLES

What is EUREPGAP?

EUREPGAP started in 1997 as an initiative of retailers belonging to the Euro-Retailer Produce Working Group (EUREP). It has subsequently evolved into an 'equal partnership of agricultural producers and their retail customers'. The mission being to develop widely accepted standards and procedures for the global certification of Good Agricultural Practices (GAP).

Technically EUREPGAP is a set of normative documents suitable to be accredited to internationally recognised certification criteria such as ISO Guide 65. Representatives from around the globe and all stages of the food chain have been involved in the development of these documents. In addition the views from stakeholders outside the industry including consumer and environmental organisations and governments have helped shape the protocols. This wide consultation has produced a robust and challenging but nonetheless achievable private-based protocol which farmers around the world can use to demonstrate compliance with GAP. It is possible for producer organisations to seek an independent and transparent recognition of equivalence with the EUREPGAP standards and procedures through a benchmarking system thereby facilitating global trade and aiding the harmonisation of technical criteria.

EUREPGAP members include retailers, producers/farmers and associate members from the input and service side of agriculture. Governance is by sector specific EUREPGAP Steering Committees which are chaired by an independent Chairperson. Both the standard and the certification system is approved by the Technical and Standards Committees working in each product sector. These committees have 50% retailer and 50% producer representation creating what is seen as an 'effective and efficient partnership in the supply chain'. The work of the Committees is supported by FoodPLUS a non-profit limited company based in Cologne, Germany.

Factors Leading to the Development of EUREPGAP/GlobalGAP

EUREPGAP was driven by the retailers desire to reassure consumers. Following food safety scares such as BSE, pesticide concerns and the rapid introduction of GM foods consumers throughout the world were asking how food is produced; and they needed reassuring that it is both safe and sustainable. Food safety is a global issue and transcends international boundaries. Many of the EUREPGAP leading members are global players in the retail industry and obtain food products from around the world. For these reasons a need arose for a commonly recognised and applied reference standard of Good Agricultural Practice which has at its centre a consumer assurance focus.

Goals of EUREPGAP/GlobalGAP

By adhering to good agricultural practices risks in intensive FFV production is reduced. EUREPGAP provides the tools to objectively verify best practice in a systematic and consistent way throughout the world. This is achieved through the protocol and compliance criteria. There are about 214 control points divided into 49 major musts, 99 minor musts and 66 recommended, a diagrammatic representation is given in Figure 7.6. EUREPGAP's scope is primarily concerned with practices on the farm, once the product leaves the farm they come under the control of other Codes of Conduct and certification schemes relevant to food packing and processing. That way the whole chain is assured right through to the supermarket shelf.

Another key goal is to provide a forum for continuous improvement. The technical and standards committees, consisting of producer and retail members, have a formal agenda to review emerging issues and carry-out risk assessments. This is a private but arguably rigorous process, following the principles of HACCP, and involves experts in their field leading to revised versions of the protocol.

In 2007, EurepGAP was renamed GlobalGAP, representing the enhanced global ambitions of the retailer-led protocol. This has also involved a process of evolution of the scheme from one initially based upon a broad range of sustainability issues towards a protocol which is now more focused on food safety and hygiene issues (see Van Der Grijp, 2008). This reinforces the rationalisation of production, record keeping and traceability requirements. A major reason for this shift in focus has been the higher priorities for food safety at the EU and member state level (as outlined in Chapters 5 and 6 of this volume). Membership of GlobalGAP has been increasing as more retailers see the non-competitive advantages of dealing with the EU food law through setting their own agreed standards for food safety. This is a clear example of how the hybrid—both public and private—EU model of regulation has been working.

Other Competitive Strategies Adopted by Retailers

Several supermarkets are trying to generate more competitive advantage through superior environmental performance over and above the EUREPGAP/GlobalGAP protocol. As one leading retailer argued:

> . . . the main thing with retailing, because selling products and anything can be copied, then the real bit of advantage is to do whatever it is first. Industry leadership means lead first to do the right thing, which

means speed of action and second-guessing what your competitors are going to do on a whole range of different issues; making sure you don't get wrong footed . . . (Retailer)

As well as being a part of EUREPGAP, Tesco, for example runs its own assurance scheme, Nature's Choice, which is 'significantly broader and deeper than EUREP'. This food labelling scheme, is essentially a code of practice and Tesco has adopted a policy that they would only accept produce accredited with the Nature's Choice label. Through this scheme, accredited growers are audited against seven criteria, one of which is that growers have to demonstrate that they are maintaining and enhancing the nature conservation and landscape values of their properties. Nature's Choice is underpinned by a 'green' philosophy of stewardship and essentially aims to combine production efficiency and conservation values through the Code of Practice.

To achieve accreditation under Nature's Choice, a policy statement (effectively an action plan) needs to be developed for each of the seven elements. Grower adoption of the Code of Practice must be demonstrated beyond a six-month period before Nature's Choice certificates are issued. The code

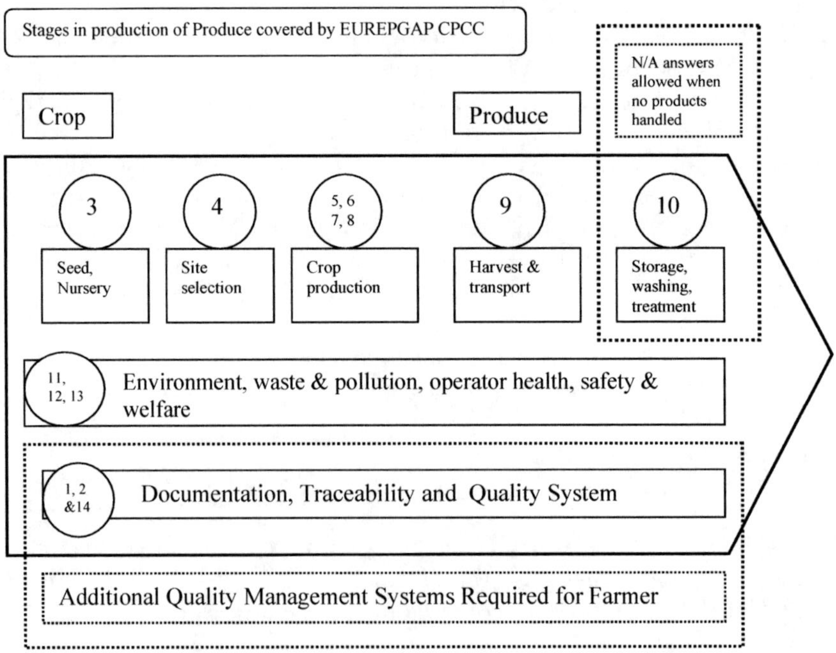

Figure 7.6 EUREPGAP's control points and compliance criteria for fresh fruits and vegetables. Source: Control points and compliance criteria, Fruit and vegetables version 2 2004. www.eurep.org

of practice includes guidelines on the use of chemical inputs, energy and water efficiency, worker health and safety, and wildlife and landscape conservation. At least 95% of Tesco's fresh produce sourced in the UK is now certified under the scheme and the standards are being introduced to suppliers worldwide.

Sainsbury's, developed a policy on the sourcing of wild products, which seeks to ensure that threatened species and habitats are not harmed, for example, shells, moss, crocodile meat, plant bulbs and sea food (based on the CITES Convention and consumer concerns). It is also working with suppliers on an initiative that encourages farm- level biodiversity action plans. Views were expressed by various actors in the supply chain, as is evident from the following excerpts:

> . . . we have these games that go on, so. It's a fiercely competitive market at the present time and that can get a little bit excited. (Retailer)

> . . . in terms of the salt-reduction program, Tesco's already announced they're doing this traffic light system on products, and that's obviously jumping ahead of what the FSA are wanting to do. They (FSA) want to develop it in conjunction with everybody so everybody's singing off the hymn sheet. (Retailer)

> . . . that's (self-regulation) something that we are seeing an advantage to, to our competitors. Everybody has got the same produce so in some ways we have to, it has to be competitive with the competitors, and also because it's always important to look a little bit ahead to . . . (Vegetable Auction body)

REGIONAL AND OTHER KEY ASSURANCE SYSTEMS

The Flandaria Label

In 1995, the Belgian auctions introduced the Flandria quality label. Flandria label is recognised across most European countries for excellent quality, which is cultivated by family businesses in an environmental friendly way. The tomato was the first vegetable sold under the Flandria quality label. Currently, more than fifty vegetables bear the Flandria quality label.

The cultivation of Flandria products is subject to strict conditions for production. In addition, an ecological balance is established with the use of a balanced set of natural cultivation measures. Minimum requirements for Flandria products are set for the varieties used (very important for taste, shelf life, etc.), shape, grading, ripeness, the firmness, and the lack of foreign substances.

In order to meet the requirements of the people in the trade and of the government, the auctions 'Mechelse Veilingen' and 'Veiling Hoogstraten' have taken the decision to extend the content of the quality label Flandria by adding the FlandriaGap Specifications. As a result of these specifications, the strict standards for hygiene, environmental friendly planting and sustainable horticulture, that apply to Flandria, are now set even higher.

FlandariaGap

FlandriaGap is a new specification for the production of Flandria produce. The Flandria label, though will continue to exist, but at the auctions 'Mechelse Veilingen' and 'Veiling Hoogstraten' it is combined with new specifications. The FlandriaGap specifications, encompasses the already stringent standards for hygiene, environmentally-friendly production methods and sustainable horticulture which apply to Flandria, but are more stringent. Extra attention is being paid to food safety and traceability, care for the environment and the workforce (accident procedures, safety, etc). FlandriaGap is an integrated system which combines quality and Good Agricultural Practice.

FlandriaGap has been introduced in anticipation of new legislation—self-assessment and duty to report—from the Federal Food Chain Safety Agency (Federaal Agentschap voor de Veiligheid van de Voedselketen [FAVV]). FlandriaGap is an alternative for existing and future specifications, such as HACCP, BRC, QS, EUREPGAP. FlandriaGap's real asset is its residue monitoring programme. Every year, approximately 14,000, mostly carefully directed samples are taken at the LAVA auctions, and this at the most critical points. In the case of most other specifications, this sampling is not carefully directed.

Hygiene is another strong criteria. Approximately 70 of the 148 inspection points within FlandriaGap relate to hygiene. Under Flandria, the grower had to achieve a score of 80% on the hygiene inspection points, regardless of the type of directive, whereas FlandriaGap comprises a number of compulsory hygiene directives. Another strength of FlandriaGap is that the emphasis is on verifying whether there effectively is compliance with the directives or not. Whereas the emphasis of EUREPGAP/GlobalGAP tends to be on registration.

Even if higher environmental standards can enhance brand reputation, retailers face another challenge getting the message across to consumers. As one of the major retailer states:

> The key, is to . . . develop tangible, quantifiable measures that assure customers that we are taking responsible decisions with our suppliers to protect and enhance the environment. This needs to be done in a way that customers can relate to easily. (Retailer)

In a culture of harsh retailer price competition, fuelled by over supply and governed by the power imbalances of market concentration at the retail level and fragmentation at the farmer level, retailers will inevitably pass on the added costs to the weakest link in the supply chain-and that is the farmers. The following quote highlights the issue.

> When they (retailers) have a problem, instead of trying to find a fundamental solution for their problem, they try to find a solution which should be placed, or the effort should come always from the grower. (Vegetable Auction body)

Some producers are calling for mechanisms to allow more transparent reciprocal auditing. This would enable them to check how their produce is being labelled and marketed. Such measures would help reassure farmers that food assurance schemes are legitimate commitments.

> . . . why should we risk taking the freedom of a supplier to contract with other people if there's no need for us to do that. In a way, it would look improper to do that. . . . So we don't put any restrictions on any of our suppliers as to who else they trade with. We wouldn't do that. Philosophically it's not something we would do.' (Retailer)

The Global Food Safety Initiative (GFSI)

In 2000, a group of international retailer CEOs identified the need to enhance food safety, ensure consumer protection, strengthen consumer confidence, to set requirements for food safety schemes and to improve cost efficiency throughout the food supply chain. Following their lead, the Global Food Safety Initiative (GFSI) was launched. The initiative is facilitated by CIES and was launched in the aftermath of the Dioxin Crisis of 1999. In its origins, GFSI is a retailer-led initiative, but manufacturers and other stakeholders are wholeheartedly invited to participate in GFSI projects. One of the key projects of the Global Food Safety Initiative is to implement a scheme to benchmark food safety management standards world-wide. Retailers accept certificates based on standards in order to be able to make an assessment of their suppliers of private label products and fresh produce (fruits, vegetables and meat), to ensure that production is carried out in a safe manner. There are many of these standards and the plethora of criteria used for audits means that suppliers with many customers are audited many times per year, at a high cost and with little added-benefit. GFSI has issued a series of Guidance documents containing commonly agreed criteria for food safety standards, against which any food safety standard can be benchmarked. GFSI does not undertake any accreditation or certification activities but encourages instead the use of third-party audits against benchmarked standards, with the goal of enabling suppliers to work more effectively through less audits and reducing travel costs for retailers so that resources can be redirected to continually ensure the quality of food produced and sold world-wide.

The mission of GFSI is to strengthen consumer confidence in the food they buy in retail outlets. GFSI aims to:

- implement a scheme to benchmark food safety standards (for private label products) world-wide;
- facilitate mutual recognition between standard owners; and
- ensure world-wide integrity in the quality and the accreditation of food safety auditors.

Pesticides Initiative Programme (PIP)

The sector of fresh fruit and vegetable exports from Africa-Caribbean-Pacific (ACP) countries to the European Union is faced with serious difficulties that stem from the harmonisation of European regulations on pesticide residues under way and the growing demands of European distributors in terms of the quality and safety of the products. It is seen as imperative that fresh fruit and vegetable producers and exporters from ACP countries make their products comply with these regulatory and commercial requirements as soon as possible. If they fail to do so, they are in danger of losing their market shares in the EU, which would threaten an important source of earnings for the ACP countries and the jobs of a large number of those employed in the sector.

The Pesticides Initiative Programme (PIP) responds to applications from private companies in the ACP fresh fruit and vegetable export sector to the European Union. They are confronted with strengthening of European buyers' requirements in terms of food safety (pesticide residues) and traceability. The European Commission and the ACP Group of States placed management of the PIP in the hands of the sector's inter-professional association. This decision demonstrates their will to enable the sector itself to define its own expectations and to focus the programme on the private sector.

The PIP was set up by the European Union at the request of the ACP Group of States in order to forestall any negative effects on the ACP export sector resulting from ongoing regulatory changes in the EU and ensure the sector's long-term sustainability. This is done mainly by helping enterprises revise their practices and implement food safety and traceability systems.

More generally, the PIP aims to contribute to the development of safe and sustainable trade between responsible partners and to:

- ensure that the specific needs of tropical crops (so-called minor crops—excluding bananas) are taken into account in the harmonisation of European Union regulations.

- provide support for building the local capacity necessary for the sustainable development of the sector by supporting so-called intermediary structures (professional organisations, local consultants and experts, laboratories, etc).

International Federation of Organic Agriculture Movements (IFOAM)

IFOAM was founded in 1972 and represents the complete spectrum of stakeholders in organic agriculture movements worldwide. IFOAM provides a market guarantee for integrity of organic claims. The Organic Guarantee System (OGS) unites the organic world through a common system of standards, verification, and market identity. It fosters equivalence among participating IFOAM accredited certifiers, paving the way for more orderly and reliable trade whilst acknowledging consumer trust in the organic 'brand'.

IFOAM aims to

- provide authoritative information about organic agriculture, promote its worldwide application and exchange the knowledge.
- represent the organic movement at international policy-making forums.
- make an agreed international guarantee of organic quality a reality.
- establish, maintain and regularly revise the international 'IFOAM Basic Standard'
- as well as the 'IFOAM Accreditation Criteria for Certifying Programs'.
- build a common agenda for all stakeholders in the organic sector.

IFOAM's Basic Standards and Accreditation Criteria (the IFOAM Norms) are the international guidelines for organic agriculture. Members build their own standards on the basis of the IBS and Accreditation Criteria, and they are also utilized as models for setting national and intergovernmental standards. Additionally the norms form the basis for harmonised inspection and certification of organic products by over thirty internationally recognized IFOAM accredited certification bodies (ACBs).

IFOAM Basic Standards are a keystone of the organic movement. They define the principles, recommendations, and required baseline standards that guide operators in producing their organic crops and maintaining organic integrity in the further handling and processing of organic commodities. IFOAM Accreditation Criteria are strictly based upon ISO sixty-five requirements, adapted to the specific needs of organic agriculture and manufacturing using a process-based approach. The criteria require that accredited certification bodies have effective quality systems. One might argue that this is bringing forth a much more precautionary approach to intensive fresh fruit and vegetable production through private sector means, and by establishing privatised and highly specific criteria of traceability and assurance.

Together with these requirements also come highly specific mechanisms for controlling the growth, shape, aesthetics and content of the crop, such that the producer is now almost completely controlled at a distance in terms of their production strategies. It is the post-farm sections of the supply chain-led especially by the globally sourcing retailers, who are now using the banner of customer assurance and quality in order to enhance their arms- length control over selected producers. From the producer perspective, acceptance and participation in these regulatory systems becomes the only option if they wish to maintain their markets.

Consumer Involvement and the Proliferation of Competitive Standards

A race to reach the top rung on the environmental performance ladder, requires not only a more equitable sharing of the costs along the supply chain, but also customers who are well informed about the food they eat. The danger of proliferating schemes by individual supermarkets, on top of the existing national and regional assurance programs and private umbrella initiatives such as EUREP, Flandaria, FlandariaGap, as outlined previously, is that the consumer will be left more confused than ever. Research undertaken by the National Consumer Council, shows that consumers are completely baffled by the range of schemes, logos and claims that surround the food industry. Consequently, they are just as likely to see such schemes as purely marketing hype.

Further, to the proliferation of such private schemes, some key definitions and regulations vary across Europe. For example one fruit and vegetable auctioneer stated:

> It would be better if there would be one standard, one European standard. That would be a combination of most of the systems, because that is a problem that there are so many systems that you need so much paperwork and then so much work also for the producer . . .

Another fruit and vegetable auctioneer stated:

> For example, the non-uniformisation in Europe of food safety residue harmonisation, in Europe started in 1991 to uniformise the pesticide regulations. They have not even achieved 15% of it, so there's the problem. And that's not only a problem for the farmers, there's a problem for the co-ops, and there's a problem for the retailers, too. The big discussion with the retailers now is . . . should there be compliance with country of production or country of destination? And then farmers will say, we can't comply with country of destination because we don't know where it will be heading to . . . (FFV auctioneer)

IMPACT OF RETAIL GOVERNANCE ON FFV PRODUCTION IN THE DEVELOPING COUNTRIES

Over recent years, sizeable FFV export-oriented horticulture industries have developed in some of the African countries for the European market. A similar niche is filled by Guatemala, Costa Rica, Columbia and Mexico for exports to the US (Thrupp, 1995). This is an area where the developing countries have been able to engage in global markets in the export of tropical crops to meet supermarkets' demand for consistent year round supplies of fresh produce.

Returns however are highly concentrated at the end of the chain in the importing countries. Dolan et al.,(1999) found that for mangetouts imports from Zimbabwe, 45% of retail value is retained by supermarkets to cover costs such as wastage and to ensure a profit margin while the producer share was only 12% (see Figure 7.7). The team found very similar figures for fresh vegetable exports from Kenya, with producer and supermarket shares of 14% and 46% respectively.

Supermarkets' standards focus on food quality and management of risk (safety and traceability). Pack-houses are required to have increasingly sophisticated equipment for tracing and labelling produce which increases the scale and cost of operations. There are also standards for environmental protection and welfare of workers even specifying the brand of fire extinguisher used in packing houses, but suppliers report that these are secondary requirements of supermarket buyers.[7] But the high capital requirements associated with meeting standards for due diligence may be a major barrier to market entry and driver of differentiation.

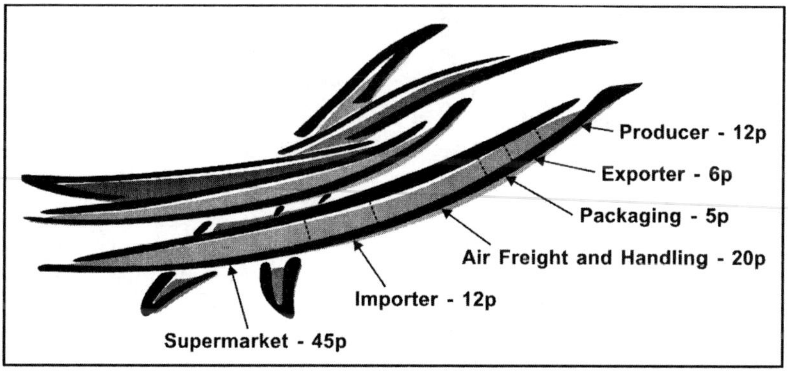

Figure 7.7 The retail value (£1.00) of mangetout exported to the UK from Zimbabwe.

Source: Dolan et al., 1999.

Quality standards may improve pesticide management and also indirectly drive quality competition in domestic markets. But as Friedburg (2003) states, 'Efforts to impose such standards on African horticultural exports thus respond more to the particular anxieties of corporate retail management rather than to the concerns of workers in the horticultural export industry themselves'. Based on research in the San Francisco valley of North-east Brazil, Cavalcanti and Marsden (2004) echo this perception of retailer imposed quality protocols as a 'Re-regulation of agriculture along private lines, around a particular construction of consumer interest which is having severe implications for farm structure' (see also Van der Grijp et al., 2005). Through their analysis at both the production and consumption ends of the FFV chain they conclude that private assurance schemes like EUREPGAP certainly provide selected groups of farmers with an impetus to change their production methods. However from a sustainability perspective these are a second-best option, their scope is limited, enforcement weak, mechanisms for meaningful participation and accountability may be insufficient; and they may exclude certain groups of farmers, thus further polarising farm structures in many exporting agri-food regions.

PRIVATE AND PUBLIC SYSTEMS OF REGULATION IN THE FFV SECTOR

A wide array of both public and private safety control systems has thus evolved for any FFV product being offered for sale to consumers in retail stores or food service operations (as detailed in Figure 7.8; Henson, 1997; Caswell, 1997; Caswell and Johnson, 1991). Public quality-control systems involve direct regulation in the form of standards, inspection, product testing, and other programmes attempt to ensure the quality of the product by specifying how it is produced and/or its final quality. Product liability involves punishing companies that produce products of insufficient quality through damage awards to those harmed by their actions. Direct regulation and product liability may complement or substitute for each other (or even conflict) in establishing incentives for companies to engage in effective quality control.

Private systems include self-regulation and various forms of certification by other parties. Self-regulation includes internal control systems that assure product quality, where the company sets, monitors, and self certifies the control parameters. It can take place at the level of the individual firm or be instituted by trade organisations that cover the predominance of market supply. Certification involves the setting of product quality standards and their monitoring and certification by parties outside the firm, for example customers, industry trade associations, or

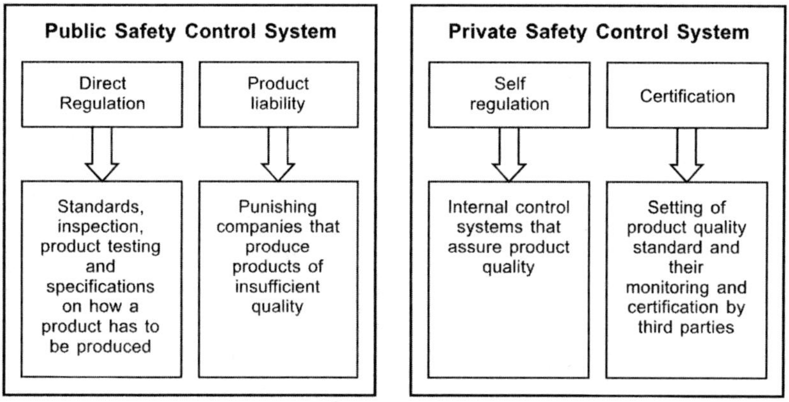

Figure 7.8 Food quality control systems.
Source: Adapted from Henson, 1997; Caswell, 1997.

bodies such as the International Organisation for Standardisation (ISO). Such certification may be voluntarily sought by the company or required by those with whom it does business. The relative importance of these public and private modes of food safety control will reflect, amongst other things, the nature of public regulation and the structure of the food supply chain. The product liability system for food products in the UK has hinged on the concept of 'due diligence'. Evidence that a company took all reasonable precautions and exercised all 'due diligence' to avoid commission of an offence provides a defence against liability. This public provision has motivated extensive retail-led private quality control activity amongst food companies that want to be able to prove they have exercised 'due diligence', based predominantly on third-party certification (Henson and Northen, 1998; Bredahl and Holleran, 1997; Zaibet and Bredahl, 1997).

The state as a regulator in food safety is far from new; while at the same time it is known that food safety has been a concern for both public and private interests, and that the distribution of responsibility among public institutions, manufacturers, distributors and individual consumers in securing safe food has changed historically. Shifts associated with the more recent development of 'the regulatory state' necessitates a change in governmental control, where traditional mechanisms of government tends to be replaced by newer mechanisms for example, privatization, contracting out and various means of standard setting linked to more or less independent agencies for monitoring and enforcement. These are examples of governing at-a-distance, often involving the 'self-regulation' or 'quasi- regulation' of businesses and consumers (Moran, 2002).

The regulatory state model has been widely criticised for its centrist conception of state power (Black, 2000; 2002). Private actors, like firms, industries, private associations and NGOs, regulate their own members, suppliers, costumers and internal affairs (Teubner, 1998; Black, 1996). The significance of this private governance will increase with ongoing organisational growth, mergers and acquisitions. This emerging tendency is often done by means of private contracts stating the proper expectations and responsibilities of the parties involved (Shearing, 1997). The way these contracts are formulated will depend largely on the international and commercially available voluntary standards. Such standards offer procedural norms based on 'best practice', third-party-based monitoring and auditing systems and procedures for the managing of deviations from norms (Brunsson & Jacobsson, 2000; Power, 1997; Scott, 2003).

It has been noted that the balance in the FFV sector has shifted from one set of private actors (producers) to another set (retailers). This phenomenon has been very obvious in the UK, where the big retailers have more or less taken over from farmers and manufacturers in taking the lead, both in terms of initiatives towards public authorities, in private regulatory efforts, and related to consumer trust. However in Norway, for instance, there has not been a parallel shift (Jacobsen & Kjærnes, 2003), with food manufacturers and farmer cooperatives playing a more proactive role. Hence it could be assumed that these shifts are strongly country and context specific.

Stigler (1971) noted that public regulations often reflect or have been 'captured' by private interests. Based on this perspective, according to Majone (1994): 'regulation is not instituted in the interest of the public at large or some sub-class of the public, but is acquired by an industry and designed and operated primarily for its benefit'.

In the case of the FFV sector we see here a direct relationship between the proliferation of quality standards and the benefits in terms of value-capture by the retailers.

One of the retailers interviewed had the following view:

> I think the driving force has to be two things. A. is product safety and the fact that obviously we have to show due diligence, and B. obviously to protect the brand image, which is probably even more important nowadays . . .

A tension exists however concerning the need for more uniformity and consistency in standards setting; and the need for state based coordination.

> . . . we want to have it as uniform, and then our lawmakers have to provide the law for that. So we have that for two things. We have it

> for the integrated fruit production, on the one hand, and we have it also for the leafy vegetables under glass house. (FFV auctioneer)

> . . . by law it is required to have a pre-harvest residue analysis. So we have a pre-harvest residue analysis. Because 80% of the lettuce is sold through producers' organisations and is controlled, and was controlled on voluntary basis, but 20% was not controlled and there we were afraid. People who were not in order for selling through the organised markets went to the non-organised markets, with a product which is poor in quality or which had too high a residue content. If in Germany they write in the paper that the Belgian salad or Belgian lettuce has a high content in the residue our sales drop, so we want to make sure that everybody is following the same standards and that's why we want the government to step in and to make it a governmental regulation, a regulation for everybody. (FFV auctioneer)

The increased reliance on the part of the State on more indicative instruments of regulation, 'like guidance, circulars deployed with the intention of shaping the behaviour of those to whom they are directed' (Scott, 2002), without having to use laws and direct commands means that this allows for a reduction or an escape for some of the procedural costs involved. This points to a process whereby norms and standards are (still) decided in a public setting, but where the responsibility of market actors has become more emphasised, more visible and cost effective. Some of the private sector respondents agreed that:

> . . . the whole regulation environment is done on a different premise . . . Food law traditionally was all based on legislation, and in public legislation there wasn't anything. . . . people weren't expected to do anything on the basis of good will or arms research, yet on the environment side it's been different from that in arm-twisting packaging, waste regulation, and a whole plethora of other controls and climate-change levy or whatever. There's been lots of quasi-soft law. . . (Retailer)

> . . . we see different interpretations, you know, you can have two stores in two bordering countries and see two interpretations on a piece of legislation. (Retailer)

> One of the biggest issues I have is, where we do transgress is trying to convince the enforcers to actually go down the route of using the enforcement concordat. (Retailer)

> And dealing with the issue through the enforcement concordat rather than the more formal route. And whilst everybody has

> signed up with the vast majority of enforcement agencies have trading standards and environmental, health labels, have signed up to enforcement concordat. It's given lip service. They say that they've signed up to it, but in the end it still gets pushed to one side. (Retailer)

> I mean, I would say that in that area, this has been more commercially driven than government driven. I would say government is catching up with what the commercial side of the game has actually got into. I mean, I'm very pleased that it has because it then means everybody's, by law, has got to conform to the same standard, and we are, as far as I'm concerned, I think right at the front of the game. One of our objectives here has always been to provide safe food for people to eat and I don't have any problem in anybody, who ever wanted to, coming and asking us what we're doing, or if they wanted a traceability or whatever I wouldn't have any problem in providing that. I don't have any problem with that whatsoever. (Salad crop grower)

Food manufacturers and food retail outlets have a great deal of capital invested in their brand images. Legal liability and loss of consumer confidence can have devastating effects on a company's market share and long-term survival prospects in a highly competitive market. This creates a clear incentive for firms to move towards closer strategic partnering relationships with suppliers.

The current food safety legislative environment is encouraging firms to follow an organisational strategy aimed at building closer supply chain relationships. This is occurring in a number of countries despite the differences in legislation between these countries. The reasons for these similar strategic developments given the differences in regulation is perhaps due to the core problem at the heart of food safety, *that it automatically creates information asymmetries along the supply chain*. Closer supply chain relationships are one way in which to reduce these information asymmetries and the resulting transaction costs.

The quality and safety of FFV produce are controlled by different public and private entities at different points in the supply chain. Figure 7.9 maps the various stages of the fresh fruit and vegetable supply chain in the UK and the EU and the corresponding stages where public and private standards operate in the chain. The research indicates that in the FFV sector, more retailers have developed their own 'codes of practice' including good agricultural practice (GAP) and specifications related to intrinsic and extrinsic qualities. These private specifications are based on and prompted by national and EU food safety and quality regulations, and in most cases exceed these regulations.

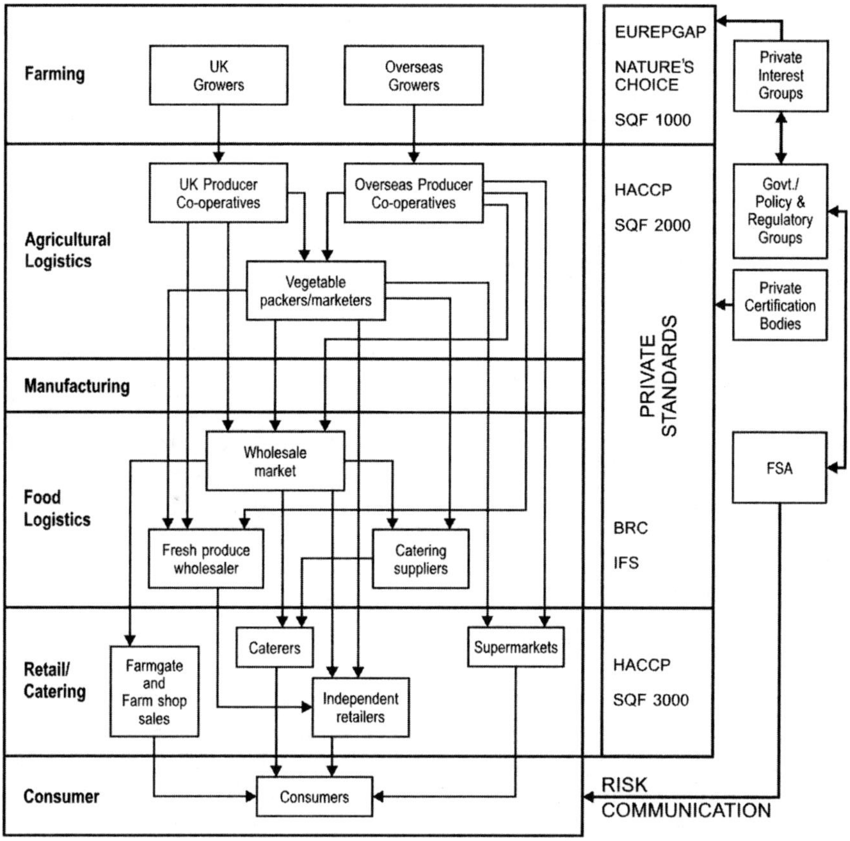

Figure 7.9 Fresh fruit and vegetable supply chain and its regulation.

CONCLUSIONS: THE FFV PUBLIC–PRIVATE MODEL IN PRACTICE

Our earlier chapters indicated that retailers are becoming more influential in food policy-making in the UK and EU, in the name of the consumer and public interest. Consumers are increasingly influencing the food system by selection or rejection of food considered healthy or hazardous; and large-scale retailer's organisations acting as intermediaries between the production and consumption are both very sensitive to these and attempt to shape consumers' preferences. This represents the development of a more complex public/private set of relationships, which now embodies new public institutions (like the EFSA and the UK FSA) and a greater competitiveness to react to consumer and media concerns. In this chapter, the case of the fresh fruit and vegetable sector is used to explore this complex hybrid model which is playing a pivotal role in reshaping both EU and UK food policy. This chapter has sought to provide an overview of the complex regulation of the fresh fruit and vegetable supply chain. It has concentrated on the extent to which the retailing industry is actively managing its FFV supply chain by the introduction of proliferating private standards to ensure food quality and safety all along the chain.

Over recent years, the UK consumers are giving more emphasis to aspects of quality and convenience rather than just to price and quantity. Further, there is an increasing demand for healthy foods and foods from market 'niches' often reflecting ethnic variety and traditions. This change in demand is 'consumer- led' and is articulated and promoted in the UK by the retailers, who are increasingly adopting a global sourcing and standard-setting policy to satisfy these new demands. Governance of the chain resides at the retail end. One example of this in practice is the case of pesticides. Retailers are constantly seeking to reduce pesticide residues on the fruit and vegetable products sold in their stores and have required that the level of residues should be below what is required by baseline public regulatory standards. This position of the retailers is made possible in the FFV sector because: uniformity and high quality are necessary for further processing, branding and large-scale buying by food service and retailers. For the UK supermarkets, FFV is a key item in the competition for broader market share as it is not only profitable but it has some of the highest profit margins per square metre of shelf space of any product category in the store rivalled only by wine and chilled products. It is also one of the few products that influence consumer's wider choice of stores. Buyer-driven chains have therefore evolved in this sector.

These chains are more regulated and characterised by high levels of private governance and long-term vertical co-ordination between the producers, supplier-integrators, processors and retailers. The resulting chains have barriers to entry for many producers such as voluntary standards, codes and benchmarks. The growing and competitive emphasis on quality standards and public concern about food safety have led both governments and retailers to set increasingly high standards on production and processing methods.

There has been an associated proliferation and differentiation of private standards often as part of Corporate Social Responsibility (CSR) or risk management initiatives. Some of the key private standards operating in the fresh fruit and vegetable sector are: EurepGap, The Global Food Safety Initiative and IFOAM.

The retailers have developed their own quality assurance and traceability systems to demonstrate due diligence as a defence against any food safety breakdown. This has led to more integration and control of supply over and above that implemented by state bodies. Retailers use private standards to standardise product requirements over suppliers. Nevertheless, this is also promoting more differentiation of product range and fragmentation of specific quality assurance schemes.

Such private quality and safety standards imposed by the retailers relate to the physical aspects of the products, as well as to cost, delivery and volume requirements, thereby enhancing a particular model of supply chain efficiency and lowering transaction costs. Private standards of a given chain are also designed to ensure (at a minimum) that public standards are met in all the markets in which the retail chain operates. Often, retailers design private standards as substitutes for missing or inadequate public standards (Reardon and Farina, 2002). In this respect, private standards can function *as a means of competition against other retail outlets* by supporting claims of superior product quality attributes. Such standards also begin to structure the competition between suppliers, processes and producers.

It is evident from this analysis that large-scale retailers are restructuring the agri-food chains from which they buy their products, in several crucial and potentially irreversible ways. This form of 'top-up' regulation by private interests in the name of consumer interests will have serious implications for the farm sector (see Van der Grijp et al., 2005). In short, retailers have taken on the responsibility of the state for assuring FFV standards. The costs of this process are largely paid for, however by the upstream actors in the chain.

Hence both quality, safety and sustainability as a set of private standards may provide leverage for large enterprises to control markets and raise barriers to competition. Therefore, when a retailer develops a strategy for sourcing more 'sustainable products', they as governors of the supply chain can push compliance costs and risks down to the suppliers. Standards and codes of practice therefore favour the well-capitalised farmers. The efforts to catalyse a public-private response that packages sustainability into technical, regulatory and managerial frameworks has shown that supply chains respond with another drive of marginalisation of small farmers (Vorley, 2001). A debate therefore needs to open as to what the social and sustainability effects are of these private standards, and how public policy should take them into account. So far this particular public-private regulatory compromise in the FFV sector means that the true costs of quality control tend to fall upon the upstream suppliers of the produce; even if the origins of private and public regulation emerge from downstream private and public bodies.

8 The Operation of the Hybrid Model
The Case of Red Meat

INTRODUCTION

As the main source of food law, EU Directives are continually being transposed into the UK to regulate issues such as: food composition; food labelling; food marketing; food standards; additives and contaminants in food; food nutrition; and food fraud. In addition to this hard law there has been a proliferation of 'guidance', whether through the use of protocols or of codified rules. Earlier chapters have identified the dynamics, of the gradual *Europeanisation* of UK food policy. There is a diversity of organisations within the European framework exerting an influence on, and articulating different knowledge, concerning food, health and ethics. For example, animal welfare groups and consumer groups now propound the precautionary principle in application to genetically modified organisms (GMOs) and traceability; such new concerns are added to the NGO agenda, and in turn, brings a new set of organisations into food policy debates. Europeanisation involves accommodating a wider and more disparate range of concerns and interests than those just associated with food quality and safety. In the area of red meat, concerns over safety and quality have triggered debate and stimulated regulatory reform at the EU and national levels and demonstrated that Europeanisation is not simply a one-way process but a dynamic one between different tiers of government.

Against this background and with the recognition of the strong impact of Europeanisation on food safety policies within the UK, this chapter maps the red meat supply chain, exploring the extent to which the various actors manage food quality and safety all along the chain, pursuing one of the general themes of this book, namely the interplay between public and private agencies operating at different spatial scales in regulating food standards and quality. In the mid 1980s, prior to BSE, the condition of meat entering the human food chain was a low-profile public policy issue and regulated in three ways. First, it was an offence for slaughtering to take place other than on licensed premises meeting requisite standards of hygiene. Secondly, animals whose physical condition did not meet certain standards could not be admitted to a slaughterhouse. Thirdly, the carcasses of slaughtered animals had to be inspected and passed fit for human consumption.

This chapter describes the powers and duties of state and private interests in place since that time, from 1986 onwards, and the shaping of wider governance systems. Following this introduction, the section titled 'Global Markets for Red Meat' sets a backdrop by considering the contemporary global situation in the red meat industry, including a brief overview of production and consumption trends. The section titled 'The UK Red Meat Industry' then reviews the UK red meat industry by reference to market statistics outlining trends in production and consumption of each type of meat (beef, lamb and pork). That section is followed by a section that outlines key market trends. An overview of the regulatory structure that the sector works within is provided in 'Industry Processes and Controls'. The structure of the supply chains for beef, lamb and pork and for organic supply are analysed in detail in the following section. As trade organisations play a central role in both the promotion and the ordering of the red meat industry, the 'Key Trade Organisations' section gives a brief overview of the major organisations. The 'Quality Assurance Schemes: The Private Face of Regulation' section reviews quality assurance schemes operating within the industry. Finally, the 'Conclusions' draws together observations on the red meat supply chain in the wider context of the book. The aim is to illustrate by practical example the highly hybrid nature of the regulation of that chain both in terms of public and private functions and domestic and European controls.

GLOBAL MARKETS FOR RED MEAT

The red meat industry has long engaged in international trade but the level of global trade and its geography has changed since the mid 1990s. Traditional meat producing countries in South America, such as Brazil and Argentina, have been joined by Asian countries as an increasingly globalised red meat industry has been subject to much greater volatility, particularly as a result of the risks within the system (see Chapter 2). Whilst food risks, notably BSE, have been the most high profile feature of the red meat industry, and have clearly shaped consumption patterns, there have also been wider shifts in meat eating practices. In short, the red meat industry exhibits many of the dynamics at work in the contemporary food system.

Global consumption of red meat was about 99m tonnes (with 70m tonnes consumed in the developed countries) and by 2002 had reached 244m tonnes (of which 105m tonnes were consumed in the developed world). These headlines figures display a dramatic change in the geography of meat consumption. Whilst meat consumption in the developed world grew slowly but steadily from the 1970s onwards by the 1980s it had reached a plateau, only increasing from 103m tonnes in 1990 to 105m tonnes in 2002, and shifting from the consumption of red to white meat. Meanwhile, in developing countries meat consumption grew rapidly from 47m tonnes in 1980, to 74m tonnes in 1990 and 139m tonnes in 2002 (Steinfeld and Chilonda, 2006: 4). The gap in meat consumption between developing and developed countries shows every sign of continuing to widen for the foreseeable future (Rosgrant et al., 2001).

Growing consumption of meat in the developing world drives global demand. As Steinfeld and Chilonda (2006: 3) have noted:

> Until the early 1980s, diets with daily consumption of milk and meat were the privilege of OECD country citizens and a small wealthy class elsewhere. . . For most people in Africa and Asia, meat, milk and eggs were an unaffordable luxury, consumed only on rare occasions.

Now, though, rising living standards, changing tastes and a growing urban population are increasing demand for meat. Between 1990 and 2002 the per capita consumption of meat per year in developing countries increased from 19kg to 29kg (Steinfeld and Chilonda, 2006: 4). This figure, though, is still well below that of developed countries where the annual per caput consumption of meat in 2002 was 80kg. China is the largest consumer of livestock products in Asia and although per caput consumption is lower than that for other developed countries it is rising rapidly at about 5% per year since the mid 1990s on the back of economic growth (Steinfeld and Chilonda, 2006: 4). The sheer scale of consumption of meat in China means that 'relatively small changes in livestock inventory growth and demand for livestock products can have significant implications for global trade in livestock feed and livestock products' (Steinfeld and Chilonda, 2006: 6).

The shifting geography of meat consumption has been matched by that of its supply. Developments in supply have been most spectacular in developing countries with the greatest economic growth. China, for example, accounted for 57% of the increase in total meat supply in developing countries (Steinfeld and Chilonda, 2006: 4). An indication of the nature of change is that in the early 1980s 'China overtook the United States and the entire European Union of then fifteen countries in terms of meat production' (ibid.). Overall, in the mid 1990s meat volume produced in developing countries exceeded that of developed countries and since then the gap between the two has continued to grow in 'a substantial shift of the "centre of gravity" of livestock production from the North to the South, from temperate regions, to tropical and sub-tropical environments' (Steinfeld and Chilonda, 2006: 3).

In the developed world the saturation of the meat market has been accompanied by a shift from red to white meat (Haley, 2001). Consumer concerns about the health affects of the consumption of red meat, alongside lengthy and long running food scares, have made the meat market more volatile. Disease related export restrictions can have a noticeable impact on world trade (FAO, 2002: 7). With BSE the most prominent food safety scare attaching to red meat, other concerns have included the presence of antibiotics and growth hormones in meat (see Chapter 1). Diseases such as foot and mouth while having no human health impacts have nonetheless affected both meat production and consumption (for the latter see Chapter 2). The financial cost of tackling such food scares can be significant. For example, it has been estimated that the cost arising from animal disease outbreaks in six countries between 1996 and 2000 was a loss in GDP of between 0.2% and 0.75% (FAO, 2002: 3). The beef market has been particularly affected by food scares as trends in developed world consumption illustrate. Table 8.1 shows that across the developed world, particularly in the USA and European Union, there has been a general decline in per capita consumption of beef since the mid 1990s (see also Aumaitre and Boyazoglu, 2002).

We detail, now, how the UK red meat industry has responded to a series of high profile food crises and changes in consumer prefence. In particular we identify the growth of niche markets, such as organic, and the role of public and private interest regulatory mechanisms in seeking to bolster confidence amongst economic actors in the food chain, and to reassure consumers of the safety of their meat.

Table 8.1 Per Capita Consumption of Beef in Selected Countries by Volume (Kg), 1995 and 2005

Country	*1995*	*2005*
Argentina	60.7	55.1
United States	44.6	39.5
Brazil	36.7	37.4
Australia	36.0	34.2
New Zealand	28.5	31.4
Canada	34.1	29.3
Mexico	20.1	22.9
Russia	22.9	21.9
Former Soviet Union	16.9	19.8
European Union	19.9	15.4
South Korea	9.2	14.2
Japan	12.1	12.8
China	3.4	5.5

Source: Cattle Today [Online]. Available from http://www.cattletoday.com/archive/2002/July/CT213.shtml

THE UK RED MEAT INDUSTRY

The UK farming and meat industries have experienced a number of severe setbacks, including the BSE crisis in the 1990s and the loss of stock following in the foot and-mouth outbreak of 2001. Since 2002, however, the industry has benefited from a revival in consumer confidence, with the value of UK livestock production increasing in 2003 (Table 8.2).

Whilst there are annual fluctuations in numbers there are longer-term trends in livestock numbers. For example, the dairy herd has been in long term decline, owing to restrictions on milk production and increasing yields from dairy cows. The number of sheep and lambs has shown greater stability. Pig numbers, meanwhile, have been contracting since the late1990s.

Table 8.3 offers an analysis of the financial results of the major companies involved in the production of meat and poultry meat products. The figures show, as is to be expected, that larger companies enjoy much higher profit margins than smaller ones.

According to National Statistics, 915 VAT-registered enterprises were engaged in the production, processing and preserving of meat and meat products in 2005 (Table 8.4) which is a reduction from 990 enterprises in 2002 and 1,505 in 2000. These figures reflect the restructuring of the meat-processing industry that has taken place in recent years, involving a large number of plant closures. At the same time, businesses are becoming larger as more vertically integrated operations are created.

Table 8.2 Livestock Production in the UK by Value (£m) and Livestock Numbers in the UK by Type of Animal (000 head), 1992–1994, 2002 and 2003

Livestock Production	**1992–1994*	*2002*	*2003*
Livestock production	6,738	5,751	5,997
Livestock products	3,613	2,966	3,218
Total	10,351	8,717	**9,216
Livestock Numbers	**1992–1994*	*2002*	*2003*
Cattle and calves	11,910	10,345	10,517
Sheep and lambs	44,263	35,834	35,846
Pigs	7,817	5,588	5,047
Fowl	127,530	155,005	165,324

* Averages over the period

** Does not sum due to rounding

Note: 'livestock production' refers to animals that are reared primarily for meat, whereas 'livestock products' refers to foods such as milk and eggs.

Source: DEFRA website, http://statistics.defra.gov.uk/esg/

Table 8.3 Key Financial Ratios for UK Producers of Meat and Poultry Meat Products (£000, % and £) 2004–2005

	Lower	*Median*	*Upper*
Turnover (£000)	311	7,091	30,460
Pre-tax profit (£000)	-8	65	658
Pre-tax profit margin (%)	-0.86	2.38	7.51
Turnover per employee (£)	65,669	121,704	220,426
Average remuneration per employee (£)	14,170	18,098	23,194
Working capital/turnover (%)	11.40	0.44	-7.83
Turnover/fixed assets (%)	2.79	4.39	7.28
Total debt/net worth (%)	171.43	62.67	14.32
Current ratio	0.60	1.00	1.66

Note: The 'lower', 'median' and 'upper' denote the size of the food and drinks manufacturers.
Source: ADAS 2007, Research into UK Food & Drink Manufacturing: Final Report https://www.fdf.org.uk/speeches/ADASreportDeskResearchFinal.pdf

Table 8.4 Number of UK VAT-Based Enterprises Engaged in the Production, Preservation and Processing of Meat or Meat Products by Turnover Size band (£000, number and %), 2005

Turnover (£000)	*Number of enterprises*	*% of Total*
1–49	65	7.1
50–99	65	7.1
100–249	120	13.1
250–499	100	10.9
500–999	110	12.0
1,000–4,999	240	26.2
5,000+	235	25.7
Total	915	

Source: ADAS(2007)Research into UK Food & Drink Manufacturing –Final Report.https://www.fdf.org.uk/speeches/ADASreportDeskResearchFinal.pdf

Regional Markets and Market Distribution

There are two distinct types of sheep farming in the UK: hill/upland sheep farming and lowland sheep farming. Hill farming is an 'extensive' system found in areas such as Dartmoor, parts of Wales, the Lake District and the Yorkshire Dales. Lowland sheep farming is a more intensive system and is found in various parts of the UK. Beef farming is concentrated in the uplands of Britain and the West Country; pig farming is concentrated in the south east of England. Some of the largest commercial pig units are located in the Chilterns, Oxfordshire, Berkshire and the Wiltshire border. Most of the leading meat suppliers have processing plants, cold stores and distribution centres around the UK, but meat-processing plants tend to be located close to the areas where the animals are reared. This is because of the cost of transporting relatively low-value, high-bulk items, as well as the need to meet animal-welfare regulations.

Specialist butchers account for around 15% of meat sales by value but their share of the market is declining (Key Note, 2003). Over the past few decades, the supermarkets have gradually established a stronghold in the UK food market. More than 90% of the population shop mainly at supermarkets. As a result, the major multiples have huge bargaining power, which they have used to squeeze the prices they pay producers and other suppliers.

MARKET TRENDS

Meat as part of the UK diet accounted for 24.2% of household expenditure on food in 2003 (National Statistics). Meat's share of the food bill rose sharply in 2003, reflecting price increases driven in part by a recovery in consumer confidence in and demand for meat. Other key trends include increasing demand for convenience foods, such as ready-to-cook meat products and ready meals, and growing concern about the sources of foods, fuelling demand for organic and free-range produce. Since the 1970s there has been increasing demand for convenience products in every sector of the food market, driven by the accelerating pace of life and the growing number of working women. In the red meat industry, this trend initially increased sales of frozen foods. Since the late 1990s, however, chilled products have seen the greatest growth in sales. A wide range of ready to cook chilled meat products is available from supermarkets.

The outbreak of BSE in the 1990s prompted many consumers to reduce their consumption of beef, to switch to other meats (such as poultry) or even to cut meat out of their diets completely. In 2003, the volume of sales of beef increased by around 3% (Key Note, 2003) and spending on red

Table 8.5 UK Beef Market Trends (1990–2004)

Beef Supplies '000 tonnes	*1990*	*1995*	*1996*	*1997*	*1998*	*1999*	*2000*	*2001*	*2002*	*2003*	*2004*
Production	1001	974	702	696	697	678	707	652	692	696	709
Imports a	174	173	187	217	160	191	188	256	314	330	343
Exports a	124	274	58	0	0	0	0	0	0	10	10
Total consumption	983	901	740	842	874	914	940	922	987	1015	1035
UK Market share %	82	81	75	74	82	79	80	72	68	67	67

[a] Carcass weight equivalent
Source: Key Note (2005) Meat and meat products market report.

meat rose sharply, partly triggered by the popularity of the Atkins Diet. Consumers also appear to have regained their confidence in beef as the BSE crisis faded from the public consciousness (see Table 8.5).

Rising incomes and growing demand for convenience foods are driving sales of added-value products. A wide range of cooked meats and ready-to-cook products in sauces are now available chilled, and take-away-food such as ready-to-eat chickens, spare ribs and other meat cuts are available in the supermarket. The success of added-value products has encouraged suppliers to develop brands in an attempt to de-commoditise the sector. Sainsbury's, for example, has focused on premium opportunities with its 'Taste the Difference' range.

The instability in the beef market caused by BSE has been one of the most significant features in the red meat industry. The ripples in the market, though, went well beyond domestic production and consumption. Imports declined through much of the 1990s as the result of changing food tastes and food scares. By the early 2000s, though, imports are once again surpassing the level of a decade earlier (see Table 8.5.).

The growing production of meat in emerging economies such as Brazil has enabled retailers to source lower-cost supplies from overseas, and UK producers, which have much higher costs in terms of land and labour, have struggled to compete. British beef exporters have been hampered by controls introduced as a result of the BSE outbreak in the 1990s. Although the ban on beef exports ended in 1999, strict traceability rules mean that only a small amount of British beef goes abroad.

UK Eating Out Market and the Meat Industry

The total income generated in 2000 from catering services was estimated to be £56bn by the Office of National Statistics. The value of restaurant brands was estimated by Mintel at £11.5bn in 2000, rising to £12.2bn in 2001. More and more people are eating out and are becoming more sophisticated in their choices (Tragus, 2004). This makes for a very dynamic and buoyant market. Leisure dining is changing and becoming more innovative. New concepts and formats are emerging whilst more mature sectors are now consolidating and their growth rates slowing. The market is highly competitive with providers incorporating the best elements of each other in order to grab a bigger slice of market share.

The fast food burger market is a well-defined segment of this market. In the UK, the major players include McDonalds, Burger King, Whitbread, TDR/Capricorn group and Wimpy. Over the period between 1974, when the McDonalds chain started in the UK, to 1995, the fast food market grew significantly in the UK at the expense of established fast food businesses, primarily fish and chips. McDonald's is the world's leading provider of quick service food with over 31,000 restaurants in 118 countries at the end of 2007 (McDonald's Corporation, 2007: 24).

In Europe, McDonald's key markets are France, Germany and the UK. The company is the largest user of beef in Europe. Eight to nine thousand cattle a week are required to satisfy their beef requirement in the UK (FCC, 2003). Fourteen abattoirs in the UK and Ireland provide all of McDonalds' British Isles beef. Forequarter and flank is used to produce the hamburger patty, which has been the traditional staple of McDonald's. Each abattoir, therefore, also needs a good outlet for the hindquarter and this is mainly achieved through long-term relationships with multiple retailers.

UK Lamb and Pork Market Trends

Volume sales of lamb, supplies of which were hit hard by the foot-and-mouth outbreak in 2001 continued to decline in 2003 but were showing signs of growth by the end of 2004.

Tables 8.6 and 8.7 highlight key trends in the UK lamb market. Compared to the volatility in the beef market, production and consumption of lamb have remained much more stable. There has also been much more stability in the domestic market for UK producers whose market share has remained largely unchanged since the early 1990s.

As Table 8.7 illustrates imports are dominated by traditional food trading relationships. In 2004 New Zealand and Australia accounted for nearly three quarters of UK lamb imports. Meanwhile, exports are to the UK's newer trading partners in Europe, especially France.

The bacon and ham sector grew by 6.2% in value terms between 2000 and 2004. Slices of bacon (or rashers) account for around 90% of bacon sales by value, with joints, chops and steaks making up the remainder. Ham accounts for around half of the £1.6bn cooked-meats market in the UK. Demand for convenience foods has boosted sales of both ham and other cooked meats over the past five years. Tables 8.8 and 8.9 show the market trends in the UK pork sector.

Table 8.6 UK Lamb Market Trends

Lamb Supplies '000 tonnes	*1990*	*1995*	*1996*	*1997*	*1998*	*1999*	*2000*	*2001*	*2002*	*2003*	*2004*
Production	370	364	345	321	351	361	361	259	300	300	306
Imports[a]	145	138	149	141	131	127	123	106	115	127	132
Exports[a]	80	147	130	108	109	110	99	31	62	77	74
Total consumption	429	351	366	352	373	380	390	335	353	350	366
UK Market share %	66	61	59	60	65	67	68	68	67	64	64

[a]Carcass weight equivalent

Source: Keynote (2005) Meat and meat products market report.

As Table 8.9 shows Britain is a large net importer of pork and once again a traditional trading relationship preceding Britain's membership of the EU—this time with Denmark whose EU membership was linked to Britain's—remains important.

Table 8.7 Lamb Meat Imports and Exports from Top Five Countries in the Year 2004

Imports		
Countries	*'000 tonnes*	*Percentage*
New Zealand	82.3	62.3
Australia	13.8	10.5
Italy	11.9	9.0
Ireland	7.5	5.7
Netherlands	3.5	2.7
Other countries	13.0	9.9
Total	132.1	100
Exports		
Countries	*'000 tonnes*	*Percentage*
France	55.8	75.6
Belgium	5.2	7.1
Germany	4.0	5.4
Italy	3.1	4.2
Ireland	2.2	2.9
Other countries	3.5	4.8
Total	73.8	100

Source: Key Note (2005) Meat and meat products market report.

Table 8.8 UK Pork Market Trends

*Pork Supplies * '000 tonnes*	*1990*	*1995*	*1996*	*1997*	*1998*	*1999*	*2000*	*2001*	*2002*	*2003*	*2004*
Production	735	759	776	872	920	825	728	606	632	584	590
Imports a	85	138	165	161	175	235	266	260	302	418	419
Exports (excl. pork for curing)	73	83	103	104	117	180	213	199	233	311	310
Exports a	51	150	156	229	283	235	209	39	95	74	91
Total consumption	757	691	721	744	751	774	740	743	772	822	810
UK Market share %	90	88	86	86	84	77	71	73	70	62	62

[a] Carcass weight equivalent
[*] including processed pig meat
Source: Key Note (2005) Meat and meat products market report.

Table 8.9 Pork Imports and Exports from Top Five Countries in the Year 2004

Imports		
Countries	*'000 tonnes*	*Percentage*
Denmark	147.1	35.1
Netherlands	77.2	18.4
Ireland	49.7	11.9
Germany	45.9	11.0
France	45.6	10.9
Other countries	99.1	23.6
Total	419.0	100
Exports		
Countries	*'000 tonnes*	*Percentage*
Germany	29.7	32.7
Ireland	18.8	20.7
Netherlands	8.9	9.8
Hong Kong	4.7	5.2
Denmark	4.4	4.9
Other countries	28.8	31.7
Total	90.9	100

Source: Key Note (2005) Meat and meat products market report.

INDUSTRY PROCESSES AND CONTROLS

The EUROP Classification System

When an animal arrives at the slaughterhouse in the EU, it is slaughtered, cut into two half carcasses and classified according to a standard obligatory classification system called EUROP. There are five main classes in the EUROP standard ranging from E (the best class) to P, and there are a number of sub-classes within each main class. The classification is based on a visual inspection of the carcass, where shape (the distribution of meat on the carcass), and fatness of the meat are judged by a certified cattle-classifier employed by the slaughterhouse. Controlled by domestic authorities, the EUROP standard directs the settling of payments with farmers sometimes employing additional criteria for sorting the meat including, for example, colour and veterinary history.

The Slaughtering Industry

All meat sold in the UK for human consumption comes from a licensed abattoir/slaughterhouse. For this reason, abattoirs have traditionally been a checkpoint for inspecting meat to ensure its fitness and quality (Phillips Report 2000, vol. 13: para. 2.3). Abattoirs seek to boost profits by maximising their throughput (the number of animals killed). As the Phillips Inquiry into BSE reported:

> This results in an emphasis on processing animals quickly, which can conflict with the interests of hygiene. The slaughterhouse depends crucially on downstream agents, particularly the renderers, to handle the by-products and waste it produces . . . While meat is the primary and most valuable product of the slaughterhouses, by-products are significant, as traditionally their sale has covered slaughtering costs. Indeed they are often referred to as the 'fifth quarter' of the animal (Phillips Report 2000, vol. 13: para. 2.4).

Since the 1970s the structure and ownership of slaughterhouses has changed. From the 1970s onwards public slaughterhouses have dwindled into insignificance, and from the 1980s onwards the number of abattoirs has fallen steeply in the UK, as many smaller ones have gone out of business (Phillips Report 2000, vol. 13: para. 2.6). This decline has been due to a number of factors, including a drive towards economies of scale, and the need to comply with higher environmental and health standards. The operations of a large slaughterhouse differ markedly from those of smaller premises, many of the latter, for example, will open for a limited period during the week to deal with a few animals.

Before the introduction of a single European standard on 1 January 1993 there was, effectively, a two-tier system of regulation—one for domestic consumption and the other for export—for the hygienic production of meat. The Regulations required that every carcass slaughtered in a domestic slaughterhouse be subjected to inspection by a qualified inspector so as to establish the fitness for human consumption of all, or part, of the carcass. The Regulations for export slaughterhouses were largely the same as those for domestic plants but as the Phillips Report noted (vol. 13: para. 2.10):

> The most important differences were in the level of inspection. For instance, in domestic slaughterhouses ante-mortem inspection of animals (ie, before slaughter) was not required until January 1991 and, before 1 January 1993, there was no requirement for veterinary supervision of meat inspection.

Meanwhile, each export slaughterhouse was supervised by an Official Veterinary Surgeon (OVS), appointed by the local authority responsible for hygiene and meat inspection. Ministers were responsible for designating individual veterinary surgeons as suitable for OVS work and local authorities could only appoint such designated veterinarians as OVSs. According to the Phiilips Report (Phillips, 2000: vol. 14–3) if a plant was producing meat for the domestic market for some or all of the time, the OVS could attend for as little as one hour a day and delegate much of the responsibility for hygiene to local Environmental Health Officers (EHO).

Subsequent changes to regulatory practice in the meat sector provide a good example of the interactions between EU and national legislation and policy delivery. EU efforts to reshape food policy in the early 2000s were marked by a determination to manage the safety of the food supply chain from farm to fork (see Chapter 4). Although the legislation was presented by the Commission in 2000, the lengthy law making process meant that it was not until 2004 that it was adopted by Member States. Even then, the proposals were not applied until January 2006 (FSA, 2005: 2). Amongst the Commission legislation were Regulation (EC) 852/2004 on the hygiene of foodstuffs, and two measures directly targeting the meat industry Regulation (EC) 853/2004 laying down specific hygiene rules for food of animal origin and Regulation 854/2004 laying down specific hygiene rules for the organisation of official controls on products of animal origin intended for human consumption. The new legislation simplified previous food hygiene legislation to allow for its better application and enforcement (FSA, 2005: 7). The legislation required that food businesses (except farmers and growers) put in place procedures based on Hazard Analysis and Critical Control Point principles. Since in practice, the Regulations did not 'substantially alter any requirements in respect of premises or equipment from the current legislation' (FSA, 2005: 9) and reinforced a risk-based approach the UK meat industry was sympathetic to the approach (FSA, 2005: 6). From a food enforcement perspective it meant that in the slaughterhouse officials in the Meat Hygiene Service, who undertake inspection duties, move from 'supervision to audit' (FSA, 2005: 24).

While these regulations have become common practice in Western European plants, and have been adopted in the USA and Australia and New Zealand, some parts of the industry in the accession states to the European Union have found it difficult to comply with every part of the regulations. Also, demands from developed countries such as the USA and the EU states has meant that many of the developing countries reliant on meat exports, have had to adopt EU and US systems to market entry.

Meat Processing Industry

Butchers and meat processors take meat that is fit for human consumption and package it for purchase and consumption. As the meat products sector has become larger and more diverse, large meat processors, independent specialist butchers, supermarket butchers and even some slaughterhouses have become involved in the manufacture of processed meat products (Phillips Report, 2000: vol. 13, para. 8.4).

The meat processing industry is largely a product of the post-war era, when consumers began gradually to move away from traditional cuts of meat, as the increased availability of refrigeration allowed the introduction of a greater range of products (Phillips Report, 2000: vol. 13, para. 8.9). The processed meat sector covers a variety of products such as burgers, sausages, pies and other pastries, canned meats, meat spreads and pâtés, cured and smoked meats, ready meals and convenience foods. Re-formed meats are used to make many different types of product, including some beef roasts and various 'rolls' of meat. The popularity of processed meat products has meant that fresh carcass meat is no longer the largest sector of the market.

STRUCTURE OF THE SUPPLY CHAINS

Beef Supply Chain

The UK has one of the largest cattle herds in the EU, along with France and Germany. In Europe, beef is produced from two sectors: dairy beef produced as a 'sideline' from dairying operations, and specialist beef producers. Beef farms are typically small and specialist beef producers are at the lower end of the income scale of farmers. UK specialist beef farms tend to be of a small size in hilly areas with few alternative enterprises, often in disadvantaged regions. The supply chain is illustrated in Figure 8.1.

Four major beef systems can be identified operating at varying levels of intensity (Winter et al., 1998; Entec, 1996). Lowland and upland suckler systems are based on breeding and rearing specifically for beef. Some of these farms fatten all or a proportion of their own stock. Others sell only store cattle to either of the remaining two systems. There are two systems of purchasing cattle and feeding to slaughter weight. Semi-intensive finishing takes calves from both dairy and suckler herds and relies on outdoor grazing for fattening. In contrast, intensive finishing takes calves predominantly from the dairy herd with animals housed and fed controlled rations.

There are few farm systems that are solely reliant on beef enterprises. In lowland areas, beef herds are established as a secondary enterprise in predominantly arable and dairy systems. In upland areas, beef cattle typically exist alongside sheep. In the EU, there has been a general trend towards a more concentrated slaughtering industry both in terms of ownership, and in terms of production plants. The closure of small slaughterhouses has accelerated in recent years due to the requirements of the still larger retail chains and hygiene requirements in the Fresh Meat Directive. The large retail chains use their buying power to demand products and services that meet their pre-specified standards, i.e. descriptions of the various products and services supplied by slaughtering companies (weight of quarters, muscles, packaging, production methods etc.) and they demand these standardised products in large quantities on which they expect discounts and guaranteed regularity of supply. Only large slaughtering companies are able to meet these demands from the retailers. Therefore, as large retail chains become more dominant, concentration in slaughtering companies follows.

Slaughterhouses source their cattle from individuals, farmers, producer groups/cooperatives or cattle markets. Cattle markets are still an important part of the distribution chain in many countries but their importance is declining. In the United Kingdom, the role of co-operatives is small especially in beef. At the turn of the century slaughterhouses are still purchasing just over half of their cattle from auction markets (according to an industry interviewee) and remainder is sourced directly from farmers or producer groups. The share of cattle going through cattle markets is declining. Pressure from both private and public sectors for greater traceability and quality assurance, nationally and at the EU level, is likely to increase the monitoring costs that slaughtering companies and retailers incur through auctions and occasional supply relationships (Hobbs, 1996). These costs may become prohibitive leading to increasing pressure from downstream firms to move toward closer forms of vertical co-ordination. The role of independent wholesalers in the industry is declining with greater integration by slaughtering companies or large retail chains via their central buying units. The decreasing sales of beef through butchers, who are the principal customers of many wholesaling companies, puts additional pressure on wholesalers. Wholesalers try to avoid being placed on the fringe by marketing a broader range of products and by taking on processing activities like cutting and consumer packaging, thus increasing the value which they add to the product.

Meat is often perceived as an unbranded commodity leading to low promotional expenditure on meat and meat products in general. Slaughtering or cutting and boning companies do not sell beef with a manufacturer's trademark. Branding hardly exists in the beef sector other than that normally carried out by national trade organisations on a generic basis or by a retail chain that wants to stand as the guarantor of quality for the consumer. The major retail chains all have their own superior quality programme. In some cases a beef product is branded with place of origin, e.g. 'Scottish Beef'. Supermarkets trying to create their own quality brand of beef contract with slaughtering companies and farmers, usually in a specific region, to supply beef that has been treated in a pre-specified way by farmers and slaughterhouses. All the major retail chains in the United Kingdom have established such 'quality assurance schemes', a development which has accelerated since the BSE crisis.

The lack of branding, notwithstanding differences in product quality and new product development in the beef sector has led to competition between both slaughtering companies and retailers based largely on price given the difficulties in differentiating quality. In general, the relations between retail chains and slaughtering companies are informal though long-term. The retail chains tend to buy their beef from the same suppliers, but also like to be able to shop around for the most attractive offer. Prices are negotiated each week on the basis of auction prices.

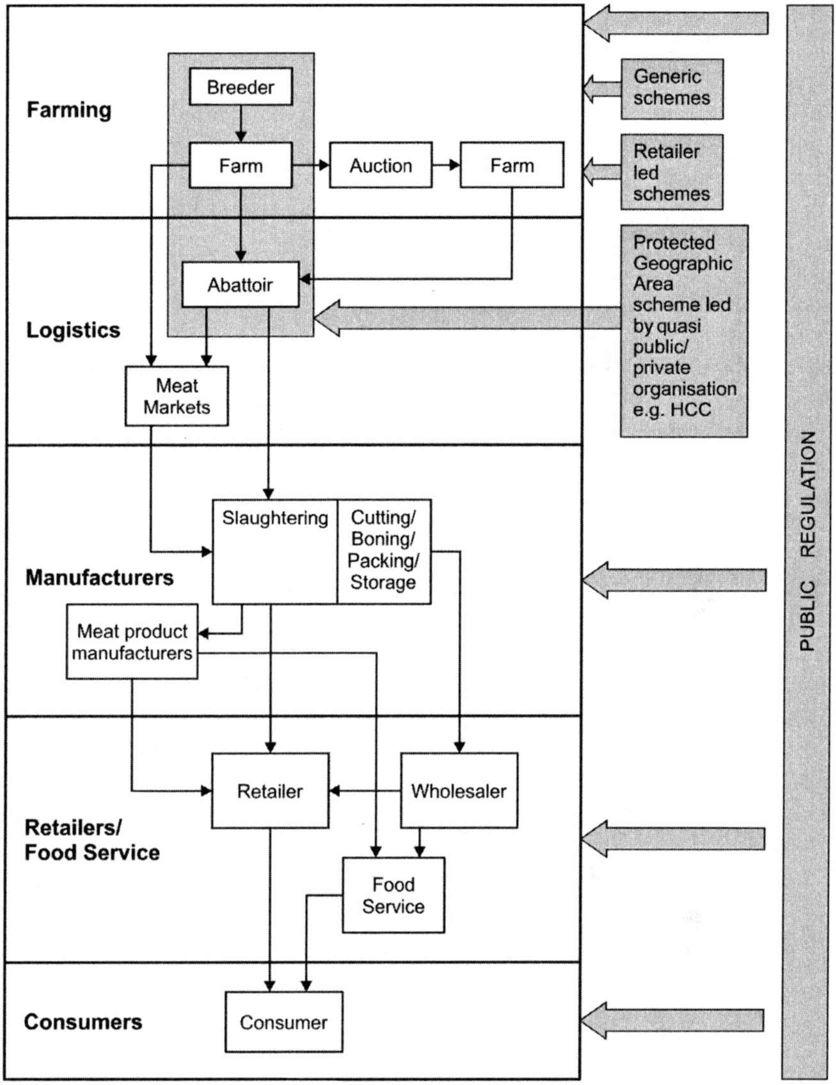

Figure 8.1 Beef supple chain.

Since the BSE crisis, traceability has become more important. Reliability of delivery and price are also important buying criteria. A number of initiatives have been launched in the EU in the aftermath of the BSE crises, to produce beef under specifications which are set up for all links in the supply chain. These schemes have been primarily aimed at assurance of characteristics, such as food safety and animal welfare, but are now also being extended to include quality characteristics like tenderness and taste. This may be seen as an attempt to employ quality control and product development to differentiate the market and ease the price competition among slaughtering companies and retailers.

Lamb Supply Chain

Sheep farming is a heavily subsidised sector and of historic importance to the UK (Fogerty et al., 2001). Since the late 1980s, the total size of the UK sheep flock has remained constant at between forty-two and forty-five million sheep—the largest in the European Union (Anderson, 2002). The UK lamb supply chain has a traditional system, which links hill and lowland producers. The principle behind the system is the movement of breeding ewes and store lambs from the uplands to the lowlands where they are ultimately fattened ('finished') for sale live at auctions, or to abattoirs and then deadweight, to processors, retailers and food service firms. Owing to the climate and topography of upland Britain, most livestock is 'finished' on the lowland, and this is generally outside the county in which the livestock is initially bred.

The continuity of the system is therefore dependent on animal movements. More recently, the sheep market has become less profitable and this has led to a situation that became apparent during the FMD outbreak of 2001 when some livestock dealers and farmers were buying and selling stock several times within a few days—an issued covered in Chapter 2.

Liveweight sales by farmers to abattoirs, processors and retailers (where possible) are the preferred mode of transaction between the live and dead stages of the supply chain. In the early 2000s just over half of all lamb sales occurred through livestock auctions and the remainder are sold deadweight to abattoirs. The auction and abattoir sectors of the UK meat and lamb supply chains are nowadays more highly concentrated and larger-scale, for example, in the early 2000s thirty-seven abattoirs were responsible for 76% of sheep slaughtered, with the top ten abattoirs accounting for almost 47% of total sheep slaughtered in the UK (MLC, 2001b).

Pork Supply Chain

The pig industry in the UK has undergone major structural change over the past quarter of a century in terms of scale, types of systems and the size of the average herds. The industry has been beset by a succession of economic and health crises. The average total herd size peaked at 585 in 1999, 35% more than in 1990 and as much as 140% more than in 1980. Since the peak year of 1999, there has been a major change in the average size of operation. The average number of total pigs per holding fell to 500 in the year 2003, with the decline being particularly marked between 2001 and 2003 (Fowler, 2004). The organisation of the supply chain is shown in Figure 8.2.

The number of pig holdings has declined more or less continuously since the 1980s. At the same time, average holdings sizes have increased very substantially as more small and medium producers left the industry under pressures of economies of scale. These changes have been far more marked for the pig sector than the cattle or sheep sector, as pig producers have not been protected, by subsidies, from underlying changes in the economy. The average pig holding size registered a decline in 2002 for the first time since the 1970s. This may also be associated with Post-weaning Multi-systemic Wasting Syndrome (PMWS) and reducing stocking densities in an attempt to reduce the incidence of the disease. The number of pig holdings continued to decline in 2002 and was 27% lower than in 1998. Pig production is established in most areas but is prevalent in eastern and northern England to take advantage of cereal production, which forms the basis of pig diets.

The production of pigs has several stages (Agra CEAS, 2003: 12):

- piglet (weaner) production takes place in 'sow herds' or 'breeding herds';
- the production of slaughter pigs produced from purchased piglets takes place in 'fattening herds', 'finishing herds' or 'feeding herds;
- piglets can also be produced and fattened within the same unit and are known as 'farrow to finish herds' or 'breeding and feeding herds'.

In their review of the UK pig industry Agra CEAS (2003: 12) note that breeding herds generally sell the weaners at between 20kg and 30kg liveweight (when they are approximately 9–12 weeks of age). National consumer preferences partly dictate the size of pigs at slaughter. For example, in the Netherlands and Belgium, slaughter pigs are sold at 110kg liveweight but in the UK they are usually sold onto the market at around 90kg liveweight. Young females (gilts) and boars are generally bought from specialist breeders at between five and six months of age, although they can be purchased earlier and reared on-farm within the herd.

Large and small pig producers have distinctive systems (Agra CEAS, 2003: 13). Larger units will operate continually as farrowing, weaning and servicing will take place every week. Meanwhile, smaller units will operate sequentially with the production cycles of all sows synchronised. An alternative, and ever more popular method, involves separating sows into divisions, farrowing at three week intervals as this enables better management of each stage of production. To prevent disease transmission between pigs of different ages each type of pig (sows, weaned piglets and finishing pigs) can be kept on different sites

The majority of pigs (75–80% in the UK) are kept indoors in intensive units with high capital investment in specialist buildings and equipment (Agra CEAS, 2003: 13). As a response to welfare and environmental concerns an increasing, proportion of pigs are kept outdoors in low cost units.

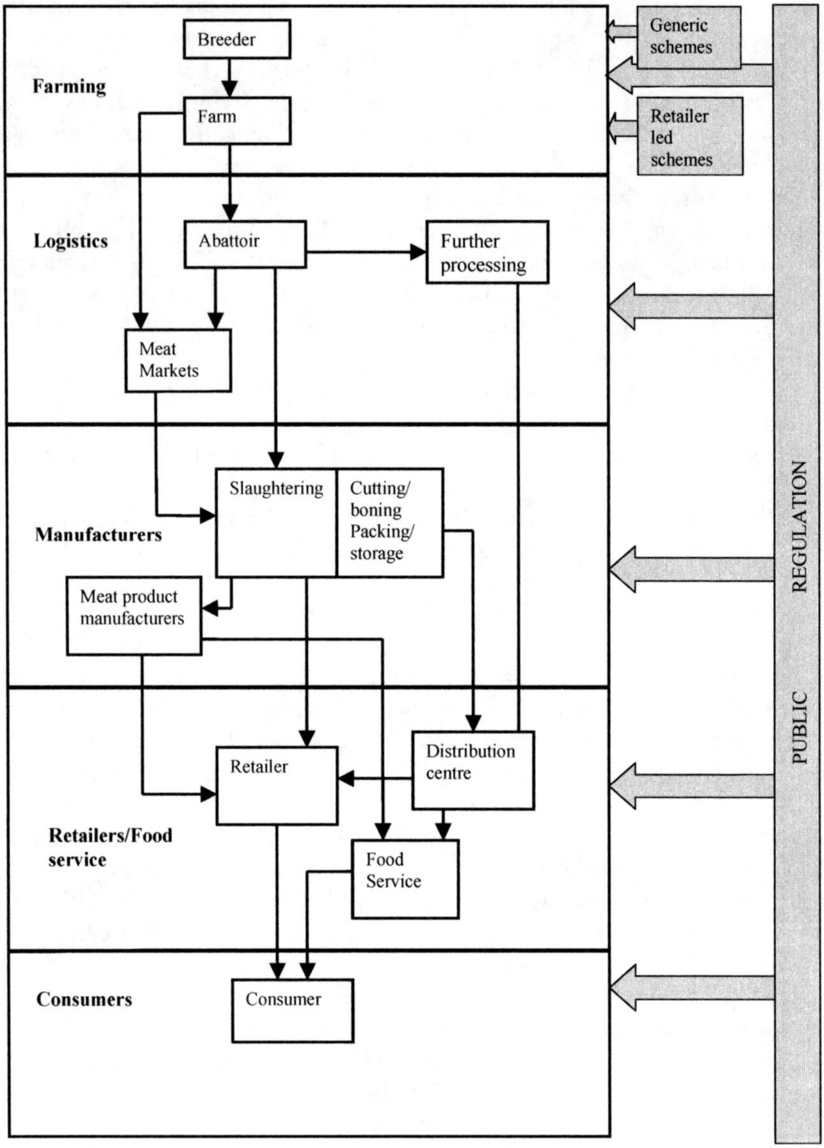

Figure 8.2 Pork supply chain.

Organic Supply Chains

Although still accounting for a relatively small proportion of the market, sales of organic and free-range meats have increased rapidly in recent years. Concern about the sources of foods, following the BSE crisis in 1996 and, more recently, the controversy over genetically modified (GM) foods, as well as an apparent increase in food allergies and growing consumer interest in food and health matters, have helped to fuel this growth.

According to one observer of the organic market, the organic meat products' market is the fastest growing in the UK organic sector (Organic Monitor, 2005). Although sales volume expanded by 139% between 2001 and 2004 it was starting from a low base. High growth rates have made the UK organic meat market the second largest in the world. The Soil Association, an organisation that promotes and certifies organic food, reported that an increase in total sales of organic food of more than 10% in the year ending April 2004. At a time when organic sales appeared to be rising inexorably the Association noted that retail sale of organic food was now worth £1.12bn and growing by £2m a week—double the rate of growth in the general grocery market (Soil Association, 2004).

Apart from the retail trade, there has been high demand for organic meats from food processors and the catering sector. The increase in organic food processing has led to a surge in demand from companies making organic sausages, bacon, ready-meals, and baby food. Over a half of British organic pork went to food processors in 2004. There is also rising demand from restaurants, schools, hospitals and government buildings. However, while sales volume has expanded considerably, the market share of organic meats remains below 4% in most retailers. Organic meats are mostly marketed under supermarket private labels, which account for over 80% of fresh cut sales. Brands are more evident on organic processed meats. Despite the concentration within the conventional meat industry the supply-side for organic meats remains fragmented with less influence from supermarkets' sourcing policies in comparison to conventional meat supply.

KEY TRADE ORGANISATIONS

The nature of risk in the meat industry means that it is relatively heavily regulated. It is also an industry where market support has bolstered farmers' incomes. As a result, a complex pattern of governance has emerged in which promotional bodies work alongside market regulatory bodies. Within the UK there is also a significant geographical dimension to these bodies, partly reflecting regional geographies of supply chains but more importantly political boundaries.

Amongst the most significant organisations are:

British Meat Processors Association (BMPA): represents the interests of companies involved in the slaughtering, processing, manufacturing, wholesale distribution and packaging sectors of the meat industry.

Meat and Livestock Commission (MLC): set up under the Agriculture Act 1967 to maintain and improve the competitiveness of the livestock industry. Its income comes from a levy on producers and abattoirs. The MLC's promotional activities have now been devolved to four separate bodies, reflecting a mixture of markets and politics:

- British Pig Executive (BPEX);
- English Beef and Lamb Executive (EBLEX);
- Hybu Cig Cymru/Meat Promotion Wales (HCC);
- Quality Meat Scotland (QMS).

QUALITY ASSURANCE SCHEMES: THE PRIVATE FACE OF REGULATION

There are a variety of quality assurance schemes in operation, ranging from those that focus on the farm to those that seek to bind together actors in a supply chain. In the UK, a number of schemes have been developed that are targeted at the red meat industry. These assurance schemes, as we shall see, are inextricably linked with public forms of food safety regulation. In analyses of farm assurance schemes for livestock producers (Fearne and Walters, 2004) and specifically of the beef industry (Fearne, 1998) four factors are identified that have facilitated the growth of partnerships or vertical collaborative exercises. The most important driver for assurance schemes is food safety legislation and particularly the 1990 Food Safety Act and its requirement that the food industry must exercise 'due diligence' in ensuring the safety of food (Marsden et al., 2000). In practice, as Fearne (1998) notes this has meant that major retailers, but also we can add food manufacturers, have

> taken extraordinary steps to ensure the safety of products reaching them from their suppliers. . . . [T]he 1990 Food Safety Act compelled . . . [retailers] to effectively take control [of their supply chain], by instituting stringent quality assurance programmes with their suppliers, with a particular emphasis on traceability. In effect, risk management took over from added value as the key driver for greater co-ordination in the meat supply chain. (p. 220)

Another factor that promoted assurance schemes was BSE. Interestingly, Fearne (1998) argues that responding to BSE though a food safety issue played out in a quite different way to the impact food risk management. He claims that

> the real significance of the BSE crisis, in terms of its impact on vertical co-ordination, is that it shifted the emphasis away from

> risk management at the retail level and the need to conform to food safety legislation . . . to the restoration of consumer confidence. (p. 221)

Here public and private forms of regulation meshed together. For example, the government established a cattle passport system to trace cattle movements and played a part in the launch of Associated British Meats, an industry body, that promoted an industry-wide assurance scheme to establish minimum safety standards (Fearne, 1998: 221).

A third factor encouraging the development of assurance schemes has been changing consumer attitudes and behaviour (Fearne, 1998: 217–219). The decline in beef sales that had begun in the 1970s and continued in the 1980s was exacerbated by the BSE crisis. In an attempt to restore consumer confidence and move away from what had become a commodity product efforts were made to add value by creating regional brand identities and premium supermarket labels.

The final factor identified relates to the competitive strategies of supermarkets (Fearne, 1998: 219). As supermarkets become ever more influential in food supply chains but find it difficult to grow through the opening of new outlets, retailers compete for market share. To protect their customer base supermarkets compete on price and notions of quality and this directly impacts on their suppliers. For example, supermarket owned labels have embedded within them ideas of quality and rely upon the development of exclusive supply chains. As a result, there is increasing competition amongst retailer-led supply chains rather than between economic actors (such as food processors) within supply chains. Retailers seek out supply chain partners who can best meet their quality and price requirements.

Retailers' assurance schemes become a condition of entry of supply (Fearne and Walters, 2004: 13). Partnerships will involve farmers and abattoirs, abattoirs and supermarkets, and may even include breeders and feed companies (Fearne, 1998: 214). From the retailers' perspective they now have an assured system of quality control that can run from the farm to the shop. Despite the variety of assurance schemes they will all include: feeding, animal health, animal welfare, traceability, and transport and handling (Fearne, 1998: 220).

Although assurance schemes have now become widespread and a complement to public sector regulation doubts have been expressed as to whether they will help to raise standards. In their review of farm assurance in the red meat industry Fearne and Walters (2004: 88) conclude that provided farmers are complying with existing food law, then 'the costs of complying with farm assurance standards should be minimal.' In other words, producer assurance schemes may not act to ratchet up standards on the farm. Perhaps even more damning is the extension of UK assurance schemes overseas has revealed that a two-tier system operates:

> the level of farm assurance in Continental Europe and South America is not as high or as rigidly monitored as it is in the UK. Thus, in theory the UK share of domestic meat, beef in particular, should be increasing if retailers and large-scale food services operators apply their diligent strategies consistently. However, this is something that retailers have been reluctant to do. As long as consumers remain blissfully ignorant of the provenance of their meat and whether or not it is farm assured and why knowing either of these things might be of interest to them, it is not in the commercial interests of either the retailer or the processor, because imported meat is often sold at a discount to farm assured British meat. (Fearne and Walters, 2004: 89).

Assurance schemes can help bind together retailer supply chains and assist retailers (and manufacturers) in their responsibilities to manage risk. These schemes dovetail well with requirements on the traceability of beef imposed by the EU. Under Regulations 1760/2000 and 1825/2000 the Commission has established a mandatory and voluntary labelling scheme (Souza-Monteiro and Caswell, 2004). The former involves ear tags, animal passports and the maintenance of databases and links animals to slaughterhouses, and from slaughterhouses to retailers. The latter allows producers to provide additional information. In their review of traceability in major beef producing and trading countries Souza-Monteiro and Caswell (2004: 22) point out that the mandatory systems in the EU and Japan provide the most systematic means of providing information on the origin of the animal to the consumer. The importance of these two major beef markets to exporters, such as Australia and Brazil means that they too are adopting traceability schemes that can link individual animals to beef products.

CONCLUSIONS

As suggested in Part II of this volume, a complex model of food governance has emerged, in which public and private interests are bound together in ever more sophisticated ways to deliver safe food. In a red meat industry, subject to considerable volatility since the 1980s, crises around the safety of food have coalesced with longer-term changes of consumer preferences for healthier foods leading to greater competition from white meat, notably chicken. These trends all have potential negative impacts on the red meat industry, and, for UK producers, are compounded by threats from imported meat.

One outcome has been that regulatory and market practices have converged. Traceability of animals through production, slaughter and onto supermarket shelves is both a regulatory requirement and a source of competitive advantage. Red meat is not a branded product in the manner of other foods. It is dominated by the supermarkets' own labels. But a source of market differentiation for both producers and retailers arises out of geographical origin of animals as a substitute for branding (e.g. Scottish beef or Welsh lamb).

Supermarkets have sought to create their own supreme quality brands by contracting with slaughtering companies and farmers, usually in a specific region, to supply (perhaps) beef that has been treated in a way prespecified by farmers, slaughterhouses and the retail chain. All of the major retail chains in the UK have established such 'quality assurance schemes', a development which has accelerated since the BSE crisis. The lamb and beef supply chains are similar in their nature and performance whereas in comparison the pork supply chain has a higher degree of vertical co-ordination and concentration of supply. Hence, traceability is relatively easier with a reduced need for specific schemes to improve traceability.

The emergence of strategic collaboration of different actors in 'value' supply chains to meet specific market objectives over the long term and for the mutual (though not equal) benefit of all 'links' of the chain, is noticeable. The increasing dominance of supermarkets, and their own label products, has led to the development of distinctive supply chains and competition between rather than within supply chains. This increased competition has been a major factor driving partnerships between specific retailers, abattoirs and producers (Fearne, 1998). The competition between major UK food retailers surrounds product quality and high service standards offered by different retailers. Alliances and direct contracting between input suppliers, processor-suppliers and retailers are compressing the red meat supply chains. According to Vorley (1999), this vertical coordination is driven by the need for traceability and 'due diligence', consistency of product, assurance of supply and avoidance of contamination by pathogens (e.g. BSE, E. coli).

Producer clubs are a good example of dedicated producer partnerships that have developed over the recent years in the red meat supply chain. These producer clubs aim to ensure traceability and quality of production and also partnership relationships between the farmers, processor and the supermarket. Major processors like St Merryn Meats (part of Grampian country foods) who supply to Tesco, ABP (supplier to Asda and Sainsbury's), Foyle (supplier to Tesco and Albert Heijn) have dedicated producer clubs.

Assurance and certification schemes both help in market differentiation and in meeting general hygiene, traceability and quality assurance concerns in the European Union meat sector. Subscription to a private standard in the red meat industry may go much of the way to ensuring compliance with publicly-set standards, illustrating the interplay between public and private regulatory practices, an experience prevalent more generally within UK food supply.

Part IV

Key Contemporary Dynamics of Regulation

9 The New Institutional Fabric
The Public Management of Food Risks

INTRODUCTION

The governance of food in Britain and Europe has been in a state of flux in recent years (see Chapter 4). In Britain, for over a decade, from the mid 1980s to the late 1990s, the then Ministry of Agriculture, Fisheries and Food (MAFF) found itself mired in a series of food controversies. Eventually, partly overwhelmed by its inability to reassure consumers or the food industry on the safety of food in Britain the Ministry was replaced by the Food Standards Agency (FSA). Meanwhile, British food controversies exposed weaknesses in the management of food at the European level and stimulated a similar bout of institutional reform, culminating in DGXXIV and the European Food Safety Authority (EFSA).

In this chapter we trace in detail the background to the FSA and review that for the EFSA (since for the latter much relevant material has already been covered in Chapter 4), two new agencies that have helped to transform the nature of food governance. Although both agencies arose out of crises and attempts to restore credibility to public forms of regulation, their relative authority is markedly different. EFSA, like a number of other EU agencies, lacks the independence and powers of regulatory bodies found at the Member State level. Consequently, in this chapter we will devote more attention to the working and achievements of the FSA.

Following the review the background to the formation of the FSA and its formal role, we then describe how the creation of the FSA has changed the relationship with local government and how these patterns have shifted the nature of food governance in Britain. To analyse the changing nature of food governance two models are outlined; one coercive and the other partnership based. An assessment of the extent to which the FSA works with one or other of these models is then made by exploring how the FSA approaches the enforcement activities of local government since these are reshaping the landscape of food governance. Finally, the chapter addresses the role and remit of the EFSA and how it may contribute to food safety across Europe.

BACKGROUND TO THE FSA

In part the creation of the FSA was simply a changing of organisational labels since the FSA took over many of the food safety responsibilities of MAFF but gained very few additional powers. However, the changing governance of food in Britain is a much more complex story. The FSA has wanted to make a difference to food governance. At the most obvious level the FSA represents a move to a more transparent and inclusive process of governance that sharply contrasts with the widely perceived closed style of government that characterised the Ministry of Agriculture. As one senior figure in the FSA has commented:

> Our experience so far is that the powers we have are certainly adequate. It is the way we use them that is critical and the work we do and the new ways we find of doing work which has not been done before. The openness agenda was a new approach to that (Bell, 2003)

As part of the changed approach to governance, the FSA has sought to alter existing relationships, such as the food enforcement activities of local government, and to engage with stakeholders in a way quite different from MAFF. Patterns of food governance in Britain, though, have also been shaped by a broader restructuring of risk, and within the food sector have increasingly involved a European level regulatory dimension (see Smith et al., 2004 for a much fuller analysis of these trends).

The system of food safety that was dominant under MAFF regarded food and agricultural production systems as being safe unless proven otherwise by technical and quantitative analyses. In this way, government (and the food industry) had a rational and scientific basis on which to rest relevant public health and food quality assurance policies. The transformation, since the mid-1980s, in how food risk is perceived and the new regulatory framework that has emerged to mediate the new concerns, have been traced by Marsden et al. (2000). In depicting the evolution that was taking place in food safety assurance strategies in the UK from the 1980s into 1990s, they pointed to a transition from a traditional government-led corporatist regulatory and monitoring model (conservative, proof-based approach enforced at the local level by Environmental Health and Trading Standards Officers) to a new phase dominated by supply-chain management, and food standards strategies, designed and applied by the large multiple food retailers. In this case, food-safety issues are perceived by large food retailers; the public sector, principally local government is left to act mainly as an auditor rather than a standard-setter and enforcer of the mainstream process.

In terms of understanding food safety, the FSA has found itself having to operate with classic issues of governance. The debate about governance is about understanding how to steer society towards collective goals, in this case improved food safety. The FSA represents one of the ways in which we are witnessing the wider 'hollowing out' of the state, since it is the removal of formerly central government responsibilities to a Non-Ministerial Department (NPD). Since the food industry has complex and globalised supply chains with sophisticated notions of quality, governments at a national and European level have to seek to engage in new forms of intervention to retain a regulatory and enforcement role. In relation to food safety, as in many other policy areas, governments cannot simply exercise their authority through traditional top-down models. Long-standing government structures and interventions seem anachronistic. Governments now face challenges of policy co-ordination and power sharing as more actors engage in policy making and implementation. In other words, the traditional clear divide between government and other actors begins to dissolve. Public policy goals of food safety and quality increasingly depend upon the standards promoted in their food supply chains by private sector companies. In a context in which the boundaries between public and private sectors are becoming more blurred than before we are interested to critically examine the extent to which the FSA can make a difference to the regulation of food in Britain and to do that we need to analyse the ways in which it tries to promote regulation through the enforcement activities of local government. As we shall see, improving local government enforcement activities as a means to improve food safety is a key role for the FSA.

Food controversies during the 1990s for the most part concerned issues of safety (e.g. salmonella, E.coli, BSE) and raised searching questions about the source and method of food regulation, especially the variability of local government enforcement practices. A high point of political and public concern occurred in the late 1990s, when within the same month (April 1997) eminent commentators were reporting for the government on E.coli (The Pennington Group, 1997) and for the then Labour opposition on a Food Standards Agency (James, 1997). Both reports documented the changing nature of food regulation processes, highlighted weaknesses in current implementation practices, and pointed to the confusing range of responsibilities and professionals involved in food regulation. Both reports concerned themselves with a range of food regulators and regulatory activities, and pinpointed the key role of environmental health and trading standards departments in ensuring food standards and safety (James, 1997: 11). The major change in regulatory structures that the outgoing Conservative and incoming Labour governments envisaged was the Food Standards Agency (FSA). The creation of a new body (largely) untainted by the food scares of the 1980s and 1990s was widely welcomed.

The Labour Government elected in 1997 published in January of the following year (1998) a White Paper (Cm3830) setting out its proposals for the FSA. The Bill to establish the FSA received Royal Assent in November 1999 and became operational on 3 April 2000. The speedy passage of the Bill through a crowded parliamentary timetable demonstrated the Government's commitment to the idea of a new food safety agency.

WHY ESTABLISH THE FSA?

The Government's thinking on the FSA largely followed that of the earlier James Report. The White Paper (Cm3830) on the FSA identified three factors that had eroded confidence in food safety. First, there was the conflict of interest within the Ministry of Agriculture, Fisheries and Food (MAFF) between its responsibilities for sponsoring the food and farm industries and ensuring the safety of food. Critics alleged that too often MAFF favoured producer over consumer interests. Second, the fragmentation of responsibilities for food within government between MAFF and the Department of Health was believed to lead to confusion. Third, there was uneven enforcement of food law by local government environmental health officers (EHOs). For some local authorities food was a high priority but for others it was not.

To address these problems the FSA had transferred to it from MAFF and the Department of Health most food safety matters to which were added limited but more extensive powers still. In consequence the FSA does not face the internal tensions that so bedevilled MAFF. The Agency also has responsibility for the Meat Hygiene Service, an executive agency. Moreover, the Agency reports to the Department of Health and not Agriculture (now DEFRA) so removing it as far as possible from the latter's productivist link, and ensuring a single line of command to government. The FSA also oversees enforcement by setting standards and auditing local authorities' compliance with them, so trying to directly tackle the problem of uneven enforcement. On the face of it, then, the creation of the FSA makes good many of the deficiencies that had been identified in the regulation of food.

The FSA's main objective as set out in the Food Safety Act 1999 is 'to protect public health from risks which may arise in connection with the consumption of food (including risks caused by the way in which it is produced or supplied) and otherwise to protect the interests of consumers in relation to food'. Restoring consumer confidence in the safety of food is, therefore, at the heart of the Agency. It is a task that MAFF especially and to a lesser extent the Department of Health proved unable to perform (see Barling and Lang, 2003). The Agency has marked out its distinctiveness from what has gone before by interpreting its responsibility to public health as three core values: they are to (a) put the consumer first, (b) to be open and accessible, and (c) to be an independent voice.

Whilst these values might have been shared by MAFF its reputation in relation to food safety had been so damaged that it could not have credibly promoted them. As one former senior MAFF official put it: 'the FSA was set up so that we could put the consumer first and part of that structure seems to me . . . that we must keep the food industry at arms length, and we shouldn't be seen to be associated with them because they're not nice people' . In large part, the FSA has been successful in achieving its core values (Dean Review, 2005).

Formally the key functions of the FSA are to:

- provide advice to the public and Ministers on food safety from farm to fork, food standards and nutrition;
- protect consumers through effective enforcement; and
- support consumer choice through effective labelling.

In the following section we outline how patterns of governance relate to structures and networks of responsibility and how these have changed with the creation of the FSA.

Patterns of Governance: Structures and Networks of Accountability and Responsibility

Figures 9.1 and 9.2 show the difference in organisational lines of responsibility and accountability pre and post the creation of the FSA. It is important to note, however, that there has been a broader dynamic of organisational change in food management of which the FSA has been a part. So, Figure 9.2 does show a changed organisational landscape but it is not one that is simply due to the creation of the FSA. Amongst the major organisational changes at a national level are the demise of MAFF, the creation of the Department of Communities and Local Government and the reform of LACOTS into LACORS. The creation of devolved administrations for Scotland and Wales has also compounded the sense of organisational change, since they will have responsibility for local government within their countries. At a European level too there has been organisational change with the development of DG SANCO to represent consumer affairs and the creation of the European Food Safety Authority (EFSA).

The two figures represent merely the public side of regulation and do not include the private supply chain regulation of food that also takes place (see Flynn et al., 1999). They indicate a dense network of formal relationships that has if anything become more complex over time. In terms of political accountability the FSA in England is responsible to Parliament through the Secretary of State for Health. What is also clear is that food remains a policy area with diffused responsibilities. For example, the Agency also has to co-operate on food issues with the DEFRA which has responsibility for issues like animal welfare, food labelling, GM foods and animal feeding-stuffs. The Department of Health retains responsibility for nutrition (HC 524, 2003: 23), foodborne diseases and the handling of emergencies (HC 524, 2003: 26). With both Departments the FSA has Framework Agreements to establish the roles and responsibilities of the different bodies. In its role as a Non-Ministerial Department the FSA negotiates in EU on behalf of the UK government and then leads on the implementation of EU food law in the UK.

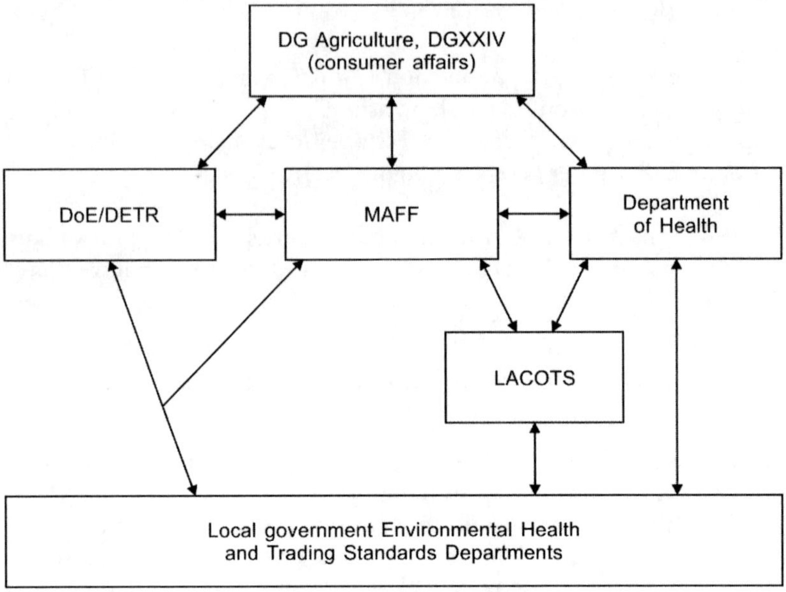

Notes:
DoE is the Department of the Environment
DETR is the Department of the Environment, Transport and the Regions
MAFF is the Ministry of Agriculture, Fisheries and Food
LACOTS is Local Authority Committee on Trading Standards

Figure 9.1 The structure of food regulation—pre-FSA.

As a body largely created from the staff and food standard safety responsibilities of MAFF and DoH the FSA is now at the centre of a network of food governance. But what do the changes arising from the creation of the FSA mean in practice? First, the FSA has become the national focal point for food issues. It is the key intermediary between European, national and devolved governments on the one side and local government on the other. What the Figures do not reveal however is that funding for local authority food hygiene and standards work remains the responsibility of central government. This key lever for promoting change remains outside of the remit of the FSA. Here is the conundrum faced by the FSA as it seeks to deliver on its remit: the Agency has the authority (as the authoritative voice on food safety) but limited power over key delivery agents (local government). Whilst both the FSA and local government have their own sources of legitimacy—the FSA's established by an Act of Parliament, and local governments as a unit of local democracy it can be difficult for the former to hold the latter to account since the constituencies that will hold them to account are so different.

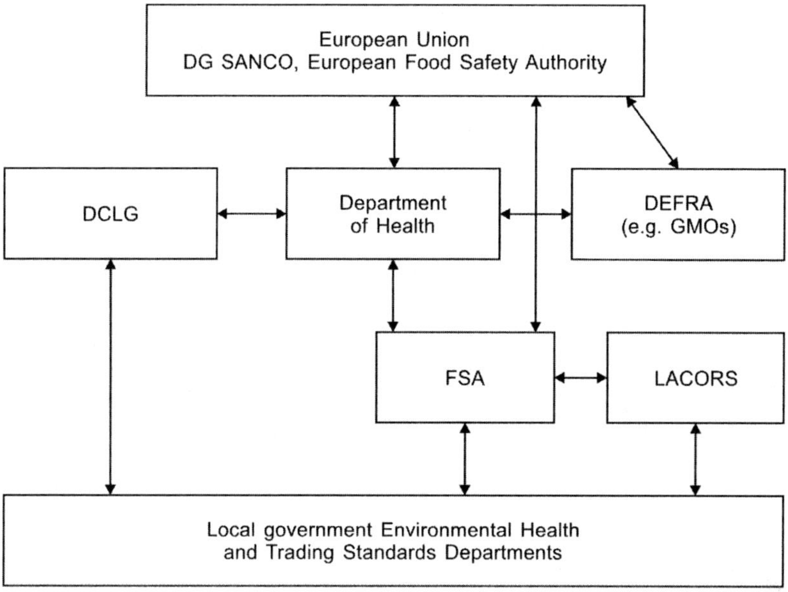

Notes:

The diagram above does not show the impact of the devolved administrations for Wales and Scotland. In Wales the Welsh Assembly Government and in Scotland the Scottish Executive will play the part of the Office of the Deputy Prime Minister.

DCLG is the Department of Communities and Local Government and replaced the Office of the Deputy Prime Minister (ODPM)
DoH is Department of Health.
DEFRA is Department of Food and Rural Affairs
LACORS is Local Authority Co-ordinators of Regulatory Services

Figure 9.2 The structure of food regulation in England: The FSA.

This context has important implications for our understanding of food governance.

Second, at a national level the likely overlap between the functions of LACOTS and the FSA in relation to promoting good practice and consistent enforcement practices seems to have been resolved. LACOTS which changed its name in April 2000 to LACORS (Local Authorities Co-ordinators of Regulatory Services) are bodies created by the Local Government Associations to co-ordinate local government activities. Pre-FSA, LACOTS performed a number of food law roles such as an interpreter of law, communicator between central and local government and general trouble-shooter. It also issued guidance notes to local authorities, participated in consultation with government and industry, co-ordinated operational practices of authorities and ensured revised patterns of enforcement, often arising from EC membership, were effective. In short, it sought to achieve greater consistency in local government enforcement practice. Given that these functions were given to the FSA, it is necessary to consider what role LACOTS had after the creation of the FSA in April 2000. The possibility of overlap of functions was addressed in a Concordat between the FSA and LACOTS, which sets out the framework for co-operation between the bodies.

Nevertheless the question remains, why was LACOTS not dissolved upon the creation of the Agency in order to avoid duplication of efforts? The answer is that the FSA and LACORS are creatures of different levels of government. LACORS is a representative body of local government and therefore seeks to protect and promote local government activities. The FSA was a creation of national government and although it has very close relations with local government it is not part of local government and will not always share its agenda and therefore a role remains for a body such as LACORS.

Third, that there is a role for LACORS alongside the FSA illustrates how complex patterns of food governance can emerge. Indeed, Figures 9.1 and 9.2 present a much simplified picture of food governance. Although the FSA is the pre-eminent food regulatory body a number of other bodies have food enforcement responsibilities (FSA, 2002a: 3):

Meat Hygiene Service—responsible for enforcing legislation in slaughterhouses and cutting plants. This is an executive agency that reports to the FSA.

Horticultural Marketing Inspectorate—responsible for checking the quality of fruit and vegetables in the UK.

Dairy Hygiene Inspectorate—responsible for checking standards at milk production holdings.

Egg Marketing Inspectorate—responsible for checking standards in egg production, packing and distribution centres.

Wine Standards Board—responsible for monitoring standards in wine making.

Port Health Authorities and Border Inspection Posts—responsible for checking food imports and products of animal origin. These can only enter the UK through authorised Border Inspection Posts.

Apart from the Meat Hygiene Service the other bodies are in large part independent of the FSA, though Port Health Authorities and Border Inspection Posts fall within the FSAs inspection remit.

FOOD GOVERNANCE

Over the last decade, the concept of governance has gained a central place in contemporary debates in the social sciences and has informed a wide array of policy documents. 'Governance'—as opposed to 'government'—has become an important concept of describing and proposing strategies for policy-making (Pierre and Peters, 2000). Or as Hooghe and Marks (2003: 233) succinctly express it, governance is the study of binding decision making in the public sphere. The debate about governance arose when political, social and economic framework conditions brought about a questioning of traditional forms of government intervention and policy-making (Jessop, 2000). Governance, therefore, represents both a means to analyse changes in the making and delivering of policy, and of a normative dimension that favours negotiation and the active involvement of all levels of government (European, national, regional and local), societal stakeholders and civil society organizations in the policy process.

The tension between analytical and normative perspectives on governance is also present in debates on multi-level governance. At a prescriptive level, multi-level governance refers to the stronger inclusion of all tiers of government in the design, formulation and implementation of policies. There is, though, a particular twist to these debates with regard to food safety policy, since it involves both horizontal integration (across policy areas, for instance embracing obesity and nutrition) as well as vertical integration. Vertical policy integration stands for coordinated policymaking and it is about matching 'the geographical space of the affected environment [with] the institutional space of the relevant authorities' (Liberatore, 1997: 116). However, as Hajer (2003: 183) argues, at a territorial level institutions are losing their effectiveness and legitimacy. This is because new actors are contributing to policy debates, such as NGOs, and decision making is now taking place over much more diverse spatial scales than in the past (e.g. as a result of moves upwards to more decisions at the supranational scale, such as by the European Union or World Trade Organisation, or downwards to devolved administrations).

From a governance perspective, therefore, the FSA raises a number of interesting questions. First, how does a UK body seek to assert its legitimacy when, as Hajer (2003) suggests, territorial institutions are facing novel challenges? Second, a key task for the FSA has been to promote more even standards of enforcement activity by local government, but in seeking to achieve this goal has the Agency recognised how devolution will have changed the governance landscape? Third, how do vertical relations of governance work in practice? Whilst multi-level governance often implies inclusivity, it tends to ignore relations of power. Here we need to think of governance as hierarchies, as part of the everyday practice of political life (Rhodes, 2000). For the FSA vertical relations will be important in its dealings with the European Union, but of more importance for this paper, is how the Agency seeks to invoke its power and authority over local government.

In answering these questions it is essential to analyse the manner in which the FSA seeks to engage in relationships with local government. The types of relationship in which the FSA might be involved are complex. Hooghe and Marks (2003: 236) have distinguished between two types of multi-level governance. Type I 'bundle together multiple functions, including a range of policy responsibilities' and operate at the territorial level and different scales of territory are nested one within another. As Figure 9.1 illustrates, Type I governance is a reasonable description of the organisation of food safety prior to the formation of the FSA. At the UK government level multi-functional departments shared responsibility for formulating policy, which was then largely delivered by multi-purpose local authorities. Type II governance is 'fragmented into functionally specific pieces—say, providing a particular local service, solving a particular common resource problem [and so on]'. The task specific nature of the organization of food safety following the creation of the FSA is illustrated in Figure 9.2. Food safety operates on multiple spatial scales but the FSA provides a focal point at the level of UK government and works largely with food specialists in local government rather than the range of tasks that local government performs. The FSA is separating out the food expertise in local government from the other tasks that are performed. As Figure 9.2 shows the FSA is likely to be involved in a set of hierarchical rather than horizontal relationships.

Type I and Type II models of multi-level governance are not mutually exclusive. Indeed, as Hooghe and Marks (2003: 238) note Type II governance is generally embedded in Type I governance. This raises particularly interesting issues for the way in which the FSA will seek to realise its goals in relation to improving local government enforcement practices. Does the FSA seek to coerce local authorities or work in partnership with them? Or does the FSA seek to establish a more variable geometry of relationships with local government in which it works with both coercive and partnership models of governance? What are the resources that the FSA can bring to the networks in which it operates to try and promote its agenda?

Governance is not only about structures and institutions but also actors, processes and outcomes. It is important to understand the interactions and networks that exist between structures. One way of seeking to understand the interactions between institutions, actors, processes and how this may produce different outcomes is to develop two ideal types of food governance in Britain and then explore them for the activities of the FSA. In Table 9.1 we outline an ideal-type model of coercive and partnership-based multi-level governance. The features in the ideal type draw on some of the themes identified by May et al. (1996) in their study of co-operative and coercive environmental intergovernmentalism.

If we select some of the key features of Table 9.1 for further discussion in relation to the FSA's approach to local authority enforcement strategies the dynamic between the two ideal types of governance becomes clearer. For instance, with regard to targets, the FSA to distinguish itself from the former food safety regime was keen to impose targets on local government, for example, the number of councils to have their food

Table 9.1 Ideal Types of Food Governance

Feature	*Coercive*	*Partnership*
Targets	Set from centre, prescriptive	Agreed by consent
Means to achieve goals	Hold to account and audit, rule bound relationships	Educate and spread knowledge
Accountable to	Higher level of government	Public, stakeholder groups and government
Agendas	Likely to be different agendas held by different actors	Seek shared agenda
Lower-level autonomy	Minimise local discretion	Accept local discretion and autonomy
Knowledge	Concentrated at the centre and to be dispersed from the centre outwards	Knowledge diffused and seek means to utilise local knowledge
Openness	Limited and to favoured few	Consultative and participatory
Views of lower-tier of government	Hierarchy	Partner in policy delivery
Funding	Ring fence budgets	Budgets determined according to local priorities within a common agenda
Policy outcomes	Seek uniformity around a baseline because monitoring for compliance with targets	Accept variability above baseline because seeking improvements in practice and spreading knowledge

service delivery audited. The setting of targets was also an important early indicator of the way in which the FSA intended to achieve its goals. With responsibility for nearly 500 food authorities, the FSA believed it would be easier to hold them to account by setting prescriptive targets and establishing a rule-bound framework that limited councils freedom of manoeuvre, than by seeking to establish a more collaborative (and resource intensive) way of working. Such a stance is quite understandable since the FSA was established at a time of crisis in food regulation in the UK and needed to demonstrate to consumers, the food industry, consumer NGOs and ministers that it could raise standards of food regulation. The profile of the Agency and its credibility were much more likely to be enhanced by the perception that it was setting tough targets and rigorously holding to account local authorities whose enforcement practices were too often regarded as lax. As a result, the FSA has consistently sought to constrain local autonomy. In its early years in particular, it meant that the FSA was likely to adopt a hectoring tone towards local government and exhibit low levels of trust in its ability to deliver higher standards of food safety. Here, there was little sense of local government being a partner in policy delivery.

The model of food governance is not suggesting that organisations will engage in either co-operative or coercive relationships since the features of the models are not necessarily mutually exclusive. Nevertheless some of the features are likely to reinforce one another. What is also clear is that the FSA's relationship with local government is a dynamic one, and there are pointers to suggest that the FSA is seeking to establish a more partnership-based style of working. A partnership model of governance will have both more complex sets of relationships by which to achieve goals and also for establishing and reporting on the accountability of an organisation. For example, whilst the FSA has been unwilling to relax its approach to limiting local discretion it has sought to engage local authorities in developing a common agenda on enforcement (such as themes for partial audits or in the work of the Enforcement Liaison Group). It is here that the tensions in the Agency's approach to local government may be most apparent: its drive for consistency is reflected in a more coercive style of governance but this potentially clashes with the more partnership styles of governance that have been nurtured in Scotland and especially Wales following devolution. (The spatial variability of governance is discussed further in this chapter). In practice, therefore, the FSA vacillates between a coercive and partnership model of governance as it pushes and probes for opportunities and leverage with which to pursue its goals.

We can now explore how the model may operate in relation to the FSA's approach to enforcement.

Enforcement Strategy

Analysis of the FSA's approach to the work of local government enforcement activities needs to concentrate on two areas: the enforcement activities and the auditing regime. Before that, though, it is worth putting into context the resource that the FSA devotes to enforcement activities and how this may influence its engagement with local government.

Data on FSA expenditure for 2002 indicates that only 5% of the budget was allocated to food law enforcement. The lion's share of the budget was taken up with tackling BSE (27% of expenditure). By the following year with BSE less prominent as a public policy issue expenditure on it had fallen to 21% whilst that on food law enforcement had jumped to 26%. Data on 2004 expenditure shows that the proportion devoted to food law enforcement continued to grow to 34% and the next most important item was 'food safety: BSE' which continued to decline to 18% (FSA, 2002b; 2003a; 2004).

The shifts in expenditure within a short time frame are remarkable. In the earliest years of the FSA the limited resourcing of food law enforcement is revealing of its initial (political) priorities (i.e. the prominence of BSE) and inevitably shaped the nature of governance relationships and responsibilities. With limited funding Agency staff would have found it very difficult to invest in the resources to develop the capacity to engage in partnership building with local government. In any case, with levels of trust so low in local government food enforcement it would have been difficult to justify such resourcing. So, the favoured approach was for the FSA to act in a much more coercive manner towards local government but in doing so lacked a key lever, namely control of funding. Here the FSA faces one of the classic challenges of governance: how can it steer others to achieve its own policy goals?

Lax enforcement of food law was perceived by the FSA to have been a key factor in the number of food borne illnesses in the UK. The assumption was that more effective enforcement would raise standards in food businesses and thus improve the safety of food that people eat and so meet the Agency's strategic aim of reducing food borne illnesses by 20% by 2006. (FSA , 2002a: para 2.4). A clear indication of the Agency's lack of faith in local government was contained in its Departmental Report for 2001 which noted:

> 'Effective enforcement of measures to protect the public is essential. We look closely at the evidence for effective enforcement, *or otherwise.* This is an important part of our role in relation to local authority enforcement of food law' (FSA 2001: para 2.15) (emphasis added).

An improvement in food law enforcement was a key priority of the Agency's first strategic plan for 2001–2006, and marked an important break with the past. An indication of how the FSA wished to tackle the challenge it faced is provided by how it was going to measure its own performance. For example, two key objectives related to local authority performance and their measurement included the provision of reports to the Board on local authority enforcement activity and of Agency audits (FSA, 2001).

The Agency's drive for consistency in local government enforcement activities by adopting a more coercive approach may have been in sympathy with the general approach of central government to local authorities in England. However, in the Devolved Administrations of Scotland and especially Wales an alternative more partnership-based approach to governance was being developed. The development of a more inclusive style of decision-making has become one of the defining features of devolved governance in Wales. In their review of the impact of devolution on the voluntary sector in Wales, Cheney and Fevre (2001) trace the centrality of inclusiveness in Wales to devolution debates in the mid 1990s. They argue that subsequently inclusiveness has come to dominate the discourse of devolution in Wales. They add that 'so central was . . . inclusiveness that it became prioritized and enshrined in the Assembly's legal framework'

(Cheney and Fevre, 2001: 152). Commentators have argued that Government of Wales Act placed a unique statutory obligation on the NAW to consult with business, the voluntary sector and local government (Kay, 2003) when making policy. Perhaps the best practical expression of a more inclusive style of governance in Wales is that of partnership working. For Entwhistle (2006: 229) partnership is a form of governance that emphasises the benefits of long-term relationships based on trust, common values, equality and reciprocity. Policy problems are to be solved through co-operation rather than coercion. Co-ordination of policy is increasingly through networks that exchange information rather than through central organisations that seek to impose solutions (see also Day, 2006: 647). The contrast between the styles of governance promoted by the Welsh Office (characterised as coercive) and National Assembly (characterised as partnership) are potentially marked. Although, the Agency has subsequently made efforts to adopt a more cooperative approach to local government, there are indications that it may still not have done enough to fully embrace the changes in governance that have taken place in Wales and Scotland. The Dean Review (2005: 37) of the FSA though concerned with slightly different issues has pointed out that there is a 'general view . . . in the devolved countries that the Agency is fundamentally an England-centric organisation'. In a report on food safety in Scotland, produced by the Scottish Consumer Council (2004), it was claimed that a common experience of local authority staff was that the FSA seems to place too much importance on auditing and statistics rather than on actual enforcement. One officer summarised this perspective:

> The FSA sees environmental health departments as a means of doing their "donkey work". No credit is offered—merely criticism during audits. They are more interested in paper work, statistics etc. (quoted in SCC, 2004:18).

FSA Enforcement Activities

Food enforcement work is shared between the FSA and local government. Local authorities are the frontline, the primary food enforcement body at the local level; the FSA is responsible for the development of food enforcement policy and support functions for local government. Within local government, enforcement is carried out by Trading Standards Officers (TSOs) and Environmental Health Officers (EHOs). TSOs cover such issues as legislation on food standards and labelling. EHOs are responsible for work on food hygiene, including food safety and microbiological contamination. The FSA is consistent in its message that it is working with local government to promote better food standards (see, for example, FSA, 2005: para 2.43, for a message that is almost word-for-word that of previous annual Departmental Reports). The Food Standards Act 1999 provides the FSA

with a package of statutory powers to strengthen its influence over enforcement activity (FSA, 2002c: 3). The Act gives the Agency powers to:
Set standards of performance in relation to the enforcement of food law

- Monitor and audit the performance of local government.
- Require information from local authorities relating to food law enforcement and inspect any records.
- Enter local government premises to inspect records and take samples.
- Publish information on the performance of local government.
- Make reports to individual local authorities, including guidance on improving performance.
- Require local government to publish these reports and state what action they will take as a response.

These powers appear to be wide-ranging and interventionist. They also fit well in a coercive model of governance with the emphasis on inspection, audit, standard setting and monitoring. Whilst the powers are significant they do not in themselves provide the levers to make local authorities single-mindedly pursue an FSA agenda. Powers to influence local government agendas remain well outside the remit of the FSA, for example in the hands of the Department of Communities and Local Government and the Devolved Administrations. So a potentially coercive style of governance has to be nuanced by the FSA: the Agency can hector and cajole but it would find it difficult to coerce local government. Even where the FSA may be able to act in a more coercive style through its audit powers it finds them potentially undermined by the actions of the Audit Commission which has its own food enforcement performance indicators and which is accorded a higher priority in local government than the FSA (local government interview).

THE FSA ENFORCEMENT AGENDA

The FSA recognises that the effectiveness of food law depends on how well it is enforced. '[A] key role for the Agency is to work with local authorities to ensure the effectiveness of UK food law enforcement' (FSA, 2002c: 6). In an early statement of its approach the FSA stated that it would promote more effective enforcement by (FSA, 2002c: 6):

- Providing guidance and support for local enforcement staff.
- Ensuring proportionate and more consistent enforcement.
- Providing more information about standards of food safety.
- Improving the transparency of enforcement arrangements for stakeholders.

- Promoting the wider implementation of risk-based systems for improving safety standards across the food chain.

Key features of the model for improving local enforcement are that first it is partnership based—local government is to be guided and supported. This would seem to be partly a result of the philosophy of governance that promotes partnership as a preferred way of working but also partly recognition of the limitations of FSA powers over local government. It has very limited authority to dictate to local government and a dictatorial stance might lead to a breakdown in relations with local government and undermine the FSAs enforcement strategy. Indeed, over time there is every indication that the FSA is moving towards a more partnership based model of governance. For example, more emphasis has been given to the Enforcement Liason Group that brings together Agency and local government staff with other key stakeholders and has played a formative role in helping to reshape the FSA's enforcement approach. It has discussed much more sophisticated notions of what is meant by consistency of enforcement (ELG, 2002) and helped to inform the Agency's approach to regulation. During 2006 a new approach to local government working was developed following a review of the Framework agreement between the FSA and local government. In part, a revised approach in which 'We [the FSA] want to move . . . [from] measuring inputs to outcomes' (ELG, 2006) was informed by broader government thinking on regulation (e.g. the Hampton report 2005) and in part to respond to the concerns of a key partner:

> 'Local Authorities have told us [the FSA] that they want to move away from an inspection based system and tick box approach to enforcement'. (ELG, 2006)

Second, the FSA is keen to promote consistent and transparent enforcement by local government. Here a more coercive model of relations between the FSA and local government is implied. Consistency and proportionality in enforcement activity will mean that decisions are not made according to local circumstances but by centrally based (and probably centrally developed) criteria. An indicator of the Agency's thinking is the comment that:

> One key area of the Agency's work has been to strengthen links with LAs. To help achieve this a Framework Agreement on Local Authority Food Law Enforcement was developed with a joint Government/local authority group (the Local Authority Enforcement Liaison Group). The Framework Agreement includes the standards and arrangements through which the Agency sets, monitors and audits local enforcement services. (FSA, 2002c: 6)

This would seem to undermine the local discretion implicit within a partnership model.

Third, the approach is typical of the rational model of decision making with the belief that providing actors with information on their performance will make them better informed and so willing to improve their performance. Such a belief, however, tends to ignore the realities of enforcement activity where actors find themselves confronted by competing demands for their time and resources and where local politics may play a big part in their activities—all often undermine a rational mode of behaviour.

The Framework Agreement on Food Law came into force on 1 April 2001 and is but one of a number of such agreements that have been negotiated between the Local Government Association (or the Welsh Local Government Association) and government and its agencies across the range of local governments work. The Framework was developed through the Local Authority Enforcement Liaison Group (now the Enforcement Liaison Group). Typically Framework documents set out the responsibilities of the different actors and the expectations that they may have of each other's performance. For central government the Framework Agreements are a means of trying to ensure that local government shares its agenda and policy priorities. In other words, they are a mechanism for trying to overcome the diversity of local government by promoting greater consistency in its behaviour. So, the Framework Agreement on Food Law does not provide for any new powers or resources for local government or the FSA but in one document makes clear FSA expectations of local authority responsibilities for food law enforcement. It thus provides the Agency with a mechanism for implementing its powers under the Food Standards Act to influence and oversee local authority enforcement activity. The Agreement applies to local enforcement of all food laws, and incorporates the latest guidance and standards on food law enforcement.

There are four elements to the Agreement:

1. Publicly available local service plans to increase transparency of local enforcement services.
2. Agreed food law enforcement standards for local authorities.
3. Monitoring scheme with greater focus on inspection outcomes which provides more detailed information on local authority performance.
4. An audit scheme aimed at securing improvements and sharing good practice.

An interesting feature of the Framework is the demand that local authorities should develop Service Plans that outline their food enforcement activities and resourcing and these will provide the basis for FSA monitoring and auditing of individual authorities. Service Plans are to be drawn up by officers but should be approved by councillors to ensure political buy-in. Again Service Plans are a typical feature of other Framework Agreements.

Promoting greater consistency of enforcement by local government is one of the key messages emerging from the FSA. At first the Agency produced and then revised twenty Codes of Practice on food enforcement. The FSA has recognised that there would be considerable benefit in consolidating into a single document the separate Codes of Practice and this was achieved in 2006. The Agency is keen to promote even enforcement practices and to do this by ensuring that local government food officers work from a common knowledge base. As the preface to the Code notes 'The purpose of enforcement is to ensure compliance with legislation . . . The effective discharge of the duty relies on officers being familiar with the law' (FSA, 2006).

If the FSA can rationalise the knowledge base under which local government staff operate, then the belief is that there will be more consistency in enforcement. But does the available evidence back up this assumption? The FSA, in line with its commitment, to openness and transparency, has made available on its website individual local authority enforcement returns. Based upon the data, the FSA also began producing reports that could provide a league table of local government performance. The information, as we shall see in subsequent text is a double-edged sword. On the one side the FSA appears to hope that exposing instances of poor performance will force recalcitrant authorities into line through embarrassment or local political concern. On the other side the data exposes the weakness of local government food enforcement activities and so opens up to critical scrutiny the role of the FSA. Whilst the report based on data for 2000 was produced in early 2002, and the report for 2001 was prepared in 2003 (FSA, 2002c; FSA, 2003b), subsequent data on local government enforcement activities has not been subject to analysis.

The two reports produced by the FSA are classic examples of coercive approaches to governance. All local authorities are evaluated against common criteria and poor performing authorities are named and shamed. The policy implications are that further control of local government is required. The reports, perhaps, mark the high point of the FSA's adversarial approach to local government and also clearly illustrate the Agency's weakness in seeking to 'control' local government. As was to be expected, local government had a mixed response to the FSA's aggressive tactics—for some it could enhance the profile of food regulation, for others it led to disengagement or resistance to the Agency's approach. It is, perhaps, no coincidence that the quality of data returns by local government to the FSA reached a low point in 2002 and was so poor that they have never been published. The FSA was simply unable to exercise sufficient authority over local government to ensure data that was integral to a coercive style of governance could be collected. Subsequently the FSA was keener to adopt a more partnership style of governance. By the end of the following year (2003) the Agency had organised the first meeting of a new Enforcement Stakeholder Forum. At the inaugural meeting it was explained that

> 'The main principles behind the forum were:
> to provide an informal communication vehicle;
> to give stakeholders opportunity to discuss current and emerging issues;
> to *explore possibilities for productive partnership working*.' (Enforcement Stakeholder Meeting, 2 December 2003)

We now turn to consider how the FSA might have influenced local authority food enforcement.

LOCAL AUTHORITY ENFORCEMENT

The enforcement of food legislation is mainly carried out by of local government Environmental Health and Trading Standards Services (so-called enforcement authorities) in 499 food authorities. The food enforcement duties vary depending on the type of local authority:

English County Councils are responsible for enforcing food standards (e.g. checking food composition, labelling, claims and presentation matters). This work is carried out by Trading Standards Services.

English District Councils are responsible for enforcing food hygiene controls (e.g. staff hygiene, hygiene structures and equipment, level of hygiene and HACCP training, temperature controls etc). This is carried out by Environmental Health Services.

Unitary authorities (e.g. those in Wales), Metropolitan Borough Councils and London Boroughs are responsible for enforcing both food hygiene and food standards.

The statutory Code of Practice issued under Section 40 of the Food Safety Act 1990 lays down minimum inspection frequencies for premises according to their risk rating (see FSA, 2006: Appendix 5). Local authorities should aim to carry out 100% of the inspections due in each of the premises risk categories. For food hygiene (the work of EHOs) these currently are:

Category A—at least every six months.
Category B—at least every twelve months.
Category C—at least every eighteen months.
Category D—at least every two years.
Category E—these are low risk food businesses which should be visited at least once every three years.

Minimum frequencies for food standards inspections (by TSOs) currently are:

Category A—at least once every year.
Category B—at least once every two years.
Category C—at least once every five years.

The risks for different types of food premise are set by combining a variety of factors including: type of food and method of handling, and level of current compliance and confidence in management of the business.

Analysis of authorities reporting at least 100% of programmed inspections for premises risk rated Category A for food hygiene and high risk for food stands reveals considerable variation in performance by local authorities (FSA, 2002c: 14–15). First, the figures show that food standards inspections (i.e. the TSO role) are achieving a consistently better performance than the food hygiene work (i.e. the EHO role). For instance Welsh unitary authorities are amongst the worst performers (only one authority met the 100% target) in meeting their food hygiene targets but achieve the highest percentage (41%) for inspection of high risk premises. This may in part reflect the greater professional standing of TSOs compared to EHOs and/or greater ring fencing of the budgets of the former. Second, that for some types of authority (e.g. Welsh unitary, English district councils for food hygiene and the London Boroughs for food standards) there is a higher rate of inspection activity across lower rated risk premises for their food hygiene and food standards work (FSA, 2002c: 16–17). The FSA does not have a full explanation as to why some types of local authority should focus their efforts on lower risk rated premises but dryly notes 'as a national statistic it is of concern' (FSA, 2002c: 16). The implication is, of course, that when one activity measure is number of visits to food premises, and departments are perhaps under-resourced and under-staffed, that they concentrate on the less demanding low risk premises. The FSA has now recognised the problem and warned that:

> Establishments that are due or overdue for inspection should be inspected according to their respective inspection ratings, with those having higher ratings being prioritised for inspection over those with lower ratings. The practice of completing the inspection programme of lower rated establishments that have not been visited during an earlier programme before commencing the inspection of higher rated establishments cannot be supported' (FSA, 2006: Appendix 5, point vii).

Third, there is considerable variability in levels of enforcement activity. Metropolitan councils are the most active in taking enforcement action and district councils the least active. There is also a large degree of variation in enforcement action within authorities of the same type (FSA, 2002c: 18).

Finally, there is also considerable variation in sampling rates both between and within different types of local authority (FSA, 2002c: 23). In follow-up work with local authorities the FSA reported 'that there was a tendency for authorities to give much higher status and priority to food premises inspection work compared to food sampling. This may be partly due to inspection work being included as an Audit Commission performance indicator, whereas sampling has not' (FSA, 2002c: 24). The message here is simple: local authorities find themselves operating in a complex web of relationships and not surprisingly sometimes receive inconsistent messages from central government or its agencies. Local authorities respond to the pressures that they regard as most acute and in this case the Audit Commission is regarded as more important than the FSA. It also illustrates the ways in which other agencies, which have no obvious food remit, can impinge on the regulation of food.

Why Do Inconsistencies Remain with Enforcement?

The FSA has identified what it believes are three key factors that account for poor performance of some local authorities. These are:

1. Local authorities had to devote resources to dealing with foot and mouth disease.
2. There are problems with staff retention and recruitment.
3. Software problems have meant that some local authorities could not record their enforcement activities.

What is interesting about the FSA analysis is that it points to resource and software issues that can be resolved but not to ones of intergovernmentalism that are much more challenging. The FSA response is therefore a classic one of further control and management of a problem as it intends to:

- Check that poorly performing local authorities do meet their inspection targets by subjecting them to an audit.
- Name (and shame) poor performers are identified on the FSA website (see FSA, 2003b: Appendix 2). Public identification it is hoped will allow citizens, officers and councillors to find out who the poor performers are and then to put pressure on them to improve.
- Meet with stakeholders to discuss why problems have arisen.
- Start assessing local authority performance against very limited indicators of enforcement activity.

Statutory Codes of Practice require local authorities to have a risk based inspection programme with an expectation that all high-risk food businesses will be visited at least once a year. Whilst this is the expectation of the FSA they have used a measure of under 50% of high- risk inspections being carried out as a basis for identifying local authorities with 'clearly unacceptable levels of enforcement' (FSA, 2003b: para 19). The vast majority of local authorities are operating well in advance of these levels. In view of this and to encourage further improvements in local authority performance the FSA propose to increase measures of inspection levels by 5% each year for the next five years (FSA, 2003b: para 19).

There is clearly an implementation deficit between the requirement of at least one visit per year to high-risk food businesses and what is happening in practice. It is not clear how big the deficit is or whether it is closing. It is also not clear that simply setting more testing targets by which local authorities are assessed as unacceptable performers will lead to an improvement in performance. This is in large part because enforcement seems to be dependent on issues that even the FSA identifies as outside of its control. These include external issues making resource demands on local government, different local political priorities (that presumably accept naming and shaming and/or an audit by the FSA as an acceptable price to pay), and problems with staff recruitment and retention. As the FSA admits: 'enforcement is a matter which resides with local authorities. Our power there [for enforcement] concerns the audit of local authorities and being able to say when they need to do more and we will help them to do more' (Bell, 2003). (Details of the FSA audits of local food authorities are explained further in this chapter).

The FSA's commitment to transparency has made clear the extent of the variability in local government enforcement activities that have been alluded to over a number of years (for example going back to the James report). Until now though there had been little publicly available data on the topic. Having exposed the variability in performance the FSA has the challenge of reducing it. However, it has only limited tools by which to 'manage' local government and so overcoming its diversity is going to be an issue on which the FSA may find itself in a rather vulnerable position.

More recently, there has been recognition that simply seeking to exercise further controls on local government may not be sufficient. In a major policy statement the FSA has heralded a new vision for enforcement. In a letter to local authority chief executives in England (November 2006) it was explained that the Agency 'propose[s] that the current focus on inspections will be augmented by a suite of interventions, so giving local authorities the *flexibility* to choose the appropriate intervention for each premises' (emphasis added).

The shift in emphasis here is significant: from its previous approach of prescription and seeking to constrain the freedom of manoeuvre of local government food enforcement staff, the Agency will now be permitting variation in practice between authorities and encouraging the development of thinking on shared outcomes; an approach that is much more sympathetic to the partnership model of food governance.

AUDITING LOCAL GOVERNMENT

Initially the Agency aimed to audit forty local authorities in England each year. Its counterparts in Scotland, Wales and Northern Ireland each operate their own audit programmes. However, by 2002, and the signs of a greater rapprochement with local government, the audit programme was revised to include themed audits. Although full audits continue, and by the end of March 2005 some ninety-nine authorities (seventy in England, all twenty-two in Wales and seven in Northern Ireland) had been subject to a full audit (FSA, 2005: para 2.49), themed audits, based around a particular topic, have become increasingly popular and have been applied to 105 authorities (eighty-eight in England, nine in Northern Ireland and eight in Scotland). In Scotland a rather different approach applies, as there authorities receive a partial audit once a year for three years.

An audit programme is published quarterly in advance of the audits. Local authorities are selected to represent a cross-section of local authority types, geographical location and level of enforcement activity as indicated by quarterly monitoring returns. Audits employ a pre-visit questionnaire requesting information from local authorities and sent three months prior to the on-site audit; an audit protocol and audit checklists; and on-site officer interviews. The on-site visits for a full audit will typically last two to three days and may also include visits to local food business. In line with its commitment to openness and transparency, the Agency publishes the reports from these audits, together with the local authorities' action plans to address the recommendations made. In order to secure improvement, follow-up action is undertaken by the Agency approximately six months after the audit report is published, to assess the progress local authorities have made in implementing their action plans. In some circumstances this will entail a re-visit to local authorities. In others, correspondence between the Agency and the local authority may suffice. Agreed revised action plans are published with the audit reports. The audit regime clearly fits into the coercive style of governance.

Audits may well prove to be a useful way of focussing the minds of local government staff on food enforcement. The audit reports may also be a good way of feeding back to individual local authorities' good practice in food management. Audits could thus prove to be a useful tool for raising food enforcement standards in local government. The problem for the FSA is that if audits and inspections are its key tools of management (by coercion) they are unlikely to engender the broader change that it wishes to see in commitment to local food enforcement. This is because the Agency cannot offer other coercive tools such as ring fencing funding to support its position. It therefore also has to work with more partnership-based tools such as Framework Agreements in the hope that these will raise the profile of food enforcement within local government. In a frank assessment of the difficulties that the FSA faces, one of its then senior figures, Jon Bell has admitted when questioned by the Commons Public Accounts Committee:

> We [the FSA] are very much there supporting the environmental health departments in doing their job and if they feel they have inadequate resources to meet the sort of targets we are setting, then we are very much there to support them, in making the case to the council for more resource. At the end of the day in the democratic system, the way it is set up, the council has to decide how to apportion its resources. (Bell, 2003)

EUROPEAN FOOD SAFETY AUTHORITY

The creation of DG SANCO may have eased some of the immediate political pressures within Europe on food safety and the consumer but it could not remove them. Two problems in particular remained difficult to handle. One was that there were continued controversies over food safety. Within Europe the speed and distance at which foods move along supply chains means that it can be very difficult for regulators to geographically confine a food safety problem. By the time regulators are aware of a problem in one location the product may have moved to another location or locations. The result is that regulators firefight along a supply chain whose start and end point they may not even be fully aware of. Speaking in 2001 the then Commissioner responsible for DG SANCO, Byrne, expressed the problem clearly: 'we face common food safety problems—they respect no national boundaries. . . a food safety concern in one member state very quickly becomes a concern in another, and has implications for all the Community.' The second problem was that the science of food safety was often questioned. The answer to both problems was further organisational reform and the creation of the European Food Standards Agency (EFSA).

So, where did the initiative for EFSA come from? One starting point was the commissioning of a report in May 1999 by Philip James (who had drafted the James Report on the British Food Standards Agency) and two colleagues on how the EU might improve its provision of scientific advice in relation to food. They recommended in December 1999 the creation of an Agency that could provide 'scientific advice which is independent, transparent, of excellent scientific quality and capable of being readily understood by non-experts, by parliament, Member States and industry, as well as by the Commission. There is also the need to have the capacity to respond rapidly and effectively to issues of public, industrial and political concern' (James et al., 1999: 6). In parallel to the specific work of James and his colleagues the Commission had been drafting a major statement of food, published in January 2000 as the *White Paper on Food Safety* (COM[1999]719 final). The White Paper took forward ideas from a 1997 Commission Green Paper on food law (COM[97]176 final) and argued that the EU should exercise responsibility for food safety from 'farm to table' (i.e. the whole of the food chain). Primary responsibility for safe food was to rest with industry, producers and suppliers. The centrepiece of the White Paper, however, was the European Food Authority (the word safety was inserted later by the Parliament). The EFSA was officially formed in early 2002 on the basis of Regulation (EC) No 178/2002.

The White Paper argued that the EFSA was necessary 'to protect public health and to restore consumer confidence. . . the primary focus of . . .[the EFSA] will be the public interest' (COM[1997] 719 final: 14). Whilst the Commission may have regarded the term 'public interest' as unproblematic, Rothstein (2006) has pointed out that the public interest will be shaped by private interests, NGOs and professionals. In practice, 'assessment of the public interest entails complex trade-offs between different interests such as consumer choice and consumer health and conflicting business interests' (Rothestein, 2006: 175). Nevertheless, the Commission believed that EFSA could reach considered judgements on the public interest because of the way in which in which it would handle safety issues by allowing the separation of risk assessment from risk management.

Commissioner Byrne subsequently outlined the line of thinking behind the separation of risk responsibilities. In a speech on 18 September 2002 he claimed that the EFSAs independence would ensure that scientific risk assessment (an ESFA duty) is not swayed by policy or other external considerations. Risk management would remain within the domain of the Commission, Parliament and Council. Byrne argued, 'The final risk management decisions taking into account all relevant aspects, must be the function of accountable, political structures. Risk managers, therefore, have to take into consideration not only science but also many other matters for example economic, societal, traditional, ethical or environmental factors, as well as the feasibility of controls'.

While Byrne could provide a robust justification for the separation of risk management from risk assessment, behind the scenes there had been debates about the relevant competences of EFSA. In the end a number of countries led by France successfully argued that EFSA should not have any role in risk management (Borraz et al., 2006: 144). From a French perspective, their own food agency AFSSA was restricted to the function of scientific expertise and risk management remained a central government function and they wished to see a similar model at the European level. Moreover, the French were also unwilling to cede national expertise in risk assessment to the European level. There had been strong differences of opinion in the late 1990s between European, British and French scientists over the risks associated with British beef (Borraz et al., 2006: 146–147). Thus, as we saw in Chapter 4, EFSA does not have the authority to impose its views on other scientific bodies.

The implication would appear to be that national sensitivities surrounding food safety need to be accommodated at the political level in the EU, though, this will have important implications for the relationship with the science based approach of the EFSA. For instance, as food safety is such a sensitive issue how will risk managers actually manage any recommendations that emerge from the EFSA? Alternatively, how will risk managers seek to shape the questions or the issues that are asked of the risk assessors in the EFSA?

The separation of risk assessment and risk management highlights different approaches to decision making in Europe. From a British perspective, where risk assessment and management are integrated in the FSA, it is not possible to disentangle them in practice. From this perspective the lesson to be drawn from the French experience where risk assessment and management are divorced is that the assessors 'can make a maverick assessment because they don't have any responsibility for working out conclusions and solutions, and that will be an embarrassment to the risk management people and may force them to make extreme solutions which the circumstances may not really justify' (interview). In other words, the very independence of the risk assessors may make it difficult for risk managers to act in a practical way. On this view it is possible to separate risk communication because that calls on a quite separate set of skills; communication skills that are quite different from the scientific skills in assessment. Risk communication, however, is an EFSA role. Both economic and consumer interests are aware of the context in which EFSA must operate, in which science is not neutral. As BEUC put it, 'as soon as you communicate on a risk you are already political' (interview). Eurocommerce are also very sensitive to the difficulties of communicating risks when there is scientific uncertainty because they do not want unnecessary consumer panic. Retailers could find themselves in a no-win situation if there should be a food scare. Some retailers may withdraw the product but then later face claims for damages for removing the product too hastily before a fuller picture emerged of its safety. If they do not withdraw the product they might then leave themselves open to legal redress by consumers for not taking all measures to protect their health. Eurocommerce would therefore rather see risk communicators linked to risk managers. Whilst retailers are very close to consumers and could provide a communication platform, they are reluctant to do so because they fear losing credibility if the advice that they give to consumers should change in a short time period (Eurocommerce interview).

Perspectives on the EFSA

Although the EFSA is a new organisation there are already signs that organisations will approach it in different ways. On one side BEUC are keen to be able to observe meetings of the EFSA Management Board and on the other side Eurocommerce believe that although EFSA is an important organisation it is a scientific body. It does not have any legislative powers and policy will continue to be made by the Commission. So 'we [Eurocommerce] will certainly follow, and must follow, their [the EFSA] work very carefully, but the legislative process will not come from them' and so Eurocommerce will continue to devote as much attention as it can to DG SANCO.

Membership of the EFSA Management Board has raised some controversy. Basically the discussion has surrounded the expectations that different groups had of what interests would be represented on the Board. To begin with consumer organisations had very high expectations that because the EFSA was a response to consumer crises in food and early documentation had suggested that consumer groups might expect to have at least two members of the Board they were disappointed to only gain one (BEUC interview). A Eurocoop official explained how they saw what had happened: 'We were hoping to squeeze in two consumer representatives, one from BEUC and one from ourselves (Eurocoop) given that we are the two largest [consumer organisations] and have worked longest on food issues. But in the end it was the member states that decided on the makeup of the Board. Each member state put forward one candidate and there was no discussion and no arguments.' So there is geographic representation (by member state) but also functional representation because the EFSAs terms of reference had referred to particular interests (e.g. farmers). 'In the end we [consumer groups] only got one, we were even more aghast when we discovered that they gave four times as many seats to farmers and food producers, and six times as many seats to other interests in the food industry. So we are not happy with the composition [of the Board]'. (Eurocoop interview)

Retailers meanwhile appeared almost to the end to have no representative and so engaged in last ditch lobbying to ensure that like other elements of the food system they too should have a representative—what Eurocommerce termed 'fair representation' (interview). In the end, when the final decision on the Board's membership was made, a retailer was included. According to DG SANCO they highly value the retailers knowledge of the consumer 'and we were very careful to make sure that they [retailers] were there [on the Board]' (DG SANCO interview). Interestingly the retailer representative has subsequently been portrayed as a consumer much to the annoyance of consumer organisations (Eurocoop interview).

The composition of the management board is raising doubts amongst consumer groups about the independence of the EFSA and whether it will be able to gain consumer confidence. 'We took the view that . . . [the EFSA] is really the agency to help reassure . . . [consumers] . . . and lo and behold the consumers only have one seat on it'. (Eurocoop interview). The lowering of expectations about EFSA amongst consumer groups is palpable: 'I am not sure it [EFSA] is going to be very independent because of the management. I don't think it will change many things'. Or again: 'It's only the embellishment that has changed because they are taking more less the whole structure lock, stock and barrel from the Commission and just transplanting it into the new framework' (Eurocoop interview).

Consumer groups are well aware that the EFSA may simply be a means of carrying on business as usual. A key test for EFSA will be the transparency with which it makes it decisions, and by which it is guided by DG SANCO (interview). More than economic interests, consumer groups want to actively work with EFSA, for example, to be asked to present their views. Such wishes, though, hint at the weakness of the consumer groups compared to the key economic actors: the latter are more confident that their arguments will be 'heard' by officials in the Commission, while the former seek new opportunities to present their ideas.

CONCLUSION

A key task for the FSA is to promote higher and more consistent levels of enforcement amongst local authority food safety staff. In seeking to realise this goal the FSA works with two different models of governance—coercive and partnership-based and seems to vacillate between the two. Particularly in its early years, the FSA appeared to favour a more coercive model of governance in which it sought to impose its will on local government. Here it has the ultimate sanction of taking over the food enforcement activities of a local authority. However, to do so would raise at least two problems, and may help to explain the apparent reluctance of the FSA to intervene when faced with very poor local authority performance. First, if the Agency takes over a food authority it will face the same issues that it has identified as contributing to underperformance, such as staff recruitment and retention and which it is likely to find equally difficult to solve at a local level. The second factor to be borne in mind, and the other side of the governance spectrum, is a partnership model that the FSA also wishes to adopt in its dealings with local government. To take over a local authority would undermine the partnership model. Partnership is predicated on consensus, goal sharing and accepting difference and has become an increasingly attractive style of operation for the FSA.

The irony is that as the FSA makes more information available on the levels of performance of local government food enforcement it shows how poor they are and then exposes its own weaknesses in raising standards. One of the key tasks of the FSA is to improve on that level of performance, but as Figure 9.2 illustrates and the discussion of food enforcement shows it lacks crucial levers to exercise power over local government. One member of staff in the FSA reflecting on the difference between regulation prior to the formation of the Agency and currently noted that 'What has changed is [that] we [the FSA] have greater oversight than before . . . we have a responsibility for a co-ordinating role'.

The interviewee continued 'we can't direct local authorities obviously but we work with them' (interview).

The temptation for the FSA is to seek to hold local government to account but having to share authority over local government with other bodies, such as the Audit Commission, the Department for Communities and Local Government and the Devolved Administrations, means it must also work with local government as a partner to help deliver food enforcement. The FSA has faced particularly acute problems with regard to the food enforcement activities of local government and these have significant implications for the emergent patterns of governance. Both in terms of the FSA agenda to promote consistency in local government performance and how it is held to account for variation in local government performance by the NAO and Public Accounts Committee, local variability is much more likely to be discouraged rather than celebrated. However, the more partnership style of working that the Agency is now seeking to develop will result in more flexible patterns of enforcement and diversity, and will result in greater monitoring of outcomes than inputs.

In practice, some tiers of government will act in a coercive manner because they are able to exercise power, they can impose their views. Other actors must adopt a partnership model because they must work with those who deliver services. The latter model may well be more resource intensive and involve capacity building in lower tiers of government which may not be sympathetic to annual reporting and auditing where much shorter time horizons come into play. Having helped to diffuse food safety controversies and secured its own legitimacy, the FSA is now in a position to think much more long term about the nature of its relationship with local government.

For the EFSA a partnership style of working is a prerequisite. It lacks the regulatory functions of the FSA. Rather, as we saw in Chapter 4, the EFSA works within an EU model of food governance that privileges networks and relationships. These networks are sources of advice and expertise and also help to bolster the credibility and authority of key public institutions. EFSA operates within networks at both the European level and the Member States. As the agency itself explains:

> To ensure that the [food safety] system works effectively, it is critical that EFSA works closely with partners throughout Europe. These include . . . risk managers in the European Commission, the European Parliament and the Member States. EFSA also works with national food safety authorities responsible for risk assessment . . .
>
> As EFSA is a listening organization, we also meet with civil society stakeholders such as consumer groups, non-governmental organizations (NGOs), and market operators such as farmers, food manufacturers, distributors or processors and science professionals to exchange

views and information" (http://www.efsa.europa.eu/EFSA/AboutEfsa/efsa_locale-1178620753812_WhoWeWorkWith.htm)

Both EFSA and the FSA were formed out of crises. Traditional government actors lacked the legitimacy and authority to provide credible solutions to food safety problems. Whilst notions of independence from government and private interests are central to the FSA, the EFSA operates in a context of interdepencies. Most notably, the Commission, Member State governments and commercial interests have an important role to play in the management of food risk.

10 Food Risk and Precaution
The Precautionary Principle in Practice

INTRODUCTION

Ulrich Beck in his Risk Society thesis (Beck, 1992) suggests a move away from Industrial Society with its focus on the production and distribution of wealth towards a risk society in which there is an increasing concern about the costs of attaching to development. The costs may be measured in risks—not simply in the form of dangers but made up of wider uncertainties and consequent insecurities (Giddens, 1999) attaching often to developments in science and technology that mark out modernity. Not least among the uncertainty is how, where and upon whom such risks may materialise given their random nature and realisation. While we focus still on production, the production of manufactured risk is starkly drawn to our attention and in the words of Lash and Wynne (1992) we see a shift from the distribution of goods in industrial society to the distribution of 'bads' in risk society.

Although the talk is of a comparator with industrial society this term denotes as much as a temporal idea as one concerned only with modes of production. It reflects a movement away from a time when we feared as the forces of nature (earthquake, tempest etc) to a time when we no longer understand what lies within the realm of the natural. Much of Beck's writing concerns this theme and in his own word: 'what no-one saw and no-one wanted—self endangerment and devastation of nature—is becoming a major force of history' (Beck, 1995). This was written before climate change became headline news through events like Hurricane Katrina at which point it became difficult indeed to separate out what was natural and what amounted to self-endangerment. This adds to spiralling uncertainty in which we know that risks may materialise but we do not know which ones those are. Alternatively we can perceive the risk (such as that inherent in climate change) but have only hazy perceptions of its consequences (will it get hotter or colder? will we face drought or flood?). We become increasingly transfixed by a request for certainty in an attempt to normalise and thereby control risk amidst 'a diversity of possible futures' (Giddens, 1992).

But as for modes of production, there is much in this literature that concerns the cost attaching to techno-economic growth and the beginnings of a suspicion that the much heralded benefits of technological innovation may actually be exceeded by the costs—if only the cost of uncertainty. Indeed what once might have been described indubitably as 'progress' becomes the subject of fierce debate amidst fears that the increasingly short term gain of technological innovation may carry longer-term price tags. In a world in which biotechnology, biomedicine and nanotechnology might offer choices not previously or ordinarily available to us it may not be clear how we reject these offerings, indeed it may be that we have no choice to reject them at all. Although we may fear that these technological advances may lead us into a wilderness that is filled with threats the prospect of being left behind may seem of little comfort too.

There is always a danger that Beck's thesis is sufficiently widely drawn that it is easy to discern trends which seem to fit it. Nonetheless in the food area we do see a move away from simple questions of food hygiene to a much wider range of health questions about food ranging from problems of allergens, through nutrition to obesity. It is also possible to observe a new range of issues that are not health related such biodiversity loss or food shortage and security as food prices begin to rise in a number of staple commodities. Many of these issues are rooted in and prompt further debate about technological aspects of food production.

It is also interesting to consider the risk thesis in terms of patterns of food consumption. One obvious demand in conditions of uncertainty is the greater availability of information. This manifests itself increasingly in food provision, whether it takes the form of 'scores on doors' hygiene ratings developed through local systems, and soon to turn national, or 'traffic light' labelling to indicate the nutritional values of food. Where consumer interest is mobilised these schemes may become mandatory as with tracing and labelling of GM foods. But much more profound changes may follow consumer reactions in the face of uncertainty. The effective working of markets depends upon the signalling of available choices and the prices that attach to these. The assumption is that in a functioning market consumer choice will be rational in that it will seek to maximise the utility of that consumer. But market models assume that significant transaction costs do not attach and that the flow of information is such that consumer sovereignty can exist. Suppose, however, that in the midst of informational asymmetries endemic in uncertainty we discern no clear pattern of consumer behaviour, since it is hard for each consumer to know where utility lies. Or suppose that in such conditions the rational choice appears to be to quit the market completely—at least for certain sets of goods?

Beck's sub-title and sub-text is that of 'reflexive modernisation'—the individualisation of responses as we learn to cope with the risks of modernisation. Reflexive modernisation represents the feeling of a way ahead in the dark shadow of progress to the point that society turns back in on modernity. This may involve a questioning of progress and a challenge to find mechanisms by which it becomes possible to adjust or redefine the goals of modernity. If this reflexivity involves this type of continual re-evaluation it may well begin in individual (consumer) responses to everyday choices (such as whether to buy certain foodstuffs). These simple choices may occasion a fragmentation of developed markets and generate even greater conditions of uncertainty as those involved in food production seek to identify, track, understand, label and ultimately collectivise these patterns of behaviour.

Beck would argue that reflexive modernisation is distrustful of science, in part because society may view itself as the subject of experimentation. It is an irony that in seeking to control nature, the boundaries between the natural world have become blurred to the point of confusion (Lee and Morgan, 2001)—the death of nature, strangled by human hands (Lee, 2002). Reflexive modernisation involves our relationships with science and scientists and charts a growing doubt about the authority and even the rationality of science. The concept speaks of other movements away from or set against science so that science becomes seen not only as value-laden but also in opposition to other values. It suggests other forums in which science may be pursued—the internet now more than the laboratory. In relation to food and food science there are clear examples of resentful attempts to reclaim the territory for science (Hathcock, 1999). And it is here that the precautionary principle takes its place, namely on the battle ground of risk society and pitched between the forces of science and scepticism.

This chapter goes on to examine where one finds the precautionary principle within European food regulation and it views the practical working of precaution through an analysis of a Commission decision to ban types of antibiotic product in animal feed, examining the challenges made to this policy. By way of contrast it reviews the considerably more limited scope for precautionary measures in the WTO framework on the basis that the infrastructure put in place in Europe has been shaped to some degree by the need to justify precautionary action, which may be readily castigated as protective or anti-competitive, in the context of global trade. Finally it attempts to chart the place of the principle in the developing framework on food safety in Europe, concluding that precautionary action can do relatively little to assuage the uncertainties that arise out of modern conditions of food production.

LOCATING THE PRECAUTIONARY PRINCIPLE

There are ample analyses of the precautionary principle (O'Riordan and Cameron, 1994; Freestone, 1991). Much of the writing follows the adoption of what is now the most commonly accepted statement of the precautionary principle, Article 15 of the UNCED Rio Declaration of 1992 (Freestone, 1994), which states that:

> In order to protect the Environment, the precautionary principle shall be widely applied by States according to their capabilities. Where there are threats of serious or irreversible damage, lack of full scientific certainty shall not be used as a reason for postponing cost-effective measures to prevent environmental degradation.

Many would accept that this principle has 'crystallised' into a norm of customary international law (McIntyre and Mosedale, 1997; see also Freestone and Hey, 1996; and Backes and Verschuuren, 1997) but it comes with an environmental rider and some would assert that its acceptance and applicability in the realm of food policy is much more open to doubt (Hanson and Carswell, 1999). For Europe, the development of a general principle based on Article 15 is helpful given the lack of precise definition in EU Law, notwithstanding the incorporation of the precautionary principle into Article 174(2) of the EC Treaty. Mention in Article 174 provides a clear indication of that it should inform legislative action but it is less than clear that it offers substantive legal rights for example as a directly applicable doctrine (Hession and Macrory, 1994).

The principle should now be considered in the light of the EU Communication, which addresses other Community Institutions and the Member States on the manner in which the Commission will seek to arrive at decisions on risk containment (European Commission, 2000). There would seem to be little doubt that one motivating factor behind the Communication is to articulate the basis on which precaution might operate within EU decision making structures in order to better protect Europe from challenge particularly within the WTO context. The principles by which risk decision-making might be subject to review are now clearly laid down in the Commission's Communication. It aims

> to inform all interested parties, in particular the European Parliament, the Council and Member States of the manner in which the Commission applies or intends to apply the precautionary principle when faced with taking decisions relating to the containment of risk. (European Commission 2000: 8)

It clearly envisages a gradual move towards the working of the precautionary principle at a formal, procedural level. The Communication propounds a consistent response to risk through a proper process of balancing environmental costs and benefits. Action based on the precautionary principle where deemed necessary ought to be proportionate, non-discriminatory, consistent with previous action, based on a cost-benefit analysis, and subject to future review. By incorporating such well developed concepts, the Communication provides a yardstick for court supervision of administrative decisions. A limited transformation from high-sounding principle to more mundane process may disappoint some but it does begin to put the principle into practical operation.

The principle as espoused in Article 15 centres upon a threat of serious or irreversible damage to the environment suggesting that in other areas of Community policy there may be no room for the application of the principle, On the other hand, food regulation generally rests upon frameworks of risk assessment which seek to balance a series of differing demands from stakeholders and which in particular may concern pressure for food safety from consumers in the context of innovation by producers. Processes of risk governance provide the structures for managing such pressures but the incorporation of the precautionary principle may be seen as generating imbalance and placing much too great a burden on those seeking to innovate by the introduction of 'a deeply conservative Luddite reaction to social advances and ecological change' (Holder, 1997). Although this may seem a harsh evaluation of the principle, it is worth reflecting that it may have a technology freezing capacity since, in the nature of things, we will always know least about and will have less experience of technologies that are newly developed (Marchant and Sylvester, 2006). In general these early stage developments are most beset by uncertainty.

The European Commission (European Commission, 2000) conscious of this view stresses the need to remember the impossibility of removing all risks of an activity. But if the principle is applied only where irreversible damage might result, then one can hardly quibble at the caution in demanding that, in line with Collingridge's dilemma of control, there is a degree of corrigibility such that steps are not taken that would prove impossible or enormously costly or disruptive to control (Collingridge, 1980). Indeed in relation to the planting of GM crops, the perceived irreversibility of the effects on biodiversity helps explain the opposition generated by the technology (Levidow et al., 2000). This assumes that a certain element of threat can at least be hypothesised, but the European Commission perhaps go further than this and suggest that the precautionary principle presupposes that potentially dangerous effects of an activity have been identified, even though the precise impact cannot be determined with certainty. If one follows this line then arguably the precautionary principle is not dealing with uncertainty as such but with an identified risk, for which the probability of its materialising is unknown. In discussing European food safety regulation Hanson and Caswell (1999) depict overlapping arenas of risk assessment, management and communication, but if one is to take into account this model of precaution it becomes necessary to add an initial task of risk characterisation (Klinke et al., 2006) because it is necessary to identify a threat, albeit one shrouded in uncertainty not as to its magnitude (as it must be capable of serious or irreversible damage) but as to the likelihood of its being occasioned. In other words, we can foresee the possibility of serious harm but remain entirely unsure of its actual existence.

In such situations, as the use of the word 'postponing' in Article 15 indicates the imperative is to move to regulatory action lest this irreversible damage be occasioned. These actions should not be postponed pending attempts to move towards a position of greater scientific certainty. A criticism is therefore that the principle mandates action in the absence of scientific certainty (Sandin et al., 2002). But such certainty may not be readily achievable. Laying aside the time which it might take to generate data, study toxicity, write up studies and the like, the very idea of scientific certainty suggests some defined point at which clear action, such as product placement, is authorised. It is the task of risk governance frameworks to reach such a point but it must do so on the understanding that science is a matter of interpretation. Scientific proof is simply a point at which consensus is reached on a particular hypothesis rather than an absolute position and is likely to be based on all manner of soft assumptions (Wynne and Mayer, 1993). Moreover this task is largely one for the risk assessment stage of the governance process and it may or may not offer clear leads for risk management not least because many of these assumptions, shared by the scientific community, may not be apparent to or relevant for the policy makers (Lee, 2000). One of the strengths of the precautionary principle, then, is that it recognises a realm outside of the 'scientific' and begins to address risk perceptions.

Once in play, if we follow the Article 15 formulation, the precautionary principle demands consideration of cost-effective measures. In other words, it triggers risk assessment, albeit that it might need to invoke some form of interim measure (Bennett, 2000). A common misunderstanding of the principle is that it must lead a to ban rather than a protective measure proportionate to the hypothesised risk. European Commission Directorate for Health and Consumer Protection suggested the following:

> The Precautionary Principle is an approach to risk management that is applied in circumstances of scientific uncertainty reflecting the need to take action in the face of a potentially serious risk without waiting for the results of scientific research. (NCC, 2000)

But it is implied here that the results should follow and the Commission Communication emphasises that the principle sets up 'a structured decision–making process' with the structure 'provided by the three elements of risk analysis' namely assessment, management and communication (European Commission, 2000: 8). It is to the elements of the risk analysis process that we now turn particularly by exploring the legal framework of these structures.

The Precautionary Principle as a Legal Concept: Additives and Animal Foodstuff

At the point at which the European Communication set out an agenda for how the Commission intended to operate the precautionary principle it was only a matter of time, given the mention of the principle in Article 174 (2), before the European Court of Justice was asked to determine the legality of the Commission's risk governance in accordance with the principle. The development of the jurisprudence of precaution, which will doubtless stretch into the future has its strongest foundation in a review of the significant decision of the Court of First Instance in relation to the banning of antibiotics in animal foodstuff (*Pfizer v European Commission,* 2002) under Directive 70/524/EC (as amended by Directive 96/51/EC). Under this regime only additives (such as vitamins, trace elements, binders, preservatives, and antibiotics) on the authorised list, and subject to certain conditions, can be incorporated into animal feeds. A Member State could halt the use of an additive thought to pose a risk to animal / human health or the environment, though subject to a notification procedure under which the Member State is obliged to inform the European Commission and other Member States of its action. Thereafter, the Commission is required to seek advice from the Standing Committee on Foodstuffs and may seek guidance from the Scientific Committee for Animal Nutrition (SCAN). Should the Commission reject the advice from the Standing Committee, it is obliged to consult the Council of Ministers.

Denmark banned the use of virginiamycin, an antibiotic, in animal foodstuffs in 1998 following national scrutiny. The Commission followed the procedure set out previously including the reception of scientific advice from SCAN, before recommending to Council that the antibiotic be banned. Council followed this advice and issued Regulation (EC) No. 2821/98, banning the use of four antibiotics—of which virginiamycin was one—in animal foodstuff. The risk as characterised was that antibiotic resistance in humans might follow the consumption of meat from animals fed with food containing antibiotic additives. The Regulation triggered a procedure allowing the amendment of the list of authorised antibiotics. Authorisation for the use of four antibiotics as additives was withdrawn, and the Council expressed the opinion that, in relation to virginiamycin in particular, the decision was justified on the grounds that the effectiveness of certain human medicinal products could be endangered (Regulation 2821/98, Recital 21). It is important to note that this decision was taken despite the fact that SCAN concluded that the use of virginiamycin did not create an immediate risk to human health in Denmark

Pfizer Animal Health SA ('Pfizer') was the sole producer in the world of virginiamycin and brought proceedings before the European Court of First Instance challenging the adoption of the regulation by Council. In the interim Pfizer was not allowed to market the product in Europe. Pfizer, joined in the action by Alpharma (Case T-70/99) as manufacturers of a second antibiotic, bacitracin zinc, proposed eight independent grounds upon which the Regulation ought to be regarded as a nullity. Essentially these grounds rested on the contention that the assessment and management of potential risks to human health posed by the use of virginiamycin in animal foodstuffs was flawed and in particular that there was no room for precautionary action of the type taken. This challenge was made possible by the agreement of Council that, when the Regulation was adopted, the existence of the risk had not been scientifically proven. As such, the precautionary principle was used to justify the adoption of the regulation. While Pfizer accepted that the Community institutions are not legally bound by SCAN's at the risk management stage, it claimed that it was impermissible for Community institutions to discount the risk assessment altogether.

While it was clear that the Directive allowed that measures might be adopted on a precautionary basis, this left arguments concerning the interpretation and application of the precautionary principle. Pfizer argued that any precautionary prohibition must be based, nonetheless, on scientific risk assessment of the risks, and that such assessment should demonstrate some degree of probability of the risk materialising. According to Pfizer unless this was the case, measures denying authorisation would be effectively demanding that there be no risk present and leave producers with the seemingly impossible task of demonstrating zero risk to human health presently or in the future. While there might be a 'hazard to human health' presented by antibiotics in feed, this was not of itself sufficient to allow the withdrawal of virginiamycin from the market. Some identifiable health effect such as evidence of the transfer of resistance to the human population was necessary to then trigger precautionary restrictions.

The Court found that it could not accept this interpretation of the precautionary principle on the basis that the territory occupied by the principle is that in which uncertainty prevails and it is 'impossible to carry out a full risk assessment in the time available'. In such situations competent authorities may regard preventive protective measures as essential, given the level of risk to human health. In the view of the Court, although the application of the precautionary principle could not be based upon a purely hypothetical risk, there was room for the application of the principle where there exists a risk to human health, even though this cannot be fully demonstrated. It was open therefore for the relevant institutions to conclude that there was a proper scientific foundation for a possible connection between the use of virginiamycin in animal feed and the development of streptogramin resistance in humans. Interestingly the Court implies that the precautionary principle is applicable at the risk assessment stage for it is critical of the lack of account given to it by SCAN, which it said allowed a departure from the SCAN opinion at the risk management stage.

The decision in *Pfizer* is a significant step in the transition of the principle from a policy to a legal instrument but it leaves much unsaid. Because both parties accepted that measures could be adopted on a precautionary basis under the Directive, at least where there was more than a zero risk, there is very little in the judgment about how risk might be characterised. The acceptance of the Court that there was some level of ascertained risk was implicit rather than explicit, which hardly helps to identify that level of risk above which precautionary action may be invoked. It might have been more enlightening had Pfizer as a party to the litigation challenged the very right to take precautionary measures relying upon SCAN's determination that virginiamycin did not create an immediate threat to human health for the purposes of such an argument. Such a claim would have opened up at least the debate upon the degree of scientific uncertainty needed to invoke the principle in risk management.

As is the case in relation to WTO approaches to risk assessment, considered in further discussion, the thinking of the European Court of First Instance appears to be that if a risk can be perceived, it can and should then be assessed. However, valuable and relevant though risk perceptions might be, these will not be sufficient in themselves and it will be necessary to move beyond these in a careful and structured manner (Short, 1989). This is because risk perceptions will always be contested, being derided as unscientific on one hand and prompted as a reason for precautionary action on the other. This ignores the critical role of characterising the realm of risk in order to frame the risk assessment. This first stage becomes all the more crucial in situations in which there is a known lack of scientific study because a clarification of the degree of uncertainty which prevails might then shape any risk assessment such that it can allow for contingency and indeterminacy. In such a context perceptions of risk can be given a role in assisting with questions of acceptability of or tolerance to risk (Renn, 1998).

The court in its judgment depicts a process of risk management, which follows chronologically though not necessarily ideologically the process of risk assessment. These separate and different stages are the domain of different groups, scientists in first stage and politicians and bureaucrats thereafter. This picture emerged at an institutional level in the course of research with DG Trade stating that the EFSA could go a long way in helping to 'separate out science from legislation.' DG SANCO expressed the hope that science-based decision-making in the EFSA would 'protect against political indiscretion especially regarding precautionary measures'. However, Eurocommerce, a major private interest umbrella organisation, bemoaned the lack of legislative capacity, stating that:

> the EFSA has a very important role to play but since it does not have any legislative powers, its impact will be somewhat similar to that of a scientific lobby body. Food safety policy itself will continue to be made by the European Commission with DG SANCO [at the heart of the process] whilst the EFSA will be responsible for communicating food risks to member states and the public. (Interview)

The *Pfizer* decision would tend to re-enforce this type of concern that science is given an advisory function subsidiary to and separate from decision-making. Many would welcome, however, the recognition in *Pfizer* that there is a space for precautionary action even in a context in which there appears little concrete evidence of risk. Against this there may be good reasons borne out of ecological modernisation to have scientific advisors around the table at the risk management stage and it is no less true that a wider range of stakeholder beyond those from within scientific expert communities ought to participate in risk assessment processes. Without this, there is a danger that the risk assessment process will revert to a reductive quantitative tradition, with ethical and social aspects of risk remaining entirely divorced from the framing of issues at any point prior to the risk management process. By that stage policy options may have been foreshortened, which would be undesirable since, as Wynne (1996) has argued, non-expert assessments may be instrumental in shaping the risk assessment process itself.

Particularly in the precautionary settings of uncertainty risk assessment will involve the shaping of assumptions which must then be tested. Such assumptions imply choice and deny the possibility of definitive answers (Shackley and Wynne, 1996). A two-stage model tends to bolster notions of scientific neutrality free from any such value judgements. Just as the risk management context is reserved for policy makers, the risk assessment stage is reserved for 'science'. Yet in uncertainty the determination of questions relating to magnitude and/or likelihood of risk may be usefully informed by a variety of real world experiences not exclusively the domain of an 'expert' community as risks are played out in social, temporal and spatial conditions subject to considerable diversity and complexity. A similar point might be made in relation not simply to risks as both benefits and burdens may flow from technological advance. We see from the GM example in Chapter 3 that a scepticism about benefits of the technology underpinned thinking about risk (Pidgeon et al., 2005) and it is an important lesson that societal views may be no less strongly held simply because they follow a risk benefit equation that is at odds with that offered by expert determination.

One fascinating feature of the Court's conclusion is whether a refusal to link risk management decisions to risk assessment is an implicit acceptance that there may be competing and even contradictory interpretations of risk such that it is necessary to leave room for tentative conclusions in the face of uncertain futures. This would seem to leave room for ignorance (Stirling, 2003) in the form of unascertained knowledge (Van Zwanenberg and Millstone, 2001). Although this may be imbuing the *Pfizer* judgment with a depth that it may not fully deserve, its refusal to mandate action that simply replicates the lead offered by risk assessment is a brave step since it demonstrates scepticism of scientific closure and in so doing supports a much more holistic approach to risk governance than simple appeal to sound science. In the light of food scares of the type considered in further discussion, it may be necessary to recognise and accept distrust and scepticism in order to rebuild confidence in scientific determinations and this may be better done in a more integrated process of risk governance than in isolating and ring fencing risk-related tasks.

One final issue relating to *Pfizer* is the space allowed for the type of precautionary ban pursued in the case of virginiamycin. While in the EU it is perfectly open to the European Court of Justice to assess precautionary action in the context and against the language of relevant legal instruments within which the precautionary principle is incorporated, there may be a limit to how far its writ will run. This is because many precautionary measures will apply to products that might otherwise circulate freely on the Single European Market. That is a market which non-European countries wish to exploit and which in line with world trade principles ought to be open to them. Conformity with the requirements of world trade law explains the stress given in the Commission's Communication on the precautionary principle to see the doctrine operate as part of a structured programme and explains the Court's emphasis on scrutiny of the process underpinning the risk governance.

PRECAUTION AND THE WTO

This limited, procedural and process-based application of the precautionary principle is much less than environmental NGOs might hope for (Van den Belt, 2003). It is one to which Europe is tied, however, not least because of its obligations under World Trade Agreements. It is clear, however, that models of risk assessment built into the fabric of the WTO framework offer little room for the application of the precautionary principle. The closest that one would come would be the weak model of precaution built into Article 5.7 of the Sanitary and Phytosanitary (SPS) Agreement. Following the GM dispute before the WTO Panel (Biotech Products, 2006) a measure restricting the trade of foodstuffs which is claimed to protect human, animal or plant life or health case will be regarded as an SPS measure and will fall into the SPS Agreement to the exclusion of other agreements which might appear to apply (Zedalis, 2002). It follows that if the EU wishes to defend measures from challenge it must meet the requirements for risk assessment under the formal models (Salmon, 2002) and narrow conceptions of ('sound') science that are recognised in the SPS Agreement.

It is worth pointing out that whatever the shortfalls of this precautionary model (which are considered in subsequent text) at least the possibility of some form of precautionary measure is recognised under the SPS Agreement. Elsewhere in the WTO structure any restriction designed to protect health and environment must be backed by scientific risk assessment. The extent to which the precautionary principle is regarded as a customary principle of international law to be applied nonetheless is not clear and in the *Biotech* dispute the Panel offered no comment on this point, despite the strong presence of precautionary arguments. In fact, in Article 5.7 there is no express mention of the principle, but there is an allowance that interim measures to restrict imports may be taken pending reasonably prompt scientific risk assessment. Moreover it is now accepted that there is an independent right to take interim measures (*Biotech Products*) so that these are not as such a an exception to the primary rule in Article 5.1 that WTO Members shall ensure that their sanitary or phytosanitary measures are based on an assessment, as appropriate to the circumstances, of the risks to human, animal or plant life or health.

Thereafter, however, there is relatively little room for the application of such measures. To begin with, rather than action in the face of some hypothesised threat, Article 5.7 appears to work not where there is scientific uncertainty but where there is an 'insufficiency of scientific evidence' (Japan—Agricultural Products II; Biotech Products). Indeed according to the Appellate Body, the interim measure itself should be adopted on the basis of available pertinent information, suggesting something other than action in the face of ambiguity. Moreover, this begs the question of the point at which scientific evidence can be described as sufficient, but it is clearly thought to be the case that once there is available data to conduct some form of risk assessment (and data generation is demanded—*Japan—Agricultural Products II*), then risk management action based on that risk assessment will displace precaution. This generates what has been described as a 'firewall' between scientific certainty and risk assessment (Matsushita et al;, 2006; Gollier et al., 2000). It paints a highly artificial picture of scientific development in which rather than assimilate knowledge and understanding we move sharply from states of bewilderment to absolute conviction. An opportunity to clarify what might be regarded as sufficient evidence for risk assessment arose in the *Biotech* case but this opportunity was ignored by the Panel.

In the *Japan—Agricultural Products II* dispute it was said that the timeframe within which risk assessment must be conducted, thereby putting an end to interim measures, should be decided on a case by case basis. This was also an issue in the dispute between the EU and the American States in relation to GM food and feed the so-called *Biotech Products* case. In that dispute, the background to which is considered in detail in Chapter 3, notwithstanding the precautionary language built into Article 5 of the SPS Agreement, the USA (USA, 2004) strongly argued that the EU moratorium in terms of a refusal to process applications for GM crops at Member State level constituted a measure under the SPS Agreement likely to affect international trade. At the very least this amounted to undue delay under Article 8 of the Agreement and was procedurally flawed under Article 8 and Article 7 (in the latter case because of a failure to publish promptly details of the moratorium). But the submission points also to the need for any moratorium to be based upon risk assessment in line with the requirements of Article 5.1. Article 5.1 demands:

> an assessment, as appropriate to the circumstances, of the risks to human, animal or plant life or health, taking into account risk assessment techniques developed by the relevant international organizations.

According to the USA the moratorium was not based on scientific principles and was maintained without sufficient scientific evidence contrary to Article 2.2. As such, the USA argued, these measures were said to be discriminatory in their effect (infringing Article 5.5) and constituted disguised restrictions on imports contrary to Article 2.3 of the Agreement.

In the *Biotech* report, the Panel ruled that because procedures for approvals must be undertaken and completed without due delay under Annex C (1)(a) the fact of a moratorium led to such delay, and because Article 8 of the Agreement demanded observance of the approval procedures in Annex C, there was a breach of the SPS Agreement. The Panel noted that the Annex required not only that approval procedures are started but that they are then 'carried out from beginning to end'. No time periods were fixed for undue delay. Time lost by inaction would constitute delay and this would be 'undue' if not warranted or justifiable, but the precise period would have to be determined on a case-by-case basis having regard to the need for a State to act in good faith in processing approvals. On this narrow ground the EC was found in breach of the SPS Agreement in failing to consider applications relating to GM approvals during the period from 1998 to 2004. Because of the limited nature of the judgment many of the more substantive issues relating to precaution in a biosecurity context were not considered. The Panel avoided consideration of risk assessment questions to a large degree by finding that the moratorium did not constitute a 'measure' for the purposes of Article 5.1, thereby avoiding consideration of Article 2.2 which states that:

> Members shall ensure that any sanitary or phytosanitary measure is applied only to the extent necessary to protect human, animal or plant life or health, is based on scientific principles and is not maintained without sufficient scientific evidence.

An interim precautionary measure under Article 5.7 would be the one occasion on which this requirement might be circumvented, but once again because the moratorium was not as such a measure (formally taken at EC level) wider consideration of the need for precaution was avoided. However, even had the moratorium been considered a measure, it is unlikely to have met the requirements of Article 5, not being based on risk assessment for the purposes of Article 5.1 and not really an interim measure under 5.7 since there was probably sufficient available information on GM and human health (particularly from the USA) to have undertaken a risk assessment which could then have provided the foundation for a risk management response.

In an earlier EU/US dispute regarding the use of hormones in beef production an Appellate Body found that:

> by maintaining sanitary measures which are not based on a risk assessment, (the EU) has acted inconsistently with the requirements of

> contained in Article 5.1 of the Sanitary and Phytosanitary Agreement. (*Hormones*)

Risk assessments are required therefore to support protective measures and these must be aimed at matters such as threats of pests or disease or the effects of food or feed on human or animal health. This narrowly drawn framework leaves little room for wider concerns. Moreover the room for public engagement is unclear, but in Europe, in the aftermath of a series of food scares, it may be that the restoration of trust and confidence in the regulation of food risks may require more than the pronouncement of scientific experts following a risk assessment. Nonetheless in the *Hormones* example the European Community found itself having to justify a permanent rather than merely a provisional ban in the absence of any plausible risk assessment. In this case the Appellate Body rejected EU claims that a ban on the importation of beef from cattle reared using certain hormones could be justified by general scientific evidence where no formal risk assessment had been conducted because it was not simply a question of whether a particular substance had potential effects:

> The EU side simply had not produced any evidence that indicated that growth hormones were being used on a scale that allowed intakes to vary significantly from those to which people are naturally exposed. (Holmes, 2000)

Had the ban on beef taken the form of an interim measure based on science, while the EU might have been left with the task of explaining why it allowed the same hormones in the pig meat chain, it might have been easier to defend, especially if further risk assessment was scheduled.

The reluctance of the Panel in the *Biotech* dispute to engage in wider debate about the role of precaution by determining the dispute on the narrowest possible grounds is instructive. Not only did it avoid highly contentious issues that might otherwise have arisen—such as whether GM crops were like products when compared to non-GM equivalents—but it allows a little something for everyone. The American States succeeded in their action and, as explained in Chapter 3, the EC took steps to ensure future GM approvals, but it remained open to claim that interim precautionary measures might be possible under certain conditions providing that sufficient formality attached to any 'measure' taken. Having said that, the scope for precautionary action remains doubtful, for under a system with a primary objective to allow goods to circulate freely it is easy to castigate precautionary action as naked trade protectionism (Groth, 2000). Moreover, different communities may have different perceptions of what is taken to constitute effective risk assessment (Jasonoff, 2000), especially when grappling with uncertainty, and background food cultures may strongly affect this. Indeed one explanation of the difference that arose between America and Europe in relation to GM is that the former proceeded on the basis of risk assessment on an incremental and product-by-product basis, whereas the latter doubted the very enterprise heralded by the technology.

EMBEDDING PRECAUTION IN EUROPEAN FOOD POLICY

Taking the Rio Declaration of 1992 as a most significant step in the formalization of the precautionary principle its institutionalization within Europe soon followed. It may not be accidental that this development of the principle took place alongside a series of food scares (McIntrye and Mosedale, 1997) and although the principle itself is by no means confined to concerns related to food, episodes such as salmonella in British eggs and dioxin in Belgian chicken feed only helped to promote its application in this context. Such episodes are located within national systems of food safety within the wider multi-level governance system of the EU. This too may have added to the increasing invocation of the precautionary principle within legislation at a European level (Vogel, 2002) following models developed in Member States such as Sweden (Löfstedt, 2003). It is true also that as challenges to the increasingly precautionary stance within EU legislation came forward they were often fought out in relation to foodstuff as with hormones in beef and milk, aflatoxins in ground nuts and genetic modification of crops. Such challenges not only occurred as between the EU market and third countries such as the USA but within the market also as became apparent when member states continued to resist the importation of products long after EC law demanded that they must do so—BSE, foot and mouth and GM all provide examples.

This offers a picture of genuine public concern for food safety, albeit one that may be transient in relation to particular products though with some longer tail effects (Böcker and Hanf, 2000). Nonetheless, it is open to states to exploit this concern in a seemingly protectionist manner. Moreover where action is to be taken, its most obvious form might be the withdrawal of products from the market in the manner adopted by the UK FSA in February 2005 when the non-food dye Sudan I had been used to colour chilli powder which had then been incorporated into Worcester sauce and in turn into ready meals. Notwithstanding contradictory scientific evidence of the health impacts of the dye in such tiny quantities in any particular food, the decision was taken to remove all relevant products as a precautionary measure. This type of precautionary response is open to national regulators by virtue of Article 7 of EC Regulation 178/2002 (often referred to as the 'general food law'), which adopts the principle and sets out the circumstances of its use. It positions it as a tool that might be applied alongside and as part of other mechanism of risk governance. It doubtless does so to fit within mechanisms that might be compatible to WTO principles. However, before the Codex Alimentarius Commission, where the USA have resisted the adoption of even a weak version of the precautionary principle, the USA have argued that this is not an appropriate approach because if there is room for risk assessment then this must replace precautionary action—the two being mutually exclusive (Editorial, 1999).

This is not a view that European regulation has endorsed largely on the back of BSE, where it seemed that waiting for firm conclusions from science was an inherent cause of the regulatory failure (Winter, 1996). Indeed the European Court in reviewing the validity of the Commission's response of banning export of beef from the UK endorsing the language of Article 174 and in particular stressing the requirement of a high level of protection endorsed a strategy of pursuing protective measures 'without having to wait until the reality and seriousness of those risks become fully apparent' (*UK V EC Commission,* 1998). Indeed the Court has suggested that the rule might be even stronger than this such that the lack of full scientific proof is not a permissible reason for inaction (Greenpeace, 1999). Cazala (2004) has argued that there is a 'progressive corpus of decisions' now emanating from the Community Courts and although this may appear to be less protective of human health than widely held doctrinal conceptions, the jurisprudence of the Court has the advantage of being effective and capable of practical application.

It follows then that on the back of experience Europe has realised the need for the availability of precautionary responses as a component in the regulatory toolbox. On the other hand, it is aware, acutely aware following GM, that Member States may too readily invoke precaution as a political or a protectionist response. Where this has led, within a multi-level governance framework, is to increasing centralisation which is now very marked in the realm of food hygiene and which is likely to spread to other areas of regulation. This is an interesting development when placed in the history of EC food regulation. Initial attempts at harmonisation of standards for mainstream food products failed to displace national systems (Van der Meulen and Van der Velde, 2004) and were forced to give way to processes built upon mutual recognition of national difference. The free circulation of goods across borders became heavily dependent on the work of international standard setting bodies with the assumption that goods which met standards satisfied EU requirements for marketing. Judge made law laid down the general principles on which food imports might be restricted (Cassis de Dijon, 1979) but new 'horizontal' rules that could apply across the board to all or most foods were clearly needed if a single market was to function in Europe. The main horizontal directives introduced from the mid 1980s onwards covered areas such as: food additives; labelling; contaminants; food contact materials; foods for particular nutritional uses; and the enforcement of food regulation.

The review of food legislation by the White Paper (EU Commission, 2000) heralded a new and more coherent and comprehensive approach with a strong emphasis on regulatory enforcement across the whole of the food chain. Scientific advice as the basis for action was expressly endorsed but the role of precautionary action was also acknowledged, not least because of the identified need for a system that could respond with rapid, safeguard actions in the face of health threats. This hints at concerns regarding the quality and credibility of regulatory action at Member State level and among the citizens of those Member States (Löfstedt and Vogel, 2001) forming a pressure for greater precautionary action. On the whole this has led to greater centralisation of regulation in the European rather than the national framework and this has given rise to increasingly contested governance in the area of food safety as attempts are made to move away from fragmented national approaches. However, Member States are conscious that this draining away of regulatory competence reduces the scope to act in terms of national advantage. These opportunities arise amid food scares which might legitimate precautionary action such as import bans or labelling requirements which seemed justified in the light of the particular scare (Majone, 2002) but which have obvious protective tendencies. There is little doubt that the EU wishes to move in favour of regulatory federalism but this increases the contested nature of regulation.

Within this contest the EU institutions have drawn upon an unlikely ally in terms of the private sector. This has been done by placing reliance on the type of controls first generated within private-sector supply-chains. The present European model of Hazard Analysis and Critical Control Point (HACCP) unashamedly draws upon the experience of audit of private supply chains. This type of system implies a move from more traditional command and control models based on inspection to a more process based oversight. It would seem likely that larger multi-national enterprises represented in lobbying within Brussels would invoke little objection in principle to a model which replicates their own approach (but which possibly demand a lower level of assurance) and reduces regulatory fragmentation in the European markets in which they operate. However, as Caduff and Bernauer (2006) indicate, many food enterprises are small in nature and considerable leeway has been allowed in introducing the system. In general terms, however, an important legal tightening of the system has taken place with the consolidation of material previously contained in Directives now taking the form of Regulations, which are directly applicable and will apply without more in the Member States. To some degree we see the move to a central system of regulation that speaks to private actors and reduces the sphere of public regulation at national level. Recent regulation of food hygiene in Europe suggests a move from multi-level governance to regulatory federalism.

If one asks where the precautionary principle sits in all of these changes, some writers have argued that when confidence in food safety is restored, precautionary approaches will wane (Löfstedt, 2004) especially when the costs of precaution are factored in (Carduff and Bernauer, 2006). An alternative analysis is that this move to centralisation achieves better control of precaution under centralised scientific models. This is likely to leave less room for precautionary responses if these are centred at European level. On the other hand there is no necessary reason to believe that concerns with food safety will be short lived or that the precautionary principle will be abandoned. Arguably the system now balances the downsides of working with what is essentially a private interest models (and therefore more open to capture) with the potential for strong precautionary action on a European scale if necessary as and when uncertainties give way to real doubts about food safety.

CONCLUSION

To date the influence of food safety on the development of regulatory ideas promoting precaution has been considerable. Strong models of precaution have been applied in regulatory decision-making and have been endorsed by the European Court of Justice. This has not cured all of the definitional problems attaching to the concept, but given that weak models only apply within the world trade arena, Europe has been moving to make the employment of precautionary regulation defensible by greater articulation of its place in risk assessment. At the same time it has cut down the leeway for national precautionary measures through legislative reform. In part this has been made necessary by the vagueness and fluidity of the precautionary principle itself.

It is in the nature of the principle that its use will be contested, as a measure taken on this basis generally restricts the market access of another party, whether State Government or private actor. To this end the incorporation of the principle in a model increasingly driven by science is significant, for it re-directs attention from the definitional shortfalls of the principle to the process by which an expert community has made a determination. It is of course the case that in the face of uncertainty the room for the operation of scientific risk assessment may be highly restricted, but that has not prevented the European Commission propounding a model which can provide the foundation of precautionary action and in which the science, notwithstanding its limited sphere of operation, provides a strong legitimating force. On the other hand, we see that at a risk management level, as in the *Pfizer* (2002) case, the limited utility of risk assessment generated in conditions of uncertainty may allow politicians to feel free to depart from messages emerging from that process.

The precautionary principle is anticipatory and proactive, but because it is brought into operation in conditions of uncertainty, there must be room to doubt its efficacy. This is all the more true, oddly, when it is located within scientific risk assessment if only because of the experiential dimensions of scientific learning which might frame issues in narrow or incomplete contexts. This might suggest that, while one can appreciate the reasons for the adoption of this type of model, not least under the pressures of world trade rules, its future success may be open to doubt. Whether or not this is the case may depend on the credence given to writers such as Beck and Giddens, who have suggested that, in modernity, risks are incalculable and uncontrollable. If this is the case then the structures adopted cannot ensure in the face of uncertainty that the risk assessment has addressed the appropriate risks and has generated an effective precautionary response.

All that this is saying is that some faith is still placed in models of scientific risk assessment notwithstanding increasing doubts as to its capacity to cope with prevailing uncertainties. Indeed it is more than possible that scientific exploration in such areas will generate greater not less uncertainty (Applegate, 2006). Inherent in the Beck analysis is a notion that the new forms of risk within risk society are tied into reflexive modernisation with its notion of technological and scientific advance turning in on itself. If this is so, it may be necessary to view BSE not as a freak event but as an inevitable cost attaching to modern forms of agricultural production. It is sobering but worth remembering that, in that context, attempts at scientific assessment of future outcomes and hazards proved a failure, largely because science saw itself in a role that marginalised uncertainty through available institutional mechanisms (Stokes, 2000) and arguably because of the commitment to prevailing productive enterprises that were not easily opened to question. All of this suggests that one might change regulatory frameworks, as Europe has done, but it will not resolve or even necessarily address wider question that arise in modern food production.

11 From Europeanisation to Globalisation of the Public-Private Model of Food Regulation

INTRODUCTION

We have seen in earlier chapters how food regulation is now deep rooted and integrated into the European political mission. Though agricultural corporatism has declined in its political and economic power in European policy-making, it has laid a foundation for a more comprehensive and commercially-led regulatory system, a hybrid model, that is more sensitive to the consumer and private sector concerns. It is increasingly universal, scientific and normative; global as well as local in reach as well as inter-sectoral. And, as observed in our earlier findings, it is being sustained by the interaction of a larger diversity of actors and policy networks. This makes the development of public policy all the more complex.

As we have seen the food and retailing industry is increasingly paying more attention to food quality and safety issues by actively managing its supply chains of food products. A plethora of private safety control systems, standards, and certification programmes are responding to more demanding consumer requirements. Many leading retailers in Europe have developed programmes for integrated production; thus paving a way for playing a pivotal role in bringing about a change in the way crops are cultivated in a safe and sustainable manner. These private standards have evolved in response to regulatory developments and, more directly, consumer concerns, and as a means of competitive positioning in markets for high-value agricultural and food products (World Bank, 2005). More generally, the evolution of private standards reflects the preponderance of 'soft law' in the governance of economic national and international systems (Morth, 2004) and the innovation of regulatory systems (Black et al., 2005), including a move towards the use of co-regulation (Garcia Martinez et al., 2005). As a result, it seems as though private standards are becoming the predominant drivers of agri-food systems (Henson and Hooker, 2001; Bingen and Busch, 2006). Further, there is evidence that private standards, which are well established in many industrialised countries, are fast becoming a global phenomenon, and permeating the developing country agri-food markets (Reardon et al., 2001; Reardon and Berdegue, 2002; Henson and Reardon, 2005). While there are signs that the role that private standards play in international markets for agricultural and food products is beginning to be recognised (Jaffe and Henson, 2005; World Bank, 2005), there is a paucity of empirical studies.

This final chapter provides a broader perspective—beyond our European focus—of the significance of private standards in the international food arena, and examines the extent to which private standards are affecting the regulatory actions of governments and the resultant impacts on trade. At the same time, the evolution of private food safety and quality standards is to a certain extent testing the role and remit of global organisations, for example the World Trade Organization (WTO). The chapter reviews the role of global organisations in the light of the growing private standards in the food sector and presents an argument that private standards are fast becoming a primary determinant of market access. In many respects this represents a diffusion of our European model of food regulation outlined in this volume to a global level. And it raises new questions and pressures for established global institutions like the WTO and FAO.

FOOD SAFETY AND TRADE

Consumers in the industrialised world have had adequate quantities of food, and they can spend resources to ensure that their food is safer. Baker (1999) found that consumers are willing to pay a premium for reduced pesticide residues in produce. Another study found that the premium consumers were willing to pay for food with low pesticide residues increased with income (Huang et al., 2000). In various surveys and studies, consumers have indicated that they would be willing to pay more for food with lower disease risks; however, these experiments might not reflect how consumers will actually behave in a market setting, as consumers' attitudes on surveys sometimes differ from their documented behaviour over time (Caswell et al., 1998). Food safety scares, like the Bovine Spongiform Encephalopathy and the E.coli outbreak in the UK have raised awareness about food safety issues. Additionally, food travels long distances from producer to consumer, and many foods are perishable. As consumers know that there are technologies available, that entail improved food safety, they are more likely hold producers to a high standard.

Since consumers demand some degree of food safety, businesses have an incentive to supply safe food (Holleran et al., 1999). The market has incentives to provide some degree of food safety, as businesses depend on their reputations for repeat sales. However, for two reasons the market generally does not provide the socially desirable amount of food safety. First, consumers cannot determine how safe food is before buying it. Second, when consumers eat unsafe food and become ill, costs extend beyond consumers themselves to healthcare workers, employers, and family members (Mitchell, 2003).

As we have seen, government regulation is an attempt to increase the amount of food safety provided by the market, as the market alone will usually not provide the socially desirable level of food safety. Government regulations or industry standards for goods can impact on trade in at least three ways: they can facilitate exchange by clearly defining product characteristics and improving compatibility and usability; they also advance domestic social goals like public health by establishing minimum standards or prescribing safety requirements; finally, they can hide protectionist policies. During the Uruguay Round of multilateral trade negotiations, member nations established The Agreement on the Application of Sanitary and Phytosanitary (SPS) Measures and the Agreement on Technical Barriers to Trade (TBT) to address the emerging debate over the use of standards in international trade. The SPS and TBT Agreements balance the competing demands for domestic regulatory autonomy and the global harmonization of product standards. At the same time, the agreements attempt to prevent standards from becoming a protectionist device.

Global regulations are broadly categorised as *product standards* and *process standards*. Product standards specify characteristics that a product must attain before it is considered safe to sell. For example, most industrialised countries have maximum residue levels (MRLs) for pesticides. If a food has pesticide residues above this amount, a vendor cannot legally sell that food. The UK government, under the due diligence principle, assigns the responsibility for verifying food safety to food retailers, rather than setting specific procedures for processing foods. Process standards specify techniques that must be used to process or package foods; with the belief that certain production techniques make food more likely to be safe.

Global food trade is continuously expanding and providing consumers with access to a year-round array of foods. Expanding trade has brought into sharper focus the divergence among countries' food safety regulations and standards. The relationship between public regulation and private-sector standards is rarely clear. However, some have argued that the regulatory and standard-setting activities of governments and the private sector may be mutually supportive in important respects. Each focuses on a separate aspect of risk management. Public regulations aim at *outcomes* i.e., the characteristics of the finished product is specified, and producers and importers are responsible for ensuring, that these requirements are met. Private-sector standards, by contrast, focus on *processes*, which are requirements set for the entire system of production and supply, with specific instructions on production methodologies and testing procedures (Chia-Hui Lee, 2006). This separation of objectives may bring benefits to both government legislators and private sector standard setters.

The International Food Standard (IFS) provides a case in point. Its main role is the creation and implementation of safety standards, mainly through contractual agreements, monitored by a pool of major European retailers. In order to prevent future food scares, retailers have defined and imposed norms on their suppliers for guaranteeing the safety of their deliverables. A new generation of 'referential products' has emerged that must conform to the HACCP method. This strategy of building self-regulation through a private institution is innovative in two ways. First, with respect to the standardisation process involved: whereas the traditional approach to standardisation (for example, norms from the International Standard Organisation (ISO)) is based on mutual agreements among parties that define norms thereafter implemented by delegation to a third party, the IFS proceeds differently: its constituents agree on standards established by experts that they have selected, and then they impose these standards on their suppliers. Second, it differs in its application. Traditionally, whereas public regulations prevail for all parties concerned, norms defined by private institutions are not compulsory. In the case of the IFS system, in agreeing norms of safety that they impose on all suppliers, the pool of retailers actually creates a universal obligation usually viewed as the privilege of public regulators. As a matter of fact, standards defined by the IFS substitute for public regulation by imposing norms that are significantly more demanding than the statutory requirements. However, public authorities continue to play their role of *certifiers of last resort*, as the monitoring function is delegated by the pool of retailers to autonomous organisations that are certified by public.

THE BACKGROUND OF GLOBAL REGULATORY ENVIRONMENTAL TRENDS

Several changes in the global food system, e.g. increased scientific understanding of foodborne hazards, increased international trade in food products, and changes in how consumers obtain and prepare food, have brought renewed attention to food safety regulation in many countries. Henson and Reardon (2005) point out seven main trends in regulation worldwide: (1) the growing use of risk analysis, (2) establishing public health as the primary goal of food safety regulation, (3) emphasizing a farm-to-table approach in addressing food safety hazards, (4) adopting the Hazard Analysis and Critical Control Point (HACCP) system to regulate microbial pathogens in food, (5) increasing the stringency of standards for many food safety hazards, (6) adding new and more extensive regulation to handle newly identified hazards, and, (7) improving market performance in food safety through provision of information.

Within the public sector there has occurred a substantial shift of food safety governance responsibilities from Ministries of agriculture to Ministries of Health and Consumer affairs. In several countries specialised food safety agencies have been created to conduct scientific assessments, to advise policy-makers and to communicate with the general public. Examples include the UK Food Standards Agency and the French Food Safety Agency. A similar institutional shift has taken place at the Community level. Oversight for an array of food safety matters has been shifted to a greatly empowered Health and Consumer Protection Directorate General (DG SANCO).

Regulatory agencies increasingly recognise that a farm to fork approach is often desirable for addressing food safety hazards. Many foodborne hazards can enter food at many points during the production process. When present in food, some hazards can multiply or cross contaminate other foods during transportation, processing, and preparation. The farm to fork approach is clearly articulated in the new EU Food Law as a principle for future food safety regulation. However, the EU policy also recognises that different kinds of regulatory measures may be needed at the farm level, due to the difficulties of controlling hazards in the farm environment.

In addition to more stringent food safety standards, newly identified hazards have brought about new and more extensive regulation. For example, BSE poses both animal and human health risks. Its mode of transmission among cattle or between animals and people is not fully understood. New regulations in the UK and elsewhere, regarding animal age at slaughter, monitoring of animal herds, testing of animal brains at slaughter, exclusion of specified risk materials (brain, spinal cord, etc.) from meat products and exclusion of certain products from cattle feed are designed to reduce the risk of transmission. These regulations are extensive, covering every step of the food production and distribution system from animal feed to meat butchering. They also have had an impact on a wide range of by products, including gelatine used in pharmaceuticals.

Other approaches to food safety regulation include the use of voluntary guidelines or standards, provision of third-party certification, provision of information through labelling, establishing legal liability for food safety, and establishing voluntary or mandatory systems for traceability (see Table 11.1). Such interventions may improve performance by providing information or incentives that encourage consumers to choose safe food and reward producers for its provision. The public role in these new approaches, and the degree to which they are mandatory or voluntary, varies among countries.

As these trends are still evolving in many countries, there are certain public policy issues that remain unresolved. First, the role of scientific and economic analysis in risk management varies widely among countries. For example in the EU, risk management decisions may include 'other legitimate factors' that extend beyond scientific and economic analysis (Henson, 2001). Such factors include consumer concerns, the environment, animal welfare, and other political or economic factors, such as the impact on small farms. Second, controversy surrounds the role of standards. In the EU, for example, the mandate for HACCP in all parts of the food production and

Table 11.1 Information-Based Approaches to Food-Safety Interventions

Approach	*Example*	*Public sector role*	*Advantage to food safety*
Guidelines	UK voluntary guidelines for farms to reduce Salmonella in pigs	Public sector can develop science-based guidelines or certification directed towards public health and consumers	Reduces food risks, but only where guidelines or certification adopted; and reduces transaction cost in markets for safety
Third party certification	Netherlands IKB programs for livestock producers		
Labelling	EU novel food regulation requires labelling of novel foods	Identify where information critical to facilitate consumer choice; respond to consumer demand for information	Reduces market failure where information was previously lacking; alters risk incidence in certain cases
Liability	UK 1990 Food Safety Act	Establishes responsibility for food safety	Improves safety by providing incentives for producers to follow practices that minimises risks.
Traceability	EU Food Law establishes as principle for food safety policy	Establish information and marketing channel requirements	Facilitates tracing problems in case of outbreak; can provide incentives for producers to improve safety

Source: Henson, 2006.

distribution system is not always practical for small retail establishments, so in many cases regulation instead relies on codes of hygienic practice (Jansen, 2001).

IMPLICATIONS FOR INTERNATIONAL FOOD TRADE

Regulatory trends, public policy issues, and the growth in world food trade have several implications for how food safety standards affect international trade in food products. The simultaneous move toward improved safety among industrialised countries creates the potential for convergence around higher standards (as developed countries with major markets adopt new regulations, there is incentive for other countries to follow suit (Vogel, 1995). New regulations are thus undertaken in some countries in response to other countries' actions.

Although some new regulatory developments might mitigate potential barriers to trade, the appearance of new hazards, or increased trade volumes from new sources, can lead to food safety incidents or disputes in trade. A disease outbreak or newly identified hazard often leads to disruptions in trade and may strain relations with trading partners. In the Belgium dioxin crisis in 1999, when high levels of dioxin were discovered in eggs and chickens and traced back to dioxin contaminated animal feed, the Belgian government was criticised for not providing timely information to other countries that imported affected products, which included chicken, eggs, meat, and any products containing eggs or milk. The discovery of BSE in the UK disrupted trade between that country and other members of the EU. The imposition of new, higher standards, as well as remaining differences among countries in how standards are developed and applied, can also lead to trade disputes. In particular, rising standards and the rapid change in food safety regulation in the industrialized countries creates challenges for developing countries, many of which have seen rapid growth in food exports since the 1990s (Unnevehr, 2000; Henson and Loader, 1999). For example, the proposed new standards for aflatoxin in the EU had a disproportionate impact on exports from developing countries (Otsuki et al., 2001). These countries may lack infrastructure to ensure basic sanitation in processing and transport, as well as public oversight to certify certain kinds of safety. New or more stringent process standards entail greater difficulties in determining whether an equivalent safety outcome has been achieved. While HACCP may be widely accepted as an approach to food safety, specific HACCP regulations for specific food sectors may result in different outcomes. As required HACCP systems may or may not be linked to specific performance standards, it can be difficult to determine if imported products are as safe as those produced domestically (Hathaway, 1995). Other kinds of process controls, such as recordkeeping or traceability requirements, can impose undue costs on trading partners. Whether such requirements are necessary to achieve equivalent-risk outcomes can be a matter of dispute.

The uncertainties that afflict some of food science highlight the question of what role scientific information and advice has played, can and should play in food policy making. This is especially so in the light of the UK government's initiative in creating the Food Standards Agency (FSA) with a mandate to provide objective and reliable scientific advice to policy makers (Chapter 9). Science-based evidence no longer generates a ready trust on the part of many consumers, at least so far, because it does not seem to necessarily respond well to diffuse consumer fears, and it too often fails to explain underpinning assumptions critical to assessments made. Considerable efforts have been made by scholars in the fields of science policy and political analysis to foster greater understanding of the ways in which science-based risk management policies are made. But the key issue continues to be the role of scientific information and advice in the assessment and management of food risks.

Strong differences remain with respect to consumer risk preferences, consumer perceptions, and the role of non-science issues in regulatory decision-making. Both consumer risk preferences and consumer perceptions are at issue in the longstanding disagreement between the US and the EU over use of growth hormones in beef. Non-science issues such as the preservation of small farms are a consideration in EU decisions about inputs like growth hormones or r-BST.[1] Differences in perception and willingness to assume unknown risks are evident in more recent disagreements over the acceptability of genetically modified organisms (GMOs) and labelling of foods produced through modern biotechnology (Chapter 3). Furthermore, non-science issues such as ethical concerns about genetic modification are at play in the dispute over modern biotechnology. Food safety issues may be difficult to separate from other contentious issues in cases like these. In summary, changes in regulatory approach may lead to some convergence in food safety standards, but the dynamic nature of food trade, the onset of new hazards, and differences in regulatory approach and capacity still instigate disputes and disruptions to global trade.

PUBLIC AND PRIVATE STANDARDS IN REGULATING INTERNATIONAL FOOD MARKETS

Standards can be mandatory in a legal sense or can be voluntary. While mandatory standards are generally the only safeguard of public institutions, both public and private institutions can be involved in the governance of voluntary standards. Mandatory standards are standards set by public institutions (in particular regulatory agencies) with which compliance is obligatory. Voluntary standards arise from a formal coordinated process involving participants in a market with or without the participation of government. Broadly, the international standards developed by the International Organization for Standardisation (ISO) and national and/or regional standards bodies take this form. The standards developed by private standards-setting bodies, for example the Safe Quality Food (SQF) Institute and the British Retail Consortium (BRC) are examples specific to food safety and quality. Members of the groups attempt to achieve consensus on the best technical specifications to meet their collective needs. A variety of private entities may be involved in the establishment of voluntary consensus standards including industry and trade organisations, professional societies, standards-setting membership organisations and industry consortia, which in some cases may be coordinated by a public entity. Use of the standards resulting from this process is generally voluntary, although they may be applied by the majority of suppliers, reflecting the economic advantage associated with standardisation or market requirements. *De Facto* mandatory standards arise from an uncoordinated process of market-based competition between the actions of private firms (Henson, 2005).

Attempts have been made in the international sphere, to overcome the potential negative trade effects of food safety and quality standards. The WTO, through the Sanitary and Phytosanitary (SPS) and Technical Barrier to Trade (TBT) Agreements, has laid down the rights and obligations of WTO Members with respect to the application of public food safety and quality measures (Josling et al., 2004; Roberts, 2004). Broadly, these agreements permit governments to apply food safety and quality standards in pursuit of legitimate policy objectives. Attempts have also been made to harmonise food safety and quality standards across nation states, through the setting up of international standards by the Codex Alimentarius Commission (more details on Codex Alimentarius Commission are discussed subsequently). The dual impact of the WTO and international standards setting bodies has been to bring about greater discipline, and certainly enhanced transparency, in the use of public food safety and quality measures (Roberts, 2004), while defining a more common vocabulary through which national governments can communicate their food safety and quality objectives.

Analogous to the development of public food safety and quality standards there have been moves by the private sector to address consumer concerns regarding food safety and quality. Much of the motivation behind this trend has been to avert commercial risks associated with the safety of food products. More broadly, a wide range of market and firm-level factors motivate the implementation of enhanced food safety and quality controls (Segersen, 1999; Henson and Caswell, 1999). Thus, there is a rapidly increasing plethora of private 'codes of practice', standards and other forms of supply chain governance (Jaffee and Henson, 2004). As we have seen, these efforts have been especially prominent among large food retailers, food manufacturers and food service operators, reflecting both their considerable market power and competitive strategies based around 'own' or private brands that tie a firm's reputation and performance to the quality supplied by its products (Berges-Sennou et al., 2004).

Thus, contemporary agri-food systems are increasingly governed by an array of inter-related public and private standards, both of which are becoming evidently (either de jure or de facto) mandatory. It has been recognised that private standards can play a key role in governing food safety and quality and that public and private controls should be coordinated (Henson and Caswell, 1999), such that co-regulatory approaches (Garcia et al., 2005) are being employed as part of efforts to achieve social food safety and quality objectives in a more competent way.

In earlier chapters we have observed a shift from mandatory standards as the predominant form of governance over food safety and quality, which is inevitably positioned within the public sector, to more voluntary forms of governance, paving a way for a more actively driven private sector. The dissimilarity and the shift between public and private standards can be seen through both the growing role of standards set by private processes and/or the emergence of private standards as *de facto* mandatory in agricultural and food markets (Henson and Northen, 1998).

Contemporary global agri-food systems are governed not only by public and private standards, but also by *public and private modes of enforcement* as they are increasingly permeating public regulations (for example, as in the inclusion of HACCP among the regulatory requirements for meat and meat products in the United States, Canada, EU, etc.) such that the relations between public and private food safety and quality standards are increasingly complex. Regulators are now increasingly adopting the mechanisms employed by private standards, and indeed even referencing private standards, in their rule making (Henson and Northen 1998; Henson and Hooker, 2001).

The development of private governance structures for food safety and quality raises considerable challenges for the analysis of trade in agricultural and food products. On the one hand, private standards are a relatively new element of the food safety and quality landscape and continue to evolve over time. On the other, the extent of private food safety and quality standards differs widely across countries, products and customers. Private standards remain far from universal and in certain contexts, for example broad commodity markets in food processing, public standards continue to predominate (World Bank, 2005). At the same time, however, it is possible to distinguish the factors that influence the development or adoption of public and private standards, providing guidance on where private modes of governance are more all-encompassing or are likely to dominate over time.

There is a growing recognition among large food retailers for a collective private standard that would enable them to reduce the costs of governing food safety along their supply chains, while expanding the population of suppliers from which they could procure. In the UK most major food retailers have collaborated in the development of a harmonised private food safety standard through the British Retail Consortium (BRC). Similar efforts by German and French food retailers have led to the International Food Standard (IFS).

Casella (2001) argues that firm-level coalitions for the formation of harmonized collective standards will shift from national to predominantly international as markets become more globally integrated. This trend is now being observed through the formation of the Global Food Safety Initiative (GFSI) through the Food Business Forum (CIES), which is developing guidelines for the benchmarking of national and regional private food safety standards in order to bring about mutual recognition of differing codes. Similarly (as we discuss in relation to fresh fruit and vegetables in Chapter 7), a league of several major food retailers across Europe in the late 1990s formed the Euro-Retailer Produce Working Group (EUREP) that has developed a common private protocol on good agricultural practice (GlobalGap).

GLOBAL ORGANISATIONS IN THE GOVERNANCE FRAMEWORK

International standards for food safety are developed and adjusted by a small number of international organisations, each of whom are strongly interlinked. At the focus of this is the World Trade Organisation and the commitments laid out in its Sanitary and Phytosanitary Measures (SPS) agreement.

All 150 WTO member states are legally bound to abide by the principles set out in the SPS agreement when developing standards that may have a direct or indirect influence on international trade. Established in 1995, the agreement takes a risk-based approach to food and agricultural standards that aims to encourage the standardisation of national standards under the principles of 'sound science' and 'non-discrimination'. A primary tenet of the Agreement is that signatory states must 'ensure that their sanitary and phytosanitary measures are based on an assessment, as appropriate to the circumstances, of the risks to human, animal, or plant life or health, taking into account risk assessment techniques developed by the relevant international organisations".'[2] WTO members are able to develop their own specifications within these principles. Should trade disputes be brought to the WTO, however, they will be ruled with reference to international standards which have been mandated with developing standards based on the WTO SPS agreement.

These organisations are the Codex Alimentarius Commission (Codex), which is overseen jointly by the World Health Organisation (WHO) and the UN Food and Agriculture Organisation (FAO) and has responsibility for food standards; the World Organisation for Animal Health (OIE) who has responsibility for animal standards; and the International Plant Protection Convention (IPPC) who, are mandated with Phytosanitary measures. Each of these organisations, work closely with each other as well as with the WTO and other stakeholders (see Figure 11.1).

The SPS states that member states must use the standards set by these organisations as reference points on which to base their own. They may only adopt higher or stricter standards if they can demonstrate a scientific justification. WTO Member states have a duty to notify the WTO of any proposed SPS regulations which are not the same as international

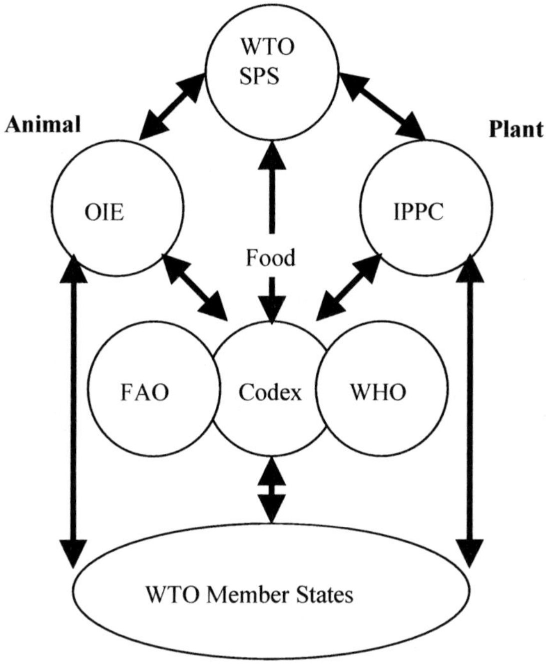

Figure 11.1 Global standard-setting organisations.

(Codex, OIE or IPPC) standards and may have a significant effect on international trade.

Codex Alimentarius Commission (Codex)

Codex Alimentarius Commission is an intergovernmental body jointly sponsored by the Food and Agriculture Organisation (FAO) and the World Health Organisation (WHO), and its aim is to establish worldwide standards for foods in the broadest sense. The Codex Alimentarius Commission, established by the two Organisations in the 1960s, has become the single most important international reference point for developments associated with food standards. Food legislation in many countries is based on Codex Standards, although it is not mandatory to implement them in all cases.

The Codex Alimentarius, or the food code, has become the global reference point for consumers, food producers and processors, national food control agencies and the international food trade. The Codex Alimentarius system presents a unique opportunity for all countries to join the international community in formulating and harmonising food standards and ensuring their global implementation. It also allows them a role in the development of codes governing hygienic processing practices and recommendations relating to compliance with those standards.

Given that food standards are becoming more important as international trade in food accelerates and consumers are more concerned about safety and quality; Codex is recognised in the relevant World Trade Organisation (WTO) agreements as the international body able to provide these guarantees. In the event of a trade dispute Codex standards would become accepted reference documents for its settlement. This underlines the increasing importance of Codex in international law.

The significance of the food code for consumer health protection was accentuated in 1985 by the United Nations Resolution 39/248, whereby guidelines were adopted for use in the elaboration and reinforcement of consumer protection policies. The guidelines advise that: 'When formulating national policies and plans with regard to food, Governments should take into account the need of all consumers for food security and should support and, as far as possible, adopt standards from the . . . Codex Alimentarius or, in their absence, other generally accepted international food standards.'

The Codex Alimentarius has relevance to the international food trade. With respect to the ever-increasing global market, in particular, the advantages of having universally uniform food standards for the protection of consumers are self-evident. It is not surprising, therefore, that the Agreement on the Application of Sanitary and Phytosanitary Measures (SPS Agreement) and the Agreement on Technical Barriers to Trade (TBT Agreement) both encourage the international harmonisation of food standards. Products of the Uruguay Round of multinational trade negotiations, these Agreements cite international standards, guidelines and recommendations as the preferred measures for facilitating international trade in food. As such, Codex standards have become the benchmarks against which national food measures and regulations are evaluated within the legal parameters of the World Trade Organization (WTO) Agreements.

By providing an international focal point and forum for informed dialogue on issues relevant to food, the Codex Alimentarius Commission fulfils a crucial role. In support of its work on food standards and codes of practice, it generates texts for the management of food safety and consumer protection based on the work of the best-informed individuals and organisations concerned with food and related fields.

While the growing world interest in all Codex activities clearly indicates global acceptance of the Codex, (embracing harmonisation, consumer protection and facilitation of international trade), in practice it is difficult for many countries to accept Codex standards in the statutory sense. Differing legal formats and administrative systems, varying political systems and sometimes the influence of national attitudes and concepts of sovereign rights, impede the progress of harmonisation and deter the acceptance of Codex standards.

One of the strengths of the Codex and FAO and WHO relationship in scientific matters is its flexibility. In recent years, FAO and WHO have held expert scientific consultations on a broad range of matters. Not all of these have resulted in the development of new Codex standards, as sometimes the best way of managing food safety risks is *determined* to be through other means. FAO and WHO also provide advice on how alternative means of risk management can be brought about.

The following excerpt from an interview with an FAO official brings out the essence of the working relationship between Codex, FAO and the WHO:

> . . . our collaboration particularly in the area of provision of scientific advice is very strong, any requests that we get from Codex we tend to work on jointly in all the activities relating to microbiological risk assessment, these are all joint FAO/WHO activities. On other levels over the past few years we've also worked with the WHO to implement the regional and global conferences for food safety. Recently as well, in the past very much in terms of capacity building or projects we have tended to work independently but now, following on from these conferences and also this more integrated approach to food safety, when it comes to establishing projects in particular countries or maybe small regional projects, both organisations try to work together so that there's a common approach to food safety. So one project maybe FAO led would have WHO input or vice versa and of course the other areas, that we're working on at the moment I think like the avian flu, FAO is working on it very much from the veterinary perspective whereas WHO are working on it from the health perspective so any issues like that that tend to require this two prong approach in terms of food safety and training health, we try to have a joint initiative with the WHO.

It is quite evident from the following excerpts of the interview with an IAEA official, the FAO and the WHO are not the only sources of scientific advice on which Codex depends. Codex encourages other scientifically based intergovernmental organizations to contribute to the joint FAO and WHO scientific system. The International Atomic Energy Agency (IAEA) provides advice and support on levels of radionuclide contamination in foods and on food irradiation.

> . . . it was recognised by both FAO and IAEA that there was a place for technical expertise related to nuclear technologies food group, the joint division (FAO/IAEA) works in two major project areas one project area is the applicatory role and the development of standards related to radiation, the use of radiation for food also the application of other standards, we are not just restricted doing the radiation we are also very much involved in the review of radio-nuclei contamination, geological events like terrorist activities. We are very much involved in the not only the interpretation but the application of conventions and agreements between UN bodies and emergency preparedness.

World Organisation for Animal Health (OIE)

The World Organisation for Animal Health (OIE) provides advice on animal health, on animal diseases affecting humans and on the linkages between animal health and food safety. Based in Paris, the Office International des Epizooties was created in 1924 as the result of an international agreement between 24 nations seeking to improve cooperation to fight against the spread of animal disease. Renamed as the World Organisation for Animal Health (but confusingly retaining its original acronym), the organisation currently has 167 full members and acts as a coordinating partner for SPS standard setting.

A central mission of the organisation is 'to safeguard world trade by publishing health standards for international trade in animals and animal products'. This sits along side objectives to communicate, analyse and provide expertise to nations to combat issues of animal disease. The organisation is also increasingly active in global animal welfare issues.

The OIE publishes a set of normative documents that put forward rules that member countries can use to protect themselves from animal diseases and pathogens without constructing undue barriers to trade. These documents include: the Terrestrial Animal Health Code, the Manual of Diagnostic Tests and Vaccines for Terrestrial Animals, the Aquatic Animal Health Code and the Manual of Diagnostic Tests for Aquatic Animals.[3]

Standards are adopted by an OIE International Committee using recommendations drawn up by specialist scientific commissions and working groups.[4] A working group on food safety was established in 2002.[5]

International Plant Protection Convention (IPPC)

Unlike Codex and the OIE, official standards and guidance for plant related trade are based on an international convention. The International Plant Protection Convention was established in 1951 and currently has 158 signatory members. The Convention works to prevent the introduction and spread of plant and plant product pests, and promote appropriate control measures. Convention activities are coordinated by an IPPC Secretariat which is hosted by the FAO and governed by the Commission on Phytosanitary Measures (CPM), which was established in 2005. A major element of the Convention's activities is the development and promotion of International Standards for Phytosanitary Measures (ISPMs). The IPPC official interviewed during our research clarified the Convention's activities as follows:

> Basically because nobody thought really about standard setting in the fields of plant health before the SPS Agreement came into being, so, at the time of the negotiations of the Uruguay round, this issue came up. Do we need to have international standards in the field of plant health?

> There was certainly some doubt at that time whether anything could be done . . . it was agreed that there was scope for that and then the countries looked for an institution basically that could do so. Therefore, the IPPC was recognised as the institution that could start working on that. So as a standard setting body the IPPC is very new although the convention itself is very old.

ISPMs are used as a reference for WTO trade rulings. WTO members are required to base their phytosanitary measures on IPPC standards. There are currently 24 ISPM standards in existence. Measures that deviate from these standards or exist in areas without current standards must be developed through risk assessment and based on scientific principles and evidence. The IPPC also provides dispute settlement procedures through the CPM, which although non-binding, act as indicators for potential WTO SPS level procedures.

The CPM meets annually to establish the priorities for standard-setting and the harmonisation of phytosanitary measures, in coordination with the IPPC Secretariat. Membership is open to all signatories of the IPPC. Governmental non-members and non-governmental organisations may attend CPM events in an observer status. As a young organisation, the CPM is regarded as still establishing its authority and efficacy, particularly in the area of information dissemination and expert links. Nine Regional Plant Protection Organisations (RPPOs) also exist. Their remit is to coordinate the work of the IPPC in their respective regions.[6]

World Health Organisation (WHO)

Both the WHO and FAO are also individually involved in other aspects of international food safety. The WHO, for example, provides expert advice and assistance to its members through activities such as, surveillance/monitoring, sharing of information, providing guidance & training, QA and testing services, appraisals of new food technologies, and the promotion of cooperation between nations and between agencies. WHO activity is concentrated in countries with public health problems and a lack of means to combat them, the WHO official interviewed during our research succinctly argues:

> . . . the FAO and WHO have a long history of multilateral efforts to promote food security and public health and have worked to develop a consensus about the implications of biotechnology for their areas of interest. Meanwhile, the IPPC and OIE are multilateral treaties that seek to protect plants and animals from the spread of pathogens through international trade, thereby providing much of the scientific consensus that underlies domestic food safety systems. Both institutions have their own nonbinding dispute avoidance and settlement systems, but

their most important role in international trade is through the WTO Sanitary and Phytosanitary Agreement (SPS), which uses the IPPC and OIE standards as the basis for evaluating SPS disputes.

The World Health Assembly, who oversee the development of WHO's activities, agreed in 2000 to an expansion of WHO's global food safety remit. This included the development of a WHO Global Strategy for Food Safety, which was endorsed in 2002 and seeks to identify global food safety needs and coordinate global approaches to combating foodborne safety issues. Individual nations are urged to use the strategy as a source of guidance when developing or reforming their own national food safety strategies.[7]

FOOD AND AGRICULTURE ORGANISATION (FAO)

FAO activity in food safety is focused through its joint implementation of the FAO/WHO Food Standards Programme and its main manifestation, the Codex Alimentarius Commission.

Food safety is an important aspect of much FAO work, although the organisation lacks a discrete internal food safety arm. Nevertheless, food safety issues are integral to the workings of FAO departments such as Animal Production and Health Division, Plant Production and Protection Division, Agricultural Support Systems Division and the Agricultural and Economic Development Analysis Division.[8]

The organisation also works closely with partners on a number of programmes related to food safety and standards. The FAO philosophy on food safety issues is based on promoting food supply chain approaches. This approach is laid out in the organisation's guiding document on this subject: 'Strategy for a Food Chain Approach to Food Safety and Quality: a framework document for the development of future strategic direction' which outlines the organisation's aims to produce a comprehensive strategy document on the issue.[9]

Inter-Agency Cooperation

The degree of inter-agency cooperation and collaboration between the standard setting organisations is variable. There has been increasing emphasis in recent years, however, on coordinating and cross-referencing texts and standards between relevant organisations.[10]

Cooperation between the standard setting organisations and the WTO SPS process are well established. All three organisations attend relevant SPS meetings as observers.[11] Ties between the standard setting organisations themselves vary. The OIE, for example, describes its cooperation with Codex as encompassing:

a) the use of a common text in the elaboration of a standard and harmonisation of definition;
b) co-operation through mutual exchange of information and participation in meetings;
c) cross-referencing to the other organisation's standards;
d) the construction of complementary texts taking into account the existing standards.[12]

OIE representatives have observer status on a number of Codex committees, for instance, including a Committee on Food Import and Export Inspection and Certification Systems, a Committee on Milk and Milk Products and one on Residues of Veterinary Drugs in Food.[13] Links between the IPPC and its two sister organisations are generally less formal.[14]

FAO has a very close working relationship with the WHO, while with the WTO is more of a distant relationship. This is evident from the excerpts from our interview with an FAO official:

> We have quite a significant working relationship with WHO in the area of nutrition, there's a very big debate, extensive work going on at the moment on diet and product issues which is not necessarily a food standards issue. . . There's a slight area of interaction which is in labelling where you have nutrition information on labels which I must say has only just started in the European Union. . . Actually the affiliation with WTO is a curious one, they're not a United Nations body, they have their own statutes and their own rules, whereas the work of Codex and the work of FAO, the work of WHO for the most part, is always advisory.

All the organisations have collaborated to produce an online information source called The International Portal on Food Safety, Animal and Plant Health which provides a single information point for official information, both international and national, on issues of food safety, animal and plant health.[15]

Links with National and Regional Bodies

Each national member of these organisations has a point of contact, usually located within the country's ministry for food & agriculture (or equivalent). Their duties revolve around the coordination of information flows between national stakeholders and the international standard setting organisation, either through answering domestic enquiries, coordinating and compiling stakeholder responses as part of consultation processes and notifying domestic interests of changes to the relevant international standards. In the UK, for example, WTO SPS 'enquiry point', OIE 'official delegate' and the IPPC 'National Plant Protection

Organisation Contact' all reside with DEFRA representatives. The Codex 'contact point' is within the Food Standards Agency. In the UK, the National Codex Consultative Committee is open to all stakeholders and attended by representatives of industry, enforcement and consumer groups.[16]

All the standard setting organisations allow national governments to propose and develop initiatives which then may be developed within the established procedural process. Standard setting organisations generally use a mixture of in-house and external expertise. The OIE, for example, has a network of 156 collaborating centres and reference laboratories that provide expertise on the specialist commissions and working groups who are charged with preparing their official guideline documents. One of the FAO officials interviewed in our research had the following to say on their involvement with the national bodies like FSA.

> . . . we make quite a distinction between the scientific advice which determines whether or not something is safe and that is done by individual experts drawn from institutions around the world in their own capacity; that's very similar to the model which is used by FSA. In the implementation side, most food regulation is implemented, through food law. So, we have to deal directly with the government, now the government may involve experts from the Food Standards Agency or they may bring policy people from the ministry in these discussions. Sometimes they do both. And there's one other difference, in the scientific side of things we work with experts in the individual capacity whereas in the setting of standards codes of practice, guidelines and so forth, it's government negotiation, it's the government that is represented with the powers of the government not as individuals.

The European Union has steadily increased its influence at SPS and partner organisation proceedings, at the expense of individual EU member state involvement.[17] In 2003, the European Commission achieved full member status in the Codex Commission and now represents all EU members on matters of EU competence.[18] The EU has a similar position within the IPPC[19] and although it is currently without full member status in the OIE,[20] the Commission does coordinate a common community position on issues.

PRIVATE STANDARDS AND THE ROLE OF GLOBAL ORGANISATIONS

The evolution of private standards simultaneously does not imply that such regulatory food safety and quality requirements will fade away. This was reflected in the views presented by an FAO official

> I should point out that codex was, is and probably will always be a voluntary standardising body. We have an acceptance procedure with the ultimate goal of course is to have people harmonise their standards from government to government, unless there is scientific reasons to deviate from this.

While private food safety and quality standards are emerging as an important trade issue for agricultural and food products, it is evident that such standards fall *outside of the scope of existing global institutions* aimed at providing discipline in the use of food safety and quality measures. There have been occasional concerns regarding private standards acting as barriers to trade; however, it has been recognised that the actions of private firms are compatible, as is reflected in the following excerpts during our interview with a WTO official:

> This is an issue that has never been discussed in the SPS Committee although it has been raised in the Technical Barriers to Trade (TBT) Committee. . . The search for a framework that could prevent these private standards from becoming barriers to trade must start with the acknowledgement that WTO Agreements are not enough to deal with this issue, since private requirements were not the central issue during WTO trade negotiations. If we consider both mandatory and voluntary environmental requirements, we have to admit that full implementation of WTO agreements is important and may have a considerable role in solving part of the problems concerning market access, but a more global solution requires the development of new tools outside WTO. However having said that, I think personally that it is very difficult for the WTO to set standards to so many different aspects so in a way what the private sector are doing is good. Their (private sector) efforts frequently involve international trade, and often exports from less developed countries. They may also utilise new technologies or management approaches that facilitate quality control and assurance. This market evolution is encouraging, because it demonstrates that private incentives can sometimes overcome technical barriers to trade. The WTO is the place of last resort for disagreements over such technical barriers.

An FAO official interviewed also shared similar views:

> . . . basically I am very much in favour of these private initiatives and private standards, . . . but I think the important thing for governments to realise is that these are in fact private initiatives and that what we want to be careful, I don't mean national legislation but also international initiatives that have by default so to speak become quite mandatory once in the trading environment. . . but I think these private initiatives in some respects are much further along than what the

UN is doing. I am very enthusiastic about these private initiatives but I think the UN should continue to play the coordinating role to make sure that these do not duplicate each other.

Another FAO official interviewed was of the opinion that private retailers should not be entrusted with the responsibility of deciding on the food safety requirements of a nation:

> . . . the ideal situation would be to leave the international harmonised arena for the Governments. They have the big value and their open and transparent consultative process. And then on special needs, you would have private standards that would compliment. But I would not recommend or I would not see how a private retailer should decide on the food safety requirements for a country, I mean that's crazy.

While private food safety and quality standards might challenge the dominance of the WTO as the main forum through which trade issues related to food safety and quality measures are addressed, it is hard to conceive of a situation where an international agreement or treaty can be brought to bear on the private commercial transactions of buyers within agricultural and food supply chains. Indeed, private standards, whether taking the form of business-to-business specifications or collective standards, are (and have arguably always been) integral to the private contractual relations between buyers and sellers. An FAO official interviewed had the following comment to make:

> . . . EUREPGAP is very successful in that they are truly governing from the farmer level all the way to Safeways. This to me is where the private sector can play a really crucial role. The point I am trying to make is the UN bodies all input to this process at different stages. We have manuals, we have fantastic manuals and GAP production and Dairy production but one other problem with the UN bodies is that they are not basically licensing or certifying bodies or accreditation bodies or anything related to formally accepting or promulgating or promoting these different standards and that's good. I think that's good, because the UN organisations have to show a very independent, very unbiased view otherwise they lose all their credibility.

During our research interviews it was clear from the responses from our interviewees that global organisations cannot do much about the proliferation of private standards. When asked about their view on WTO's possible interest in the growth of private standards because it could be contravening the notions of free market, an FAO official had the following response:

> The WTO has basically said that they cannot do anything about the private standards. The question was raised in the SPS committee some

> time ago by Jamaica and some others and the response was because these are not government to government arrangements and WTO is explicitly a government to government body, WTO cannot do anything with them.

CONCLUSION

With heightened awareness of food safety concerns and the globalising food system, food safety standards are becoming more stringent and responsive to new hazards. Countries that trade internationally may have different desired levels of food safety and food safety regimes, as well as different costs of complying with regulations. Food safety, both domestically and internationally, is managed and ensured by both private and public sector efforts.

In essence, the private and public sectors have responded to consumer demand for quality and safety by developing and implementing common approaches for quality and safety control, management, and assurance, often working in partnership. The extent of public versus private responsibility varies among commodities and food products. Public and private approaches are often intertwined with each other and with multilateral coordination mechanisms (e.g. Codex and HACCP).

As more safety and quality attributes are increasingly demanded by consumers, the private sector responds. In general, the private sector pioneers food safety advances. Importers often target their food safety efforts to sell to large supermarket chains with particular food standards (e.g., regarding produce). Private approaches fostering food safety include self regulation, vertical integration, third-party certification, and common approaches to risk identification, assessment, and management such as Hazard Analysis and Critical Control Point (HACCP) systems and voluntary guidelines or Good Agricultural Practices (GAPs) (see Figure 11.2).

One of the foremost concerns regarding the growth of private food safety and quality standards is their potential impact on the *transparency of regulatory processes*. While the WTO commits Member states to notifying all new public food safety and quality standards and providing time for trade partners to voice concerns and engaged in bilateral dialogue, this does not apply to private standards. On the other hand, a wide constituency of stakeholders, both along the supply chain and geographically, is often involved in the promulgation of 'collaborative' or 'partnership' type private food safety and quality standards. For example, the GlobalGAP and SGQ standards are all developed by technical committees that include representatives of food retailers and suppliers from multiple countries. This might suggest that, in some cases, private standards are more open to influence by trading partners than national regulatory requirements.

The findings of the earlier chapters indicates that there is a significant trend towards Europeanisation of food policy in the UK, and a growing

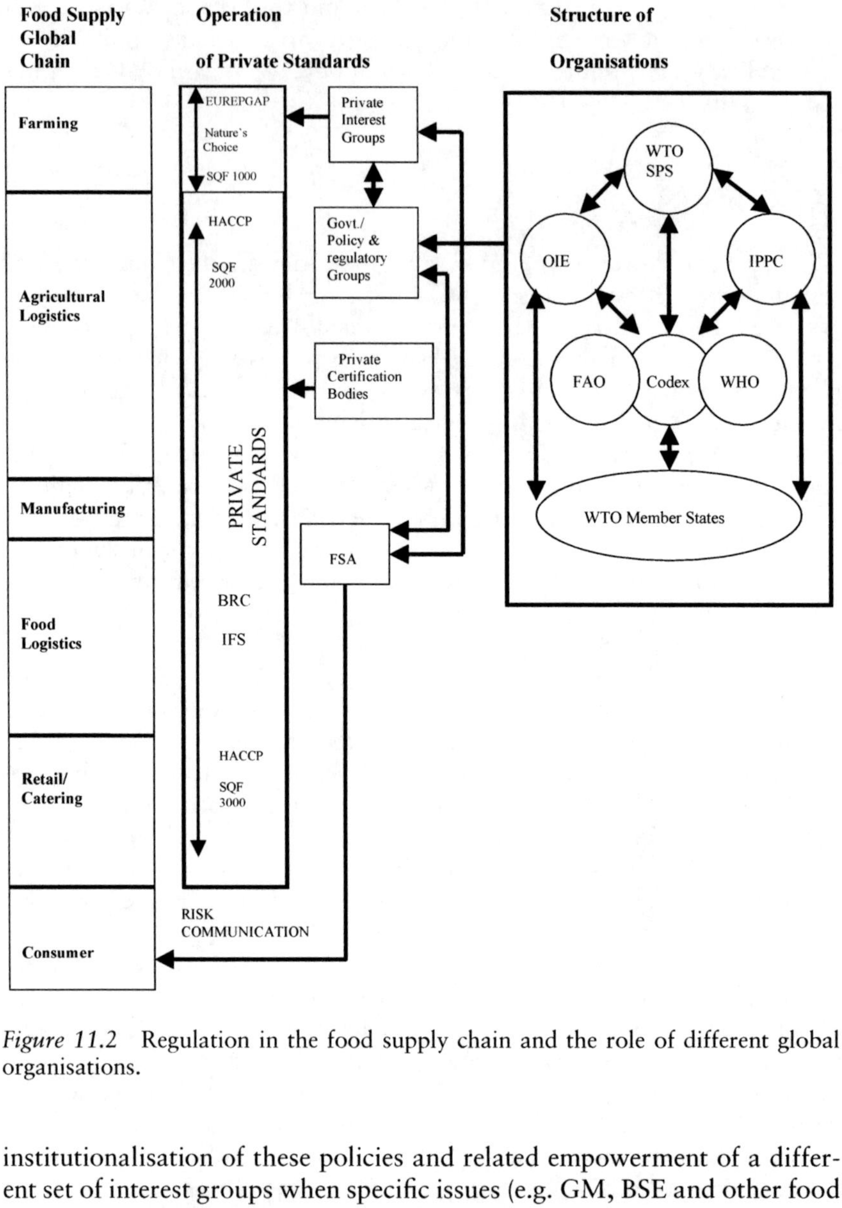

Figure 11.2 Regulation in the food supply chain and the role of different global organisations.

institutionalisation of these policies and related empowerment of a different set of interest groups when specific issues (e.g. GM, BSE and other food safety issues) are concerned. Private interest groups are increasingly playing a pivotal role in reshaping the UK food policy. This chapter has also shown that in many ways the European public-private regulatory model is itself becoming internationalised.

From our research it is clearly evident that global organisations believe that the EU-based work being carried out by the private sector is laudable and the ability of the private sector to bring about a market evolution is encouraging, as this demonstrates that private incentives can sometimes overcome technical barriers to trade. Member nations bestow global organisations a fairly open hand in developing new ideas, but are very wary of conferring with any authority over their trade or over their internal regulation.

An FAO official interviewed had the following to say:

> The mixed model (Public-Private model) that you're looking at is with us for some time. Whether it will succeed in the long run is hard to say. . . . But I think it's got a better chance of succeeding than a government-only model or an industry-only model.

Clearly, private standards are fast becoming a primary determinant of market access, simultaneously paving a way for the evolution of private food safety and quality standards that is now even looking like challenging the role of the global organisations e.g. the World Trade Organisation (WTO). The actual views and tensions/concerns surrounding the private food safety and quality standards is reflected in a closing statement of an interview with one of the FAO officials interviewed:

> For the most part they (retailers) are not imposing too many new standards, but they are imposing much more rigorous control all the way along the line. Partly because of, what used to be called due diligence, but has now been folded into the new European food law to protect themselves against liability . . . It's a marketing ploy. I honestly don't think it has anything to do with protecting consumer's health. I think it's exclusively a marketing issue and playing to consumers perceptions about food safety but not about the food safety itself.

Alternatively the FAO operates in a more public realm:

> And of course we have workshops and meetings and training and expert consultations. Everything we do, we try to be 'bottom up'. We have strict rules and an open transparent process for the selection of experts, they come under their own responsibility and they don't represent anything. If they do have a conflict of interest they have to explain it such as regarding a patent or something; and either be removed or be excused. So the expert consultations are very widely based and then hold a normative element that we then work with the countries to implement it.

From this analysis of the global regulatory bodies and their degree of interaction with private standards, a set of concluding points can be made.

Global public bodies are based upon regulating trade across nation states and in opening up markets which can then be exploited by the imposition of private and corporately controlled standards. This is now the global reality of the hybrid model outlined with reference to Europe and the UK in earlier chapters. There is thus a system of co-regulation (public nation-state/ private supply chain) at a global level which presides over the growing proliferation of private standards. These are, in effect, publicly underwritten by defining consistent state regulations on the movement and trade in food goods.

From the point of view of the global public bodies, private standards are seen to fall outside the scope of existing instructions, although there has been growing concerns (for instance by Argentina and Jamaica) among some member states about these private standards acting as barriers to trade. This is seen as largely a non-issue by the WTO (in contrast to the FAO, for instance), with the private standards seen as largely complimentary and bringing forth new innovations in technologies and management approaches.

Hence we have global institutions which ensure nation state regulation compliance leaving internationalised supply chain regulation to the private sector. Here there are serious questions of regulatory transparency and questions about the continued marginalisation of sustainable rural development as part of the governance frameworks. This is likely only to create more opposition outside these global institutions.

As Busch (2006) has shown, the greatest paradox of these complementary systems of (hybrid) governance, especially at the global level, is that they are by far market structuring mechanisms rather than market liberalising ones. They provide a regulatory framework of both public and private collaboration which at the global level provides a rich but lop-sided competitive terrain in which corporate players can exploit local and national agro-food systems in ways which continue to capture value in the manufacture, processing and retailing ends of supply chains. For instance, the WTO and the private standard setters may promote the view that they are separate from each other, but in reality their distinctive regulatory functions are complimentary in framing 'markets' for foods. This continues (as many of our respondents in the FAO recognised) to put local producers and their local and regional supply chain linkages very much at risk. As we showed in the introductory chapter this is fuelling the further international embeddedness of corporate supply chain management and the decline of local and regional systems of marketing and wholesaling (Riordan, 2007). These economic realities fall out, and are a clear expression of, the emerging global hybrid regulatory system outlined in this chapter.

12 Conclusions
Continuities and Challenges

In this book we have critically analysed the regulation of the contemporary food system, paying particular attention to the ways in which food safety (and food risk) is dynamically constructed between public, private and consumer interests, operating at a variety of spatial scales. Among the key points drawn out is the complexity of the contemporary food system, such that it cannot simply be understood by focussing on selected private actors, such as farmers or retailers. The ways in which food supply chains as a whole operate can be at least as important as the parts played by individual or groups of actors in delivering foods. There is variety in the way in which food supply chains operate, as we demonstrate in relation to red meat and fresh fruit and vegetables, so it is necessary to be able to understand both the singularities and commonalities of supply chains. The role of governments, and patterns of governance, in food safety needs to be explored at a variety of scales, since neither a national nor a European level of analysis is sufficient. The making and delivery of food policy is taking place at multiple scales and this understanding must be incorporated into, and reflected by, analytical models. The nature of contemporary food governance means that an institutional analysis can only provide a partial picture of food safety management. Whilst bodies such as the European Food Safety Authority and the Food Standards Agency (see Chapters 4 and 9) are important objects of analysis, as we have consistently argued, it is the *interactions* between public and private sectors that are essential to a fuller understanding of the food system.

To further reflect upon the aforementioned themes, and drawing upon the analysis of the volume, this chapter is organised around five topics. First, we examine the recent history of the relationship between markets, state and regulation. Over time, we are witnessing a blurring of the boundaries between state and private interests as they coalesce in ever more complex arrangements. In the second section we pursue further the nature of contemporary food governance and argue that the state is increasingly acting to legitimate private supply chain activities as a means of delivering safe and plentiful foods. Matters, though, are made more complex since private forms of supply chain regulation do not necessarily coincide with the scales of public regulation. In the third section, on globalised and national food systems, we point out that the globalisation of food supply chains is integrally linked to current patterns of governance. The fourth section analyses the adaptability that the conventional food system has shown when faced with a number of food scares and challenges from alternative food models. As we point out, however, whilst the dominant food system has proved to be remarkably resilient when faced with food based challenges it is a moot point as to whether it can be so adaptable when confronting major global external shocks, such as climate change. Finally, we suggest that factors such as 'peak oil, 'peak food' and climate change are leading to a rapid reassessment of the nature of European agricultural and food policies and of the potential role of the nation state.

MARKETS, STATE AND FOOD SAFETY REGULATION

In this volume and earlier analysis (Marsden et al 2000) we have sought to distinguish three phases in the ongoing development of food safety regulation since the 1980s. In the first phase, up to the mid 1980s, food hygiene and public health were the highest concerns on the food safety regulatory agenda, strategies to manage food risk depended heavily upon science-based, technological approaches. Under the regulatory regimes that were in place then, food and agricultural production systems were regarded as being safe unless proven otherwise by technical and quantitative analyses. In this way, the State had a rational and scientific basis on which to rest relevant public health and food quality assurance policies. This time-honoured food regulatory approach, along with periodic on-site monitoring reinforced by a graduated scheme of penalties for breaches, allowed the state to play a key role in the food supply sector (Marsden et al. 2000).

The second phase in the evolution of food regulation in the UK was driven primarily by the way food safety issues were perceived by large food retailers; leaving the State to act mainly as auditors rather than standard-setters and enforcers of the mainstream process. This two-tiered approach, whereby the state-centred system of spatial regulation continues for non-corporate producers and retailers on the one hand, but a new private-sector regulated supply chain approach operates for corporate retailers on the other, became an embedded feature of food regulation in the UK by the mid 1990s. But, despite offering certain clear improvements in food quality assurance, this two-tiered approach allowed corporate retailers to distinguish themselves from their non-corporate competitors, and from each other, on the basis of the assurance of quality that they were able to deliver through stringent supply chain management.

However, because the greater assurance of food quality that the second phase (private–public) food regulation regime engenders does not encompass the entire food supply chain, and, given the continuing diversity and intensity of food risks, the pressure for further changes became apparent. This third phase (i.e. the 2000s) is marked by a new phase of institutionalism in food safety. High profile organisational reforms take place at both the national level (e.g. the Food Standards Agency and Department of the Environment, Food and Rural Affairs) and European level (e.g. European Food Safety Authority and DG SANCO). As we saw in Chapter 4, institutional reforms are in large part a long legacy of the BSE crisis and help shape three distinctive features of the current model of food safety management. First, there is the 'spillover' between national and European food crises that mark a new phase in the integration of European food policy. Second, governments make efforts to reassert a public interest legitimacy into food safety management through the creation of new, more consumerist-oriented institutions. Third, as we explore further below, the most recent phase of food regulation blurs public and private, regulation and market, in ways that can make it difficult to distinguish clear boundaries.

Academic and critical arguments about neo-liberalism (Macarthy 2006, Potter and Tilzey 2006) tend rather paradoxically to assume the unproblematic diminution of the public realm over the private. Such approaches assume that the neo-liberal hegemony is sacrosanct. Rather, as we have demonstrated in this volume, we see the public and the private as a contested and interlocking regulatory terrain; and one not just reacting to a neo-liberal agenda. Despite the increasing assertion of a private sector role in food safety regulation there is always a public realm, but how key interests perceive the public and how they value it are subject to ongoing debate and contestation.

At present the public–private interface is being shaped by three macro-features. First, food and food production issues are becoming more embedded in both society and polity. Second, science continues to play a key, though contested, role. Science remains important in the construction of food risk as demonstrated by the efforts of the EFSA to assert its authority (see Chapter 4). Science, particularly bioscience, is also centrally involved in attempts to 'solve' the various crises engendered in the intensive conventional food system. Third, there are continual efforts by states and corporations to open up markets in ways which increase the flow and trade of goods around the globe; attempts which are then creating new oppositional sites for ecological localisation (McMichael 2005, Friedmann 2005).

It is an attempt to 'manage' the interaction and tensions between the three macro-factors previously mentioned that has fuelled the development of a sophisticated and complex public-private model of food regulation. In Figure 12.1 and below we outline our model of food governance. Food, if it ever was a simple product, now performs multiple functions and is subject to multiple meanings: both encompassing economic appropriation and moral appropriation. As new actors seek to become involved or are drawn into food issues, debates on food metamorphose. Debates blend and coalesce and actors enter into temporary alliances; for example, small farmers and consumer groups can both champion the benefits and wholesomeness of local foods. In attempting to 'solve' both the continuing legitimation crises of the conventional food system and, at the same time, to appease and fragment these oppositional movements we can observe processes of constructive and marketised fragmentation. Three related market and regulatory forces come into play here. First, the expansion of food-based accumulation through corporations; second, that such corporate-based accumulation delivers public (e.g. plentiful and relatively cheap food) and publicly accountable benefits; and third, but not least, to create a condition in the market place which encourages *at the same time* as it fragments and neuters alternatives to the conventional system. For example, economic actors seeking to extract value find themselves having to construct food in different ways (e.g. functional, nutritional, healthy and local) and to keep at arms length those actors and interests that may impinge negatively on their activities. Here, the corporate sector can also show its versatility and power to shape or incorporate potentially competing visions of the food system: 'local' foods, for instance, now have well established spaces on the shelves of the corporate retailers. Indeed, one key feature of the public-private model is to allow the corporate sector to 'commercialise' and appropriate what might otherwise develop as real oppositional alternatives (see Friedland 2008).

Perhaps the one area where there is the greatest blurring between public and private in food safety is in relation to risk. This is because both public and private sectors have complementary interests in managing food risks to secure public confidence in the foods that they consume. In the period up to the early 1980s, regulatory and accountability approaches focused primarily on managing age-old food risks, such as illnesses that were caused by direct microbial contamination of foods, elevated microbacterial counts, unhygienic food handling, poor transportation and storage of foods, and improper food preparation. Since the mid-1980s a discernible change in the perception, nature and extent of food risk began to emerge. In the case of the UK, public rejection of British beef following the outbreak of BSE, and the subsequent EU export ban on British beef, had adverse economic as well as social impacts on local farmers. And, the ensuing regulatory response to this threat (as well as to others such as pesticides, GMOs and junk food) to human health, as well as to the rural and national economies, resulted in a fundamental shift in the way safety within the food supply chain would be assured in the future. The BSE crisis created wider recognition of the spatialities of food risk in two ways: First, it affected broader consumer perceptions of risk across conventional food chains. Second, it highlighted the rise of the globalised nature of movements of food across large geographical and temporal distances.

The globalisation of food supply chains now means that food crises can quickly move beyond national boundaries and also draw in different national governments and levels of government. The severity of food crises in Europe, notably that of BSE and FMD, showed that they can take place over wide spatial scales, involve many different economic and consumer interests as well multiple levels of government. As a result, Europe found that food crises can be very difficult to manage and the credibility of existing systems of governance are severely tested. Political crises, though, often result in institutional innovations, and that of food was no exception (Hellebo, 2004: 9).

Whilst food safety governance has shown itself to be highly dynamic in its scale, institutional innovation and balance of public and private interests, cannot remove food crises from the system. So, although both governments and private sector interests have significantly adjusted to the BSE crisis it has in turn been followed by the proliferation of other risks, for instance, those associated with Foot and Mouth Disease, GM, Avian flu, or 'Blue-tongue'. Food risks are particularly inherent in the industrial model of food production and consumption. Nevertheless, in the face of food scares, the growth of 'careful consumption' and alternative food systems, conventional food supply chains have been quite strikingly resilient, and in many cases have tightened their grip upon not only UK and European, but also global food systems and spaces. Perhaps paradoxically, what is so striking about the contemporary governance of food is the ways in which it has built up resilience (or adaptability) in dealing with it own vulnerabilities at the same time as protecting its abilities to create surplus values and profits. It is to this issue that we now turn.

FOOD GOVERNANCE: THE CHALLENGE OF MANAGING FOOD SPACES AND SUPPLY CHAINS

Over the last decade, the concept of governance has come to occupy a central place in contemporary social science debates and has informed a wide array of policy initiatives. 'Governance'—as opposed to 'government'—has become an important concept in describing and proposing strategies for policy-making (Pierre and Peters, 2000). Or as Hooghe and Marks (2003: 233) succinctly express it, governance is the study of binding decision making in the public sphere. The debate about governance arose when political, social and economic framework conditions brought about a questioning of traditional forms of government intervention and policy-making (Jessop, 2000). Governance, therefore, represents a means to analyse changes in the making and delivering of policy, while presenting a normative dimension that favours negotiation and the active involvement of all levels of government (European, national, regional and local), societal stakeholders and civil society organizations in the policy process. With regard to food, both dimensions of governance can be important and intertwine. For example, the normative element of governance has been important for those seeking to argue for a greater involvement of consumer groups in policy making at a national and European level. In the UK the public *GM Nation* debate was recognition that there should be a broader range of constituencies engaged in this discussion but provided legitimation as a wider range of stakeholders were consulted on a more sympathetic approach to GM foods (Horlick-Jones, 2007).

The tension between analytical and normative perspectives on governance is also present in debates on the multi-level governance of food. At a prescriptive level, multi-level governance refers to the stronger inclusion of all tiers of government in the design, formulation and implementation of policies. Aside from the formal processes of governance, different levels of government will, therefore, continually be making claims as to their need to be involved in the making and/or delivery of policy. These claims may take a number of forms, including consultation, participation, sharing of responsibility or veto, and the credibility, strength and nature of these claims will vary according to the prominence of food safety issues on the public policy agenda.

Vertical policy integration stands for coordinated policymaking and it is about matching "the geographical space of the affected environment [with] the institutional space of the relevant authorities" (Liberatore, 1997: 116). For food safety the relationship between scale and governance is sophisticated and plays out in a number ways. As we have seen, one of the major challenges for the State in seeking to manage food safety is that regulatory spaces do not necessarily spatially or temporally coincide with those for production, manufacturing/processing, distribution or consumption. Even the upscaling and extension of the regulatory reach from a national to a European level does not correspond with the globalised dynamics of food supply chains. Extending food safety management to a European stage means that the State remains constrained in exercising its responsibilities within a defined politico-administrative boundary. Nevertheless, within the boundaries of European food safety management, we have shown that much has happened to develop a more systematic and coordinated process of governance despite these constraints.

Amongst the key developments to promote vertical policy integration have been institutional innovations, policy initiatives and reporting of activities. For example the European Food Safety Authority is a high profile institutional innovation that works across and within Member States. A key initiative is EFSA's Advisory Forum as this connects EFSA with the national food safety authorities of all twenty-seven EU Member States. The Forum works as a two-way means of communication in which EFSA can inform partners in the Member States of a European perspective on risk assessment and risk communication, whilst those working within a national context can draw attention to their perspectives on risk science and EFSA priorities. In terms of policy the Commission's White Paper on Food Safety (COM [1999] 719 final) provided a significant advance in relation to the Member States of the development and legitimation of a

European level food policy. The Europeanisation of policy has been further bolstered by efforts to consolidate and standardize the reporting by Member States of their inspection data. Traditionally much reporting of data has taken place in relation Directive 95/53/EEC (fixing the principles governing the organization of official inspections in the field of animal nutrition) and Directive 89/397/EEC (on the official control of foodstuffs). More recently, the EU has sought to systematize matters still further under EU Regulation 882/2004 on official controls. This requires that competent authorities in Member States, in the case of the UK the FSA, must produce a single, integrated, multi-annual (three to five year), National Control Plan (NCP). NCPs are to ensure more effective and even implementation of EU food and feed law. Whilst the EU is moving towards a more sophisticated pattern of engagement with Member States in relation to food safety it is important to remember that the Commission and EFSA remain weak institutions in the development of new policy and policy delivery. In both cases Member States continue to play a key role, for instance, in relation to inspection practices.

The European dimension to food policy making and delivery, as well as the different responsibilities within nation states for formulating policy and undertaking inspection activities means that structures and processes of governance have an important vertical dimension to them (Pierre and Peters, 2000: 17–18). Governance is not necessarily a partnership of equals but a more complex interaction between actors and institutions which bring to the table variable levels of power and influence. This indicates the importance of governance not only as a set of structures but also as a process shaping the interactions between institutions and actors. In this process actors and networks will operate with different resources, they may conflict with one another and their influence and power will be subject to continual re-creation and challenge. Moreover, we have witnessed in the 2000s the widening of the spectrum of issues and concerns around the consumption and production of food. This will mean that an increasing variety of actors will seek to shape institutions and networks to serve their interests.

Networks are key, therefore, to the way in which governance operates (Rhodes 2000; Chandler et al., 2008). Networks are the means by which the different social actors structure and shape their interactions. One of the most notable features of networks in relation to food is their density and complexity. Networks operate at a number of scales: within different levels of government; within supply chains; and between governments and the private sector. These networks will have varying degrees of intensity and forms. For example, some networks will coalesce around regulatory behaviour. This will involve, for instance: defining the nature of inspection regimes; assessing risks; and engaging in reporting. Other networks will form around policy-making, for instance the drafting of a new food law or the creation of a standard. Such networks may be short-lived—lasting little more than the drafting and adoption of the legislation—but its membership will be drawn from and will return to more established networks engaged in deliberating on the nature of food policy. A third type of network relationship that is especially significant in domestic settings, relates to competitiveness. Here network actors seek to shape perceptions about the nature of competition between actors within and across supply chains. Within the UK, for example, the Competition Commission and the Office of Fair Trading have undertaken a number of high profile investigations into the relationship between retailers and their suppliers. These networks can be particularly instructive in illuminating beliefs about the nature of corporate and consumer interests.

Of course, government has always had to deal with different actors in developing and delivering policy but what is novel is the declining control that government exerts over these actors or networks. This arises out of both a lack of legitimacy in the face of private processes of regulation and the complexity of the policy process. Network actors, drawn from the public and private sectors, are increasingly drawn into relationships of interdependency. These interdependencies may imply a shift from a hierarchical form of governance, and one particularly well suited to a European context, to a more co-operative form of network governance in which there is a much greater dispersion of power from the centre. This suggests that networks are much more diffuse and less aligned than before to structures and institutions of government—hence the emergence of bodies like the FSA—and more attuned to the needs of the corporate sector.

Whereas formerly a scalar politics of networks based around state institutions responsible for the making and/or regulation of policy prevailed, now networks led by the corporate sector are controlling ever larger spaces through their supply chains (e.g. to promote product innovation, or secure food hygiene). Private forms of supply chain regulation are largely indifferent to public regulatory spaces—they run through and between levels of government; as nation states are 'hollowed out', and markets and globalisation further restrict the ability of governments to govern. Governments in the area of food now face challenges of policy co-ordination and power sharing with more actors engaged in policy-making and implementation. In other words, the traditional clear divide between government and other actors begins to dissolve (see Figure 12.1). As we analysed in Part II and Part III, public, private and civil society interests are involved in making and delivering public policy goals and the boundaries between them are less clear with time.

One consequence of the new relationships between public and private actors is that the state acts to legitimate private supply chain activities as a means of delivering safe and plentiful food. For example, HACCP is expounded in key national and European food policy documents but its realisation depends upon the management of the private sector. HACCP for the most part works beyond the gaze of the public sector (and the consumer) until there is an inspection of premises (operated by a retailer or processor) or a food safety problem emerges. The co-operative relationship

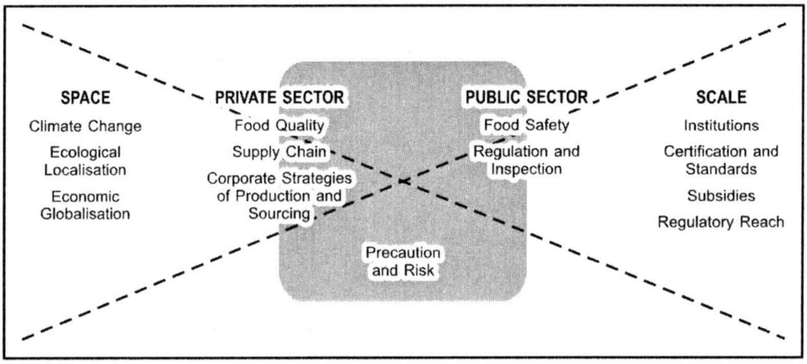

Figure 12.1 Arenas of food governance.

between the public and private sectors has to depend upon a constructed coincidence of interests. From a retailer perspective, private supply management is designed to ensure security and quality (including safety) of supply; shelves are never to be empty and waste needs to be kept to a minimum. At a time of consumption-oriented politics, the fate of governments and consumers are inextricably bound together and so governments too are sympathetic to the fostering of a market place in which the corporate sector can prosper.

A more co-operative network of relationships between public and private interests, whereby both sets of interests respect each others roles and responsibilities, costs and benefits, also has implications for our perspective on the *nature of regulatory practice.* Governments need to assure citizens that food is safe as part of a wider process of assurance befalling government in risk society. Meanwhile the private sector needs to assure consumers that food is safe to retain confidence in, and expand, markets. The mutual benefits for both sides from a co-operative relationship mean that we should by no means regard the relationship between the public and private sectors as a zero sum game. Although at times one of the public or the private sector will play a more prominent role, it is not necessarily at the expense of the other. Rather the mutual dependencies between public and private sectors mean that the regulatory relationship creates positive outcomes for both sides. However, the pattern of governance is dynamic and contingent; it needs to be constantly constructed by public and private actors and legitimated both between each other and to the wider public.

Such co-operation of key actors does not, however, mean that contestation, conflict or struggle between the different interests disappears. Political and economic tensions between farmers, manufacturers and retailers emerge as they seek to shape food systems in their interests. The boundary between public and private regulatory spheres and areas of authority is itself an arena of struggle. There is contestation too between the power and expertise of different tiers of government. The upscaling of policy making to a European stage has challenged traditional politico-administrative boundaries and competences, previously rooted at the level of the nation state, and has disrupted longstanding networks.

The move from national to European level decision-making amalgamates together different food cultures and different approaches to food safety and innovation; as indicated by attitudes in Member States towards the licensing of GMOs. As Morgan et al. (2006) have concluded 'we will continue to have different worlds of food', but those food worlds in Europe are likely to be rather different as a result of the impact of the EU as we have depicted in this volume. EU food decision-making is a consensus driven process that results in harmonisation by the lowest common denominator. In seeking to achieve minimum food safety standards and ensure a common baseline across Europe the EU is asserting one aspect of the public domain. Its role is to try to establish a level (spatial and vertical) regulatory playing field against a highly mobile and competitive food supply system.

Within the corporate food sector there is a collective belief in the importance of food safety, as the new food governance model has developed they have seen it as a non-competitive 'issue'. Instead, the private sector seeks now to assert its authority around differentiated notions of quality and consistency of products. This can lead to a paradoxical situation with regard to local spaces. On the one side the distinctiveness of local food spaces can be valued by local states, farmers and consumers, though less often by the corporate sector (at least until local foods become a significant source of added value). On the other side, the corporate sector strives for uniformity and standardisation of products across geographical spaces, to the point that they lose their distinctiveness and provenance as sites of consumption (Bingen and Busch, 2006). Since notions of food quality are constructed by retailers and manufacturers and are a source of competition and differentiation then (as we saw in the case of fresh fruit and vegetables and red meat) the corporate sector is to the fore in defining private standards. But this does not mean that the State plays no role anymore. Rather as we have seen at national, European and global scales it now becomes the complimentary role of the state to provide the baseline playing field upon which competitive, standardised and differentiated quality conventions can continue to be privately constructed. In this sense, the State provides a 'stage' or regulatory infrastructure upon which corporate competition can develop and exploit consumers' choice. Both public and private interests are thus, in their own complementary ways, continually constructing spaces of food production and consumption; the former by setting and integrating actions within spatial boundaries and hierarchies; the latter through innovative 'quality' supply chain management across space (See Figure 12.1).

Though food safety policy has an increasing European dimension, it is important not to underplay the continued salience of the *nation state.* A challenging analytical task is to further elucidate the role of the nation state during a period in which multi-level governance becomes increasingly prominent. It is clear that many contemporary political challenges in which food is embedded (e.g. food security, food prices) are realised at a political level in the nation state. So, a key question becomes within a European context, to what extent can nation states steer development? Moreover, matters of governance, at least in relation to food, are made more complex because of the nature of the development of the food system. This prompts a second question: to what extent can national (or sub-national) food systems prevail in an increasingly globalised system of food production, processing, distribution and consumption?

GLOBALISED FOODS AND NATIONAL FOOD SYSTEMS

As Oosterveer (2005) has recently pointed out the production and consumption of food has changed dramatically over the past three decades. More of our food is sourced and manufactured or processed overseas. In 2001–2002 the trade in manufactured foods was greater than that for unprocessed agricultural products (Oosterveer, 2005: 16). Increasingly, the trade in food is organised by retailers and manufacturers whose brands have a global resonance. It is no longer the case that produce is exported from one country to another but rather that agricultural products produced in one location are inputs for the food processing industry located elsewhere and consumed in a third location.

Oosterveer (2005: 27–30) has usefully summarised the parameters of the food globalisation debate. On the one side, there are the *hyperglobalists* (such as Bonanno et al., 1994; Friedland et al., 1981; Hendrickson and Heffernan, 2002) who focus on the subordination of food producing regions to global food supply chains dominated by transnational food companies. Heffernan and Constance (1994) for example, have analysed in detail a small number of emergent global food clusters. For hyperglobalists the international trade in food has developed over three distinct stages. The period between 1870–1914 is characterised as colonialist in which agrarian raw materials were exported from colonies in exchange for finished goods; the second stage fully emerged after 1945 and is characterised as Fordism in which energy intensive agriculture was locked into a mass manufacturing and consumption system and in which there was increasing separation in time and space between production and consumption. The third, post-fordist, phase has emerged since the mid 1980s and recognises that the state is withdrawing from agrarian markets, and that international economic actors, especially retailers, seek highly flexible supply chains to meet the increasingly differentiated demands of consumers in the developed world.

On the other side of the globalisation debate are the *transformationalists* who point out that globalisation is contingent, multidimensional and may take many different forms. In the context of food this means that rather than standardisation there may emerge heterogeneity in which agri-food networks involving different social actors construct notions of food in different ways. So, according to Oosterveer (2005: 30):

> Hyperglobalists underline the growing dominance of private firms in the organisation of food supply. Transformationalists point to the flexibility and heterogeneity in recent transitions and at the importance of combining local and global dynamics in the conceptualisation of globalisation and food.

The implications of Oosterveer's categories are twofold. First, that more attention needs to be given to the ways in which globalisation may act as a force for heterogeneity rather than simply homogeneity. Second, uncovering the variety of globalisations requires that the process is analysed through a variety of scales and objects of analysis, for example, in terms of governance (as Oosterveer himself does), in terms of supply or commodity chains, in terms of food networks, and of the roles that national food systems may continue to perform.

Oosterveer's recognition of the significance of governance in understanding globalisation is important for our thesis in this volume. Whilst there has been much debate about the nature and extent of food globalisation, commentators tend to ignore or underplay the role of the State. The State is in the background and often rather passive. The point is that it chooses to act 'passive'. The relationship between public and private actors—the nature of governance arrangements—is, however, central to the development of globalisation. It is the *form of governance* that has enabled globalisation to take place. Here we can briefly point to two key features. First, at the market level as we saw in Chapter 11, the State has created trade rules, at both a European and global scale for instance with the EU and WTO, that facilitate *a trade* in agricultural products. It is, perhaps, when those rules are challenged or conflict with other social or political values, as in the case of GM (see Chapter 3), that the ways in which the State and private interests interact to construct markets are most apparent. Second, it is the *practices of governance* that legitimate globalised food markets and the food choices and food safety standards that go with them. Our model of food governance recognises that food supply chains are not neatly nested within administrative boundaries but run through and between them. Scales of governance and spaces of supply chains do not necessarily coincide. The public–private model of food safety regulation legitimates the supply chain management activities of the corporate sector. As we have also argued, food governance has to be analysed at multiple scales, including the global and the national. There are always tensions and contingencies below the arenas of spatial and supply chain governance.

Turning briefly to the specificities of globalisation and national food systems in their Introduction to *From Columbus to ConAgra* Bonanno et al. (1994) laid out the interface between the nation state and processes of globalisation. They pointed to both the relevance of the nation state at a political and regulatory level and its irrelevance at an economic level. Moreover, despite much talk of globalisation, world trade in food products is dominated by a small number of countries, notably in North America (the USA and Canada), in Europe by countries such as France, the Netherlands, Germany and the UK, and from Asia (China and Thailand). Similarly world trade is dominated by a small number of products with highly specific trade flows (Oosterveer, 2005: 15–16). For example, meat exports are largely undertaken by a small group of developed countries who tend to specialise; for example, poultry is exported by the USA and the EU.

Bonanno et al. (1994) have pointed out that food commodities expose different aspects of globalisation. Using the example of Heffernan's (1984) work on the chicken they note that

> in a large spatial area such as the United States with its enormous market, can be fairly well nationalized. Yet, the globalization of chicken production is well underway, with the production of eggs in one location, the raising of chickens in another, the slaughter in a third, the deboning of meat (for some markets) in yet another, and finally, the shipment of chicken meat into different markets (Bonanno et al., 1994: 10).

It is important, though, to extend a note of caution here. Bonnano et al. (1994) suggest that the discrete activities in rearing, slaughtering and processing a chicken will take place in separate locations, but equally the integrated nature of the chicken supply chain means that they may take place in co-locations or at least in neighbouring locations. As Bonanno et al. (1994: 10) themselves recognise 'there is not yet, in fact, a global chicken. Rather chickens as a commodity, while beginning to become internationalized, are still more or a regional commodity intended for localized markets'. Two further notes of caution follow from this. First, that national or regional studies of even 'world foods' will remain important. Janet Dixon's (2002) study of the Australian chicken set in the context of the American poultry industry is a case in point. Second, that local, regional or national consumption practices also remain important. As Marsden et al. (1994: 105) argued it is important to retain a focus on the 'nature of a national food system within the changing context of international forces'. The reason for the national focus was not to deny the potency of international restructuring but rather to draw attention to the progressive incorporation into the polity and economies of different national regulatory structures. They went on to argue that 'nationally constructed systems of regulation, food consumption, and legitimation are crucial in assessing the changes of direction and the relative sustainability of the international food system . . . [I]t is at the national level that the most comprehensive (and relevant) food crises (as opposed to farm crises) are realized and that, given specific political and cultural conditions, severe constraints can be placed on the tendencies towards industrialized and homogenized food production and consumption' (Marsden et al., 1994: 107).

It is also necessary to outline how recent changes to the global food system will have more national or sub-national impacts. For example, a number of commentators have highlighted the role of retailers in restructuring and directing food supply chains (see, for instance, Marsden et al., 2000; and Hendrickson and Heffernan, 2002). As American commentators have noted, however, the increasing dominance of food retailers is newer to the USA than it is to Europe (Hendrickson and Heffernan, 2002: 357; Guptil and Wilkins, 2002: 40) where the Dutch and UK markets, for example, have for some time been dominated by a small number of highly influential supermarkets. Hendrickson et al. (2001) have suggested that over time it is likely that six or fewer global retailers will evolve. Most of these are likely to be European-based transnationals, such as Tesco (UK), Ahold (Netherlands) and Carrefour (France). WalMart is likely to be the only major US-based global retailer. Although the US has relatively recently witnessed the levels of dominance of a small number of key players that have been found for some time in countries such as the UK and the Netherlands, the results are similar: retailers dictate terms to food manufacturers who then force changes back through the food system (Hendrickson et al., 2001; Konefal et al., 2005). Another feature of European retailer-led food systems is that many also have a more marked trend to own label brands than is to be found in the US. In the UK, for example, 45% of sales are retailers own label goods, in the US, meanwhile, Kroger estimates that its own label accounts for 25% of sales (Hendrickson et al., 2001: 13). The prominence of retailers in the UK food system and the increasing identification of branding with a supermarket (rather than a product) allows the food system to ride out crises and continually reproduce itself. Thus, the corporate retailers have largely been able to diffuse food crises to other parts of the system and retain confidence in their outlets.

NEW FRAGILITY AND ADAPTABILITY: THE CRISIS OF THE EUROPEAN FOOD STATE

As we have argued the European food system is based around a dense network of relationships between the public and private sectors. Generally, these networks have been internally focussed, concerned to maintain competitive markets and secure safe and plentiful food. To maintain the present system of governance involves a considerable investment by both public and private sectors in institutions and processes. The sheer scale of human and capital investment in the conventional food system is enormous. Despite the inevitable 'lock-in' that takes place in technologies and processes, the conventional food system is remarkably resilient and able to ride out crises and challenges. For example, the UK food system has had to cope with BSE, FMD and a number of other food scares and yet appears to have emerged remarkably unchanged. Other challenges to the food system have come from the organic movement and local/regional food supply chains. Once again, though, the conventional food system has shown itself to be surprisingly robust. Where market value can be obtained, for example, the conventional system has shown itself sufficiently adaptable to be able to absorb potential challenges.

In practice, it is only at the stage of agricultural production that the organic supply chain differs from conventional supply chains, and even here the differences, at least for one set of producers, chicken growers, are not perceived to be radical (though for a different perspective based on a survey of Belgian conventional farmers [see Baecke et al., 2002]). Similarly, Hendrickson and Heffernan (2002: 360) have pointed out that US Department for Agriculture Standards for organic production 'point to a standardization of organic that will fit an essentially philosophical vision of food and agriculture into an industrial model of mass production and consumption'. At the stage of rearing there are distinct differences in breed, feed, period of growing and manner of keeping chickens. However, at the stages of food processing and distribution the two food systems are almost identical. In the stage of processing although slaughterhouses must be certified as organic, the equipment is identical to that in conventional primary processing. Indeed, in one case, farmers have recently purchased slaughtering equipment from a conventional grower and, once again, like their conventional counterparts, have a highly integrated production system, so that they can retain as much value added as possible. The use of chilling and freezing is at a similar level in both supply chains. Innovations present in conventional food supply chains such as refrigeration, packaging and cooking also apply to organic foods. Perhaps one of the best indications of the similarities between the conventional and organic chains is that conventional producers will now often have organic sidelines. Kirwan (2004: 396) too has noted that alternative food systems 'are open to appropriation, and the possible (re-)absorption . . . within broader industrialised production differentiation strategies.'

In terms of the structure of the supply chain, the analysis shows that from being marginal supply chains, organic food production and distribution has now been adopted by large mainstream producers, processors and retailers as part of their diversification strategy: it has become, essentially, a "branded" form of production, which may offer all parties in the chain an opportunity to extract higher profits. Manufacturers are responding in kind to promote their brands in new markets. As Howard (2003: 3) reports 'Many organic brands have been acquired by giant food processors such as General Mills, Kraft (Philip Morris) and Kellogg . . . Slightly smaller global food processors are also establishing their own organic product lines (such as Dole, Chiquita and McCormick & Co) or acquiring organic brands'.

Thus, the UK experience of the operation of the organic and conventional supply chains is by no means unique:

> in California agribusiness involvement does more than create a soft path of sustainability—an 'organic lite' if you will. For the conditions it sets undermine the ability of even the most committed producers to practice a purely alternative form of organic farming. (Guthman, 2004: 301–302).

Guthman (2004: 307) suggests that agribusiness threatens organic farming in three ways. Firstly, there is a political threat which leads to a lowering of organic standards. Secondly, there is the direct economic threat of agribusiness that reduces economic returns for organic farmers. Thirdly, agribusiness may practice organic farming in a more shallow fashion that reduces the distinctiveness of organic production. To Guthman's list we might add a fourth point, that the close supply chain relationship between major conventional growers and the retailers allows the latter to encourage the former to enter organic markets. Large supermarket chains now sell organic foods alongside their conventional products. Currently, around 80% of UK organic chicken sales are through the supermarkets and ironically this is a higher figure than for conventional chicken because the latter are also widely distributed in the burgeoning food service industry (e.g. takeaways, restaurants and snack bars).

What the previously mentioned account of the interrelationship between conventional and organic food systems demonstrates is the flexibility and adaptability of the former when faced by the potential challenge of the latter. The conventional food system shows considerable resilience when faced with food-based challenges, such as alternative food systems or food risks. It is our contention that it is the density and sophistication of the prevailing pattern of food governance—as explored in this volume—that provides much of the capacity for such system adaptability. Key actors share a common interest in ensuring that the system is reproduced; the system adapts over time. Thus far, the conventional food system has been able to make these changes because it has had to adapt to changes and challenges from within. However, the basis of this resilience in the food system may also mean that when confronted with major external shocks, which demand a response that goes beyond the thinking and relationships that pervade the conventional food system, there is some chance of fragility. In other words, the very density of network relationships results in an inward-looking, introverted, perspective in which potential external shocks are ignored and their relevance for the system is denied or the common response of absorption of a challenge is promoted.

There is a very real possibility that the food system has locked within it a crisis of modernisation. Now, major challenges to the food system, such as peak oil or climate change, can only be partially successfully tackled by adapting the current system. For example, novel foods, new growing areas, less intensive farming are all ways of adapting to climate change and reducing dependence upon oil-based inputs. What these responses do not do, though, is to confront the more fundamental challenge that is raised: how, at a time of climate change, do we adopt a low carbon food system? Debates are thus now moving from those not just of food safety and quality, but also to food security and into territory that key players in the conventional food system can no longer internally manage. Thinking on food security demands revised notions of governance. As we are already seeing when faced with citizen concerns about rising food prices and food security there is a reassertion of the role of the nation state and what national governments can and cannot do. The nation state once more reasserts itself as the primary site for food production and consumption for its own citizens. National food policies come to the fore. In this context our EU hybrid model of food governance, however adaptable or resilient it has been in the 2000s, may prove to be rather fragile. It is not only the public sector that may need to rethink its role and how it asserts its authority. If food safety is played down in favour of food security, what are the implications for the corporate sector and its globalised food supply chains?

CONTESTATION, TRANSFORMATION AND THE RISE OF NEO-PRODUCTIVISM

In a European, and indeed a global context we have seen the development and diffusion over the past decade of a highly sophisticated hybrid model of public–private food regulation. The analysis in this volume has seen these developments very much as a palliative to dealing with the conundrum of the economic globalisation of food supply and consumption, on the one hand, and the growing public need to appease concerns about food risks on the other. Clearly these tensions have not dissipated as the first decade of the 21st century draws to a close. New institutions, like the EFSA and the FSA are now firmly established in the new food governance model. These bodies, however, face a wider spectrum of public and private concerns than envisaged at the time of their formation. Such worries are associated with the corporate-controlled technological race to establish new innovations in food supply (like functional foods, health products, genetically modified seeds, foods and feeds, and nano-tech marking and tracing, see EFSA, 2008). Moreover, private sector standard setting, as

Bingen and Busch (2006) outline, is now so entrenched in global food systems that it is unlikely to reduce its capabilities to set rules and to control access to an increasing array of marketing opportunities. The major retailers increasingly set the frameworks for power relations in the food chains (as we saw in section 3, regarding fresh fruit and vegetables and red meats), by influencing 'who gets what, where and how'.

So we have argued that there are considerable path dependencies and continuities now built into the conventional regulatory system as depicted in this volume (not least in its appropriation of a particular scientific/policy paradigm). However, there is also growing evidence that the regulatory model's very prominence has indeed created an uneven and fragmented basis for new oppositional forces to this current dominant model of food governance (Marsden, 2008). This has so far been depicted as a moral economy of food, or what in a generic sense we might term ecological re-localisation (see Morgan et al., 2006; Allen, 2005). However, much of the literature on re-localisation (Marsden and Sonnino, 2008) has taken for granted the continuance of a 'cheap-food economy' built on continuing over supply of food goods and relatively cheap transport costs.

As we conclude the book the effects of climate change, the growth of protein exchange in newly developing countries, and the restrictions in oil supplies (whether politically or geologically created) have by 2007–2008 significantly begun to challenge these 'post-productionist' assumptions. Moreover, from a European perspective in particular there has been a marked and rapid challenge to EU agricultural and food policies and a recognition that the creation of European food policy cannot necessarily protect its producers and consumers in the ways that had been assumed a decade earlier. In short the political, economic and ecological boundaries between the EU and the rest of the world are becoming weaker.

With increasing concerns for global food security, growing numbers of food riots, and the unanticipated introduction of national export embargoes now featuring daily in debates about and responses to global food systems, the EU food governance infrastructure looks increasingly out of step and not quite so 'fit for purpose'. How these new more turbulent macro-economic conditions will begin to affect the food governance models outlined in this volume is thus far too difficult to predict. However, there is evidence that the period of a plentiful supply or over supply of food is now over, with grain and meat stocks disappearing, and moves to eradicate such policy instruments as milk quotas and set-aside of land in the EU.

More fundamentally, these changes may become to be seen as radical in that they represent the first clear signal of both 'peak oil' and, indeed 'peak-food', as we hit against resource constraints not merely in relation to hydrocarbons but also in relation to other inputs such as soil and water that are also under pressure from climate change, intensive agricultural regimes and their globalised supply chains. If alongside this the conventional system continues to be prone to crisis tendencies, such as those analysed in this book, then we may begin to witness a truly 'transformational moment' in the development of global food systems. Some scholars (e.g. van der Ploeg, 2008; Marsden and Sonnino, 2008) argue that this might provide the opportunity for many nation states and regions to *radically rupture* with the conventional—high energy/water/soil-system. More likely, however, and there are clear examples of this in Europe, is a process of intensified contestation between different interests and groups, bringing with it a capacity to severely weaken the public-private food governance model depicted in our analysis here.

For instance, we are beginning to see growing tensions amongst member states in the EU around either continuing the technologically driven model of food supply in order to boost production of national and EU foods (as in the UK, and the Netherlands); as opposed to taking the opportunities to move into a more sustainable rural and agro-food model (as in Italy, Denmark, and Sweden). Moreover, in the political sphere, 'food,' and especially food costs and quality is becoming an ever more heated political concern. This is evidenced by the UK Government's Strategy Unit report on food (Strategy Office, 2008) and the FAO's international summit in Rome 2008 (FAO, 2008). The latter demonstrates widely differing nation state views regarding the role of biofuels (see Mol, 2008) in deepening the problems of food and feed costs.

It is clear that these pressures could contribute to more re-nationalisation of food governance as, perhaps paradoxically, the 'silent tsunami' (Economist, 2008) of peak food and fuel affect the highly, globally interconnected and governed food system. Also such pressures are likely to affect the competitive supply chain practices of the large food firms. How are they to transfer these higher transport costs? How can they maintain their political status both in and outside government brought about as the harbingers of a low inflation economy? Is it possible to continue to employ such a vast array of quality conventions (and indeed more differentiated discounted lines) as points of competition in supply chain management?

Clearly the rather dramatic realisation of resource constraints currently affecting fuel and food are highly interconnected and may well put pressure on corporate retailers to further tighten their margins and to generate a new raft of supply chain relationships with their 'preferred suppliers'. Rising costs and scarcity of resources could in the short-term lead to a further deepening, therefore, of corporate retailer power (as outlined in the introductory chapter). The question will be, however, whether national governments and EU bodies, faced with a new round of consumer pressures and wider political problems surrounding foods, will be quite so sanguine about allowing the corporate retailers to continue their historic freedom of action with regard to their supply chain innovations. In the UK, for instance, there is some call for an expansion of the responsibilities of the Food Standards Authority (FSA) to take a more comprehensive role across government departments with regard to not only food safety and communication, but also health, nutrition, food security and welfare. Nevertheless, a major problem for governments is that having devolved so many powers to the private sector in the area of standard setting in foods, the public sector now lacks the skills, innovation and sheer market power to re-regulate food around a more comprehensive set of integrating principles. The shallowness of the 'hollowed out state' is becoming all the more marked as these fundamental public concerns grow. This 'hollowing out' has been highly complex in form, as the analyses in this volume testify. What is becoming more obvious, however, is that it is producing a process of policy fragmentation especially under new, fundamental resource challenges. Indeed some early evidence, from recent research (Chatham House, 2009) suggests that key private sector actors such as major food manufacturers and retailers now wish to see national governments re-state a more comprehensive framework within which they can operate. As in the early 2000s (see Part II of this volume) the private sector players are keen for the EU and member states to again develop new institutional frameworks; at that stage to allay consumer fears and risks of the day, but now to re-establish actions and frameworks which ward off market instabilities and uncertainties, perhaps by means of new forms of intervention.

Having traced the emergence of what can be described as a very complex but nevertheless robust and hybrid European model of public-private regulation, it is clear that this now faces new profound external challenges and vulnerabilities. These can be conceptualised in two ways, and traced to two different points of origin. First, the model is becoming buffeted by the now well documented 'moral economy' surrounding food, whereby more consumers and NGO's persistently demand a more ethically and socially responsible set of food chains. Second, and more recently, we see the uncertainties, denial tendencies and highly contested debates surrounding resource constraints, as food scarcity and fuel costs drive up price. Thus our model of food governance outlined in this book, is not only now struggling with its own internal tensions and contradictory logics as we have argued earlier in this chapter, it is increasingly located within a wider external set of global conditions which stress the (disproportionately richer) consumer moral economy, on the one hand; and the (disproportionately poorer) resource depleting carbon economy on the other. More than ever these changing macro and external conditions will challenge the coherent European model of food regulation; and they could throw it increasingly out of step with national and global governance priorities in the immediate future.

Appendix to Chapter 5

List of Organisations and Bodies Interviewed

Consumer/Social Interests:

- Eurogroup for Animal Welfare
- Eurocoop
- European Food Information Council (EUFIC)
- European Consumers' Organisation (BEUC)
- Greenpeace European Unit

Private Interests:

- COPA-COGECA
- Eurocommerce
- Confederation of the Food & Drink Industries of the EU (CIAA)
- Freshfel Europe

Regulatory/Public Bodies:

- DG: Health & Consumer Protection
- DG: Agriculture
- DG: Trade
- European Food Law Association (EFLA)

Notes

NOTES TO CHAPTER 1

1. Directive on public access to environmental information.
2. Code of Conduct concerning Public Access to Council and Commission Documents.
3. Directive on the Protection of Individuals with regard to the Processing of Personal Data and on the Free Movement of such Data.

NOTES TO CHAPTER 2

1. Statement by Nick Brown—see Anderson, 2002: 89. This statement was made by the Minister on 15 March but not implemented (except for some areas of Scotland) until 28 March. In fact, the FMD Science Group eventually recommended a more restrictive approach based on a smaller radius because the 3k cull was felt to be 'neither practical nor likely to be legal' (Anderson, 2002: 93). In fact the 3k radius is not accidental but emanates from the protection zone demanded by Article 9 of EU Directive 85/511. A protection zone is not by any means a 'cull' zone.
2. But the Meat and Livestock Commission put the total of animal losses at 10,791,000 of which the vast majority (9.5m) were sheep—see unpublished work by Jane Connor of the Meat and Livestock Commission as reported by Robertson C, 'Slaughter toll three times the official figures' *Sunday Post*, 20 January 2002.
3. See Directive 85/511/EEC as amended. Vaccination could be used as an emergency measure once an outbreak had occurred but only if all vaccinated animals were then slaughtered.

NOTES TO CHAPTER 3

1. There is an obvious terminological difficulty that pervades the debate generally but when we use the term GM food in this chapter we refer to GM in this sense of the use of recombinant DNA techniques rather than traditional means of plant modification.

NOTES TO CHAPTER 6

1. Speaking at a conference on 'Risk Perception: Science, Public debate and Policy Making', 4–5 December 2003.

2. Report based on surveys with senior food executives and policy makers in nineteen countries, along with extensive market analysis from consultants Cap Gemini Ernst & Young, 2003.

NOTES TO CHAPTER 11

1. Recombinant bovine somatotropin, a synthetically produced version of a naturally occurring hormone intended to increase milk production
2. http://www.wto.org/English/tratop_e/sps_e/spsagr_e.htm
3. http://www.oie.int/eng/OIE/en_oie.htm
4. http://www.oie.int/eng/normes/en_norm.htm
5. http://www.oie.int/eng/secu_sanitaire/en_workinggr.htm
6. https://www.ippc.int/servlet/BinaryDownloaderServlet/159931_Procedural_manual_20.doc?filename=1166524691874_ProceduralManual2006_FINAL.doc&refID=159931
7. http://www.who.int/entity/foodsafety/publications/general/en/strategy_en.pdf
8. http://www.fao.org/ag/aga/agap/frg/feedsafety/special.htm
9. http://www.fao.org/DOCREP/MEETING/006/Y8350E.htm
10. http://www.fao.org/DOCREP/MEETING/006/Y9339E.htm
11. http://www.fao.org/docrep/008/y5968e/y5968e07.htm
12. http://www.oie.int/eng/secu_sanitaire/Cooperation%20CAC-OIE%20on%20food%20safety%20throughout%20the%20food%20cha%E2%80%A6.pdf
13. http://www.oie.int/eng/secu_sanitaire/en_introduction.htm
14. https://www.ippc.int/servlet/BinaryDownloaderServlet/115287_CPM2006_INF9.pdf?filename=1140709495972_CPM2006_INF9.pdf&refID=115287
15. http://www.ipfsaph.org/En/default.jsp
16. http://www.food.gov.uk/foodindustry/regulation/Codexbranch/
17. Alessandra Battaglia (2006) ‘Food Safety: Between European and Global Administration’ Global Jurist: vol. 6 : Iss. 3 (Advances), Article 8.
18. http://www.food.gov.uk/foodindustry/regulation/Codexbranch/
19. http://www.fao.org/Legal/TREATIES/004s-e.htm
20. http://www.defra.gov.uk/animalh/int-trde/oie/index.htm

Bibliography

Agra CEAS Consulting in consultation with Department of Agricultural Sciences, Imperial College, University of London (2003) Economic Evaluation of the Pig Industry Restructuring Scheme, Defra, April.

Alemanno. A. 2006. Food Safety and the Single European Market In *What's the Beef? The Contested Governance of European Food Safety*, edited by Ansell. C and Vogel. D. Cambridge, Massachusetts: MIT Press.

Allen, P. 2004. *Together at the table: sustainability and sustainance in the American agri-food system*. Pennsylvania: Penn State University Press.

Anderson. I. 2002. Foot and Mouth Disease 2001: Lessons to Be Learned Inquiry Report. London: Report to Prime Minister and the Secretary of State for Environment, Food and Rural Affairs.

Ansell, C., and Vogel, D. eds. 2006. *What's the beef? The contested governance of European Food Safety*. Cambridge, Massachussetts: MIT Press.

Applegate. J. 2006. The Government Role in Scientific Research: Who Should Bridge the Data Gap in Chemical Regulation? In *Rescuing Science From Politics: Regulation And The Distortion Of Scientific Research 261*, edited by Wagner. N. and Steinzer. R. Cambridge: Cambridge University Press.

Aumaitre. A. L., and Boyazoglu. J. G. 2002. A Note on Livestock Production and Consumption in Europe, UADY, Mexico. Available at *http://bsas.org.uk/downloads/mexico/007.pdf*

Backes. C. W., and Verschuuren. J. M. 1997. The Precautionary Principle in International, European and Dutch Wildlife Law. San Diego: Academic Press.

Baecke, E., Rogiers, G., De Cock, L., and van Huylenbroeck, G. 2002. The supply chain and conversion to organic farming in Belgium or the story of the egg and the chicken. *British Food Journal* 104(3/4/5):163–174.

Baker. G. A. 1999. Consumer Preferences for Food Safety Attribute in Fresh Apples: Market Segments, Consumer Characteristics, and Marketing Opportunities. *Journal of Agricultural and Resource Economics* 21:180–197.

Barling. D, and Lang. T. 2003. A Reluctant Food Policy? The First Five Years of Food Policy under Labour. *The Political Quarterly* 74 (1):8–18.

Barrett. H., Ilbery. B., Browne. A., and Binns. T. 1999. Globalization and the Changing Networks of Food Supply: The Importation of Fresh Horticultural Produce from Kenya into the UK. *Transactions of the Institute of British Geographers* 24 (2):159–174.

Baxter. J. 1998. Meat and Meat Products: 1998 Market Report. Cardiff: BRASS Centre.

Beck. U. 1992. *Risk Society: Towards a New Modernity*. London: Sage.

———. 1995. *Ecological Enlightenment*. Cambridge: Polity Press.

Beckmann. V., Soregaroli. C., and Wesseler. J. 2006. Governing the Co-existence of GM Crops: Ex-ante Regulation and Ex-post Liability under Uncertainty and

Irreversibility. In *ICAR Discussion Paper 12/2006*. Humboldt University, Berlin: Division of Resource Economics.

Beckwith, J. A., Colgan, A. P., and Syme, G. J. 1999. *Seeing Risk through Other Eyes*. Paper read at Contaminated Site Remediation Conference, at Centre for Groundwater Studies, CSIRO Land and Water, Western Australia.

Beers. G. 2002. State of the Art of Tracking and Tracing in Dutch Agribusiness. In *Referate der 23*, edited by Wild. K et al., Jahrestagung Dresden: GIL.

Bell. J. 2003. Reply to question 131. In *Select Committee on Public Accounts Minutes of Evidence 14 May 2003*.

Bennett. P. G. 2000. Applying the Precautionary Principle: A Conceptual Framework. In *Foresight and Precaution*, edited by Cottam. M. P., Harvey. D. W., Paper. R. P. and Tait. J. Rotterdam: Balkema.

Bèrges-Sennou, F., Bontems. P., and Rèquillart. V. 2004. Economics of Private Labels: A Survey of Literature. *Journal of Agricultural and Food Industrial Organization* 2 (3):1–23.

Bingen, J., and Busch, L. 2006. Shaping a Policy and Research Agenda. In *Agricultural Standards. The Shape of the Global Food and Fiber System*, edited by Bingen, J., and Busch, L. Dordrecht, NL: Springer.

Bingen, J., and Busch, L. eds. 2006. *Agricultural Standards: the shape of the global food and fibre system*. Dordrecht, NL: Springer.

Biotech Products. 2006. WTO Dispute DS291; EC-Approval and marketing of Biotech Products.

Black. J. 1996. Constitutionalising Self-Regulation. *Modern Law Review* 59:24–56.

———. 2000. Proceduralising Regulation: Part I. *Oxford Journal of Legal Studies* 20:597–614.

———. 2002. Regulatory Conversations. *Journal of Law and Society* 29:163–196.

Black. J., Lodge. M., and Thatcher. M., eds. 2005. *Regulatory Innovation: A Comparative Analysis*. Cheltenham: Edward Elgar.

Bock. A.-K., Lheureux. K., Libeau-Dulos. M., Nilsagård. H., and Rodriguez-Cerezo. E. 2002. Scenarios for Co-Existence of Genetically Modified, Conventional and Organic Crops in European Agriculture In *Report EUR 20394EN*. Brussels: European Commission Research Centre.

Böcker. A., and Hanf. C. H. 2000. Confidence Lost and—partially—Regained: Consumer Response to Food Scares. *Journal of Economic Behavior & Organization* 43:471–485.

Body. R. 1982. *Agriculture: The Triumph and the Shame*. London: Temple Smith.

———. 1984. *Farming in the Clouds*. London: Temple Smith.

———. 1987. *Red or Green for Farmers (and the Rest of Us)*. Saffron Walden, Essex: Broad Leys Publishing.

———. 1991. *Our Food, Our Land*. London: Rider.

Bonnano. A., Busch. L., Friedland. W., Gouveia. L., and Mingione. E., eds. 1994. *From Columbus to ConAgra: The Globalization of Agriculture and Food*. Lawrence: University Press of Kansas.

Born, M. 2001. 100 Herds Saved as Trainee Solicitor Finds Loophole. *Daily Telegraph*, 12 May.

Borraz, O., Besancon, J., and Clergeau, C., 2006. Is It Just About Trust? The Partial Reform of French Food Safety Regulation. In *What's the beef? The contested governance of European Food Safety.*, edited by Ansell, C., and Vogel, D., Cambridge, MA: MIT Press.

Bredahl. M., Northen. J., Boecker. A., and Normille. M. 2001. Consumer Demand Sparks the Growth of Quality Assurance Schemes in the European Food Sector. In *Changing Structure of Global Food Consumption and Trade WRS-01–1*. Washington DC: USDA/Economic Research Service.

Bredahl. M. E., and Holleran. E. 1997. Technical Regulations and Food Safety In NAFTA. In *Harmonization/Convergence/Compatibility in Agriculture and Agri-Food Policy: Canada, United States and Mexico*, edited by Loyns. R., Knutson. R., Meilke. K. and Summer. D. Winnipeg: University of Manitoba.

Breslin. L. 2002. *Food Quality and Safety.* Paper read at Proceedings of Framework Programme 6 Conference, 28th November 2002, at QEII Conference Centre, London.

Brousseau. E., and Codron. J. 1998. La complémentarité entre formes de gouvernance: Le cas de l'approvisionnement des grandes surfaces en fruits de contresaison. *Economie Rurale* 245–246:75–83.

Brunsson. N., and Jacobsson. B. 2000. *A World of Standards.* Oxford: Oxford University Press.

Bulmer, S., and Burch. M. 2000. The Europeanisation of British Central Government. In *Transforming British Government*, edited by Rhodes. R. A. W. London: Macmillan.

Bulmer. S, and Burch. M. 2001. The Europeanisation of Central Government: the UK and Germany Historical Institutionalist Perspective. In *The Rules of Integration*, edited by Aspinwall. M. and Schneider. G. Manchester: Manchester University Press.

Bulmer. S., and Radaelli. C. 2004. *The Europeanisation of National Policy?* Belfast: Queen's University.

Buonanno. L. 2006. The Creation of the European Food Safety Authority. In *What's the Beef? The Contested Governance of European Food Safety*, edited by Ansell. C. and Vogel. D. Cambridge, Massuchesetts: The MIT Press.

Burch. D., and Goss. J. 1999. Global Sourcing and Retail Chains: Shifting Relationships of Production in Australian Agri-Foods. *Rural Sociology* 64:334–350.

Busch, L. 2007. Performing the economy, performing science: from neoclassical to supply chain models in the agri-food sector. *Economy and Society* 36 (3):437–466.

Buttel. F. 2006. Sustaining the Unsustainable: Agro-Food Systems and Environment in the Modern World. In *Handbook of Rural Studies*, edited by Cloke. P., Marsden. T. K. and Mooney. P. London: Sage.

Cabinet Office. 2003. *Field Work: Weighing up the Costs and benefits of GM Crops: Analysis Papers.* London: Cabinet Office Strategy Unit.

Cabinet Office. 2008. The Strategy Unit Food Matters. London: HMSO.

Caduff. L, and Bernauer. T. 2006. Managing Risk and Regulation in European Food Safety Management. *Review of Policy Research* 23 (1):153.

Calvacanti, S., and Marsden, T. 2004. The globalised fruiti-culture system: new structures and agency in the north/south relationships. In *Conference on Resistance and Agency in Contemporary Agriculture and Food: Empirical Cases and New Theories*. Austin, USA.

Campbell, D., and Lee, R. 2003a. "Carnage by Computer": The Blackboard Economics of the 2001 Foot and Mouth Outbreak. *Social and Legal Studies* 12:425–460.

———. 2003b The Power to Panic: the Animal Health Act 2002. *Public Law*:382–396.

Carson. L., and Lee. R. 2005. Consumer Sovereignty and the Regulatory History of the European Market for Genetically Modified Foods. *Environmental Law Review* 7 (3):173–189.

Casella. A. 1997. Free Trade and Evolving Standards. In *Fair Trade and Harmonization: Prerequisites for Free Trade?* edited by Bhagwati. J. N and Hudec. R. E. Cambridge: MIT Press.

———. 2001. Product Standards and International Trade: Harmonization Through Private Collations? *Kyklos* 54 (2/3):243–264.

Cassis de Dijon. (1979). Case 120/78, [1979] ECR 649.

Caswell. J. (1994) *Uses of Food Labelling Regulation*. Organisation for Economic Cooperation and Development 1997. Available from http://www.oecd.org.

Caswell. J, Bredahl. M. E, and Hooker. N. 1998. How Quality Management Meta-Systems are Affecting the Food Industry. *Review of Agricultural Economics* 20 (2):547–557.

Caswell. J., and Johnson. V. 1991. Farm Strategic Response to Food Safety and Nutrition Regulation. In *Economics of Food Safety* edited by Caswell. J. A. New York: Elsevier.

Cavalcanti. B., and Marsden. T. 2004. The Globalised Fruiti-Culture System: New Structures and Agency in the North/South Relationships. In *Conference on Resistance and Agency in Contemporary Agriculture and Food: Empirical Cases and New Theories*. Austin, USA.

Cazala. J. 2004. Food Safety and the Precautionary Principle: The Legitimate Moderation of Community Courts. *European Law Journal* 10 (5):539.

CEC. 1990. Directive (EEC) 90/313 on Public Access to Environmental Information Edited by EEC: Official Journal of the European Communities (L158, 23/6/1990).

———. 1993. (EC) 93/730 on the Code of Conduct concerning Public Access to Council and Commission Document edited by EC: Official Journal of the European Communities (L340, 31/12/1993).

———. 1995. Directive (EC) 95/46 on the Protection of Individuals with Regard to the Processing of Personal Data and on the Free Movement of Such Data edited by EC: Official Journal of the European Communities (L281, 23/11/1995).

———. 2000. *White Paper of the Safety of Food*. Brussels: COM.

———. 2002. Regulation (EC) 178/2002 of the European Parliament and of the Council of 28 January 2002 Laying Down the General Principles and Requirements of Food Law, Establishing the European Food Safety Authority and Laying Down Procedures in Matters of Food Safety edited by EC: Official Journal of the European Communities (L31/24, 1/2/2002).

Chandler, D., Davidson, G., Grant, W. P., Greaves, J., and Tatchell, G. M. 2008. Microbial biopesticides for integrated crop management: an assessment of environmental and regulatory sustainability. *Trends in Food Science & Technology* 19 (5):275–283.

Chatham House. 2009. Food Futures: rethinking UK strategy. London: Chatham House.

Cheney. P., and Fevre. R. 2001. Inclusive Governance and "Minority" Groups: The Role of the Third Sector in Wales. *Voluntas: International Journal of Voluntary and Nonprofit Organizations* 12 (2):131–156.

Chia-Hui Lee. G. 2006. Private Food Standards and their Impacts on Developing Countries: European Commission DG Trade Unit G2 http://trade.ec.europa.eu/doclib/docs/2006/june/tradoc_127969.pdf

Chief Veterinary Officer (CVO). 2001. Evidence to the Anderson Enquiry. In *Foot and Mouth Disease 2001: Lessons to be Learned Inquiry Report, Annex B*, edited by Anderson. I.

Christey. M., and Woodfield. D. 2001. Coexistence of Genetically Modified and Non-Genetically Modified Crops. In *Crop & Food Research Report No. 427*. New Zealand: Ministry for the Environment.

Church of Scotland. 2001. Committee on Church and Nation Proposal to Introduce a 20 day Standstill Period following Movements of Sheep and Cattle. Edinburgh: Church of Scotland.

Clark. J., and Lowe. P. 1992. Cleaning up Agriculture: Environment, Technology and Social Science. *Sociologia Ruralis* 22 (1):11–29.

Clarke. M., Godfrey. S., and Theron. J. 2003. Globalisation, Democratisation and Regulation of the South African Labour Market. In *Globalisation, Pro-*

duction and Poverty Research Project. Labour and Enterprise Project. University of Cape Town: Institute of Development and Labour Law/Sociology Department.

Clunies-Ross. T., and Hildyard. N. 1992. *The Politics of Industrial Agriculture.* London: Earthscan.

Cm3830. 1998. *The Food Standards Agency: A Force for Change.* London: The Stationery Office.

Codron. J., Sterns. J., and Vernin. X. 2002. Grande distribution et agriculture raisonnée dans la filière fruits et légumes frais. Paris: Document INRA-CTIFL.

Cohen. M. 1997. Risk Society and Ecological Modernisation: Alternative Visions for Post-Industrial Nations. *Futures* 29 (2):105–119.

Collingridge. D. 1980. *The Social Control of Technology.* New York: St Martin's Press.

Commission of the European Communities (CEC). 1997. *Communication from the Commission, Consumer Health and Food Safety.* Brussels: COM(97).

———. 2000. *White Paper on Food Safety.* Brussels: COM (1999).

Competition Commission. 2000. Supermarkets: a report on the supply of groceries from multiple stores in the UK. HMSO, London: Cm 4842.

Competition Commission. 2006. Summary of findings. Competition Commission: HMSO.

Cook. G., Pieri. E, and Robbins. P. T. 2004. The Scientists Think and the Public Feels: Expert Perceptions of the Discourse of GM Food. *Discourse and Society* 15 (4):433–449.

Cook. R. 1998. *Production Agriculture in Transition: The Fresh Fruit and Vegetable Sector.* Paper read at Food System of the Future Conference Proceedings, at Purdue University.

Cottrell. R. 1987. *The Sacred Cow.* London: Grafton Books.

Cox. G., Lowe. P., and Winter. M. 1986. From State Direction to Self-regulation: The Historical Development of Corporatism in British Agriculture. *Policy and Politics* 14:475–490.

Curry, Sir Donald. 2002. Curry Report: Report of the Policy Commission on the Future of Farming and Food. London: Cabinet Office.

Dabrowska. P. 2004. GM Foods, Risk, Precaution and the Internal Market: Did Both Sides Win the Day in the recent Judgment of the European Court of Justice? *German Law Journal* 5 (2):151.

Day, G. 2006. Chasing the Dragon? Devolution and the Ambiguities of Civil Society in Wales. *Critical Social Policy* 88 (3):642–655.

Dean, B. 2005. Review of the Food Standards Agency. An independent review conducted by the Rt Hon Baroness Brenda Dean of Thorton-le-Fylde.

DEFRA. 2001. Position on Deliberate Foot and Mouth Disease Infection. London: Defra.

———. 2002. UK Consultation on the Animal Health Bill.

———. 2006. Consultation on Proposals for Managing the Co-existence of GM, Conventional and Organic Crops. London: Defra.

———. 2007. Agriculture in the UK. https://stastics.defra.gov.uk/esg/publications/suk/2007/excel.asp.

Defra and DCMS. 2002. The Economic Cost of Foot and Mouth in the UK: A Joint Working Paper. London: Defra.

DG Health and Consumer Protection. 2001. Press Release.

Die Zeit (2001) Absolute Purity Does Not Exist. 39 Die Ziet 20 September 2001, reproduced at: http://europa.eu.int/comm/commissioners/byrne/interviews/zeit0901_en.htm

Dixon, J. 2002. *The Changing Chicken: Chooks, Cooks and Culinary Culture.* Sydney: New South Wales Press.

Dobson Consulting. *Buyer Power and its Impact on Competition in the Food Retail Distribution Sector of the European Union*. Available from http://europa.eu.int/comm/competition/publication/studies/bpifrs/

Dobson, P., and Waterson, M. 1996. Retail power: recent developments and policy implications. *Economic Policy* 14 (28):133–164.

Dobson, P. W., and Waterson. M. 1997. Countervailing Power and Consumer Prices. *Economic Journal* 107 (441):418–430.

Dobson. P., Waterson. M., and Davies. S. 2003. The Patterns and Implications of Increasing Concentration in European Food Retailing. *Journal of Agricultural Economics* 54 (1):111–126.

Dolan. C., Humphrey. J., and Harris-Pascal. C. 1999. Horticulture Commodity Chains: The Impact of the UK Market on the African Fresh Vegetable Industry. *In Working Paper 96*. University of Sussex: Inst. Developmental Studies.

Dower. M. 2002. Northumberland Foot and Mouth Inquiry. Northumberland: Official Report.

DTI. 1993. Review of the Implementation and Enforcement of EC Law in the UK. London: Department of Trade and Industry.

———. 1994. Getting a Good Deal in Europe, Deregulatory Principles in Practice. London: Department of Trade and Industry.

Duffy. R., Fearne. A., and Healing. V. 2005. Reconnection in the UK Food Chain: Bridging the Communication Gap Between Food Producers and Consumers. *British Food Journal* 107 (1):17–33.

Duke of Northumberland. 1969. Report of the Committee of Inquiry on Foot and Mouth Disease 1967/68 (Cmnd 3999). London HMSO.

Editorial. 1999. Divisions over the Precautionary Principle. *EU Food Law Monthly* 7:89.

Ellahi, B. 1996. Genetic Modification for the Production of Food: The Food Industry's Response. *British Food Journal* 98:53–72.

Enforcement Liaison Group (ELG). *Enforcement Liaison Group Awayday Report* 2002.

———. 2006. Enforcement Strategy. In *Discussion Paper, LG 139*.

Entec. 1996. Options for Change in the CAP Beef Regime: Report to Countryside Commission, Countryside Council for Wales, English Nature and Scottish Natural Heritage.

Entwhistle. T. 2006. The Distinctiveness of the Welsh Partnership Agenda. *International Journal of Public Sector Management* 19 (3):228–237.

EUREPGAP. *Eurepgap Fruit and Vegetables* 2003. Available from http://www.eurep.org/sites/history.html.

Euro Monitor. *Grocery Stores/Food Retailers/Supermarkets in the UK* 2003. Available from http://www.marketresearch.com/product/display.asp.

European Commission. 2000 (12 January 2000 COM [1999] 719 final). *White Paper on Food Safety*.

———. (2 February 2000–COM [2000] 1 final). Communication on the Precautionary Principle.

———. 2001. Report From The Commission Based On The Reports Of Member States Concerning Their Experiences With Directive 90/219/EEC On The Contained Use Of Genetically Modified Micro-Organisms For The Period 1996–1999: COM 263 Final.

European Commission Press Release. 2003a. European Commission Regrets the Request for a WTO Panel on GMOs (IP/03/1165), 18 August 2003.

———. 2003b. Commission Rejects Request to Establish a Temporary Ban on the Use of GMOs in Upper Austria' (IP/03/1194), 2 September 2003.

———. 2004. Commission Authorises Import of Canned GM-Sweet Corn Under New Strict Labelling Conditions—consumers can choose (IP/04/663), 19 May 2004.

European Parliament. 2002a. Directorate General for Research Position of International Organisations on Vaccination against Foot and Mouth Disease.

———. 2002b. Temporary Committee on Foot and Mouth Disease. In *Conclusions of the Rapporteur, Working Document 5a.*

European Voice. 1999. *European Voice, Vol 5, No 45.*

———. 2000. *European Voice, Vol 6, No 20.*

———. 2000. *European Voice, Vol 6, No 15.*

———. 2001. *European Voice, Vol 7, No 27.*

———. 2002. *European Voice, Vol 8, No 14.*

———. 2003. *European Voice, Vol 9, No 29.*

Evans. N., Morris. C., and Winter. M. 2002. Conceptualising Agriculture: A Critique of Post Productivism as the New Orthodoxy. *Progress in Human Geography* 26 (3):313–332.

Falkner. R. 2000. Regulating Biotech Trade: The Cartagena Protocol on Biosafety. *International Affairs* 76 (2):299–313.

FAO. 2002. Animal Diseases: Implications for International Meat Trade. In *Committee on Commodity Problems, Intergovernmental Group on Meat and Dairy Products, Nineteenth Session.* Rome: FAO.

FAO STAT. Online database: http://faostat.fao.org/site/567/default.aspx#ancor.

Fearne. A. 1998. The Evolution of Partnerships in the Meat Supply Chain: Insights from British Beef Industry. *Supply Chain Management* 3 (4):214–231.

———. 1998a. Building Effective Partnerships in the Meat Supply Chain: Lessons from the UK. *Canadian Journal of Agricultural Economics* 46 (4):491–518.

Fearne, A. and R Walters (2004) The Costs and Benefits of Farm Assurance to Livestock Producers in England, Final Report, Centre for Food Chain Research, Imperial College London, February.

Fiddis, C. 1997. Manufacturers-Retailers Relationships in the Food and Drinks Industry: Strategies and Tactics in the Battle for Power. *Financial Times Retail and Consumer Publications.*

Financial Times (Leader). 2003. The Popular Verdict on GM Crops. *Financial Times.*

Finucane, M. 2000. *Improving Quarantine Risk Communication: Understanding Public Risk Perceptions.* Eugene, Oregon: Decision Research.

Flynn. A., and Marsden. T. 1992. Food Regulation in a Period of Agricultural Retreat: The British Experience. *Geoforum* 25:85–93.

Flynn. A., Marsden. T., Carson. L., Lee. R., Smith. E., Thankappan. S., and Yakovleva. N. 2004. *The Food Standards Agency: Making a difference?* Cardiff: The Centre for Business Relationships, Accountability, Sustainability and Society (BRASS).

Flynn. A., Marsden. T., and Harrison. M. 1999. The Regulation of Food in Britain in the 1990s. *Policy and Politics* 27 (4):435–446.

Flynn. A., Marsden. T., and Ward. N. 1991. Managing Food? A Critical Perspective on the British Experience. *Changement technique et restructuration de l'industrie agro-alimentaire en Europe, INRA Actes et Communications,* 7:159–181.

FoE. *Genetically modified food and feed* 2004.Available from http://www.foeeurope.org/GMOs/european_legislation/genetically_modified.htm.

Fogerty. M, Turner. M, and Barr. D. 2001. Lowland Sheep 1999: The Economics and Management of Lamb Production. In *Special studies in Agricultural Economics.* Exeter: Agricultural Economics Unit, University of Exeter.

Folkerts. H, and Koehorst. H. 1998. Challenges in International Food Supply Chains: Vertical Co-ordination in European Agribusiness and Food Industries. *British Food Journal* 100 (8):385–388.

Follett. Sir Brian. 2004. Infectious Disease in Livestock—Follow up Report: Royal Society.

Food and Agriculture Organisation of the United Kingdom. 2008. Declaration of the high-level conference on world food security: the challenges of climate change and bioenergy. Rome: FAQ.

Food Standards Agency. 2001. Statement on Food and Mouth Disease: Food Standards Agency.

———. 2002 Evaluating the Risks Associated with Using GMOs in Human Foods. London: FSA.

Foreman. S. 1989. *Loaves and Fishes*. London: HMSO.

Foster, J. B. 1999. Marx's theory of metabolic rift: classical foundations of environmental sociology. *Journal of Sociology* 105 (2): 366–405.

Fowler. T. 2004. *Structural Changes in the Pig Industry: Economic and Policy Analysis Group*. British Pig Executive. November 2004. Available at: http://www.bpex.org/technical/publications/pdf/BPEX_structures_report04.pdf.

Freestone. D. 1991. The Precautionary Principle. In *International Law and Global Climate Change*, edited by Churchill. R. and Freestone. D. London: Graham and Trotman.

———. 1994. The Road from Rio: International Environmental Law After the Earth Summit. *Journal of Environmental Law* 6 (2):193–218.

Freestone. D., and Hey. E. 1996. Origins and Development of the Precautionary Principle. In *The Precautionary Principle and International Law*, edited by Freestone. D. and Hey. E. The Hague: Kluwer.

Friedberg. S. 2003. Cleaning Up Down South: Supermarkets, Ethical Trade and African Horticulture. *Social and Cultural Geography* 4 (1):27–43.

Friedmann, H. 2005. From colonialism to green capitalism: social movements and the emergence of food regimes. In *New Directions in the Sociology of Global Development. Research in Rural Sociology and Rural Development Volume 11*, edited by Buttel, F., and Michael, P. Oxford: Elsevier.

Friedmann, H. 2008. Review article: Morgan, K., Marsden, T. K., and Murdoch, J. L.(2006). Worlds of Food. *Agriculture and Human Values* 25 (22):291–294.

Frewer. L. J. 1999. Public Risk Perceptions and Risk Communication. In *Risk Communication and Public Health*, edited by Bennett. P. and Calman. K. New York: Oxford University Press.

Friedland. W. 1994. The New Globalization: the Case of Fresh Produce. In *Columbus to ConAgra: The Globalization of Agriculture and Food*, edited by Bonanno, L. B., Friedland. W., Gouveia. L., Mingione. E. and Lawrence. K. Kansas: University of Kansas Press.

FSA. Putting Consumers First, Strategic Plan (2001–2006). Available from http://www.foodstandards.gov.uk.

———. 2001. Strategic Plan 2001–2006.

———. 2002a. Food Standards Agency Business Plan 2002–2003.

———. 2002b. Departmental Report Spring 2002, Cm5404.

———. 2002c. Report on Local Authority Food Law Enforcement Activity in the UK. London: FSA.

———. 2003a. Departmental Report Spring 2003.

———. 2003b. Report on Local Authority Food Law Enforcement Activity in the UK in 2001. London: FSA.

———. 2004. Departmental Report Spring 2004.

———. 2005. Departmental Report Spring 2005.

———. 2006. Food Law Code of Practice.

Garcia Martinez. M., Fearne. A., Caswell. J. A., and Henson. S. J. 2005. *Co- Regulation of Food Safety: Opportunities for Private-Public Partnerships*. Ashford: Imperial College at Wye.

Garcia. M., and Poole. N. 2002. *The Impact of Private Safety and Quality Standards for Fresh Produce Exports from Mediterranean Countries*. Imperial College London: Food Management Unit, Department of Agricultural Sciences.

Gaskell. G., Allum. N., Wagner. W., Kronberger. N., Torgersen. H., Hampel. J., and Bardes. J. 2004. GM Foods and the Misperception of Risk Perception. *Risk Analysis* 24:185–194.

Gent. T. N. 1999. Genetically Modified Organisms: An Analysis of the Regulatory Framework Currently Employed within the European Union. *Journal of Public Health Medicine* 21 (3):278–282.

Gereffi. G. 1994. The Organization of Buyer-Driven Global Commodity Chains: How US Retailers Shape Overseas Production Networks. In *Commodity Chains and Global Capitalism*, edited by Gereffi. G. and Korzeniewicz. M. Westport CT: Praeger.

Giddens. A. 1994. Living in a Post-Traditional Society. In *Reflexive Modernisation: Politics, Tradition and Aesthetics in the Modern Social Order*, edited by Beck. U., Giddens. A. and Scott. L. Cambridge: Polity Press.

———. 1999. Risk and Responsibility. *Modern Law Review* 62 (1):1–10.

Gill. B. 2002. Statement on the Lessons to be Learned Inquiry: NFU.

GM Nation Public Debate Steering Board. 2003. GM Nation? The Findings of a Public Debate. London: GM Nation Public Debate Steering Board.

Gollier. C, Julien. B, and Treich. N. 2000. Scientific Progress and Irreversibility: an Economic Interpretation of the "Precautionary Principle". *Journal of Public Economics* 75 (2):229–253.

Goodman. D, and Redclift. M. 1991. *Refashioning Nature. Food, Ecology and Culture*. London: Routledge.

Gordon. A. 1998. Changes in Food and Drink Consumption, and the Implications for Food Marketing. In *OECD The Future of Food: Long-Term Prospects for the Agro-Food Sector*. Paris: Organization for Economic Cooperation and Development.

Grant. W. 1983. The National Farmers' Union: The Classic Case of Incorporation. In *Pressure Politics*, edited by Marsh. D. London: Junction Books.

———. 1993. *Business and Politics in Britain*. Basingstoke: Macmillan.

Greenpeace. 1999. France V Ministere de l'Agriculture et de la peche [1999] ECR ?? at 71 (opinion of Advocate General Mischo)

Grievink, J. W. 2003. The changing face of the global food supply chain. In *OECD conference: Changing dimensions of the food economy: Exploring policy issues*.

Groth. E. 2000. *Science, Precaution and Food Safety*. New York: Consumers Union of US.

Guardian. 2004. Balancing the Benefits with the Public's Scepticism. *Guardian*.

Guptil, A., Wilkins, J. L. 2002. Buying into the food system: Trends in food retailing in the UK and implications for local foods. *Agriculture and Human Values* 19:39–51.

Guthman, J. 2004. The Trouble with 'Organic Lite' in California: a Rejoinder to the 'Conventionalisation' Debate. *Sociologia Ruralis* 44 (3): 301–316.

Gutteling. J.M., and Kuttschreuter. M. 2002. The Role of Expertise in Risk Communication: Laypeople's and Expert's Perception of Millennium Bug Risk in the Netherlands. *Journal of Risk Research* 5 (1):35–47.

Guy. C. 2007. *Planning for Retail Development: A Critical Review of the British Experience*. London: Routledge.

Hajer. M. 2003. Policy without Polity? Policy Analysis and the Institutional Void. *Policy Sciences* 36:175–195.

Haley. M. M. 2001. Changing Consumer Demand for Meat: The U.S. Example, 1970–2000. In *Changing Structures of Global Food Consumption and Trade*, edited by Regmi. A. Washington DC: US Department of Agriculture, Economic Research Service.

Hall. P. 1993. Policy Paradigms, Social Learning and the State. *Comparative Politics* 25 (3):274–296.

Hampton. P. 2005. *Reducing Administrative Burdens: Effective Inspection and Enforcement*: HM Treasury.

Hanson. S., and Caswell. J. 1999. Food Safety Regulation; An Overview of Contemporary Issues. *Food Policy* 24 (6):589–603.

Harris. S., and Pickard. D. 1979. *Livestock Slaughtering in Britain: A Changing Industry*. Ashford: Centre for European Agricultural Studies.

Harrison. M., Flynn. A., and Marsden. T. 1997. Contested Regulatory Practice and the Implementation of Food Policy: Exploring the Local and National Interface. *Transactions of the Institute of British Geographers* 22 (4), 473–487.

Harvey, M., McMeekin, A., and Warde, A., eds. 2004. *Qualities of Food*. Manchester, UK: Manchester University Press.

Hathaway. S. C. 1995. Harmonization of International Requirements Under HACCP-Based Food Control Systems. *Food Control* 6:267–276.

Hathcock. J. N. 1999. *Assuring Science-Based Decisions—No Need for a Separate Precautionary Principle in Risk Analysis for Foods*. Washington DC: Council for Responsible Nutrition.

HC 524. 2003. Improving Service Delivery: The Food Standards Agency. Report by the Comptroller and Auditor General, Session 2002–2003. London: The Stationery Office.

Hefferman, W. D. 1994. Constraints in U.S. poultry production. In *Research in Rural Sociology and Development: A research annual,* edited by S. H. K. Greenwich, CT: JAI Press.

Hefferman, W. D., and Constance, D. H. 1994. Transnational Corporations and the Globalization of the Food System. In *From Columbus to ConAgra. The Globalization of Agriculture and Food,* edited by Bonanno, A., Busch, L., Friedland, W., Gouveia, L. and Mingione, E. Kansas: University Press of Kansas.

Hellebo. L. 2004. *Food Safety at Stake—the Establishment of Food Agencies.* Bergen: Stein Rokkan Centre for Social Studies.

Henderson. M. 2001. Vets More Confident of Halting Outbreak. *The Times*, 7th March 2001.

Hendrickson, M. K., and Heffernan, W. D. 2002. Opening Spaces through Relocalization: Locating Potential Resistance in the Weaknesses of the Global Food System. *Sociologia Ruralis* 42 (4):347–369.

Hendrickson, M. K., Heffernan, W. D. Howard, P. H., and Heffernan, J. D. 2001. Consolidation in Food Retailing and Dairy: Implications for Farmers and Consumers in Global Food System. Washington, DC: National Farmers' Union.

Henson. S. 1997. The Impact of Regulations on Consumers and the Food Chain Industries. In *Management of Regulation in the Food Chain: Balancing Costs, Benefits and Effects*, edited by Marshall. B. and Miller. F. A. University of Reading: Centre for Agricultural Strategy.

———. 2001. The Appropriate Level of Protection: A European Perspective. In *The Economics of Quarantine and the SPS Agreement*, edited by Anderson. K., McRae. C. and Wilson. D. Adelaide: Centre for International Economic Studies.

———. 2001. Appropriate Level of Protection: A European Perspective. In *The Economics of Quarantine and the SPS Agreement*, edited by Anderson. K.,

McRae. C. and Wilson. D. University of Adelaide..: Centre for International Trade Studies.

———. 2006. The role of public and private standards regulating international food markets. In *IATRC Symposium*. Bonn, Germany.

Henson. S., and Loader. R. 1999. Impact of Sanitary and Phytosanitary Standards on Developing Countries and the Role of the SPS Agreement. *Agribusiness* 15:355–369.

Henson. S., and Northen. J. 1998. Economic Determinants of Food Safety Control in the Supply of Retailer Own Brand Products in the UK. *Agribusiness* 14 (2):113–126.

Henson. S. J., and Caswell. J. A. 1999. Food Safety Regulation: An Overview of Contemporary Issues. *Food Policy* 24:589–603.

Henson. S. J., and Hooker. N. H. 2001. Private Sector Management of Food Safety: Public Regulation and the Role of Private Controls. *International Food and Agribusiness Management Review* 4:7–17.

Henson. S. J., and Reardon. T. 2005. Private Agri-Food Standards: Implications for Food Policy and the Agri-Food System. *Food Policy* 30 (3):241–253.

Héritier. A. 2003. Elements of Democratic Legitimation in Europe: An Alternative Perspective. *Journal of European Public Policy* 6 (2):269–282.

Hervey. T. 2001. Regulation of Genetically Modified Products in a Multi-Level System of Governance: Science or Citizens? *Review of European Community and International Environment Law (RECIEL)* 10 (3):321–333.

Hession, M. and Macrory. R. 1994. Maastricht and the Environmental Policy of the Community: Legal Issues of a New Environment Policy. In *Legal Issues of the Maastricht Treaty*, edited by O'Keeffe and Twoney. London: Wylie.

Highfield. R. 2001. Tactics Used on Half the Farms "were inefficient". *Daily Telegraph*, 22 May 2001.

Hill. J. R., and Merton. I. 1995. Consumer Expectations as Perceived by Retailers. *Outlook on Agriculture* 24:7–10.

Hilson. C., and French. D. 2003. Regulating GM Products in the EU: Risk, Precaution and International Trade. In *Agriculture and International Trade: Law, Policy and the World Trade Organisation*, edited by Cardwell. M., Grossman. M. and Rodgers. C. Wallingford, Oxon: CABI Publishing.

HM Comptroller and Auditor General. 2002. *The 2001 Outbreak of Foot and Mouth*. London: Stationary Office.

Hobbs. J.E. 1996. A Transaction Cost Analysis of Quality, Traceability and Animal Welfare Issues in UK Beef Retailing. *British Food Journal* 98 (6):16–26.

Holder. J. 1997. Safe Science? The Precautionary Principle in UK Environmental Law. In *The Impact of EC Environmental Law in the United Kingdom* edited by Holder. J. London: Wiley.

Holleran. E., Bredahl. M. E., and Zaibet. L. 1999. Private Incentives for Adopting Food Safety and Quality Assurance. *Food Policy* 24 (6):669–683.

Holmes. P. 2000. The WTO Beef Hormones Case: A Risky Decision? *Consumer Policy Review* 10 (2):61–71.

Hooghe. L., and Marks. G. 2003. Unravelling the Central State, but How? Types of Multi-level Governance. *American Political Science Review* 97 (2):233–243.

Horlick-Jones. T. 2007. *The GM debate: risk, politics and public engagement*. London: Routledge.

Houghton Brown. M. 2001. Inoculate—Don't Prevaricate. *The Times*, 17 March 2001.

House of Lords Debates. 2002. Animal Health Bill 2001, 26 March 2002, col 167.

Howard, P. 2003. Consolidation in Food and Agriculture. *CCOF Magazine*, 2–6.

Howell. K. E. 2004. Developing Conceptualisations of Europeanisation: A Study of Financial Services. *Politics* 24:20–25.

Huang. C. L., Kamhon. K., and Tsu-Tan. F. 2000. Joint Estimation of Consumer Preferences and Willingness-to-Pay for Food Safety. *Academia Economic Papers* 28 (4):429–449.

Ilbery. B., and Bowler. I. 1998. From Agricultural Productivism to Post-Productivism. In *The Geography of Rural Change*, edited by Ilbery. B. London: Longman.

International Council for Science. 2003. *New Genetics, Food and Agriculture: Scientific Discoveries- Societal Dilemmas*. Paris: ICSU.

Jacobsen. E., and Kjærnes. U. 2003. Sikker mat til forbrukerne: et privat eller offentlig ansvar? In *Den politiserte maten*, edited by Jacobsen. E, Almas. R and Johnsen. J. Oslo.

Jaffee. S. 1995. The Many Faces of Success: The Development of Kenyan Horticultural Efforts. In *Marketing Africa's High-Value Foods*, edited by Jaffee. S. and Morton. J. Washington DC: World Bank.

Jaffee. S., and Henson, S.. 2004. Standards and Agri-food Exports from Developing Countries: Rebalancing the Debate. In *Policy Research Working Paper 3348*, edited by World Bank. Washington DC: The World Bank.

James. P. 1997. *Food Standards Agency: An Interim PProposal*. Aberdeen: Rowett Research Institute.

James. P., Kemper. F., and Pascal. G. 1999. *A European Food and Public Health Authority. The Future of Scientific Advice in the EU*. European Integration online Papers (EIoP), Vol. 6, No. 2002–019 .

Jamieson. B. Evaluation of the Organisation and Management of GMHT Farm Scale Evaluations (FSEs). London: HC Environmental Audit Committee.

Jansen. J. 2001. Netherlands Inspectorate Health Protection and Veterinary Public Health.

Jasonoff. S. 2000. Between Risk and Precaution—Reassessing the Future of GM Crops. *Journal of Risk Research* 3 (3):277–282.

Jenkins. R. 2001. Corporate Codes of Conduct: Self-Regulation in a Global Economy. In *Technology, Business and Society Programme Paper No. 2*. Geneva: UNRISD.

Jessop. B. 2000. The State and the Contradictions of the Knowledge-Driven Economy. In *Knowledge, Space, Economy*, edited by Bryson. J. R. et al. London: Routledge.

Josling. T. E., Roberts. D., and Orden. D. 2004. *Food Regulation and Trade: Toward a Safe and Open Global Food System*. Washington DC: Institute for International Economics.

Kay. A. 2003. Evaluating Devolution in Wales. *Political Studies* 52:51–66.

Kennard. R., and Young. R. 1999. *The Threat to Organic Meat from Increased Inspection Charges*. Bristol: Soil Association.

Key Note. 2003. Market Report 2003: Meat and Meat Products.

King. D. 2001. Use of Vaccination in the Current FMD Outbreak. London: DEFRA.

Kirwan, J. 2004. Alternate Strategies in the UK Agro-Food System: Interrogating the Alterity of Farmers' Markets. *Sociologia Ruralis* 44 (4):395–415.

Kjaenes, U., Harvey, M., and Warde, A. 2007. *Trust in Food: a comparative and institutional analysis*. New York: Palgrave Macmillan.

Klinke. A., Dreyer. M., Renn. O., Stirling. A., and Van Zwanenberg. P. 2006. Precautionary Risk Regulation in European Government. *Journal of Risk Research* 9 (4):373–392.

Konefal, J., Mascarenhas, M., and Hatanaka, M. 2005. Governance in the global agro-food system: Backlighting the role of transnational supermarket chains. *Agriculture and Human Values* 22:291–302.

Lang. T., Barling. D., and Caraher. M. 2001. Food, Social Policy and the Environment: Towards a New Model. *Social Policy & Administration* 35 (5):538–558.

Langford. I. H. 2002. An Existential Approach to Risk Perception. *Risk Analysis* 22 (1):101–120.

Lappe. M., and Bailey. B. 1999. *Against the Grain: The Gentic Transformation of Global Agriculture*. London: Earthscan.

Lash. S., and Wynne. B. 1992. Introduction, edited by Beck. U.

Lee. R. 2000. From the Individual to the Environmental: Tort Law in Turbulence. In *Common Law & the Environment*, edited by Edmunds. R. and Lowry. J. Oxford: Hart.

Lee R. 2005. GM Resistant: Europe and the WTO Panel Dispute on Biotech Products in Jennifer Gunning and Søren Holm, *Ethics Law and Society* (Ashgate) pp131–140.

Lee. R., and Morgan. D. 2001. *Human Fertilisation and Embryology, Regulating the Reproductive Revolution*. London: Blackstone.

Levidow. L., and Boschert. K. 2008. Coexistence or Contradiction: GM Crops versus Alternative Agricultures in Europe. *Geoforum* 39 (1):174190.

Levidow. L., Carr. S., and Wield. D. 2000. Genetically Modified Crops in the European Union: Regulatory Conflicts as Precautionary Opportunities. *Journal of Risk Research* 3 (3):189–208.

Levidow. L., and Murphy. J. 2003. Reframing Regulatory Science: Trans-Atlantic Conflicts over GM Crops. *Cahiers d'économie et sociologie rurales* (68/69):47–74.

Liberatore. A. 1997. The Integration of Sustainable Development Objectives into EU Policymaking: Barriers and Prospects. In *The Politics of Sustainable Development*, edited by Baker. S. et al. London: Routledge.

Liddell. S. 2000. *Transferability of European Food Safety and Quality Assurance Models to the United States*. Logan: Department of Economics, Utah State University.

LMC International. 2003. *Supply Chain Impacts of Further Regulation of Products Consisting of, Containing, or Derived from, Genetically Modified Organisms*. London: Defra/The Food Standards Agency.

Löfstedt. R. 2003. Swedish Chemical Regulation: An Overview and Analysis. *Risk Analysis* 23 (2):411–421.

———. 2004. The Swing of the Regulatory Pendulum in Europe: From Precautionary Principle to (Regulatory) Impact Analysis. In *AEI-Brookings Joint Center Working Paper No. 04–07.*

Löfstedt. R., and Vogel. D. 2001. The Changing Character of Regulation: A Comparison of Europe And the United States. *Risk Analysis* 21 (3):399–416.

Lucas. C. 2001. *Stopping the Great Food Swap; Re-localising Europe's Food Supply*. Strasbourg: Greens/European Free Alliance.

Lucus. C., Hart. M., and Hines. C. 2002. Looking to the Local: A Better Agriculture is Possible. In *Discussion document*. Brussels: European Parliament.

Macarthy, J. 2006. Rural geography: alternative rural economies: the search for alterity in forests, fisheries, food and fair trade. *Progress in Human Geography* 30 (6):803–812.

Macintyre. S., Reilly. J., Miller. D., and Eldridge. J. 1998. Food Choice, Food Scares and Health: The Role of the Media. In *The Nation's Diet: The Social Science of Food Choice* edited by Murcott. A. London: Longman.

MAFF. 1997. Proposals for a Food Standards Agency. In *The James Report*. London: Ministry of Agriculture, Fisheries and Food.

Majone. G. 1994. The Rise of the Regulatory State in Europe. *Western European Politics* 17:77–101.

———. 2002. What Price Food Safety? The Precautionary Principle and its Policy Implications. *Journal of Common Market Studies* 40 (1):89–109.

Marchant. G., and Sylvester. D. 2006. Transnational Models for Regulation of Nanotechnology. *Journal of Law, Medicine Ethics* 24 (4):714.

Margolis. H. 1996. *Dealing with Risk: Why the public and experts disagree on environmental issues.* Chicago: University of Chicago Press.

Marsden, T. K. 2004. Theorising food quality: some key issues in understanding its competitive production and regulation. In *Qualities of Food*, edited by Harvey, M., McMeekin, A., and Warde, A. Manchester, UK: Manchester University Press.

Marsden. T. 2008. Agri-Food Contestations in Rural Space: GM in its Regulatory Context. 39 *Geoforum* 191–203.

Marsden. T., Bridge. G., and McManis. P. 2003. Guest Editorial: The Next New Thing? Biotechnology and its Discontents. *Geoforum* 34:165–175.

Marsden. T., Flynn. A., and Harrison. M. 2000. *Consuming Interests: The Social Provision of Food Choices.* London: UCL Press.

Marsden. T., Harrison. M., and Flynn. A. 1997. Creating Competitive Space: Exploring the Social and Political Maintenance of Retail Power. *Environment and Planning A* 30:481–498.

Marsden. T., and Sonnino. R. 2008. Rural development and the regional state: denying multi-functional agriculture in the UK. *Journal of Rural Studies* 24:422–431.

Marsden. T., and Wrigley. N. 1995. Regulation, Retailing and Consumption. *Environment and Planning A* 27 (12):1180–1192.

Marsden. T. K. 2003. *The Condition of Sustainability.* The Netherlands: Van Gorcum.

Marsden. T. K., Banks. J., and Bristow. G. 2002. The Social Management of Rural Nature: Understanding Agrarian-Based Rural Development. *Environment and Planning A* 34:809–825.

Marsh. G. 2001. Community: The Concept of the community in the risk and emergency context. *Australian Journal of Emergency Management* 19 (4):6–19.

Matsushita. M., Schoenbaum. T., and Mavroidis. P. 2006. *The World Trade Organization: Law, Practice and Policy.* 2nd ed. Oxford: Oxford University Press.

May. P., Burby. R. J., Erickson. N. J., Handwer. J. W., Dixon. J. E., Michaels. S., and Ingle-Smith. D. 1996. *Environmental Management and Governance.* London: Routledge.

Mazey. S. 2001. European Integration: Unfinished Journey or Journey without End? In *European Union: Power and Policy-Making*, edited by Richardson. J. London: Routledge.

Mazey. S., and Richardson. J. 2001a. Institutionalising Promiscuity: Commission/ Interest Group Relations in the EU. In *The Institutionalisation of Europe*, edited by Fligstein. N., Sandholtz. W. and Stone-Sweet. A. Oxford: Oxford University Press.

———. 2001b. Interest Groups and EU Policy Making: Organisational Logic and Venue Shopping. In *European Union: Power and Policy Making*, edited by Richardson. J. London: Routledge.

McDonalds Corporation (2007) Annual Report.

McIntyre. O., and Mosedale. T. 1997. The Precautionary Principle as a Norm in Customary Environmental Law. *Journal of Environmental Law* 9 (2):221–241.

McMichael. P. 2005. Global development and the corporate food regime. In *New Directions in the Sociology of Global Development. Research in Rural Sociologt and Rural Development Volume 11*, edited by Buttel. F. and McMichael. P. Oxford: Elsevier.

Meacher. M. 2004. GM: The Politics of Uncertainty. *Science in Parliament* 61 (1):1.

Meat and Livestock Commission. 2002. Export Cheer for British Beef: Press Release.

———. 2006. Submission to the Competition Commission Market Investigation into the Supply of Groceries by Retailers in the United Kingdom.

Meat and Livestock Commission (MLC). 2001a. The Abattoir and Meat Processing Industry in Great Britain: MLC Economics in partnership with MLC Industry Strategy Consulting Group, UK.

———. 2001b. Towards a Sustainable Future—A Vision for the British Sheep Industry: Sheep Strategy Council, UK.

Mercer. I. 2002. *Crisis and Opportunity; Final report of the Devon Foot and Mouth Inquiry*. Tiverton: Devon Books.

Midgley. C. 2001. The Cruellest Months of All. *The Times*, 24 May 2001.

Miekle. J. 2006. Ministers Pave the Way for GM Crops as "Zero Cross-Pollination" Ruled Out. *The Guardian*, 21 July 2006.

Miele. M. and Bock. B. 2007. Competing discourses of farm animal welfare and agri-food restructuring. *International Journal of Sociology of Agriculture and Food* 15 (3):1–7.

Miller. D., and Reilly. J. 1995. Making an Issue of Food Safety: The Media, Pressure Groups and the Public Sphere. In *Eating Agendas: Food, Eating and Nutrition as Social Problems*, edited by Maurer. D. and Sobal. J. New York: Aldine De Gruyter.

Millstone. E., and van Zwanenberg. P. 2001. The Politics of Expert Advice: Lessons from the Early History of the BSE Saga. *Science and Public Policy* 28 (2):99–112.

———. 2002. The Evolution of Food Safety Policy-Making Institutions in the UK, EU and Codex Alimentarius. *Social Policy & Administration* 36 (6).

Minoli. D. 2003. A Summary Report on the Insurance Aspects of the Foot and Mouth Outbreak of 2001. Cardiff: BRASS.

MLC (Meat and Livestock Commission). 1996. Meat and Livestock Commission Press Release, No 66/96, 29 August 1996.

Mol. A. 2008. Boundless biofuels? Between environmental sustainability and vulnerability. *Sociologia Ruralis* 47 (4):297–300.

Monsanto Canada Inc., v. Percy Schmeiser, 2004 SCC 34, [2004] 1 S.C.R. 902.

Monsanto v. Homan McFarling (No. 2) 363 F.3d 1336 (Fed. Cir. 2004).

Monsanto v. Homan McFarling 302 F.3d 1291, 1296, 1299–300.

Moran. Lord. 2002. The Noble Lords were not Content. *Country Illustrated*, May 2002, 10.

Moran. M. 2002. Understanding the Regulatory State. *British Journal of Political Science* 32:391–413.

Morrison. N. 2001. RSPCA Lawyers Investigate Claims of Cruelty During Foot and Mouth Culls. *Northern Echo* 3rd September 2001.

Morth. U. 2004. Introduction. In *Soft Law in Governance and Regulation*, edited by Morth. U. Cheltenham: Edward Elgar.

National Consumer Council. 1988. *Consumers and the Common Agricultural Policy*. London: HMSO.

———. 2000. *Public Health and the Precautionary Principle*. London: NCC.

National Farmers' Union (NFU). 2001. NFU Position on Vaccination against Foot and Mouth: NFU Notice to Members, 22 April 2001.

National Foot and Mouth Group. 2001. Joint Submission on the Animal Welfare Bill from the National Foot and Mouth Group and Vets for Vaccination: NFMG.

———. 2003. Response to Consulation On Defra's FMD Contingency Plan, Decision Tree and Slaughter Protocol.

NERA. 2001. *Economic Appraisal of Options for Extension of Legislation on GM Labelling*. London: NERA Consulting..

Newsmax. *Bush Blames African Starvation on Europe* 2003. Available from http://archive.newsmax.com/archives/articles/2003/5/22/144647.shtml

Noussair. C., Robin. S., and Ruffieux. B. 2004. Do Consumers Really Refuse to Buy Genetically Modified Food? *Economic Journal* 114 (492):102–120.

NRLO. 1998. *Market Strategies and Consumer Behaviour: Future Initiatives for Knowledge and Innovation*. The Hague: National Council for Agricultural Research.

O.I.E. (Office International des Epizooties). 2000. *Manual of Standards for Diagnostic Tests and Vaccines*. 4th ed. Paris: OIE.

O'Donnell. J. 2001. Ripple Effect of Foot and Mouth Crisis. *Sunday Times*, 4 March 2001.

Organic Monitor (2005) The UK Market for Organic Meat Products, Research Report 1202–44, March

O'Riordan. T., and Cameron. J. 1994. The History and Contemporary Significance of the Precautionary Principle. In *Interpreting the Precautionary Principle* edited by O'Riordan. T. and Cameron. J. London: Earthscan.

O'Rourke. R. 2004. US–EU Trade War Looming over GM Foods. *Journal of International Biotechnology Law* 1 (1):28–31.

OECD. 2002. *Guidance for the Designation of a Unique Identifier for Transgenic Plants*. Paris: OCED.

Oosterveer, P. 2005. Global Food Governance, Wageningen University, Wageningen.

Otsuki. T., Wilson. J. S., and Sewadeh. M. 2001. Saving Two in a Billion: Quantifying the Trade Effect of European Food Safety Standards on African Exports. *Food Policy* 26 (5):495–514.

Parliamentary Office of Technology. 2001. Open Channels: public dialogue in science and technology. London: House of Commons.

PDSB. 2003. GM Nation? The Findings of the Public Debate (Report by the Public Debate Steering Board). London: Department of Trade and Industry.

Perdikis. N., Kerr, Shelburne. W., and Hobbs. J. 2001. Reforming the WTO to Defuse Potential Trade Conflicts in Genetically Modified Goods. *The World Economy* 24 (3):379–398.

Peters. B. G. 1999. *Institutional Theory in Political Science*. London: Continuum.

Petts. J., and Leach. B. 2000. *Evaluating Methods for Public Participation*. Bristol: Environmental Agency.

Pfizer v. European Commission, Case T-13/99, 11 September 2002.

Phillips of Worth Matravers. 2000. The BSE Inquiry Report: HMSO, 2000.

Phillips. Lord. 2000. Inquiry into the Emergence and Identification of Bovine Spongiform Encephalopathy (BSE) and Variant Creutzfeldt-Jakob Disease (vCJD) and the Action taken in response to it up to 20 March 1996. London: House of Commons.

Phillips. Lord (Chair). 2000. The Inquiry into BSE and Variant CJD in the UK: HMSO.

Pidgeon. N., Poortinga. W., Rowe. G., Horlick-Jones. T., Walls. J., and O'Riordan. T. 2005. Using Surveys in Public Participation Processes for Risk Decision Making: The Case of the 2003 British GM Nation? Public Debate. *Risk Analysis* 25 (2):467–479.

Pierre. J., and Peters. B. G. 2000. *Governance, Politics and the State*. London: Macmillan.

Plant Biotech Co-operative Centre. 2001. EU Urges Britain to Bosst GM Crops. In *Crop Biotech Update 23*. Available at: http://www.mardi.my/pbcc/crop2.htm.

Potter. C., and Tilzey, M. 2006. Agricultural policy discourses in the European post-fordist transition: neo liberalism, neomercantilism and multifunctionality. *Progress in Human Geography* 29 (5):581–601.

Power. M. 1997. *The Audit Society. Rituals of Verification*. Oxford: Oxford University Press.

Power A. P. and Harris S A. (1973) A cost-benefit evaluation of alternative control policies for foot and mouth disease in Great Britain, *Journal of Agricultural Economics* 24, 573–596.

Prempeh. H., Smith. R., and Muller. B. 2001. Foot and Mouth Disease: The Human Consequences are Slight, the Economic Ones Huge. *British Medical Journal* 322 (7286):565–566.

Prescott. M., and Leake. J. 2001. Ministers Hit Out at Farmers. *Sunday Times* (and see Lobby Briefing dated 26 March 2001 from 10 Downing Street), 25 March 2001.

Qualman. D. 2001. The Farm Crisis and Corporate Power. Saskatoon: National Farmers Union of Canada.

Randall. E. 2003. *Changing Perceptions of Risk in the European Union* 2002. Available from http://www.policylibrary.com/essays/RandallEFARisk1.htm.

Reardon. T., and Berdegeue. J. A. 2002. The Rapid Rise of Supermarkets in Latin America: Challenges and Opportunities for Development. *Development Policy Review* 20 (4):371–388.

Reardon. T., Codron. J.-M., Busch. L., Bingen. J., and Harris. C. 2001. Global Change in Agri-Food Grades and Standards: Agribusiness Strategic Responses in Developing Countries. *International Food and Agribusiness Management Review* 2 (3/4):421–435.

Reardon. T., and Farina. E.M.M.Q. 2002. The Rise of Private Food Quality and Safety Standards: Illustrations from Brazil. *International Food and Agricultural Management Review* 4:413–421.

Reardon. T., Henson. S., and Berdegue. J. 2007. 'Proactive fast tracking' Diffusion of supermarkets in developing countries: implications for market institutions and trade. *Journal of Economic Geography* 7 (4).

Renn. O. 1998. Three Decades of Risk Research: Accomplishments and New Challenges. *Journal of Risk Research* 1 (1):49–71.

Rhodes. R. A. W. 2000. Governance and Public Administration. In *Debating Governance Authority, Steering and Democracy*, edited by Pierre. J. Oxford: Oxford University Press.

Richardson. J. 2001. Policy-Making in the EU. In *European Union: Power and Policy-Making*, edited by Richardson. J. London: Routledge.

Richardson. K. 2000. Big Business and the European Agenda. In *Working Papers in Contemporary European Studies*. University of Sussex: Sussex European Institute.

Risse. T., Cowles. M., and Caporasso. J. 2001. Europeanisation and Domestic Change: Introduction. In *Transforming Europe*, edited by Cowles. M. Ithaca: Cornell University Press.

Roberts. D. 2001. Rural Change and the Impact of Foot and Mouth Disease. *Countryside Recreation* 9 (3/4):4–8.

———. 2004. *The Multilateral Governance Framework for Sanitary and Phytosanitary Regulations: Challenges and Prospects*. Washington DC: World Bank.

Roederer-Rynning. C. 2003. Talking Shop to "Working Parliament"? The European Parliament and Agricultural Change. *Journal of Common Market Studies* 41 (1):113–135.

Rosegrant. M. W., Paisner. M. S., Meijer. S., and Witcover. J. 2001. 2020 Global Food Outlook. Trends, Alternatives and Choices. In *A 2020 Vision for Food, Agriculture and the Environment Initiative*. Washington DC: International Food Policy Research Institute.

Rushton. J., Taylor N., Wilsmore T., Shaw A., James A. 2002. *Economic Analysis of Vaccination Strategies for Foot and Mouth Disease in the UK*. Reading: Veterinary Epidemiology and Economics Research Unit, Department of Agricultural and Food Economics, University of Reading.

Salmon. N. 2002. A European Perspective on the Precautionary Principle, Food Safety and the Free Trade Imperative of the WTO. *European Law Review* 27 (2):138–155.

Sandin. P., Peterson. M., Hannson. S., Ruden. S. O., and Juthe. A. 2002. Five Charges against the Precautionary Principle. *Journal of Risk Research* 5 (4):287–299.

Schofield, R., and Shaoul J. 2000. Food Safety and the Conflict of Interest in the Meat Industry: The Case of E.coli 0157, Public Administration 78 (3):531–554.

Scott. C. 2002. Private Regulation of the Public Sector: A Neglected Facet of Contemporary Governance. *Journal of Law and Society* 29 (1):56–76.

———. 2003. Regulation in the Age of Governance: The Rise of the Post-Regulatory State. In *The Politics of Regulation*, edited by Jordana. J and L.-F. D. Cheltenham: Edward Elgar.

Scottish Consumer Council. 2004. Food Law Enforcement. In *A Study of the Views of Environmental and Food Safety Officers in Scotland.*

Segerson. K. 1999. Mandatory versus Voluntary Approaches to Food Safety. *Agribusiness: An International Journal* 15 (1):53–70.

Select Committee on the European Union. 2002. Labelling of GM Food and Animal Feed: Informing the Consumer: Twenty Second Report, April 2002.

Self. P., and Storing. H. 1962. *The State and the Farmer.* London: Allen and Unwin.

Shaoul. J. E. 1997. BSE: For Services Rendered? The Drive for Profit in the Meat Industry. *The Ecologist*, 182.

Shaw. S., Dawson. J., and Blair. L. 1992. The Sourcing of Retailer Brand Food Products by a UK Retailer. *Journal of Marketing Management* 8:127–146.

Shearing. C. 1997. Unrecognized Origins of the New Policing: Linkage between Private and Public Policing. In *Business and Crime Prevention*, edited by Felson. M. and Clarke. R. Monsey, New York: Criminal Justice Press.

Sheenan. M., and Kearney. V. 2001. Gardai Quiz Dealer on Outbreak. *Sunday Times*, 4 March 2001.

Sheldon. I. 2002. Regulation of Biotechnology: Will We Ever Freely Trade GMOs? *European Review of Agricultural Economics* 29 (1):155–176.

Short. J. F. 1989. On Defining, Describing, and Explaining Elephants (and Reactions to Them): Hazards, Disasters, and Risk Analysis. *Mass Emergencies and Disasters* 7 (3):397–418.

Shucksmith. M. 1993. Farm Household Behaviour and the Transition to Post-Productivism. *Journal of Agricultural Economics* 44:466–478.

Siegrist. M., and Cvetovich. G. 2000. Perception of Hazards: The Role of Social Trust. *Risk Analysis* 20 (5):713–719.

Skogerbo. E. 1997. External Constraints and National Resources: Reflection on the Europeanisation of Communications Policy. *Telematics and Infomatics* 14 (4):383–393.

Skytte. H., and Blunch. N. 2001. Food Retailers' Buying Behaviour: An Analysis in 16 European Countries. *Journal on Chain and Network Science* 1:133–145.

Slovic. P. 1999. Trust, Emotion, Sex, Politics and Science: Surveying the Risk Assessment Battlefield. *Risk Analysis* 19 (4):689–701.

Smith. E. 2002. Ecological Modernisation and Organic Farming in the UK: Does it Pay to be Green?, City and Regional Planning, Cardiff University, Cardiff.

Smith. E., Marsden. T., Flynn. A., and Percival. A. 2004. Regulating Food Risks: Rebuilding Confidence in Europe's Food? *Environment and Planning* C 22 (4): 543–567.

Smith. M. J. 1990. *The Politics of Agricultural Support in Britain.* Dartmouth: Aldershot.

Soil Association (2004) Organic Food and Farming Report 2004, Soil Association.

Souza-Monteiro D. M. and J A Caswell (2004) The Economics of Implementing Traceability in Beef Supply Chains: Trends in Major Producing and Trading Countries, Department of Resource Economics, *Working Paper No. 2004–6*, University of Massachusetts Amherst.

Star. C. 1984. Risk Management, Assessment and Acceptability. In *Uncertainty in Risk Assessment, Risk Management and Decision Making*, edited by Covello. V. T., Lave. L. B., Moghissi. A. and Uppuluri. V. R. R. New York: Plenum Press.

Steinfeld. H., and Chilonda. P. 2006. Old Players, New Players in Livestock Report 2006. Rome: Food and Agriculture Organization.

Stichele. 2005.

Stigler. G. 1971. The Theory of Economic Regulation. *Bell Journal of Economics and Management Science* 2:3–21.

Stirling. A. 2003. Risk Uncertainty and Precaution. In *Negotiating Environmental Change*, edited by Berkhout. F., Leach. M. and Scoones. I. Cheltenham: Elgar.

Stokes. E. 2006. Bovine Spongiform Encephalopathy, the definition of risk, and the (in)applicability of the precautionary principle: assessing the ability of precaution to mitigate the impact of scientific uncertainty. Cardiff: Cardiff University, PhD Thesis.

Street. P. 2001. Trading in Risk: The Biosafety Protocol, Genetically Modified Organisms and the World Trade Organisation. *Environmental Law Review* 3 (4):247–263.

Sturgeon. T. 2000. How Silicon Valley Came to Be. In *Understanding Silicon Valley: the Anatomy of an Entrepreneurial Region*, edited by Martin. K. Stanford CA: Stanford University Press.

Supermarketing, week ending February 6th, 1998.

Supermarkets. 2000. A Report on the Supply of roceries from Multiple Stores in the UK. Available from http://www.competitioncommission.org.uk/rep_pub/reports/2000/446super.htm.

Teubner. G. 1998. After Privatization: The Many Autonomies of Private Law. In *Current Legal Problems*, edited by Freeman. M. Oxford: Oxford University Press.

Thankappan. S., Marsden. T., Flynn. A., and Lee. R. 2004. The Battle for the cCnsumers: Building Relationships in a New Phase of Contested Accountability in the UK Food Chain. Cardiff: Centre for Business Relationships, Accountability, Sustainability and Society (BRASS) *Working Paper no:17*.

The Economist. 2008. Silent Tsunami. The new face of Hunger: Briefing Food and the Poor. *The Economist*, 32–34.

The Pennington Group. 1997. Report on the circumstances leading to the 1996 outbreak of infection with e.coli 0157 in Central Scotland, the implications for food safety and the lessons to be learned. Edinburgh: The Stationery Office.

Thrupp. A. 1995. *Bittersweet Harvests for Global Supermarkets: Challenges in Latin America's Agricultural Export Boom*. Washington DC: World Resources Institute.

Toke. D. 2004a. A Comparative Study of the Politics of GM Food and Crops. *Political Studies* 52 (1):179–186.

———. 2004b. *The Politics of GM Foods*. London: Routledge.

Tragus. 2004. The Changing UK Leisure Dining Sector. London: Tragus Holding Limited.

Treaty of the European Union. 1992. Common Provisions: Article 1,: Official Journal of the European Communities (C340, 10/11/1997).

Trettin. L., and Musham. C. 2000. Is Trust a Realistic Goal of Environmental Risk Communication? *Environment and Behaviour* 32 (3):410–427.

Tromans. S. 2002. The Silence of the Lambs: The Foot and Mouth Crisis, Its Litigation and Its Environmental Implications. *Environmental Law and Management* 14 (4):197.

U.S. Department of Agriculture. 2002. Foot and Mouth Vaccination: USDA Animal Health Inspection Service.

UK Food Market Review. 2001. *UK Food Market Review*. Available from http://www.researchandmarkets.com/.

UK v. EC Commission (Cases 157/96 and 180/96; 5 May 1998).

United States-European Communities: Measures Affecting the Approval and Marketing of Biotech Products- First Submission of the United States (WT/DS 291, 292 and 293) 21 April 2004.

Unnevehr. L. J. 2000. Food Safety Issues and Fresh Food Product Exports from LDCs. *Agricultural Economics* 23 (3):231–240.

Van den Belt. P. 2003. Debating the Precautionary Principle: "Guilty until Proved Innocent" or "Innocent until Proven Guilty"? *Plant Physiology* 132 (2):1122–1126.

Van der Grijp. N. 2008. Regulating pesticide risk reduction: the practice and dynamics of legal pluralism. PhD Thesis, Academisch Proefschrift.

Van der Gripp. N., Campins Eritja. M., Gupata. J., Brander. L., Fernadez Pons. X., deBoer. J., Gradoni. L., and Montanari. J. 2004. Addressing Controversies in Sustainability Labelling and Certification. In *Sustainability Labelling and Certification*, edited by Campins Eritja. M. Marcial Pons: Madrid.

van der Grijp, N. M., Marsden, T. K., and Calvacanti, J. S. B. 2005. European retailers as agents of change towards sustainability: the case of fruit production in Brazil. *Environmental Sciences* 2 (4):445–460.

Van der Meulen. B., and Van der Velde. M. 2004. *Food Safety Law in the European Union*. Wageningen: Wageningen Academic Publishers.

van der Ploeg. J. D. 2006. Agricultural Production in Crisis. In *Handbook of Rural Studies*, edited by Cloke. P., Marsden. T. K. and Mooney. P. London: Sage.

van der Ploeg. J. D. 2008. *The peasantries: struggles for autonomyand sustainability in an era of empire and globalisation*. London: Earthscan.

Van Zwanenberg. P., and Millstone. E. 2001. Mad Cow Disease—1980s–2000: How Reassurances Undermined Precaution. In *Late Lessons from Early Warnings: The Precautionary Principle 1898–2000*, edited by Gee. D. et al. Copenhagen: EEA.

VAO (Valuation Office Agency). 2005. *Rating Manual, Volume 5, Section 5*.

Vidal. J., and Sample. I. 2003/September. Five to One Against GM Crops in Biggest Ever Public Survey. *Guardian* 25.

Vogel. D. 1995. *Trading Up*. Cambridge, MA: Harvard University Press.

———. 2002. *Risk Regulation in Europe and the United States*. Berkeley: Haas BS.

Vorley. B. 1999. Agribusiness and Power Relations in the Agri-Food Chain. Background paper for: International Institute for Environment and Development: UK.

———. 2001. Farming that Works: Reforms for Sustainable Agriculture and Rural Development in the EU and US. In *NTA Multi-dialogue Workshop: Sharing Responsibility for promoting Sustainable Agriculture and Rural development: The Role of EU and US Stakeholders*. Lisbon.

———. 2004. Food, Inc. Corporate concentration from farm to consumer: UK Food Group.

Voss. E. 2000. EU Food Safety Regulation in the Aftermath of the BSE Crisis. *Journal of Consumer Policy* 23:227–255.

Wales. C., and Mythen. G. 2002. Risky Discourse: The Politics of GM Food. *Environmental Politics* 11 (2):121–144.

Westlake. M. 1997. Keynote Article: Mad Cows and Englishmen—The Institutional Consequences of the BSE Crisis. *Journal of Common Market Studies* 35:11–36.

WHO. 1999. Food Safety: Report by the Director-General: World Health Organisation, EB105/10.

Williams. Lord. 1965. *Digging for Britain*. London: Hutchinson.

Wilson. G. K. 1977. *Special Interests and Policy-Making: Agricultural Policy and Politics in Britain and the USA 1956–1970.* Chichester: Riley.

Winter. M. 1996. Intersecting Departmental Responsibilities, Administrative Confusion and the Role of Science in Government: The Case of BSE *Parliamentary Affairs* 49 (4):550–556.

Winter. M., Rutherford. J., and Gaskell. P. 1998. Beef Farming in the GB LFA—The Response of Farmers to the 1992 CAP Reform Measures and the Implications for Meeting World Trade Obligations. In *Second International LSIRD Network Conference on Livestock Production in the European LFAs*. Dublin.

Woods. A. 2004. *A Manufactured Plague: A History of Foot and Mouth Disease in Britain*. London: Earthscan.

World Bank. 2005. *Food Safety and Agricultural Health Standards: Challenges and Opportunities for Developing Country Exports*. Washington DC: World Bank.

Wrigley. N. 1991. Is the "Golden Age" of British Retailing a Watershed? *Environment and Planning A* 23:1537–1544.

———. 1992. Antitrust regulation and the restructuring of grocery retailing in Britain and the USA. *Environment and Planning A* 24.

———. 1994. After the Store Wars? Towards a New Era of Retail Competition? *Journal of Retail and Consumer Services* 1:5–20.

Wrigley. N., Coe. N. M., and Currah. A. 2005. Globalising Retail: Conceptualising the Distributiion-Based Transnational Corporation (TNC). *Progess in Human Geography* 29 (4):437–457.

WTO. *SPS Measures* 2003. Available from http://www.wto.org/english/tratop_etbt_e/tbt_e.htm.

WTO Appellate Body. 1998. Report on EC Measures concerning Meat and Meat Products (Hormones)—Complaint by the USA (WT/DS26/ABAB/R; AB)—1997—4 PH June 1999, January 1998.

———. 1999. Report on Measures Affecting Agricultural Products (Japan Agricultural Products)—(WT/DS76/AB/R; AB 99–0668), 22 February 1999.

WTO Dispute Panel. 2006. Report on EC Approval and Marketing of Biotech Products Complaints by the United States (WT/DS291), Canada (WT/DS292) and Argentina (WT/DS293), 29 September 2006.

Wynne. B., Marris. C., and Simmons. P. 2001. Public Attitudes Towards Agricultural Biotechnologies in Europe (PABE). Final Report of Project with Vive partner Country Teams (Spain, Italy, Germany, France, UK), Funded by DG-Research, European Commission. Lancaster University: Centre for the Study of Environmental Change (CSEC).

Wynne. B., and Mayer. S. 1993. How Science Fails the Environment. *New Scientist*, 1876: 33.

Zaibet. L, and Bredahl. M. E. 1997. Gains from ISO Certification in the UK Meat Sector. *Agribusiness* 13 (4):375–384.

Zedalis. R. J. 2002. GMO Food Measures as "Restrictions" under GATT Article XI (1). *European Environmental Law Review* 11:16.

Zwangenburg, P. van, and Millstone, E. 2003. BSE: a paradigm of policy failure. *Political Quarterly* 74 (1):27–37.

Index

Q

R